THE LAST WARRIOR

The Last

Warrior

Peter MacDonald

and

The Navajo Nation

Peter MacDonald
with Ted Schwarz

The Library of the American Indian
Herman J. Viola, Editor

ORION BOOKS / NEW YORK

Published by Orion Books, a division of Crown Publishers, Inc., 201 East 50th Street, New York, New York 10022. Member of the Crown Publishing Group.

Random House, Inc. New York, Toronto, London, Sydney, Auckland

ORION and colophon are trademarks of Crown Publishers, Inc.

Manufactured in the United States of America

Library of Congress Cataloging-in-Publication Data

MacDonald, Peter, 1928–
    The last warrior : Peter MacDonald and the Navajo Nation/
Peter MacDonald with Ted Schwarz.
        p.   cm.—(The Library of the American Indian)
    Includes index.
    1. MacDonald, Peter, 1928–.   2. Navajo Indians—Biography.
3. Navajo Indians—Politics and government.   4. Navajo Indians—
Government relations.   I. Schwarz, Ted, 1945–.   II. Title.
III. Series.
E99.N3M27   1993
973'.04972—dc20   91-3174
[B]   CIP

ISBN 0-517-59323-8

10 9 8 7 6 5 4 3 2 1

First Edition

I dedicate this book to my wife, Wanda, my children Linda, Rocky, Hope, Faith, and Charity, and to my grandchildren Emily, Bernard, Jessica, and Larue.

They first came for Hoshkaisith with words, the white man's deadliest weapon, honed to razor sharpness on the whetstone of broken treaties and improper U.S. government subpoenas that challenged the sovereignty of the Navajo Nation. To his people, he was naat'aanii, the traditional term for leader. To his enemies, he was the Last Warrior, the spiritual survivor of the Long Walk, a man who feared neither scandal nor death so long as he was acting in the interests of the people he loved.

Hoshkaisith, like the great Navajo chiefs of centuries past, studied his enemies before doing battle. He mastered their weapons, then learned to use them against their inventors. They wanted the battle-field to be his territory, the isolated land of Arizona, Utah, and New Mexico that composed the bulk of the treaty-created Navajo Nation. It was a land so desolate that one might be born, grow into adulthood, marry, give birth, age, and die without ever seeing anyone outside one's extended family. It was a land where English was a second language, where the culture did not require television sets or radios, cars, trucks, expensive perfume, or designer clothing. To choose the Navajo Nation as a battleground was to wage war away from the prying eyes and ears of news photographers' cameras and reporters' tape recorders. The followers of Hoshkaisith might intimately know the land, but the white man's tactical advantage came from the fact that it was a world about which no outsider seemed to care.

The Last Warrior understood the problems. Instead of confronting his enemy on familiar terrain, he selected a different battlefield, one where he was seemingly at a disadvantage. He journeyed to Washington, D.C., the home of Congress and the "Great White Father." He adorned his body with the camouflage of white man's battle dress—a three-piece suit, polished shoes, a necktie, and an articulate manner. He used the Anglo name Peter MacDonald, the identity he had been given when he went to the schools required by the Bureau of Indian Affairs. And he used the tactics that had enabled the white man to triumph in the past—the lobbying of congressional representatives and senators, the cultivation of the media, and the voter registration of his people, 200,000 strong.

The year was 1972. The war had been called for the same year that Republican Richard Nixon was running for president against Democratic candidate George McGovern. Arizona was traditionally a Republican stronghold, controlled by men such as Senator Barry Goldwater, one of the most powerful congressmen, who wielded additional control in his home territory. Hoshkaisith had dared to challenge that power. His voter registration drive among the Navajo had altered the state, weakening Goldwater's hold for the first time in the senator's career by electing the state's first Democratic governor.

The Last Warrior's battle cry was self-determination for the Navajo Nation. It was a simple message—his people's right to control their own destiny. Hoshkaisith spoke of basic freedoms, including the right to use the land the Navajo owned in a manner consistent with the free enterprise to which the Republicans had been paying lip service. Few could argue with his words, and MacDonald won the battle, embarrassing Senator Goldwater, who had previously dominated the decisions concerning how the Indian land within his state would be governed.

Ostensibly, the Last Warrior's victory was almost minor. The public would not realize for almost four more years that the victory could allow the Navajo to determine how their resources would be used.

Much of the land the Navajo had been given was so surface-poor that it supported neither crops nor livestock. But the land did have coal, uranium, water—all the key elements needed to maintain white man's society. Arizona was the fastest-growing state in the nation; Phoenix and Tucson were becoming major cosmopolitan areas suitable for corporate headquarters and large-scale manufacturing. Yet those cities were in the Sonoran Desert and required power and water that had to be diverted from other parts of the state. The Navajo land was so mineral-rich that, in any given year, enough energy could be harvested from the seeming wasteland to meet the state's current needs as well as the projected needs for the next thirty years. Its resources were also deemed critical to the expanding population of California.

Billions of dollars could have been made by land speculators, crooked developers, and others if the control of those resources were turned over to white men. And many of Barry Goldwater's friends were among those who would have benefited by the shift of economic power away from the leadership of the Last Warrior.

Yet the white man's weapons—words—had failed to stop Hoshkaisith.

What follows is Peter MacDonald's own story—from the ancient Navajo teachings of a lifestyle as old as mankind itself, to the early rocket age, to a war still raging between a sovereign Navajo Nation and the corrupt developers of Arizona and California, the key states of the American West. It is the story of a sheepherder; of a World War II

Navajo code talker; of an engineer who designed the Polaris missile guidance system, one of the cold war's most important technological breakthroughs; and, ultimately, of the chairman of the Navajo Nation, a man embattled in the courts, accused of corruption and greed—the Last Warrior, who, standing alone, is willing to die for that in which he believes.

This is the story of that life.

THE LAST WARRIOR

The Reluctant Warrior

(1928–1936)

I was born into the Haskonhazohi and Betani clan as my people had been born for centuries. It was May, the time of my family's thirty-mile walk from our sturdy winter hogans in Utah to our more mountainous summer homes in Teec Nos Pos, Arizona. My grandparents and most of the others in my extended family were tending the thousands of sheep, horses, and cattle that were our primary livelihood. My father had strapped large wooden water kegs to the sides of a mule, then had gone to a distant stream to fill them in order to quench the thirst of the people and livestock. Only my mother, Glen-Habah, and her aunt were inside the tent that served as shelter from the intense heat of the midday sun. They, too, should have been working, but I had dropped low inside my mother's womb, and she was going into labor.

Childbirth was too natural a process to cause either my mother or her aunt to worry about the fact that they were many hours' travel from the nearest medical care. Instead, the aunt did what Navajo women had been doing for generations. First she found a sturdy piece of wood that would serve as a pole. Then she dug a hole deep enough so that the pole could be tightly inserted, reinforced with dirt, and made to hold fast. She tied a rope around the top of the pole so that my mother could pull down on it during the labor contractions, and she placed a goatskin pad beneath my mother so that I would have a soft resting place when I was born.

The delivery went normally. While my mother rested, her aunt cut the umbilical cord, setting it aside while she cleaned me and laid me in my mother's arms.

The umbilical cord had to be saved because it was my connection with the earth. My mother eventually carried it to Teec Nos Pos and buried it near the family farm. Then the gods would know that I belonged there, and my spirit would return to that land.

My father returned approximately an hour after my birth, and the rest of the extended family came back in the late afternoon. We stayed only an extra day or two at the makeshift camp, allowing my mother to fully regain her strength. Then we continued toward our summer home.

My father made a cradleboard when the family reached Teec Nos Pos, and from then on I was carried while the others did their work.

The lower part of our land was farmed, while the upper elevations were used for the livestock cared for primarily by the children.

Although I was born in the spring, the Bureau of Indian Affairs arbitrarily gave me the birth date of December 16, 1928. I never did question why they made that selection. It seemed as good a birth date as any other.

My people did not track time the way white men did. There was no need to be aware of anything more than the changing seasons. Sometimes your birth was known because of a major event, such as a great blizzard that had made survival difficult for everyone. But when the weather was mild, your birth was marked by the seasons, the exact date remaining unknown, unimportant. We were in harmony with nature—birth, death, and the life that was led in between were all a part of the natural pattern of human existence.

I have no idea how old I was when I first became aware of my surroundings. I know that it was wintertime, though it is unclear whether it was that first year of my life or sometime later. I can remember looking up and seeing huge sheep and cattle as far as the eye could see. And I remember moving with the family, traveling with the seemingly endless herds of livestock from Mexican Water and Bluff, Utah, to Teec Nos Pos, from Teec Nos Pos into the mountains, then back down again, reversing the travel after the fall harvest.

Our extended family was fairly wealthy by Navajo standards. We owned thousands of sheep, one of the criteria for riches among our people. We did not have fancy homes or other such possessions that the white man coveted. Our life-style was such that some of us did not even know that automobiles, radios, and similar goods existed. They would have meant little to us if we had known of them, though. They were not of our world, and were unimportant for our existence.

The Navajo were not united in the manner of other tribes of the times. There was no single leader of all our people, no chief who spoke for everyone. Instead, we were a series of extended families, often isolated from one another, but all living within the same sacred mountains and all raised with the same customs and traditions, the same beliefs, the same language and culture.

As was the tradition for all the Navajo, my maternal grandparents were the head of our family. Their children, my parents, my uncles and aunts, and their grandchildren made up the extended family that lived and worked together, adding to and caring for the livestock and farming the land to supply food to supplement our diet. The chores were divided among the families. One uncle, his wife, and their children might be responsible for the horses. Another family would take care of the cattle, and a third, the sheep.

The oldest male who was judged by the extended family to have superior wisdom, knowledge, and spiritual strength became the chief, the leader, the spokesman, for that family. Other tribes—the Ute, Hopi, Zuni, Pima—had a single chief who spoke for all. The Navajo life-style, quite different from that of the other tribes, made our ways unique on the North American continent. Our isolation and extended-family arrangement led to the need for individual spokesmen. However, it was not until the 1930s that the position of chairman of the Navajo Nation originated, and even then it was created by white men who did not feel comfortable adapting to our culture.

Other Indian tribes failed to understand that our social structure was different from theirs. For years there was a feeling that the Navajo could not be trusted, that we were treaty breakers, because a treaty agreed to by one chief would not be honored by the followers of the other chiefs. These tribes failed to understand that the chief spoke only for his extended family, not for all the people of the Navajo Nation.

Perhaps it was the isolation of my people that made us unique. Or perhaps it was the structure of our society, which was natural to the Navajo, but seemed frustratingly disjointed to other cultures. Whites, blacks, Hispanics, and other Indian tribes viewed us as people who were not trustworthy because we never accepted the practice of following any one chief.

Some of my people's activities required that several extended families work together. Farming in the summer home area of Teec Nos Pos, for example, was always a communal effort, often involving unrelated neighbors. Everyone would help clear the land. Then the men would plow the fields, moving from plot to plot until every family's section was prepared for planting. The work went quickly. The same cooperative effort was made by other farming families throughout the many small Navajo communities in the 17 million acres of the Navajo Nation I knew as a child.

Not all Navajo families had farmland. Some had only cattle or horses or sheep. But the families who earned their living from livestock often assisted their neighbors with the planting and harvesting of crops. Their reward was a good meal during the planting and, at harvest time, a share of the wheat, squash, fruit, or other crops they had helped to cultivate.

The children were assigned chores from the time they were old enough to be responsible, usually five or six years of age. They took care of the horses, sheep, and cattle. They gathered firewood for cooking and heating. They fetched water, making certain that the supply was always adequate.

All together there were ten to fifteen adults and perhaps fifteen children in each extended family. However, each couple, like my parents, maintained separate living quarters for themselves and their children, taking care of their own bedrolls, dishes, and other belongings and doing their own cooking and household chores. They also had livestock for which they were personally responsible, perhaps five or ten horses and some other animals. But the vast herds of livestock were considered community property. Everyone shared in their care and benefited from their value.

The constant work was combined with education. The women would weave when their other work was done, teaching the girls the same skill. The girls were also taught to make pottery and to prepare native foods, including such tasks as grinding corn, butchering animals, and preparing meat for cooking. The boys learned to tan the buckskins, make moccasins, handle the horses, and care for the sheep. The latter included marking the sheep for identification, either by painting the wool—a painless alternative to branding—or marking the ear by cutting it in a certain manner to distinguish its family ownership; castrating and sheering the sheep; and caring for the newborn and growing lambs. And both the boys and girls learned certain survival skills, like the identification and gathering of edible seeds. Some of the seeds were meant for seasoning. Other seeds were ground into a flour for cakes. They also gathered yucca fruit, sour berries, choke berries, cactus fruit, and similar treats.

There were hogans in the farm area, permanent homes for each immediate family. Only in the mountains were the shelters simple—tents or makeshift protection. Additional hogans, often better constructed to survive the sometimes harsh winters, could be found in Utah. But there the work was less difficult. Although the animals had to be cared for and many of the same chores were necessary, there was no farming, and the families relied on the crops they had harvested earlier and stored. As a result, we spent more time together, enjoying storytelling and other activities that helped teach the children our history, values, and religious beliefs.

We Navajo call ourselves the Diné, which means "the only human beings in the world." That sounds arrogant to those who do not understand our culture and history, and it has caused us to experience great hatred and violence. Yet the concept developed from our efforts to understand our place in the world at large and was our way of determining how we differ from the birds, the animals, and the other creatures with whom we share the earth.

From the time we were very small children, we heard stories about Coyote. The stories provided an inoffensive, impersonal way to teach us about ourselves and help us develop a code of morals and ethics. Sometimes Coyote was a positive role model. Sometimes he was an example of what human beings should not be like. The Coyote stories are one of the ways we learned to think of ourselves as unique— different from other men and women who looked like us but who were not Navajo.

For example, there is a story about the time Coyote was walking down the road. He saw some creatures taking out their eyes, tossing them into the air, catching them, and putting them back in their sockets. The creatures looked a lot like Coyote, but they were actually quite different.

Coyote thought that what the creatures were doing would be fun, so he took out his eyes and tossed them into the air. But Coyote's eyes landed in the trees, and unlike the other creatures, he could not find them to put them back.

The creatures who had been tossing their eyes in the air led Coyote over to a log and helped him sit down. Then they went to a stream and found two smooth yellow stones, which they gave to him to use as eyes. Coyote could see again, but he had learned an important lesson: just because someone looks like you doesn't mean you can do what he does. Each creature has certain skills and limitations, and you will only be hurt if you try to act like someone else.

Coyote was sometimes a hero and sometimes a villain, though it was not unusual for him to be a fool, to make the mistakes the elders wanted us to avoid. We heard stories about Coyote and the man-killing giant, Coyote and the skunk, Coyote and the rabbit, Coyote and the deer.

The deer story is particularly revealing about the beliefs of the Diné. One day Coyote came across a doe with her young fawns. The fawns were covered with beautiful spots, as are all fawns, and Coyote was extremely impressed. He told the mother what beautiful children she had, with their gorgeous coloring and the white spots on their backs. He also had children, but as they were not nearly so attractive, he asked her how she had done that.

The doe disliked Coyote because he was nosy, so she decided to play a trick on him. She told Coyote that she placed her children in a cave. Then she built a fire at the opening, and when the sparks flew, they hit her children's backs, giving them their beautiful spots.

Coyote hurried home to his puppies. He gathered them together and placed them in a cave. Then he built a large fire at the mouth of the cave.

Soon the puppies were screaming and crying.

"Don't be afraid," said Coyote. "The fire will make you beautiful."

But the puppies died from the fire, and Coyote learned a lesson. No one should change what God creates. You should be what you are and not try to be something else.

So it was with us Diné. We human beings learned about sacred places where stepping on the land could make us insane or take our lives. We learned certain rituals to follow each day in order to be right with the deities and enjoy good health. These beliefs affected everything we did. And if someone accidentally violated what we knew to be correct—if, for example, a child wandered onto an area where touching the land might cause illness or death—the person had to experience a ritual called a "sing" in order to be cleansed. These rituals *had* to be performed. Without them, the person's fate was sealed and we would be guilty of abusing or murdering that child or adult.

The owl was another creature who was a part of many Navajo stories. The owl's sound was to be feared. When the owl called your name, you could die. You needed to get a hand trembler (diagnostician) to determine why the owl was hooting and to tell you what kind of ceremony you needed to get back in good graces with the spirits.

When I was about four years old, I learned about the owl's sound. We were driving our sheep back down to the base of the mountain near Teec Nos Pos. The sheep were bedded down in a circle, the kids and adults scattered around them, some on the east side, some on the north, some on the south, and some on the west side. In this way we protected the sheep from drifting off or from becoming prey to coyotes.

One evening, my mother, my youngest sister, Betty, who was two years old, and I were sleeping on the east side of the circle. The next morning my mother told us that she heard an owl in the middle of the night calling my sister by her name. She said that the owl was saying "Betty." She woke up and realized that my sister, who had been lying next to her, was gone. A few minutes later, she saw Betty coming back toward her. When my mother asked Betty where she'd been, my sister didn't know.

The next morning my family planned to send for a hand trembler as soon as possible to determine what had happened to Betty. Nothing could be done immediately, however. My mother and my aunt first had to move the sheep another five miles to our next campsite. My grandfather and grandmother needed to round up the horses and the mule and take them to the same location.

My family had reason to think Betty would be safe at camp. There are special prayers that can be used until the hand trembler arrives, a kind of short-term protection, or spiritual First Aid, but I don't remember if the family used them. Even when they are used, there is no guarantee that they will work, and the fact that my sister and I were in a place that seemed safe may have lulled my family into a false sense of security.

It was cool out, and we had a fire for warmth at breakfast. Because Betty and I were too young to be of any help, our small selves only getting in the way, we were told to stay at the camp until my family returned after completing their work. Since it was cold and we were small, we decided to lie down by the fire, to rest and keep warm.

The next thing I knew, Betty was on fire. She had apparently gotten too close to the embers, which had set her clothing ablaze.

She began running around, screaming and crying, while I stood staring in horror as her clothing was destroyed by the flames. At first I didn't know what to do, but when she was naked, I somehow thought to wrap her in a blanket, smothering the fire. However, by the time my grandparents came back with the horses and mule, Betty was seriously burned.

My grandparents took Betty on horseback to get my mother, then they went to the trading post. They drove the thirty miles of dirt roads from Teec Nos Pos to the Shiprock Hospital in the trader's car in a desperate effort to get Betty help in time. In those days there was little that could be done for burn victims even under the best of circumstances. The unavoidable delays made it impossible to save my sister. She died three or four days later.

I never forgot that incident, nor did my mother stop reminding me. She sometimes berated herself for not getting the trembler in time. She also wondered if perhaps it had been Betty's time to die. And it all began when the owl called my sister's name.

We Diné also recognized that there were others who could go where we dared not—the animals of the forest, the birds, and the insects. A deer could walk on sacred ground and live a full life. A bird could rest on that which was taboo for us, then fly away unharmed.

Then, over time, other people came into our world. These were the Ute, Hopi, Pueblo, Zuni, and others, all of whom looked much like us, though perhaps they were not so handsome. They did not follow our ways. They walked where we dared not walk. They behaved in a manner that, for us, would have brought down the wrath of the deities unless we immediately cleansed ourselves. Yet they were not hurt. They did not die. And they did not follow our rituals for purification.

So we used the stories of Coyote and our teachings to help us understand that some creatures on earth could do certain things while others could not. What was taboo for one might be acceptable for another. Coyote took out his eyes and tossed them in the air, but he went blind, whereas the creatures who looked like him had no trouble with this sport.

We Diné had to follow certain rituals to avoid suffering. And this meant that the people who appeared on our land—the other Native Americans, the Blue Coats, the settlers—were not the Diné. To us, they were not Navajo. Their bodies might appear to be like ours, but they were different. How else could they violate our taboos? Perhaps they were part of the animal kingdom. It did not matter. What was important was that they did not have to follow our ways, and we certainly dared not imitate theirs.

We did not lack respect for other tribes, for the white, black, and Hispanic settlers. We realized that there were things they knew that we did not, things they could do that we could not. They were as important as all creatures. They simply were not Diné.

Tragically, the men and women who encountered the Navajo during the westward migration of the settlers did not take the time to understand our culture. Some of them learned enough of our language to talk in simple ways, but they failed to learn why we said and did the things we did. They made assumptions based on their own cultures, then became angry when we did not act as they thought we should.

This was true even with the early treaties. The white men did not realize that our chiefs were the patriarchs only of our extended families, not of the whole nation. If there was a war between the Navajo and the Blue Coats, and if a Blue Coat general made peace with a Navajo chief, the general assumed that the decisions were binding for all the Navajo. Yet each time the Blue Coat general and his men encountered a different extended family, new agreements would have to be made. This was simply the way we lived, the way we had lived for centuries. But it was not the way of the Zuni, the Pueblo, the Ute, and the other tribes the settlers and soldiers encountered in their travels through the Southwest.

This failure to learn the Diné's unique ways led to the most tragic era in our history, the era of Kit Carson and the Long Walk to Fort Sumner, beginning in 1863. The Diné were exiled and confined for many years before being allowed to return to their original lands in 1868. Of the estimated 12,000 Navajo taken to Fort Sumner, only 7,500 survived.

The Long Walk was to the Navajo Nation what the Holocaust was to the Jews of the Eastern European nations overrun by Hitler's Germany. The few survivors never forgot the horrors they witnessed and endured. They passed the stories on to their children and grandchildren, who were raised as though, at any moment, the events of that period might begin anew.

My great-grandmother was a survivor of the Long Walk. She was an old woman by the time I was born, yet her horror was still ingrained in her. She had watched family and friends slowly die in the summer sun. She had witnessed small babies, their stomachs bloated from starvation, cradled lovingly by young mothers desperately trying to squeeze what little milk their malnourished bodies could produce through the cracked nipples of their shriveled breasts. She had heard the keening and wailing of a people in agony, praying to God and the deities, trying to understand circumstances outside their control.

She and my great-grandfather had been children at Fort Sumner. They had seen their friends die, had been told by the survivors the stories of the war with Kit Carson that preceded the Long Walk. They had learned that there was no safety in the mountains or the valleys, in the night or in the day, and that it was impossible to relax one's vigilance despite being at peace with one's neighbor and in harmony with the land. They saw the scars on the bodies of people who had survived gunshot wounds, stabbings, and vicious beatings. They saw the results of the invisible scars on the minds of women who had been raped, of people torn from their homes before sunrise, having to watch their families separated, some to be murdered, others to be enslaved.

And they lived in fear.

My parents knew the stories of their parents and the old people. They knew some of the survivors. But they had always been safe, had never been so directly touched by the horrors of the Long Walk as had their parents and great-grandparents. They simply respected the wisdom of the old ones, wisdom gained in blood. They respected the danger. They believed it could happen again.

And they, too, lived in fear.

By the time I was born, there were no more Long Walks, no more Fort Sumners. Our enemies would be more subtle, and the attacks we experienced would be launched in ways that seemed impossible to overcome. But no one realized that, and so I, too, was raised in fear.

I was awakened each morning at dawn, as were all the other children of my generation from the moment we were able to walk. There were no exceptions for age, no exceptions for health, no exceptions for weather.

We were herded outside to face the east, a small bag of white cornmeal in our hands in order to say our prayers to the Navajo deities. We were taught that all good things come from the east at the crack of dawn, the time when you can receive the rich resources of life. If you breathe in the crisp early-morning air, you will not become lazy in life; you will become successful. Then, before the sun could rise and change the quality of the air, we were told to run. White cornmeal was male, like the east which we faced just when the sun was beginning to rise. We used yellow cornmeal at night, for it was female, like the west.

We also had yellow corn pollen, which was considered a sacrifice. For example, if we encountered the footprint of a coyote, we could sprinkle it with corn pollen. Otherwise we might be hurt because the coyote tracks crossing our path formed a warning sign. The pollen sacrifice and a prayer helped assure that we would not be hurt as would likely otherwise be the case.

All the children ran, no matter what their age. Uncles and grandfathers would run, too, to keep fit themselves and to make certain everyone completed the required mile or two.

We children were told of the Ute, the Comanche, the United States Army, and the other people who had made the Navajo their enemy over the years. We did not know what war might mean, only that the terrible experiences could occur at any moment. We were taught that we might have to run to escape the enemy, run to stay alive. Strength meant survival. Being able to run in all types of weather, under all conditions, meant that we could flee if we were surprised.

My great-grandmother told us the story of the time before the Long Walk, when the Utes and the Comanches were used by the whites to help destroy the Diné.

When she was three or four years old, a Ute war party arrived at Teec Nos Pos in the Four Corners area to steal Navajo horses, sheep, and possessions. They deliberately came when all the men were out hunting, when only the women and children were in the hogans.

Great-grandmother remembers all the women and children running. She was too small to save herself, and her tiny legs would only have slowed down the others. One of the women grabbed her and threw her into a thick bush that kept her hidden and told her not to make a sound until the Utes were gone and the Navajo had returned. Then the rest of her family fled into the surrounding terrain.

Great-grandmother recalled seeing the horses, animals that looked like giants to her, as they thundered past the bushes. The Utes spent hours there, killing anyone they caught, stealing, destroying. Great-grandmother was terrified, yet she also was silent. Only when the Utes were gone and the others returned could she relax.

We learned several lessons from Great-grandmother's story. One was a history lesson, reminding us of the struggle we endured before the time of the Long Walk. It was also a lesson to children that they must mind unquestioningly when an adult tells them to do something, not cry or carry on just because they don't understand or agree. Great-grandmother was torn by the bush and in great pain as she hid, yet by not crying, she lived to tell the story.

Another lesson was that we must prepare for the future. A time might come when we, too, would be attacked. Her actions could teach us a way to survive.

Our grandparents told us stories of hearing a cry in the distance, then having to run and hide in the woods as the enemy attacked. There were times when people survived only by running fifty to one hundred miles with as little rest along the way as was humanly possible. In a sense, the Long Walk ensured that the surviving Navajo would be strong. The weak had died. A Navajo child who lived through the birthing process, who grew into the teenage years, had to be tough.

We had to take other precautions as well. We were taught to eat squatting. We could not sit down. We could not relax. Too many of our ancestors had been ambushed while enjoying their food. We squatted so that we could drop everything and run at the first sight of the enemy.

Oddly, the adults did not squat with us. They sat down comfortably on the hogan floor. Either they felt they could react faster, or they were raising us in a way that would please their parents and grandparents, even though they no longer felt attack was imminent. We never knew why and we never dared ask. We were like Marine recruits in basic training, obeying orders. In fact, years later, when I joined the Marines during World War II, I found basic training easy. I had been in boot camp all my life and just did not realize it. In fact, we Navajo were so skilled and so fit that we used to race through the training course, then laugh at the Anglos who were struggling with it. Eventually they punished us by making us do everything twice. Yet even that was not difficult for us.

Even during the winter or the rainy season, we could not go inside the hogan to warm ourselves by the fire when we finished running. Instead, we were forced to stand around outside for a few minutes. In bad weather, we had to strip to the waist and roll in the snow. If there was no snow, we had to jump into the icy water of a nearby river or stream. By the time we returned to the hogan, our clothing was so stiff from the cold that it felt as though it was made of concrete. The training was meant to make us tough.

Running was also good for our health, though I don't know if our parents were aware of that. The Navajo had relied upon herbs and medicine men for generations while whites were developing hospitals, surgical procedures, and pharmaceuticals. Most of my people had never even seen a doctor or a hospital. They had no medical care, no aspirins or shots. If children were kept in the best physical shape possible, there was less danger from illness and a greater chance that we would survive serious injury. We were ready to endure any kind of adversity.

Not that the Navajo failed to take advantage of Anglo medicine when it was available. When I was seven years old, there was a field nurse in Teec Nos Pos who discovered that I was choking on all my food. My tonsils were bad, and I had to be taken to a hospital quite a distance from home. I would have died without having the tonsils removed, and my family approved the procedure.

When we were finally allowed inside, our grandparents would "shape" us, massaging our still-malleable bones to affect the shape of our bodies. They would heat their hands and apply pressure to our arms, our faces, our hands, our noses, all parts of our bodies. The nose would be made slender and well shaped, not flat or wide. The forehead would have a pronounced roll over the eyes. The feet would be narrowed. The back would be straightened.

The shaping was a tradition handed down through the centuries. My people believed that when First Man and First Woman were born, the Navajo gods used their hands to shape them into the best-looking human beings they could be. When their children were born, First Man and First Woman repeated the shaping procedure that had been used on them. *Their* children shaped the next generation, and so on. In this way, all Navajo women could be beautiful, all Navajo men could be handsome.

When a girl had her first menstruation, in fact, she underwent another beauty ceremony. For four days, for one hour each day, she would lie down while a Navajo woman shaped her. She made her body slender and her back straight, and adjusted the shape of her nose and the other parts of her body, as she had been shaped in infancy, according to the ancient ritual.

The woman who did the shaping was of great stature. She was considered a great beauty by Navajo standards. And her spirit, knowledge, and wisdom were respected by everyone.

After the ceremony, the men and women, who were generally in their fifties and older, would touch the young woman. They would rub their hands against their bodies and heads while praying, "My strength, my body, my spirit will be as young as this young lady." At that point, just after the ceremony, the young lady was considered a holy spirit whose youthful energy, spirit, mind, eyes, ears, and legs could be transferred to the old people.

In exchange, the elderly pass their wisdom and knowledge to the girl. Thus each generation shares what is unique and valuable to them. The old respect the young, and the young respect the old. It is a tradition that is still practiced and respected today.

After running and eating, we were ready to start the day. Education began early for Navajo children, because we were needed to work in whatever way our families earned their livelihood.

My work was with the sheep. At certain times of the year, a shepherd had to separate the lambs from the ewes, since the lambs were small and could not travel very far.

We children would chase the lambs, who had a tendency to wander off. We were like little sheepdogs, running this way and that in order to keep the lambs safely together.

When we became more coordinated, we were taught to use a sharp knife to castrate most of the male lambs. We worked alone, one or more children being responsible for as many as a thousand lambs. Only the largest, best-looking sheep were spared and allowed to grow into rams that, with luck, would pass on their superior genetic characteristics, improving the quality of the flock. The rest were prevented from breeding, and they also became docile, acting more like ewes.

Then there was the shearing, though this was done with the aid of adults, including those from neighboring families. It was similar to harvest times, when everyone worked together over a four- or five-day period. We would go from herd to herd, shearing all the sheep owned by all the neighboring families in our area.

Other children worked with the mules or donkeys, but those older children who were responsible for the horses had the most work to do. The horses were put out to graze during the periods when my people were not on the move. They chewed the plant life, moving slowly from wherever they started. Within two days they were likely to have wandered as much as ten miles from where they started grazing. The children assigned to their care had to follow their tracks, locate them, and return them to the campsite. Then they had to walk to the nearest water source and fill the water vessels attached to the mules or donkeys, much as my father did on the day I was born.

It was a life filled with work and learning, a life that was as eternal as the Navajo people. There were no Bureau of Indian Affairs (BIA) schools. There were no books. There was no separation of the children from their families.

The land itself seemed as harsh as our life-style. The land from our winter home in Utah to approximately ten miles before Teec Nos Pos was desertlike, dotted by brush and occasional grass. Water was extremely scarce, and the ground was flat, an occasional mesa breaking the monotony of the sandy soil. There were no trees and no cactus. Weeds seemed to grow in clusters, reaching a height of about eighteen inches and covering an area of a few square feet before the ground turned almost barren once again.

The harsh terrain covered the first fifteen miles of our journey to the summer home. Halfway between our two homes an earthen dam had been created to catch water, but the trip to refill the water barrels always took us several hours from our path.

Water was most precious during the walk to and from Teec Nos Pos. It was used only for drinking and cooking. No one dared wash, except to use a small cupful in order to remove the dust from our eyes and clean out our mouths.

I remember one time when I was four years old, helping my mother drive the sheep across the barren land. It was high noon, the sun was intensely hot, and our water bag was empty. The nearest water hole was three or four miles away, and we could not both leave the sheep to quench our thirst.

My mother sent me to get water first. She said that though we were both thirsty, she felt that I probably had the greater need. I could go to the water hole and get a long drink, then bring water back for her. There was a large tree growing at the water hole, the only place where there was any such growth. That tree, clearly visible from where we were herding the sheep, was my landmark, so although I was small, I had no trouble finding the water hole.

I reached it, took my drink, then realized that I had forgotten the jug necessary to carry water back to Mother. I felt terrible, and somehow knew that it would be wrong to not return with a drink for her. I don't know what possessed me to do it, but I decided that the only way I could bring her a drink was to fill my mouth with water, then hold it while I walked back.

I took as much water as I could in my mouth, closed my lips, and forced myself to breathe through my nose as I made the long trip back to where she was herding the sheep. Five minutes passed. Then ten. Then fifteen. I covered the first mile, the second, the third, fighting to keep from swallowing or spitting out the precious liquid. Finally, after a journey that seemed much longer than my original walk, I reached my mother and passed the water from my mouth to hers.

The incident seems funny to me now, but my mother was deeply moved by what I had done. I was quite small, my father having died two years earlier, yet I recognized that I had to be responsible enough to care for my mother despite being ill-equipped to do so. Somehow I knew that she would become dangerously dehydrated without that precious drink.

Within a few miles of Teec Nos Pos, water became more plentiful and the land grew more colorful. There were more mesas, and juniper, piñon, and cedar trees began to appear. Near the base of the mountain, arroyos and canyons carried water from the peak to the fertile land below.

The runoff from the mountain filled a wash that served as a source of irrigation water for Teec Nos Pos farmland. The area was quite beautiful, teeming with life. Besides the trees, there were naturally growing onions, a plant we called Navajo tea, yucca fruit, cactus containing edible berries, and other vegetation that was good to eat. We could find a wide range of healthful foods to enjoy while we planted the crops and tended to the sheep.

Teec Nos Pos itself also had beautiful cottonwood trees. In fact the name of the community means "cottonwood trees in a circle." But the most breathtaking scenery unfolded as we moved the sheep up the mountain for the summer. We could see Colorado in one direction, Utah in another. There were bears, deer, and other creatures. At the top of the mountain there grew different kinds of wild berries, which we harvested in August and September. We would climb the trees, eating the berries until our stomachs were full and our faces were streaked with juice. But there were so many that none of the elders minded. We always filled enough containers so there would be berries for everyone throughout the harsh winter.

The area had once contained an active volcano. Canyons dropped a thousand feet or more, their walls made of lava and ash from ancient eruptions. The rise to the top was steep, but at the top, approximately nine thousand feet above the valley, the weather was cool and pleasant, the ground so flat that we had no problem caring for thousands of sheep.

Up until I was six or seven years old, I was often assigned the least difficult task. Frequently the older children and adults on the mountain butchered sheep for those working on the farm. Then the carcass would be loaded on a horse or donkey and I would slowly ride with the animal down the winding, treacherous trails to the base. The distance from top to bottom was not great, less than two miles, but we had to travel a total of fifteen miles along a winding path with many switchbacks and other impediments. There was danger from bears and all manner of other wild animals that lived along the way.

The trip must have been safer than my imagination led me to believe, however, or I would not have been sent alone at that age. Undoubtedly there had not been any bear attacks against small boys on horseback. But I neither knew this nor would have believed it. I was terrified as I rode down the mountain, and terrified anew when returning with the groceries obtained from the exchange of the butchered sheep at the trading post.

Trying to show my courage as I traveled, I sang every song I knew over and over again. My voice, lifted in song, was not a pleasant one. I had no gift for music, and the sounds echoed painfully off the canyon walls. In my heart I believed it worked, though, because the bears never attacked me. I succeeded in returning to the top as I had made it to the bottom, unmolested, uneaten, and very tired.

Life on the mountain was easier than caring for the animals in our winter home. The area of Utah where we had our hogans had relatively sparse foliage. The animals would wander for several miles, then have to be brought back. But on the mountain there was plenty for them to eat. They would stay in a cluster for three or four hours, grazing one small area before moving what might be only a few hundred yards. This gave us kids plenty of time to play.

We would ride over to the camp of another extended Navajo family, meet their kids, and play games together. We had donkey races. We also had rifles and would practice target shooting. There was a lot of work, but we had a great deal of fun, too.

To some, this might sound like a primitive existence. White men had radios, talking pictures, trains, planes, indoor plumbing, and labor-saving devices. Air-conditioning had been invented more than a decade before I was born and was being used in a few businesses in southern Arizona's larger cities. Aspirin, invented in the mid-1900s, was helping to change the white people's hospitals from care stations for the dying to havens for the sick and injured, with a growing percentage of patients leaving in better health. Anglos were making some of the greatest advances in technology anyone had ever witnessed, and yet we Navajo knew only about horses, saddles, and wagons. We did not even know about cars. We were comfortable with what our ancestors had known, perhaps going back as far as First Man and First Woman.

However, a more careful examination of our life-style reveals a very different type of culture, far more advanced in ways that result in a healthy, happy life. First there was Navajo education, actually a lifelong process.

All Navajo education had a purpose: to teach wisdom, not just knowledge. We gained knowledge from the work we had to do each day. We learned how to care for the animals and the land. We learned how to use every part of the sheep and cattle that we slaughtered. We learned to make clothing, tools, and weapons from the materials all around us. We learned how to assist at birthing when necessary, and how to treat injuries in the field. We learned how to develop our bodies, and we studied the plants that could enhance our health.

We had no written laws. The rules under which we live were given to us by the Great Spirit, and thus were fair for all. They were mastered by the elders, who orally passed them from generation to generation. They were applied equally to everyone, and since they were the same laws by which the Great Spirit judged us, we had no problems with mutual respect.

During the last thirty years Anglo scientists have studied many of the herbs and plants used in our ceremonies. They have found that most of these herbs have specific components that affect disease, components that are little different from those used by pharmacists in more concentrated form in capsules and tablets. For example, for centuries, someone with a headache would drink tea made from willow bark. Scientists now know that willow bark contains salicylic acid, the main ingredient in aspirin.

Likewise, our medicine men might apply a spiderweb to a bleeding wound. I now know the web produces a chemical reaction that causes the blood to clot, thus stopping the flow. Instead of superstition, as Anglos once thought, the use of the spiderweb was based on accurate observation of its healing properties.

There is equal value in other native plants our medicine men cultivated over the centuries. They developed an understanding of the ways the plants affected the health of the Diné, adding them to the rituals they performed. It might be said that the Navajo were among the earliest holistic medical practitioners, recognizing the relationship of body, mind, and spirit.

Education is critical for both children and adults. The basic education is vocational. But the Coyote stories taught to children become more complex as the years pass, providing older children with appropriate cultural guidelines. Other, more sophisticated stories, told by the elders, especially during the harsh winter months when there is less work to do, deal with ever more complex issues of mortality, ethics, history, and religion, which adults must learn and understand. Thus, the creation story, and other stories of our early history, became more involved as the Navajo passed through the different stages of life. These stories are an oral tradition, and everyone is expected to learn them over the years.

By contrast, the white world seemed strange to my people. White people were given knowledge—the ability to read, to write, to calculate. They were prepared for a trade. They might be given a religious education or they might reject it as unimportant. They might keep track of current events, or their exposure to the world around them might be limited. They did not take the time to learn all the survival skills of their culture. Instead, they became specialists and let other specialists help with the necessities. The white hunter could not do carpenter work. The white carpenter did not know how to make moccasins. And so on, from special trade to special trade.

The members of Navajo extended families could fill all of their survival needs. We all learned to build temporary shelters and permanent hogans capable of protecting us from the harsh winters. We learned to grow and harvest food, to raise and butcher sheep and cattle, to travel on foot and on horseback. We learned to teach each succeeding generation, to ensure that neither knowledge nor wisdom was lost. We learned to respect the dream and vision of each individual, and so we were more in tune with what was important for our people than the average white person.

When I studied religion while in college, it was rather a shock to read the Ten Commandments. The Great Spirit did not have to give such rules to the Navajo. We never heard any talk about covetousness. The Navajo did not consider stealing a horse or sheep, or trying to take over someone's farmland. The laws of the Great Spirit were written in our hearts so that we would walk and breathe them. What was apparently so common for others that special laws had to be given was completely foreign to the Diné.

Not that we were arrogant. Few, if any, Navajo understood these facts at the time. It is only in hindsight that such comparisons can be made, only in hindsight that the Navajo people have come to understand that we were neither inferior nor superior to others. We did not have the technology of some surrounding cultures. But what we did have was far more complex, far more intellectually and spiritually challenging, than it appears when one first examines Navajo ways.

While my extended family prospered, there was tragedy within my immediate family. When I was two years old, my father was crushed by a horse. Given the year when this occurred and the extensiveness of the injuries, I doubt that he could have recovered no matter what treatment he received. Whatever the facts of his condition, he was too far from any hospital to be taken for help before he died. It was the burden of my mother, aided by my grandfather and uncles, to raise me until she eventually remarried.

The loss to my family was probably much greater than I understood at the time. My father had two wives—my mother and her older sister, a situation that was proof of his skills as a provider.

The Navajo did not practice polygamy like the Mormons who made their way west to Utah. They also never married women from different families. A man would marry a woman, then work hard for his family. If she had a sister who was not married, and if the man proved to be caring, a good provider, and a good husband, he would be gifted with his wife's sister, marrying her as well. If there was no unmarried sister, he would not marry another woman. Such arrangements were made only within a single family, and the single sister was never prevented from marrying during the time her brother-in-law was proving himself. It was only if she stayed single, and if her brother-in-law was a truly great man, that the second marriage would take place.

In my family, the most familiar story was that of my mother's grandmother and grandfather. After the Long Walk, when everyone returned home from Fort Sumner, some of the Navajo realized that there were going to be serious problems for them. They were exhausted, sick, horribly weakened by their time in captivity.

The Army arranged for the Navajo to use Fort Defiance as a resting place. Provisions and clothing had been stocked to help the people survive. As a result, some of my people, including my great-grandmother's family, settled at Fort Defiance rather than moving further. They wanted to get strong before considering where to spend the rest of their lives, and the fort was considered a safe place.

My maternal great-grandfather and his family did not stay at Fort Defiance. They moved to the Four Corners area to resume their lives.

I'm not certain where my maternal great-grandparents met. They were kids at Fort Sumner and knew each other from there, at least. The romance between them began when my great-grandfather and his father settled in the Four Corners region. The two men regularly took mules and rode the four days' trip to Fort Defiance to obtain needed food and clothing for their family. Although some of my great-grandfather's family had hidden from the Blue Coats in the Teec Nos Pos area, keeping much of their livestock safe until everyone returned from Fort Sumner, they did not have enough food for everyone. At least one full growing season was needed for his family to become self-sufficient again, and in the meantime they took advantage of what was available to help them at Fort Defiance.

Each time my maternal great-grandfather accompanied his father to Fort Defiance, the two of them stayed with my maternal great-grandmother's family. The young people renewed their friendship and decided to get married.

My maternal great-grandfather, whose name was Clah Cheschillige (Curly Haired Lefty), was already more prosperous than many Navajo because of the hidden livestock. Thus my great-grandmother found herself married into wealth that existed for few Navajo of the day.

Curly Haired Lefty took all of my great-grandmother's family and slowly moved them all the way to Teec Nos Pos during the first year after the marriage. There he and the others cleared land, built an orchard, increased the sheep and cattle, and made the area prosper. His in-laws were so impressed with his hard work that he was honored by also being allowed to marry my great-grandmother's younger sister.

The two unions led to a dozen children—six boys and six girls. As a result, I have a great many cousins in Teec Nos Pos, as well as on the western side of the Navajo Reservation.

Curly Haired Lefty and two of his sons became important tribal leaders. Curly Haired Lefty was a judge in the late 1800s and early 1900s, and one of his sons became the second Tribal Chairman. But the most influential was David Clah, still alive at this writing, though because he's in his nineties, he lives in an extended care facility. He was a tribal Council Delegate for approximately twenty years, from the 1940s through the 1960s, and he was also a religious activist over the years.

There were religious wars among the Navajo just before World War II. The Navajo had their own religion and culture, and Christian missionaries also became involved with the people. But a third religion, now called the Native American Church, was developing among the tribes in Oklahoma and the Dakotas. Quite different from the faith of my people, one sacrament involved the drinking of brewed peyote juice or use of peyote powder, a hallucinogenic drug. This drug was not abused, the way Anglo addicts eventually abused it, but was a serious part of the service. Although many Navajo were against the introduction of this unusual faith, David Clah became a supporter of religious tolerance among the people. However, tolerance was not always practiced, and there was a period in the 1930s when my people engaged in what came to be known as religious wars.

The wars became violent, and at times clans fought within themselves. Navajos who were against the use of peyote were deputized to infiltrate areas where the religion was practiced. Then they tried to arrest other Navajo, a highly destructive situation for the Diné. David Clah worked to end the wars and eventually became a leader in gaining the Freedom of Religion Act of the 1950s, which gave peyote use limited approval.

In the 1960s, David Clah and others won the right for all Native Americans to harvest peyote for religious use only in south Texas and Mexico. Those who truly practiced this faith were given special identification documents so they would not be arrested. And as a result of all that, today at least a third of the Navajo Nation belong to the Native American Church, whose solemn sacraments are practiced on designated Saturday nights. The remainder of the Navajo continue with the traditional religion of my people, or they are Catholic, Protestant, or Mormon. Thus David Clah is a highly respected man among the Navajo, and it was within his family that my father was proving himself after he married my mother's older sister. Eventually he showed the qualities his in-laws wanted to honor, and that was when his wife's younger sister, my mother, was given to him in marriage.

The stories of the individual family members were of interest to us within our clan, but they were not how we identified ourselves to others. Individual names meant nothing to the Navajo at the time I was born. We identified ourselves by our larger family groups, naming first the mother's clan and then that of the father. In my case, I would say: "I am Haskonhazohi born for Betani." My mother's clan was Haskonhazohi, and my father's was Betani, and the two names would tell the traditional Navajo everything they needed to know about me.

A major part of my early education was religious. The Navajo religion is complex, based on our understanding of the world as we experienced it. There are slight variations in the stories of the deities, depending on where in the Navajo Nation the stories are told, but this is because we followed an oral tradition that was carried on in isolation. The Judeo-Christian faith and most other Western religions have books that record the story of their past. The Old and New testaments of the Bible, the Koran, the Book of Mormon, and numerous other written documents provide a record of the early years of the various religions. Even then, there are slight variations, such as the ancient Jewish story that says Lilith, not Eve, was the first woman and that Eve was created later.

For the Navajo, the most important deity was Changing Woman, also known as the Turquoise Goddess or Estsánatlehi. During the time of darkness, Mother Earth rose up to meet Father Sky. A great mist appeared on the sacred mountain, and when the mist rose, a child was heard crying. This was Changing Woman, who went from infancy to adolescence to adulthood to old age in just four days. Later she would be thought of in relation to the seasons, as an infant in spring, a teenager in summer, an adult in fall, and an old woman in winter.

Changing Woman was responsible for all creation on earth. First she had intercourse with the sun and gave birth to two monster-slayers, the deities Nayenezgáni (Warrior God) and Tobadsistsini (Child of Water). Then came the Diné, all of whom lived at first in the Fourth World, a land populated by monsters, which made the Warrior Gods important protectors.

As it evolved, our religion became more complex in order to explain everything there was to know about life. Changing Woman was created after First Man and First Woman, but she is the most important deity on earth. It can be said that she is the child of the mountain, her father being the sky. With such a history, you can understand why certain mountains and other places were considered sacred to the Navajo. Such mountains defined territory that was never to be abandoned, even at the expense of one's own life.

All things that are natural—trees, rivers, rocks, mountains, the sun, the moon, and the stars—are deities. Everything on earth must be respected as a living being. The rock that to others seems immobile and without purpose to the Navajo contains a spirit, a soul, the ability to hear what is happening and to act in ways we cannot see.

Our religion nurtures a deep respect for nature. When each blade of grass has a soul, a life, and an equal place with all else in existence, it cannot be taken for granted. It is to be used properly, respected, not casually destroyed. We show reverence for all creation because all creation is filled with living spirits.

Thus, when we prayed, we looked for a piñon, juniper, or other tree that approximated our height. We then placed some objects—certain stones, perhaps—before the tree as a sacrifice. We explained to the spirit of the tree that the object was a gift in return for the spirit making contact with the Creator to express our desire to become strong like the tree.

There were also certain special trees brought from the Fourth World to the present world, and their spirits could provide more power. Likewise, when we encountered areas ravaged by the intense force of rushing water or struck by lightning, we prayed to gain the forces of water and lightning to serve as protection from harm.

Always we sought the special gift of the spirit. If a tree or rock was seen as indestructible, then the Navajo asked the spirit of the rock or tree to make him indestructible, too.

The request was based on our belief that all living things would share their spirit with the Navajo people. Some spirits are good, some are bad, and some are both good and bad. For example, the snake can be protective, but it also can be vicious, and thus it must be approached with great respect. Likewise the spider can be either protective or deadly. The positive characteristics of the spider emerge out of the legend surrounding the construction of the web. When an enemy was coming at the spider, the web could be woven very fast to stop the aggressor, much like a barbed-wire fence.

If a Navajo was going into battle, he might pray to the spirit of the spider for the ability to spin a web to stop his enemy. Against that power, an attacking enemy would suddenly find himself helpless, as though tied up. The Navajo would not expect actually to see the web, only to have its protective power, provided by the spirit of the spider.

Typically, a Navajo might take some corn pollen as a sacrifice to the spider. Then he might say something like this: "I pray to you, spider spirit, that you will accept this sacrifice. And in return, I want your spirit to protect me from my enemy by the use of your web."

Some prayers might be more elaborate, such as a prayer to one of the deities whose armor was so strong that no arrow or spear could penetrate it. These prayer songs requested the protection of the armor the deity carried: "Your impregnable shield, the shield with a lion across it and a snake sticking out, weaving back and forth, its tongue darting about ready to strike, is now my shield, my protection. Your leggings of iron are now my leggings. Your chest protector of metal is now my protection. Nothing can penetrate my body."

Every day we believed that we were living in a world in which it was possible to reach out and gain the protection of the living things all around us. We carried corn pollen, said prayers, sang sacred songs, and believed ourselves indestructible in adversity because of the powers we could receive from the spirits all around.

We never fought among ourselves. We also had deities unique to our land, which, when I was growing up, I believed formed the entire universe. There were brief mentions of other deities sacred to our enemies, but these were unfamiliar to me.

For us, medicine, psychiatry, and religion were all interconnected. For example, if we had a bad dream, we called upon a Hand Trembler, a diagnostician who first analyzed the dream and related its meaning. Next he decided upon the necessary ceremony, to be performed immediately. He might also suggest a second ceremony of a different type to be performed a few days or weeks later.

Someone in the family would seek out a medicine man trained in the necessary ceremony. The next night, when the ceremony was held, the entire family participated. There were songs and prayers. The dreamer took corn pollen and white corn meal. The ceremony might take a day or two or three, depending on the circumstances.

If someone did not feel well, the Hand Trembler might decide that he or she needed a Beauty Way Ceremony for purification. Again, the appropriate medicine man would be sought, for not all medicine men were trained in all ceremonies. And always the family would participate.

The extended family gathered for ceremonies every week or two, since there were enough people in any given area to ensure that such help was often required. While this may seem like a primitive ritual, it was actually an early form of modern-day group therapy. No one lived in isolation. No one could avoid helping the sick, the troubled, or the hurting. There were no orphanages for Navajo children who lost their families. There were no outcasts among our people. There were no prisons, no old people's homes. We were never alone within the Navajo Nation, never isolated from the loving help of others.

The entire community was responsible for everyone. If I did something wrong and someone in the family died shortly afterward, I would be told that I had caused the death. Wrong acts always had their penalties, and we were very much our brother's keepers.

Although the ceremonies served as acts of renewal for everyone, we children required the most frequent ceremonies because we were still learning what was right and wrong, still testing the limits of what was proper. For example, we were not allowed to go near graveyards because they were considered dangerous. Dead people's spirits never suffered, but there was evil connected with death, and a dead person's spirit could cause the living to suffer. And although the dead did not seek out the living, anyone who went near the burial site had to undergo a purification ceremony.

The adults understood this and respected it. When someone died, the body was either shoved into a crevice in the rocks, if such a spot existed, or buried as quickly as possible. Usually two or three people handled this chore, which was followed by the purification ceremony. Everyone then knew to stay away from the place where the Navajo had been buried, though we children used to challenge each other, trying to get up the courage to go close to it. We were being foolhardy, like city children playing chicken, running into the street to see how close they could come to moving cars without getting hurt. And invariably we would be scolded for the risk we had taken, then forced to go through the purification ceremony to protect ourselves.

One time I went to play where a dead relative had been buried. There was a board over the spot, and I began hanging from the board in full view of my mother and grandparents, who were perhaps a hundred yards away. I knew it was dangerous. All the kids knew it, but I had been dared to hang there, and, much to the horror of my family, I was more frightened of the other kids thinking I was afraid than of the danger from the grave.

My mother and grandparents were almost hysterical. They were certain I was going to die, perhaps even before they could get to the medicine man. They raced off to get him, and the purification ceremony was performed immediately, all further punishment waiting until I was spiritually safe.

According to Navajo beliefs, the only natural death was a result of extreme old age. As in all societies, some people lived through many seasons and were ninety to one hundred years old at the time of their death. We considered these exceptions the only people to have died a natural death. Everyone else died as the result of some evil spirit or in response to some offense against the deities, either their own or that of someone within the extended family. Thus we took our responsibilities to one another very seriously.

Everything we encountered was spiritual. Even enemies were filled with a spirit we had to identify, because identification allowed us to protect ourselves.

We believed that encountering other tribes in peace or war contaminated us. We frequently engaged in trade with other tribes, an important act of commerce but one that exposed us to spirits that were dangerous for the Diné. As soon as we could after each encounter, we had a Squaw Dance, the important cleansing ceremony that rid us of the influence of the dangerous spirits.

This was the custom most misunderstood by the Bureau of Indian Affairs. When I eventually went to the BIA school, there were square dances for the children that were intended to help us overcome our shyness. What the school officials did not understand was that touching a girl of the same clan, even though sex was not involved, meant that we would go blind or insane. It was part of an incest taboo.

Touching someone who was not Navajo, including the white teachers of the BIA, meant that that person's spirit would contaminate us. The spirits of others were safe for them, but could mean death to the Navajo.

Even dances between Navajo boys and girls were taboo during the teen years. A Navajo boy had to be twenty-one before he was allowed to be involved with girls. At that time the family would analyze his maturity, his skills, and his value as a man. Then they would seek a compatible girl and arrange a marriage. Yet the boarding school teachers talked with us about girlfriends and boyfriends, something we were not allowed to think about at home. They even showed us movies that included scenes in which people were kissing and chastely making love. They did not realize that that was not part of the Navajo · world. It was something teenagers might see in a theater back East, but it was foreign to us, foreign to our culture. For us, it was blatant sexuality that we neither understood nor were prepared to handle, emotionally or spiritually.

As a result, whether the non-Navajo teachers were trying to show us they cared for us through touching or were trying to entertain us with Anglo dances that white children enjoyed, they were giving us messages that led to fear and distrust. We lived in terror until we could return home to be cleansed by a Squaw Dance. It seemed to us that instead of loving and socializing us, the BIA teachers were trying to kill us. They never bothered to learn our culture and couldn't understand why we were in constant terror when we were unable to have a cleansing ceremony. They just thought we were pagan savages who were more interested in rituals than in personal growth.

Our religion defined where it was safe to live and how large an area we needed to take advantage of the strength and goodness of our deities. The elders taught that the influence of the Navajo deities, though they were all-powerful, was limited to certain areas. The land where we lived was sacred, filled with deities who would help us. But if the Navajo left the sacred land, as they had during the Long Walk to Fort Sumner, they lost the protection of most of the deities. They still had the Sun, the Moon, the Stars, the Dawn, and a few of the other deities. But they could no longer call upon the spirits that had surrounded them in their own land. They could only rely upon healing and purifying ceremonies, whose protection was limited, making them highly vulnerable to diseases, violence, and death.

Years later, when I studied the Christian religion, I found that there were many similarities between the Navajo faith and the stories in the Bible. In Genesis, God walked in the Garden of Eden, speaking to Adam (First Man) and Eve (First Woman). A talking serpent used his wiles and persuaded them to defy the Supreme Being. There is the flood story, which existed in the Navajo religion as well, and the story of Jonah swallowed by the giant sea creature. And there are numerous instances where men asked God's power to become their power, whether to enable them to heal the sick or to give them comfort and protection, as in the Twenty-third Psalm.

The practitioners of both religions are expected to be humble. In both religions, their abilities are seen as gifts from a higher power that are to be approached in a worshipful, respectful manner. In both religions, people are expected to be the stewards of all life.

What was different for us, and what added to our hardships when we were forced to live on the reservation, was that we saw the land we had known as our true home. So long as we were in the midst of all our deities, we were safe, loved, and protected from harm. We knew how to act. We knew how to get help, even when we were alone, lost in a forest, away from all other Navajo, because the deities of the sacred mountains, the rocks, the trees, the coyotes, the birds, and all other living beings were there to help us. We were one with the earth. We lost this protection and comfort when we left the Navajo land and when sections of it were denied to us. It was as bad to be denied access to our four sacred mountains, for example, as it was to be away from the Navajo land, in the midst of the deities of our enemies.

The Diné's main contact with the outside world was often through the trading post, a general store that stocked everything from fabrics to clothing, food, plows, and wheelbarrows. Most trading posts were run by white men, not because the Navajo were inferior in business but because our culture prevented us from becoming financially successful store owners.

Whereas Anglos look upon the products in a store as items for purchase, no matter who desires them, the Navajo are taught to share their goods within their extended family. If a white man walks into a trading post owned by his uncle, he will be expected to pay for whatever he wants, but the Navajo consider it wrong to deny someone something you own, even the stock from your own store. Very often a Navajo trading post operator would go broke giving merchandise to family members who desired something free or below cost. He did not understand that his actions would ruin him, and he dared not violate the tradition that required him to share.

In Navajo culture, your father's family is obligated to take care of you. The Navajo term for this obligation translates as "the person you're born for," meaning that your father's relatives can't deny you anything.

I remember as a small boy, after my father died, my aunt, my mother's sister, would urge me to visit my paternal grandmother. She knew that these visits would provide me with the things my mother could not afford. Every time my grandmother saw me, she would start to cry, saying, "My God, you would not have such raggedy clothes if your father was alive." Then she would take me to the trading post and buy me a new pair of trousers or shoes. Later she would fix food for me to take home. This was the tradition, and in the same way, people would come to my grandmother on my mother's side. This all went around and around, but it was our custom to give gifts and to take care, even if everyone was pretty well off. Gift giving was a gesture of goodwill and respect.

Since it was only within one's extended family that such courtesies had to be extended, there was occasionally a successful Navajo trader. However, he was always located in an area where he had no immediate relatives. It was the only way he could make a profit.

The trading posts changed with the times, stocking items according to the needs of the people and their ability to pay. I remember my first visit to such a place when I was a small boy. There was a U-shaped counter, which was over my head, and behind it the trader did much of his business.

Canned goods, coffee, and other staples were kept directly behind the counter. In one corner stood a glass case containing a wide variety of candy—flavored sugar sticks, licorice, chocolate, and other types, most of it sold by the penny or by the pound. There was also a scale on which to weigh potatoes and other foods.

In back was a room that held additional supplies, bags of flour and similar goods. To the left of that room was a display of utensils needed for working with the animals, such as harness parts and accessories, and tools for repairing and maintaining wagons. Farther to the left were shoes, clothing, and fabric. There were shawls, blankets, and sewing goods.

High up on the wall and hanging from the ceiling were washboards, buckets, and so forth. Soft drinks, packaged goods, and other food items were also for sale.

During the winter, five to ten Navajo would come into the store to get warm. They would arrive when the store opened, talk with the trader and one another, and watch people buy their merchandise. At noon, when the trader closed for lunch, the men would buy a tin of sardines, a box of crackers, and some soda pop. They would eat outside until the trader reopened, and then they would go back inside to continue their gossiping and people watching. It was only near closing time that they would buy the merchandise they needed and return home.

Shoes were a popular item purchased in the trading posts, but my people did not understand the idea of foot width. Moccasins were made of animal hide and had extensive stretch to them. When a moccasin was custom-made, the feet were outlined on the cowhide that was used. After that the moccasins would expand and contract, the custom pair as well as mass-produced pairs, fitting many different people with different-sized feet. But the custom-made moccasins always begin with the exact outline of the buyer's feet. Often a man with a wide foot could wear the same width pair as a man with a narrow foot, the moccasin sides stretching to fit. That was not the case with the shoes available from the trading post. These were the type worn by Anglos, their form rigid, the differences in width quite important. But my family did not know this, and the trading post operator did not say anything. Either the trader assumed my people knew how to buy shoes, or he did not bother to stock a variety of lengths and widths, since no one seemed to care.

Each time our feet grew, our parents took a string and measured the length of our feet. They tied a knot where the string went just past our toes and another knot just behind our heels. Then they took the measurement to the trading post and brought home new shoes of the proper length.

Sometimes we got lucky and the shoes fit perfectly. At other times the shoes cramped our toes, even though the length was right. When that occurred, we took a knife and slit the sides of the shoes so that our toes would have room. This made walking in wet weather rather uncomfortable, but we did not mind. We thought that all shoes were like this. We assumed that white men also occasionally had to slit the sides of the shoes they wore.

Colors and styles in shoes were also unimportant to us. We took whatever the trader had, usually somewhat narrow, but always the right length.

A hand gas pump and a weighing area for wool stood outside the trading post. The weighing area was used frequently. Only an occasional car pulled up to the gas pump.

Our family would butcher a lot of sheep or goats over three or four weeks and save the hides to sell to the trader. Then one of us children would take them to the trading post. When it was my turn, my grandfather would load my donkey with a dozen hides or more, and I would lead the animal to the trading post.

I used to dread that trip. I didn't have the best of clothes. The hides always stank. And I always felt as though the other kids laughed at me.

One day, when I was seven or eight years old, I felt so embarrassed that I decided to wait until all the children and adults had left the trading post. I sat on a hill with my donkey tied to a tree and waited for everyone to leave. It never happened. If someone left, someone else arrived. Finally I got the nerve to go see the trader. I sold the hides and bought the groceries my mother wanted me to get with the money he paid.

Every family, no matter what its circumstances, sold hides. Some families, like mine, suddenly poor after the livestock reduction, had to make do with whatever we had. We children then had to wear our clothes until they were so tattered and raggedy that they could not be mended. I don't know why I was embarrassed by this. So many families suffered during the livestock reduction that I shouldn't have felt that way. But something about the circumstances made me feel humiliated.

Other families still had money, but they were stingy and refused to spend any money on their children. In these families, even if there were two thousand head of sheep, the children still dressed in rags. All their wealth was saved, though for what, nobody knew.

Still other families were also well-to-do and liked to spend their money clothing their kids. Their children wore cowboy boots, Levi's, a nice shirt, and a nice hat.

All three types of families were shepherds. We all sold hides. We all had a similar life-style. The trader served another, more specific purpose for our family. All Navajo have one name that is special to the family and one name that is given to us when we are older. The family name is used by our parents, brothers, and sisters. It is special, almost sacred, and we do not normally use it when we are not with our family. My family's Navajo name for me was Hoshkaisith.

When we are older, we are given a second name that is based on some aspect of our life. For example, if you are related to someone important, you might be called by a name that means that person's grandson. If the older man has several grandchildren, your name would mean the first grandson, the second one, or whatever number you might be.

You might also have a name in the community that is not necessarily used to your face. For example, if you are always wearing red flannel shirts, you might be called "the man in the red shirt" behind your back. Then your name in the community would be Mr. Red Shirt.

My father, for some reason, decided that I should have an Anglo name. He went to the trader and asked him about a name of someone famous he could use for me.

The trader explained that there was a famous person in the Bible named Peter. My father discussed the name with my mother, and she agreed they would call me that. However, she never called me Peter. Instead she called me Bedo, a nickname the others sometimes used as well.

I have other memories of those days at the trading post. Once when I was seven or eight, old enough to go to the trading post on my own, my mother gave me two fifty-cent pieces to buy a sack of potatoes and some other food items. A dollar was a lot of money in those days, a big responsibility for a small child.

I was bored while walking and decided to create a game. Indian men played a game that was a little like horseshoes. They would dig a small hole in the ground, then stand back and toss a silver dollar toward the hole. The man who pitched the dollar closest to the hole was the winner.

I tossed one of my fifty-cent pieces ahead of me, being careful to notice exactly where it landed. Then I tossed the other, seeing how close I could get to it. I had been playing the game for several minutes on my way to the trading post when I lost one of the coins. I was certain that my toss had been perfect, the one half dollar landing on the other. But something had gone wrong. I didn't know if the coin had bounced in one direction or another. All I knew was that the coin was gone, my family would go hungry without the groceries, and I was in trouble.

I began searching frantically in all directions. The coin was there. It had to be. The earth couldn't have swallowed it. Yet I could not find it, no matter how hard I looked.

Desperate, I thought about my religious teachings to see if there was anything in the beliefs and religious history of my people that might help me. That was when I remembered the story of the Bear Lady.

There once was a lady who could turn herself into a bear. This was at a time when there was interaction among all creation—animals, people, and spirits. Thus it was possible for her to look like everyone else during the day and to turn into a bear whenever she chose, though at first she only did this at night so no one would know who she was.

The Bear Lady was extremely violent, killing everyone, including her relatives. The men resisted. They went on hunting parties, attacking her with arrows, but she did not die. Instead she returned to her cave, built a fire, then danced and sang while the arrows dropped harmlessly away. By morning she was a lady again, looking like everyone else.

People began to hide from the bear, knowing that was the only way to be safe. When the Bear Lady could not see them or smell them, she would pee on the ground. Whichever way the urine flowed, that would be the direction she went. Invariably she found the person in hiding.

I decided to act like the Bear Lady. I unzipped my pants and peed on the ground, watching to see which way it ran. I followed the pee, and three or four feet from where I thought it had landed, I found that fifty-cent piece. I didn't risk losing those coins again and put them inside my pocket until I got to the trading post. But I was convinced that any time in the future that I lost something, all I would have to do was pee like the Bear Lady and I would find whatever it was.

The story of the Bear Lady did not have a happy ending, as mine did. She killed everyone except her brother, the youngest child in the family and the last survivor.

The boy was told by a spirit that he was in danger of being killed and that he had to be prepared. His sister, the Bear Lady, had gotten away with killing everyone, even those who shot her full of arrows. What saved her was that she had no heart in her bear's body.

The spirit explained that the Bear Lady's heart was stored alive in a tree, not inside her body. The boy was to take his bow and arrow and go to the tree where the heart was stored. The spirit would send a bird to show him the exact location. He was to shoot his arrow just below the bird; in that way he would strike the heart and kill his sister, the Bear Lady.

The boy was uncertain what to believe, so the spirit gave him a way to know that his sister was the Bear Lady and had to die. When his sister came to him in the daylight, to fix his long hair into a beautiful knot, the boy would sit in an east-west direction, letting his sister stand behind him. In that way, he could watch her shadow and see when she began to turn into a bear to attack his neck.

Following the spirit's advice, the boy shot his arrows toward the woods, then let his sister work on his hair. Each time he saw her shadow start to change into a bear, he said that he had to be retrieve his arrows. Instantly she turned back into a lady while he went into the woods, following him so that she could continue working on his hair. She did not realize that he was searching for the bird that would show him the location of her heart.

Finally the boy saw a bird land on a branch. He aimed his arrow at the heart. His sister came racing behind him, begging him not to shoot. But he knew that she was the killer bear, and he had no sympathy for the woman who had once been his sister. He fired his arrow, striking the heart, and his sister fell, bleeding, just as blood also flowed from the heart, down the tree, and onto the ground.

The spirit warned the boy to use an arrowhead to draw a line between the two rivers of blood. Otherwise the blood from her body would touch the blood from the heart, and she would live again. He drew the line, the two streams of blood stopped without meeting, and the danger from the Bear Lady was ended.

The story of the Bear Lady was meant to illuminate several beliefs. The first was that if you draw a line with an arrowhead, your enemy cannot penetrate that protection. The second was that when something seems indestructible, as the bear did, you must just find the right place to strike your blow in order to kill it.

Another story was told about people and animals, though it was not one I thought about when searching for my missing coin. This story was meant to explain why humans and animals can no longer talk together as they were believed to have done during the early years.

According to this story, the night animals decided to have a contest with the day animals, something the deities did not want them to do. The animals held the contest, and the winner would dominate. If the night animals won, there would be night all the time. If the day animals won, there would be day all the time.

Each side struggled mightily, but the contest was a draw. Time was split evenly between day and night. However, the deities felt that a punishment was needed because of the animals' disobedience, so they made the animals unable to communicate with the human beings.

Apart from the spiritual education, the most important lesson we children were taught was to honor our parents and other adults. Our mothers loved us. Our fathers loved us. And they both demanded respect. But our grandparents were often the ones who lectured us daily, helping us to understand the reality of life, and they often had the greatest impact on our values.

We children were often harshly lectured, because we committed some social infraction almost daily. We had to look directly into the face of the adult scolding us, usually one of our grandparents, and not hide our faces. We were told not to cry, to be strong, because life would not always be easy for us.

The adults explained that there would come a time when we would be subject to ridicule, when others would call us names or call our children names. We had to learn to take it. We would not always be protected, as we were in the family. We had to be physically, emotionally, and spiritually strong to withstand any adversity that might come along.

We were told that we would marry, but there might be a divorce. A weakling would fall apart and not know what to do. We had to be strong enough to accept the shock, to carry on with life.

The lesson was especially meaningful for me, since my father had died and my mother had raised us children on her own for several years before remarrying. The same chores existed before and after Father died. The responsibilities were no lighter. She had to be strong to deal with the previously unthinkable. We had to learn to be strong so we could endure whatever might come along in our adult lives.

And so we learned to honor our elders, to listen to them, to learn from them, never to make fun of them. Leaders were feared and respected. Their lectures were the greatest punishment we could get. We cared so much for the leader that we did not want to be shamed by having him lecture us for wrongdoing.

In my childhood, the most feared adult was my great-uncle David Clah. Every time he came to the hogan, he would say to me, "Why are you sitting there? Why aren't you out chopping wood? Why aren't you going to get water?" These chores were appropriate for my small size, chores I routinely handled, but I had not been told to do such work by my mother and grandparents. Either I had completed such tasks or it was not time to do them again. I was not being bad when he came, and yet he made me feel that I was shirking my duty, being lazy.

David Clah always carried a big handkerchief in his pocket. When he arrived, he would take out that handkerchief, hand it to me, and tell me to wipe his nose.

It was a disgusting, demeaning act, but I would do it, because I was afraid of him and did not want to take his wrath.

Later I wondered why my family made me endure all that. They knew he was being unfair. They knew he was treating me badly.

Only when I was older and could better understand the Navajo way did I fully appreciate the lesson they were giving me by allowing my great-uncle to treat me as he had. David Clah was teaching me humility. He was showing me that no matter how low I had to go, I had to accept what was happening. If I could do that, I could endure anything.

Another great-uncle, Chizsi, saw me herding sheep with my mother when I was five years old. I was in brush over my head when I heard him shouting "Pete! Pete!"

I was afraid of the man and did not want to respond. My mother knew this, but when I asked her what I should do, she told me to answer him, which I did.

"Get out in the open," he shouted in Navajo. "I'm going to shoot you."

I asked my mother what I should do. I was certain he meant what he was saying, but he was my elder, someone I was to respect.

Mother told me to go into the clearing as he asked and, terrified, I complied. I realized that if I didn't obey him, I would encounter him again soon, and then I would have to answer for my disobedience. But shoot me . . . ?

Suddenly a shot rang out, but the bullet came nowhere near me. I also knew that since the bullet did not hit the ground anywhere around me, he had intended only to scare me. It was a harsh lesson in unquestioning obedience and respect. In a rather perverted way, it may also have been a lesson in trust, though it was fortunately not one he put me through again.

Years later when I joined the U.S. Marine Corps, I was put into the same kinds of situations. We had to learn to handle ourselves in combat where, at any instant, we could be wounded or killed. We had to learn to obey without question, to move against our natural inclination for self-protection in order to triumph over the enemy. During basic training, our superiors ordered us into situations in which we would be exposed to live gunfire, staying unhurt only if we did exactly as we were told. Yet my first day on the course, where many of the young men were terrified, I felt no fear. My relatives had put me through the same training as a child. The Marine Corps regimen was a familiar one for me.

And all of my abilities were the outgrowth of both the spiritual teachings of the Navajo and my knowledge of what had been endured by the survivors of the Long Walk. We children were raised to prevail over any hardship, to survive any adversity. We did not realize how soon the problems would begin anew.

CHAPTER TWO

During my childhood, changes were taking place for the Navajo, changes that began in 1923, though my family was unaware of them at the time.

In 1868 the Navajo had been allowed to leave the Fort Sumner area, the place where they had been isolated following the Long Walk that ended the early wars against my people. At that time all but 3 million acres of land had been taken from us. This was one-tenth of the 30 million acres we had considered our home before our forced removal. Much of it was outside traditional areas of religious significance as well as away from grazing land that we had used for generations.

The white men provided maps of the newly divided territory to the Navajo chiefs before their release from Fort Sumner. Treaties were signed, and the soldiers assumed the Navajo would respect the boundaries. They did not realize that the Navajo people did not know how to read maps. They told directions by their awareness of the terrain they traveled in relation to the sacred mountains. Their return to the land meant, to them, that they could return to the familiar patterns of the past. They moved back to wherever they or their relatives had lived. There they raised sheep, cattle, and horses in the midst of their special spirits.

My people had no possessions, only the clothing on their backs and perhaps a few blankets, yet the 7,500 survivors of the Long Walk were skilled at what they did. Between 1868 and the first part of the twentieth century, prosperity returned to the Navajo people. Livestock abounded, and the people regained their strength. Each extended family had thousands of sheep, horses, and cattle, and the grazing land kept expanding.

Although the westward migration of white men began with the discovery of gold in California in 1848, the Navajo land was never particularly desirable. It was only at the turn of the century that the railroad, which had expanded to such previously isolated areas as the Grand Canyon, made a concerted effort to bring travelers to see the wonders of the West. Some of these men and women chose to relocate, increasing the population of communities as small as Taos, New Mexico, and as large as Flagstaff, Arizona.

Periodically, during this era of slow white western expansion, government officials discovered that the Navajo were living outside the mapped area of the 1868 treaty. The local Indian agent would look into the problem, find that the Navajo needed the land they were using for their livestock, and request that Congress alter the treaty to allow for the additional acreage known to be in use. Since no one else wanted the land, permission was almost routine. What had been used illegally suddenly fell inside a legitimate new boundary.

At first, reclaiming the land occurred by chance. However, once the Navajo realized that this could be accomplished just by expanding their grazing area until government officials noticed, they deliberately challenged the new boundaries. They moved farther and farther from the assigned territories, until complaints forced the Indian agent to appeal for restructuring. Then they were given the land they had commandeered through expanded use.

In the early 1920s, the white settlers and ranchers began to notice that the Navajo were encroaching on territory that they wanted. The Anglos were also gaining a stronger voice in Congress than were the Indian agents, especially after the Utah, New Mexico, and Arizona territories became full states.

A new policy was established, whose goal was twofold: to try to stop the Navajo land expansion beyond borders that were already several times larger than those designated under the treaty of 1868, and to limit or reduce the numbers of Navajo livestock so that the Navajo would not need additional land.

Originally the government thought that it would not succeed in its dual goal. Expansion by white families was still limited, the population of the largest cities in the western states often being less than the current population of the smaller towns in the eastern states. The government decided to make a trade-off, telling the Navajo that if the extended families would encourage one another to reduce their livestock, they would receive more land.

In 1925 the government agencies concerned with Indian affairs realized that many people were accepting more land without making a serious livestock-reduction effort. A forced reduction of livestock was instituted by the government.

These orders did not have much effect on my family until 1934, when it was estimated that the Navajo Nation had approximately half as much livestock as it had owned a decade earlier. I was six years old when my family was ordered by the government to get rid of most of our sheep, cattle, and horses. I did not understand what was happening. I did not know that my generation would be the last to experience the old way of life, or that I would be forced to culturally advance thousands of years in the next two decades. All I knew was that everyone in my family was upset, the women crying, the men in shock.

No longer were we allowed the traditional two homes. We were given boundaries that confined us almost exclusively to the farming area of Teec Nos Pos and the mountain region where we kept the sheep in summer. We were ordered to reduce our livestock drastically or the government would destroy our animals for us. The impact of the order was the same for the Navajo as if someone came to you and took away your life savings, then cut your annual income to a fraction of what it had been in the past.

The land restrictions ensured the forced reductions of livestock. My family had been using the land in the most effective manner possible. Less land meant that it would be impossible for us to raise enough sheep to maintain our wealth.

Also in 1934 a decision was made to freeze the Navajo Nation's boundaries at between 17 million and 18 million acres. No more land would be available to my people, though we had managed to regain approximately six times what we had lost after the Long Walk. Yet this was only slightly more than half the land that the Navajo had used before the wars of the 1850s. More important, the approximately 35 million acres that had once formed the Navajo Nation were within the boundaries of the four sacred mountains of our religion. We had gained more than we had, but we were still cut off from what we regarded as our spiritual mother, father, and siblings. We had won a victory of sorts, yet parts of our heritage, our religion, and our home were denied us.

This was more than an economic issue. When we raised sheep, cattle, and horses without restrictions, when we grew whatever crops we could handle, our people had freedom. Your success was determined by how energetic you were. You could achieve anything you desired if you wished to work for it. Each day there was opportunity to experience the limitless blessings of the Great Spirit, to have pride in what you could achieve from the world we were given to nurture and share.

At first the government tried to force us to sell our livestock, insisting on prices that were ten cents on the dollar compared with the true market value. But even if the government had allowed a fair sale based on market prices throughout the country, we still would not have wanted to sell. Sheep were like money in the bank; the more you had, the better your life, your future, and your family's future. In some ways sheep were better than money because, even when market prices were depressed, the animals could be slaughtered for personal consumption.

Suddenly families with 3,000 to 5,000 sheep had to rid themselves of all but 200 to 300 animals. Grazing patterns changed, and the work load was dramatically lightened. The Navajo self-sufficiency was ended in almost every case.

The livestock reduction meant that no Navajo could ever accumulate any more wealth (sheep, cattle, and horses) than he possessed at the time of the reduction. Hard work, determination, and all of man's other admirable traits would go unrewarded forever as a result of the change. It was a situation that denied the people hope.

What happened in that year was something that all the violence of the nineteenth century had failed to accomplish. Almost overnight the Navajo Nation, as it had existed from well before our recorded history, was destroyed.

The children were the last to fully realize what was happening. We were still tending the sheep, the job that had been ours for generations. I was very small, but I worked a full day along with the older children in my family. Yet we were the only ones who worked. There was no longer any work to occupy the adults. They were suddenly without purpose, a people who no longer gained their history, their value, and their religion from being in harmony with life as they cared for the animals, tilled the soil, and worked long hours in nature. Everything they valued, and everything from which they took their value, had suddenly been taken away from them. They were instantly helpless, their daily existence seemingly without meaning.

People soon began to look for supplemental income. My grandfather and uncles worked in CCIO, the New Deal program called the Civilian Conservation Corps—Indian Division. They received a dollar a day.

Others left the reservation to work on the railroad or do migrant work. The people were forced to give up the close-knit families that had provided the Navajo way and the change began to destroy the very fabric of the Navajo society.

By the time I was of school age, the livestock reduction had become vicious. Bulldozers were brought onto the reservation to help the white men dig massive burial ditches. Then other men with rifles shot large numbers of sheep, tossed the corpses in the ditches, covered them with dirt, and left them to rot.

There was no pretense of giving us a chance to sell the animals. There was no effort to understand the damage to our culture, to even attempt to help us find an alternative means of earning a livelihood.

The official excuse was that the extensive livestock holdings were causing soil erosion. Dirt was moving into the San Juan River, which emptied into Hoover Dam. If this continued, the silt buildup in the dam would cause flooding.

No one among the Navajo was ever certain that this was true. All we knew was that our wealth, our heritage, and our culture were being shattered. Without having experienced a culture other than our own, we were expected instantly to adapt to a world few of us had even seen and almost none of us understood.

The Navajo people became sharply divided over what to do about the children. The elders all accepted the fact that the old ways were being destroyed. Some decided to give up. Some felt the need to endure. Some agreed that it was time to change.

An estimated 30 percent of Navajo adults decided that the only future their children had was with white man's education. The Navajo had always believed in training their children for survival. For generations that had meant an education that centered on working the land, hunting, being a part of their parents' life, religion, and toil. Now there was something new. A family that had owned thousands of sheep would now be allowed to keep no more than eighty-five. Only twenty-five head of cattle could be retained. And the number of horses had to be reduced to five. The land they had once traveled so freely was now restricted. But there was a greater world where white men and other Indian tribes lived and worked with tools unfamiliar to us. They lived in hogans that were far more elaborate and contained devices we had never seen. For these Navajo parents, the BIA schools seemed the only way to prepare their children for life in this unfamiliar world.

The decision to send children to the BIA schools did not change parental fears or diminish their determination to continue their religious practices. Squaw Dances would be held whenever possible. The stories of the Navajo religion would be taught when the children were home with the family. Something would be lost, of course, though no one was certain just what. Yet it seemed a price that had to be paid to ensure their children's future.

The remaining 70 percent of Navajo parents felt that the old ways were the only proper ways. Yet even here there were compromises. For example, there came a time when the law required that all Indian children attend the BIA schools. Special government agents were sent out to ensure compliance, and families that were against the BIA could get into trouble if they did not obey.

These pressures created much confusion among the Navajo even though white people's laws should not have had such an effect on us. But having just returned from the Long Walk, we hesitated to do anything that might lead to retribution. Many of us kids were being trained to survive what our families had experienced in case it occurred again. We had been a sovereign nation within the boundaries of the United States since 1868, and that had not changed. However, several laws passed by Congress in 1934 were to effect a change in the Navajo government, so that when the BIA insisted that its rulings were more powerful than Navajo clan decisions, my people feared challenging the whites openly.

Beginning in 1934, the Indian Reorganization Act instructed every Indian tribe except the Navajo to prepare a constitution based essentially on the U.S. Constitution and subject to the approval of the secretary of the interior. These tribes were to remain somewhat sovereign on the reservations, but when there was a conflict, the white laws would supersede their own. In any dispute, the whites would triumph.

For the Navajo, however, the change was less drastic. For the first time in the history of the Navajo Nation, the idea of a single leader was created. A twelve-member tribal council was established whose representatives were to replace the traditional extended family leaders. In fact, though, the men selected were under the thumb of the Bureau of Indian Affairs, little more than a front for the white man's policies. Only the tribal chairman, who was elected directly by the Navajo, represented the people. Although the system drastically changed our social customs and created divisiveness in leadership, it did give the Navajo people a greater voice in their own affairs, especially when a strong chairman, sensitive to the people's wants and needs, was in office, for the followers of many chiefs could now work together with a single voice.

The BIA government and the Navajo tribal government were to oversee all critical areas of tribal activity. These included the tribal courts—which at the time followed such traditions as using the Navajo language for all cases—the tribal police, and the disbursement of tribal funds. It was a system that would last for over fifty years, finally changing in 1989 when the BIA and Congress encouraged dissident members of the Tribal Council to declare themselves more powerful than the chairman and the people. The change in government resulted in the office of the chairman, formerly elected by all the people, suddenly being eliminated. The people lost direct control of the government. A new position of the council was also created at this time. To be elected only by the council, he was called the "speaker" of the Tribal Council, and his position eliminated the chairmanship. At this writing, there exists instead a president of the Navajo Nation whose duties and responsibilities are limited by the desires of the Tribal Council, not the people of the Navajo Nation. This is called the Title 2 Amendment to the Navajo Tribal Code. Although a very controversial action, it was encouraged by the BIA. But such problems were in the future.

During this period of rapid change, the council-chairman government was instituted and worked adequately during the harsh era of livestock reduction. Despite our acceptance of this form of government, the Navajo remained the only treaty tribe, the only sovereign nation, within the United States. All other tribes had gone along with the Indian Reorganization Act, developing constitutions, which were approved by the secretary of the interior, essentially becoming as much a part of the United States as the thirteen colonies had been when they formed the federal government. The former Indian tribal treaties, which had made other tribes as sovereign as the Navajo, were voided by these constitutions that the tribes created in the 1930s. By contrast, when we Navajo obeyed the whites' law, we did so out of fear of the unknown, not because it took precedence over the sovereignty we gained under the treaty of 1868.

The BIA forced education resulted in a quiet rebellion. For example, suppose a family wished to educate its five children in the traditional way. In the event the BIA equivalent of the truant officer showed up at their home, the parents would decide to "sacrifice" one of the children—sometimes chosen by age, sometimes selected at random—to the BIA. All the other children would be sent to hide in the woods, and the family would admit to having only that one son or daughter. That child would then go to the boarding school while the rest learned the old ways. The federal government was happy, and only a single child would be changed by the system.

There had been no talk of outside education in my home, though I had cousins attending day schools and boarding schools run by the BIA. White man's education was never a consideration for my family as long as we lived the life of sheepherders and farmers. But when this way of life was suddenly brought to a violent end, my family had to reconsider. Ultimately, I was the child selected to go to the BIA school. My brothers and sisters stayed at home. Later I would also be the one who went to war. I would experience enough separation from the poverty-stricken reservation areas that, for a while, my sense of how desperate the Navajo became during this period would be limited.

I was not aware of the anger among the Navajo families who were against the white domination and the forced changes. I later learned that it reached explosive proportions at the end of 1943, when a group of Navajo men decided to go to war against the federal agents. They went to the home of the main federal BIA agent and his wife, who were living in Teec Nos Pos, kidnapped them, and took them to a distant pit from which escape without assistance would be difficult or impossible. The Navajo tied their hands and feet, cut area telephone wires, and let it be known that they were going to fight the U.S. government's restrictions.

The government sent law enforcement officers into the Navajo Nation. They freed the federal agent and his wife from captivity. Then they pursued the Navajo war party into Utah, captured them, and returned them to Prescott, Arizona, to stand trial. The men were imprisoned, but the Navajo viewed their actions as the only way they knew to stand up against the slaughter of the livestock and the destruction of our heritage. Those Navajo heroes from Teec Nos Pos involved in the resistance are still honored today.

But that was all in the future. I was six years old when the BIA built a new day school in Teec Nos Pos. My cousins were enrolled in the school, and when they came home, I was shocked to see that they had brand-new shoes, clean trousers, and nice sweaters, all U.S. government-issued. I was jealous. I wanted clothes like that, clothes I soon learned were provided when they started going to school.

One morning my mother asked me to fetch some water. We were using the school's well, which was four miles from our home, so I took a couple of buckets over to the school.

As I approached the well area, I heard the children playing. They sounded happy, and I was curious to see what was taking place. But I was also embarrassed by my ragged appearance, the result of the sudden poverty caused by the livestock reduction. So, instead of walking around to where I could see what was happening, I left the buckets and began sneaking up on the area where the kids were playing. I cautiously hid behind a tree, then ran to a closer tree, hiding for a moment and peeking around the trunk, then raced for the next shelter.

Soon I saw all these kids running around in their beautiful clothes and new shoes. I was fascinated and stared at the children until I suddenly realized that a Navajo man, one of the school officials, was standing behind me.

The official asked me what I was doing, then took me down to the schoolyard. Before I knew it, several women surrounded me, all talking at once. I didn't know what was happening, but went along with whatever they wanted to do. The next thing I knew, I was getting a haircut. The long hair I had worn tied in a knot by my mother, the style of most young Navajo boys, was now gone.

Once my hair was cut, I was placed in a galvanized tub and given a bath. Then I was given brand-new clothes—coveralls, a shirt, sweater, shoes, and socks.

Now I looked just like the other kids, and I was sent to play with them. I felt really good and completely forgot my mission.

My mother became concerned about my long absence, so she walked to the well, where she found the two buckets I had abandoned. From there she went to the school, figuring that maybe I had gone to play with my cousins.

She was shocked when she saw the way I had been changed. The BIA officials had no right to handle me in the way they did, even though I was cooperative. They did not know my name, my age, or anything about me. Yet they had cut my hair, bathed me, given me new clothes, and sent me to join the other children.

My mother demanded an explanation of the teachers' actions, and the officials told her that I wanted to go to school. She and my grandparents had already decided that I would be the one child in the family to get an education in order to satisfy the BIA officials. Now my apparent desire convinced her to agree. The officials asked my mother my name, and she said Bedo. However, they recorded it as Peter and then asked for my last name. I did not have one.

"What is your husband's name?" they wanted to know.

My mother could not tell them. My father was dead, and it was not good to talk about dead people.

Then they asked my grandfather's name, and we said it was Dayathini (Many Whiskers) of the Tsin Secadnii clan, which apparently proved too difficult for them to pronounce. Some of the officials were Indian, and others were white, and the white people had only a limited understanding of the Navajo language. They finally decided to call me Peter Tent.

I liked day school during that first year because there was more play than work. I wore new clothes. I ate hot meals every day. And I still lived in the old way, going home each afternoon to herd the sheep, or at least what was left of them.

All of the children at the school were Navajo. All of our teachers were white women. They did not speak the Navajo language, though they learned a few words, just as we began to learn English. Somehow we got along.

I had to avoid the teachers as much as possible, though, because as my grandfather explained to me, they were non-Navajo. We were the only human beings. They looked like us, but they could do things we could not. They were probably of the bird society, since they could violate our sacred areas and still live.

I was told not to associate closely with the teachers and never to touch them. They were contaminated, and I would need a ceremony to cleanse myself.

We knew, for example, that the white people occasionally went near a gravesite. A Navajo who did that would develop swollen legs and mental illness. A medicine man would have to be called to perform a cleansing ceremony or the Navajo would become sick and would die. But white people did not have this problem, and this made them quite different. Their spirits were not in harmony with ours, so we had to be careful while we gained their knowledge.

I managed to get through that first year, the equivalent of kindergarten, without any major problems, and my family decided to enroll me in the first grade. Once again we tried to clarify my name, only this time the BIA officials decided to give me a last name based on my mother's pronunciation of my grandfather's name. The name they thought was most similar was "Donald." I had gone from Peter, to Peter Tent, to Peter Donald. It made little sense, but no one really cared. We just accepted it as the BIA way.

My name changed again when the children learned the song about Old MacDonald's farm. Soon some of them were teasing me by singing, "Peter MacDonald had a farm, ee-ye, ee-ye, oh." And eventually, everyone at the school was calling me Peter MacDonald. It was the name by which I would be known by most people for the rest of my life.

The day school educated children only through the second grade. After that, I would have to go to a boarding school thirty miles away in Shiprock, where some of my older cousins were living.

I was nine years old, and the Navajo world was in turmoil. The forced livestock reduction was in effect, and the forced education efforts were increasing. It seemed sensible to let me continue to be the child in the family who would get a BIA education, something I had enjoyed the first two years.

Although I did not realize it at the time, my attendance at the BIA school made my family's survival easier. Like all children, I accepted whatever life handed me, and I had no memory of better times because all life seemed to be whatever was happening at the moment.

The poverty caused by the livestock reduction meant that our food supply was at the level of bare subsistence, and the other kids and I were always hungry. Sometimes lunch consisted of a single dry Navajo tortilla. Instead of being upset, I simply adapted. For example, we knew where the day school put out its trash, and we had learned that some of the trash bins contained canned goods, such as jam and jelly. Since there was always some jam left at the bottom of each jar, we'd dig the jars out of the trash, then wipe the bottoms of the jars with our dry tortillas in order to get a special meal.

We did what we had to do to ease our hunger to survive. Even when we were away from the day school, we would catch locusts, prairie dogs, and rabbits while herding sheep. The locusts were the most abundant, and we would roast them over a fire and, after removing the wings, eat the soft centers. These insects have provided nourishment to impoverished people since well before the days of the New Testament's John the Baptist.

Today, after being out of the wilderness this long, I don't think I could eat locusts, prairie dogs, or rabbits—unless they were prepared in a gourmet manner.

Boarding school was like a military academy for children. We marched everywhere, to classes, around the grounds, to meals. Everything was regimented, including the way we had to make our beds. Even worse, the kids developed a hierarchy of power. The older children delighted in picking on the nine-year-olds, making our lives miserable.

For example, we frequently had fruit for dessert. Just as we were about to eat our apples or oranges, the bigger kids would steal them from us. We were mad, but we were much too little to fight the older boys with any hope of winning.

Day after day I endured the teasing, the taunting, the regimentation. I was miserable among the strangers. I longed for my home. I knew very little English and was faced with teachers who knew very little Navajo and were forbidden to use it. Everyone was to speak English on the school grounds or face severe reprimands, even the Navajo employees. I was unable to see my family, to herd the sheep, to do anything that had been familiar over the years. Desperate to escape, I decided to run away.

There were three of us from Teec Nos Pos; the other two boys were around fifteen years old. They seemed like adults to me because of the age difference, but they were as unhappy as I was. We talked, and when I learned that they were planning to flee, I asked them to let me go with them. I was six years younger, though, and they didn't want to be burdened with me, but I persisted.

The school was like a compound, with everything fenced in. Escaping was a little like fleeing a minimum-security penitentiary. It required planning to get through the gates or over the fence without being stopped. The two older boys had figured out a way to escape and knew how to get back to Teec Nos Pos. I intended to leave no matter what, but I did not want to make the trip alone.

I kept begging them to let me come along. Finally they agreed.

On a cold February morning we made our escape. The snow was four or five inches deep. It was eight o'clock, and all the students were rushing to get to class. No one noticed us sneaking out the back door, scrambling over the fence, and heading toward the big mountain that marked our home some thirty miles away.

First we had to cross a river. After that came walking, endless walking in the cold. The two other boys had been able to get a loaf of bread, though they never told me how they got it. What mattered was that it kept us from getting too hungry at first.

The snow began to deepen. I was the smallest, and soon it was almost up to my knees. Yet still we walked, mile after mile, hour after hour. It took us nine hours of steady moving, and only the extensive training of my early childhood gave me the strength to make the trip and keep up with the much taller boys.

My home was the first on our trek. The boys left me on a hill overlooking my hogan a mile away. Wet and cold, I looked at the smoke curling out of the chimney and watched the sheep being moved for the night. I desperately wanted to be inside, to be warm and fed, among those I loved. But I was terrified. I knew my mother and grandfather were going to lecture me very harshly.

I decided to stay outside a little longer. The family would finish their chores with the sheep and then go inside to eat. At that point the work would be almost over for the day, and everyone would be warm and happy. I would be welcomed more warmly than at any other time.

My mother and grandfather were shocked to see me. They looked as though they were seeing a ghost, then realized what had happened and gave me the scolding I expected before allowing me to join them to eat. It didn't matter. I was home, safe and warm.

The next day my mother walked me to the day school I had attended for three years. She knew that a coal truck traveled from Shiprock to the day schools to provide them with fuel to heat the buildings. My former teacher loaded me on the coal truck so that the driver could take me back.

The teachers at the boarding school were quite angry with me. I was assigned extra chores and watched more closely for a while. However, having succeeded in finding my way home once, I was certain I could do it again. I only had to wait for the right opportunity.

Toward the end of the school year I saw my second chance at freedom. This time I persuaded another little boy, Randolph, to go with me. He lived halfway to Teec Nos Pos and looked up to me because I was a veteran escape artist.

We got out the way I had the first time, then traveled along the river to his home. No one was there, and I still had an equal distance to go.

It was late in the day, and though the days were longer by then, I did not like the idea of having to do so much walking. Fortunately, Randolph's family had a horse. I persuaded him to saddle it, take me home on horseback, and then ride back.

We rode toward Teec Nos Pos, but it grew dark before we had gone half the distance. However, we spotted a family that Randolph knew, and they seemed happy to let us stay the night. They even knew my family, though I had never met them.

Randolph unsaddled the horse and placed it in their pen. Then we sat inside the hogan, eating fried bread, fried potatoes, and other food.

After dinner we were given a sheepskin and a thin blanket for sleeping. We would continue our journey in the morning. Randolph would take me home, then return to his parents' place.

Everyone slept inside the hogan, no matter how many people were there. Thus it was impossible for me not to hear voices whispering at one or two o'clock in the morning.

I opened my eyes a little bit, though not enough so anyone would know I was awake. The blanket was over my head, so I slowly inched my hand near my face, then poked a tiny hole in the blanket, just large enough for me to see through. I saw that a kerosene lamp was lit and realized someone new was there. That was when I saw a man's khaki pants, though I couldn't see who he was.

I nudged Randolph awake. He stared through the hole, then whispered that the man was his father. I realized then that we were in trouble, though we did nothing right then except try to go back to sleep.

We got up at the usual time for Navajo, before the sunrise. Randolph's father was waiting for us and immediately began scolding us for running away, for taking the horse, and for all our other "crimes." Since I was the leader, I got the brunt of his anger.

Once again my escape was foiled. This time we were taken to a different school, called Beclabito Day School, where another truck would drive us back to Shiprock. That was all right for Randolph, but I had no intention of experiencing such a fate again.

In order to get out of the hogan and study the surrounding terrain, I convinced the family that I needed to go to the bathroom. I saw an arroyo about three hundred yards behind the house, then a clearing about four miles wide and, beyond it, trees and rocks.

I had a choice; I could go down the arroyo and try to find a place to hide, or I could cross the arroyo, and race for the woods and rocks, where I would not be found.

There was already activity. Sheep were being brought out. Children were getting ready for school. I had to act at once or I would not be able to act at all.

I went behind the hogan, braced myself, then ran as fast as I could across the arroyo. I paused long enough to make sure that nobody had spotted me, then ran for the woods.

I had forgotten just how open the land was and that everyone knew how long it would take for me to relieve myself. The family spotted me in a few minutes and yelled at me to come back. I just tried to run that much faster.

Suddenly I heard hooves pounding in the distance. Randolph's father had mounted a horse and was coming after me. In one hand was a length of rope, which he was getting ready to swing, not as a lasso but as a whip.

The first blow stung my back and sent me stumbling. The second and third blows were even more painful. I had to give up, turn around, and head back to the hogan.

Randolph's father made me walk as fast as I could, whipping me each time I slowed down. Thirty minutes later the two of us were in a pickup truck on our way to Beclabito Day School, where we were to wait for a truck to take us back to the boarding school.

I was hungry and wanted to go home. The day school stood between two arroyos, so I told Randolph I was going to make another escape from there.

This time, thinking I was being very clever, I headed in the wrong direction, then circled around toward home—all the time unaware that I was being watched by the boys' adviser, a BIA official. Just when I thought my route was clear, the boys' adviser announced his presence and asked me where I was going. The unexpected sound of his voice terrified me, causing me to stop where I was. He then locked Randolph and me in a classroom to wait until late afternoon, when the coal truck appeared.

The boarding school teachers were irate over my second escape. This time they denied me all rights. I was not allowed to watch movies with the other children. On weekends, when the others were allowed to play in the hills or to fish in the river, I had to stay in school. Instead of playing, I faced the most devastating punishment of all—darning socks.

The government socks, like all socks, wore out in the heels and the toes first and had to be repaired and reused. Darning the socks was the chore given to those children who deserved severe punishment. It was my job to sit in the midst of a massive pile of socks, place a light bulb inside to stretch the fabric, then carefully darn each and every hole in each and every sock.

Only later did I understand what the school administration was doing. It was their job not only to educate us but to break us. We were accustomed to the freedom of the land. We were used to having homes that essentially stretched over great distances. We had a language and a culture that were different from others and that the Anglos made no effort to understand. Although we were learning white people's ways, the teachers made it clear to us that we would never have as much ability as white people. In fact, they frequently stressed that we were inferior, dirty, stupid pagans. They were working to break us, to teach us to conform, to make us into a generation of adults who would not consider resisting the government's wishes. But while I was darning those socks, I was too angry to do anything except hate the white man, the BIA, and the way I was treated.

Looking back, I realize that the BIA program was poorly planned and unrelated to the needs of the Navajo children. The hostile attitude toward my people was emotionally devastating, of course. We were taught that we were superstitious savages, and we were forced to go to church without being given an understanding of the Christian religion. We were made to feel that our parents, our grandparents, and everyone who had come before us was inferior. It was even worse for those who came to believe these teachings and who still remembered the stories of Coyote. Those stories, so inspirational in so many ways, taught us not only how we came to be the Diné but also that we could never change. The whites were different from us. We were constantly told that we were truly inferior to them and that we would always be inferior.

The educational program reinforced this attitude. We were taught reading, writing, and arithmetic. We were taught English. We were taught white history, which assumed that all Indians were uneducated, superstitious savages, and that the only advances in civilization were made by whites.

We Navajo were forced to abandon our traditional way of life. The only future for us was through jobs that were not part of our culture. We would have to work off the reservation. We needed to acquire skills that would enable us to enter the white job market, and the only way to obtain those skills was to attend the BIA schools.

The problem was that the BIA did not bother with vocational lessons. There was no thought to our gaining employment as executive secretaries, teachers, medical professionals, technicians, business people, or workers in any other field where jobs were plentiful and in which we could learn to survive. Instead, the idea seemed to be to make us fluent in English and then let us find whatever work we could. We were trained for nothing more than manual labor—digging ditches, cleaning, farming and milking cows, driving trucks—or for being clerk-typists, and the like, with only half a day devoted to academics. Yet even those jobs were foreign to us because ultimately they did not prepare us for the world in which we would have to live, and gave us no options for careers that would require self-determination.

There were a few role models at the school, though. Several Navajo men worked as boys' advisers, clerk-typists, and bus drivers. I figured that I would have to take one of those jobs.

Not that I thought that this was all bad. Since I didn't know the choices that white children had for their future, I didn't miss the opportunities available to them. I decided that it might be fun to drive a truck or bus, and it also might be enjoyable to be a clerk-typist. That job was actually the more appealing of the two. I would be able to sit down all day, working inside, away from the cold, the rain, and the mud. I would not have to go thirsty. I would not have to live in fear of wild animals. It seemed like a very pleasant future, given the only other choices I thought I had.

Years later, when I was eighteen and nineteen and an ex-Marine considering my future, those two jobs were still appealing. I came to think that the ideal would be to have a job where I would earn a salary, as well as a side business where I could make extra money. I thought I might like to work as a clerk-typist and also own a dump truck so I could haul coal, uranium, and other materials found on the reservation.

What I did not know was that going to school actually narrowed my choices for the future. After the livestock reduction, even though my family's herd was down to fewer than a hundred sheep, it was still possible to retain some of the old ways. A limited number of permits were issued to Navajo who wanted to herd on a small scale. My mother received a permit, as did my brother and sister. But they could not apply for one for me, and I could not get one because I was away at school. By the time I learned of the possibility, the limit for the number of permits had been reached. I was stuck with whatever the BIA was going to teach me, and though the future promised a couple of options that were appealing, the school's methods left me constantly upset.

And always there were the dreaded square dances. When I wasn't being punished, I lived in apprehension of Friday nights when the old Victrola would be brought out. The square dance records were placed on the turntable, the Victrola was cranked up, its massive tone arm set in place, and we were once again forced to violate one of the taboos of our culture.

Most of us didn't have the courage to fight what we were being made to do. We'd go to the room where the dance was held, and then we'd rush to the corner, knowing that the first boy or two who made it would not have to dance. The teachers would grab those closest to the dance floor, pulling them out and making them dance with a girl. Since there were more boys than teachers, the lucky ones who found a corner were able to avoid dancing.

One of my friends decided to resist one night. A teacher grabbed him and ordered him to dance. He refused. She tried to pull him toward a girl who was nervously waiting across the room, and he resisted. Finally, angry, she dragged him down the hall to his adviser.

My friend was scared, and we were frightened for him. We had no idea what these people might do to us for some infraction of the rules. Most of the punishments had been mild, along the lines of what I had endured. But our imaginations ran rampant, and because we were forced to violate our cultural heritage and do things that we knew were wrong, we fantasized the worst possible punishments. We never knew when we might get beaten or killed.

The angry adviser said to my friend, "You filthy savage! Why are you disobeying orders?"

"Because I know that girl," he said. "She is from my hometown. She's related to me by clan." He knew, as we all did, that if a boy touched or messed around with his sister, his cousins, or any of the extended family or clan members, he would go crazy. Not all clan members were related by blood, but involvement within the clan was still considered incest. Dancing may have seemed innocent to the BIA staff, but we knew the penalty for the Diné.

This girl was actually both clan and blood relation to my friend by way of his extended family, and he was respecting his cultural teaching. The adviser refused to accept his answer, and he was punished, but at least he didn't have to go to the dance.

Another time, I remember, we decided to have a Navajo Squaw Dance. Two or three of us began singing Navajo songs. One of the advisers heard us and became irate. We were not allowed to sing in Navajo any more than we were allowed to speak in Navajo. Once again I was punished, this time for two weeks, and again I was forced to endure the staff's lack of sensitivity toward my culture.

I stayed in the BIA school through the sixth grade. We were trained to do things we'd had no intention of ever doing. For example, there was a boxing team to prepare Navajo for the national Golden Gloves championship fights. At age ten or eleven, I was assigned to a boxing team to fight. I couldn't understand why I was being made to do this, because no matter how much of a friend the person you're fighting is, if he's in the same age and weight category, you fight for elimination. The best fighter in each age/weight category would attend the regional competition in Albuquerque, and then the national Golden Gloves championship in Chicago. This was encouraged by the BIA, and I eventually came to enjoy it. Yet initially it was quite difficult because the Diné were taught not to fight, even in sport.

Later I would become a member of the Marine Corps boxing team and then the boxing team at Bacone College (Golden Gloves), where I lettered in boxing. After my nose was busted and I married, I thought about joining the 1953 University of Oklahoma team. The doctor asked me if I wanted to live my life with a completely flat nose, a possible result of its being broken again. Since my grandfather had shaped it, I certainly didn't want to risk any further disfiguring of my face. I decided to stop boxing. When I dropped out of BIA school, my real education began. My grandfather, who was a medicine man, wanted me to become a medicine man, a highly respected profession taught through apprenticeship, one generation teaching the next.

The training of a medicine man is long and difficult. No ceremony used by the Navajo can be mastered in less than three years; many take seven to twelve years. Becoming a medicine man requires a lifelong series of studies, the equivalent in the Anglo world of the person who both works and goes to school, earning doctorate after doctorate throughout his life.

The medicine man is both physical healer and spiritual teacher, working in harmony with the earth, the gods, and the human beings. His training, through apprenticeship and oral tradition, is as rigorous in its own way as that of someone studying to become an M.D., a Ph.D. in physical therapy, and a doctor of divinity before being allowed to work with patients.

I understood that I would have to work for four or five years with my grandfather before I would be capable of performing a single ceremony. Then I could use that skill, or I could do what most medicine men did—take another four or five years to learn a different ceremony. Generally someone would spend ten years learning before he went out on his own, about as long as it would take to go through high school, college, and graduate school. After that I would perform the ceremonies I knew and continue the lifelong process of learning additional ceremonies.

A medicine man could not value possessions because there was no set fee for his work. Sometimes he needed a buckskin or a basket for his ceremony, which the patient or the patient's family would supply. Afterward, the medicine man could keep the item, use it, or sell it. This happened only when the item was an integral part of the ceremony, however. Many ceremonies required only chanting and singing. The patient might thank him or give him a dollar, five dollars, or a sack of corn pollen. Whatever was done, there were no complaints.

In theory, the medicine man could be given nothing. In practice, though, I had never seen a poor medicine man. And today some medicine men have a set fee schedule to ensure a minimum guaranteed income for their work. But despite the healers' success, the rewards for training an apprentice had to be spiritual, not physical.

The medicine man's apprentice had to learn the spiritual life, a life where material goods did not matter. Food and shelter were provided. All other aspects of life were ignored.

At first I had the most menial of responsibilities. I held the medicine man's horse. I carried his small medicine bag. There was no pay, though he did feed me. I simply followed him everywhere, talking with him, observing.

In many ways this was much the same kind of education that the Navajo once received all through their lives. As children we were taught the Coyote stories as a way of learning morals, ethics, and proper patterns of behavior. Traveling between summer and winter homes, the winter nights were filled with more complex stories about our religion, our history, and the myths of our culture. The older we became, the more we learned, always being taught by the elders of our extended families.

As an apprentice medicine man I simply learned these stories faster and earlier. The teaching was constant. In addition, instead of being a participant in ceremonies where I was familiar with my role, I learned to watch closely, to see exactly what was involved, because I was preparing to become a leader, a healer. It was like the difference between going to school and studying in order to pass tests that would enable you to be promoted to the next higher grade, and going to school and studying in order to be able to teach. The information available to you might be similar, but your attitude and the intensity of your study are quite different.

Later I began to learn the prayers, songs, medicines, and other information I would need to heal the body and the spirit. Each ceremony had to be enacted without any errors, and the training required a good memory and dedication. I had the memory and the ability to learn, and perhaps this was the reason my grandfather encouraged me. But I did not have the drive of some youths. Although I was interested in my people and their ways and, through my work with my grandfather, was reminded of the importance of keeping our Navajo past alive, I was restless. My dedication to follow in his footsteps came, in large part, from having no alternatives.

CHAPTER THREE

I had heard from my family that many things were happening during this period. The Japanese attacked Pearl Harbor, and the United States declared war. Many Navajo men enlisted in the army, and others found jobs off the reservation where they could make money.

My mother had remarried, but times were always hard, even with two people working. The old way of life was almost gone. Many people were extremely depressed, some turning to alcohol, others emotionally withdrawing, and still others just trying to find a way to stay alive. My family was poor, and my training as a medicine man meant that I could be of no financial help to them for several years. I did not like being in this position, so, approximately two years into my apprenticeship, I was enthusiastic when a cousin told me about high-paying jobs off the reservation.

My cousin talked about jobs I had heard of but had not understood, such as railroad work, which enabled a Navajo man to buy new pants, new shoes, even a new saddle. Possessions and money had not mattered to me when I became my grandfather's apprentice. Though I liked the idea of becoming a medicine man, when given the choice between earning money and remaining an apprentice, I chose to work with my cousin in Cortez, Colorado, the farthest I had ever been from home.

I don't know how disappointed my grandfather felt. Years later I learned that I was always considered the black sheep of the family because of my not being at home. I was proud of what I was doing, of making more money than I could possibly need so that I could send money back to my mother. However, my mother suffered much criticism from the family because I was not under control, running away first from school and then from my apprenticeship. I was to be the designated student when the BIA forced everyone to send at least one child to school. And it was a great honor to have me selected to apprentice as a medicine man.

But no one told me the criticism my mother was enduring at the time because I failed to fulfill expectations and traditions within my family. I was finding my own way, exploring my own life. I was not as aware of the feelings of others as perhaps I should have been. I just knew that I was helping my mother in a way that made me proud, and she was finally able to afford an occasional luxury, like a velveteen blouse or a nice shawl she could wear to squaw dances, ceremonies, and fairs.

In those days businesses did not worry about child labor laws, so I got a job in a lumber mill. All the employers wanted were able-bodied workers who could handle the job. I was thirteen and not a particularly big kid, but they were willing to hire me.

When I went to the office to get a Social Security number, the clerk asked me how to spell my last name. "Is it McDonald or MacDonald?" she wanted to know. I had no idea, so she wrote "MacDonald." From then on, any time I had to give my name, I just showed the person my Social Security card and he or she wrote it the same way.

I worked for a month and had never had more money in my life. I was able to buy myself a new pair of good shoes, some Levi's, a jacket, and even a suitcase to hold my new possessions. Then I returned home to visit my grandfather, who thought I was going to return to my training.

The biggest lesson I had learned in that first month on the job was that when you did work, someone paid you for it. I hadn't fully understood money before. But now that I had some, and the freedom to buy things I desired, I did not want to spend the next few years learning for no pay.

I began working harder than I ever had before, as long as someone would pay me by the hour for what I did. I stayed in the Farmington area of New Mexico, picking apples and doing similar spot-labor tasks. However, I was never going to get very far picking apples, and when another cousin told me about jobs on the Union Pacific Railroad where one could earn a lot of money, I jumped at the chance.

Navajo youths were known for their hard work and dedication, so the railroad made a special effort to recruit them. Every three or four months they would arrange an elaborate transportation system.

A truck came to the trading post in Teec Nos Pos to pick up the youths seeking jobs. They were crammed inside and driven to Farmington. There a bus would take them to Denver, where the big-money jobs were waiting for them.

I went to the trading post, boarded the truck, and rode to Farmington, where I was disappointed. The Union Pacific and Santa Fe railroads, unlike the lumber mill, would not hire anyone who was less than seventeen years old. They insisted that every male present either a birth certificate or a Selective Service card before boarding the bus.

Navajo don't have birth certificates, so I asked how I could get my Selective Service card. I was sent to the Selective Service office around the corner, a place my cousin had already been, and was asked how old I was. My cousin whispered in Navajo to say I was seventeen, though that birthday was still two years away. The clerk had no reason to question, so I was given a Selective Service card.

Now I was set to earn big money, a fact that delighted me. What I did not realize was that my ruse also assured me of a place in the armed forces.

The trip to Denver was frightening. The bus was filled with Navajo men, but the world I could see through the windows was unlike any I had known. The "mountains" were made of brick, concrete, glass, and steel. The "canyons" were paved and filled with cars. I had never seen so many buildings, or buildings that were so tall. I had never encountered such massive numbers of cars, buses, and people. Even the air smelled strange to me. I was not frightened by what I was seeing, but I was uncomfortable. Nothing was familiar.

We arrived at the train depot in Denver. That was the first time in my life I ever saw black people. The blacks wore uniforms with red caps, handling luggage and checking tickets. I thought they had very important jobs. It was only years later that I learned that these positions were low-paying, manual-labor jobs. The uniform, which I thought was related to high stature, fooled me.

We all boarded together, and started on what was my first train ride, ending in The Dalles, Oregon. There were about forty Navajo, all of us working on the railroad.

The work was hard physical labor, though we were all in shape for it because of the manner in which we were raised. Much of it involved driving spikes, pouring gravel, laying rails, placing ties under the rails, and generally both repairing existing track and expanding the line. We pulled the spikes from the ties with crowbars, then pulled the railroad ties from underneath the rails. We then placed new ties back under the rails, added a metal plate, and secured it all by driving new spikes with a sledgehammer. Today there are machines that perform these tasks, but back then it was hand labor, quite difficult, and the men who stayed with the job, as Navajo men did, were valued.

The pay was the best I had ever earned. It was probably less than a dollar an hour, yet it was far more than I imagined possible, and both my desires and my needs were modest. As extra gang workers, we lived free, using special kitchen, dining, and sleeping cars as our portable quarters. It was a good time for me.

We were paid every week or two, cashing our checks and sending most of the money to our families. I sent money to my mother for herself and my younger brother, John, who was going to school and needed shoes and trousers. I kept only a little for myself, as all I needed was money to buy clothes.

I had been working only a couple of months when my mother forwarded a letter to me from Uncle Sam. Greetings, it said, adding that it was time to report for my physical examination. I was being drafted for the war effort, though I had no understanding of what that meant.

I returned to Farmington too late to be sent to where I was supposed to report. The draft board officials chewed me out, then told me to stick around the area and wait for the next group of draftees.

Instead, I continued to work, not thinking about the passage of time or remaining in Farmington. I had no idea what the letter was all about or what Uncle Sam wanted from me. I just stayed with the railroad, completing the work in Oregon, then moving on to Montana, where I got a second letter, less friendly than the first, warning me again that it was time to report. Finally I told my boss, who told me to take care of it.

The railroad paid my train fare to Flagstaff, Arizona, which I reached around the Fourth of July. There I met some old friends who were working at the Navajo Ordnance Depot about ten miles west of Flagstaff. They suggested I go to work there, since a lot of Navajos were making good wages at the depot.

We all stayed at a government-constructed Indian camp and were trucked from there to the job site all summer. We'd spend the day at the site, working hard except during the lunch break, when we invented a rather dangerous game to play. We'd get on the small forklift trucks used to move heavy supplies, then play tag, driving after one another all around the yard. The supervisors were not around during that time, so no one knew what we were doing.

None of us knew what we were doing, since we didn't usually handle such equipment. But the forklifts were easy to drive, and we had no problems with them—until one afternoon when I misjudged what I was doing and struck a pillar, breaking a wheel and axle.

At one o'clock the boss came around after discovering the damage. He demanded to know who had caused the accident, and I admitted that I had. He took my name and employee number, then turned me in.

The next day I was called into headquarters, where one of the army officers informed me that I was guilty of destroying government property. It was a serious offense and I was fired on the spot. I hung around the camp for a couple of days, then left with two of my buddies who decided to quit their jobs and go with me to find other work.

From there, the three of us went to an old western town called Clarkdale, where a big smelter was operating. We got jobs shoveling ash for eight hours a day. It was the roughest work I had ever done, and so dangerous that we had to wear gas masks and special clothing because the ash covered our bodies to a depth of about a half-inch during the course of a work shift.

I had been working at the smelter for about six weeks when I received another forwarded letter from Uncle Sam. This time the government was very angry, warning me that someone would come for me if I failed to show up. Yet as a young teenager, I did not see the full importance of what all this meant.

It was around September of 1944, the time of the annual Northern Navajo Nation Fair in Shiprock. It was an event all of us had attended in the past, and it would give us a chance to see our families and have a good time. I figured I could go there with some of my buddies who wanted to quit working at the smelter, then take care of the draft notice. I would be able to see my mother at the fair, something I looked forward to, since I had only corresponded with her for almost a year.

After the fair, I went to Teec Nos Pos with my mother, then planned to go to Farmington to take the physical exam. But a cousin told me that they probably wouldn't take me, because they hadn't taken him. He was told that his education had been inadequate to meet the minimum requirements for a soldier.

I finally got to Farmington, and the Selective Service Board was angry with me. They told me to wait until the next morning, when a bus would take me to Santa Fe for my physical exam.

I had no trouble passing the physical, and my education was adequate. I could read, write, understand, and speak English. My vocabulary was limited compared to that of white applicants. However, I met the educational standards of the service at the time.

At that time a draftee could choose any branch of the service he wanted. I had no idea what the differences were; I didn't understand the war or the military. However, I had heard about the Navy and the Marines, including the Navajo code talkers, from some of my relatives. I had seen the Marine dress uniforms on slightly older Navajo men and thought they were snappy. I wanted to be like them.

I was almost as excited as when I wanted the new clothing worn by the children at the BIA day school. Then I had been too poor for my mother to buy me what the school provided. This time I was getting a chance to wear the best-looking uniform in the armed forces.

The following morning I was on the train from Santa Fe to San Diego. I arrived late, carrying my orders, and took a city bus to the gate of the Marine headquarters. It was around nine o'clock at night, the middle of October, and rather cold. As the guard checked on me, a vehicle that looked like a large cattle truck pulled up and the driver called to me by name. I was told to get inside, so I climbed onto the passenger seat. The private first class who was driving was outraged, informing me that a lowly recruit rode in the truck bed. Sneering, he added, "Your good old civilian days are over! "

I suddenly realized my life was never going to be the same again.

I was scared when I reached the barracks. The cold reception made me wonder what I had gotten myself into. Although I knew it was probably impossible, once again I wanted to run away. If I hadn't been afraid someone would ridicule me, I would have cried. I thought about the Navajo children sold into slavery in the 1700s and 1800s and suddenly understood their fears of the unknown. It was the most miserable time of my life, and the fact that I was more child than man added to my discomfort.

I was first sent to the supply sergeant, who gave me sheets, blankets, and the other items I needed for the night. As I waited for him to find everything for me, I kept hearing something in the distance, something familiar. It sounded like a Navajo song, though I knew it couldn't be. I was too far from home, too far from the familiar.

The sergeant seemed to know what I was feeling. He said, "You hear something? "

"Yes," I said. "It sounds like Navajo."

He smiled then and said, "Maybe it is Navajo." He took me down the hallway to a flight of stairs, up the stairs, and down another hallway. All the while the singing was getting louder. It was Navajo, yet I knew it couldn't be.

Suddenly we were inside a large room with forty-five Navajo boys. I'd had no idea that there were Navajo Marine units.

I had no idea that I would meet anyone familiar. I was so happy I could have kissed every one of them. I even knew three of the boys from the school in Shiprock.

I was still out of place. I was still the youngest Navajo in the barracks. But now it seemed as though everything might work out all right.

Marine boot camp was supposed to be tougher than any other branch of the service. But we ran up and down hills with ease. The calisthenics and other physical activities that were meant to toughen us were so easy for us that we were always sitting around waiting for the Anglo units to finish. Eventually the drill sergeant made us go through the course twice and do double the calisthenics, generally punishing us for being in such good shape. We learned to slow down a bit so he would ease off slightly, but the course was not difficult.

There was other training as well. We learned to shoot the M-1 rifle, then the standard issue. I was trained in handling grenades, hand-to-hand combat, knife fighting, and the other deadly skills Marines had to know. Then, after graduating from basic training, we were given time off to see our families before beginning the advanced schooling we needed to become code talkers.

My mother was horrified when I proudly showed off my uniform. I was fifteen years old, much too young to be in the military. No matter how much I had grown up while I was away from the reservation, no matter how hard I had worked, legally I was still a child. But my mother did not realize she could simply inform the Marines that I was underage. She thought I had no choice, so she arranged with the medicine man to hold a protection ceremony for me.

After my leave, I was sent to Camp Pendleton in Oceanside, California, and assigned to another barracks that was all Navajo, perhaps a hundred of us all together.

First we were put through jungle combat training. Live ammunition was fired over our heads, just as I had experienced with my uncle, the one who had shot at me. Booby traps were hidden, and we had to find them without setting them off. We had to "shoot" snipers out of the trees before they could "shoot" us. And we learned how to remain calm and effective in the combat situations we were likely to encounter in the war against Japan. We also trained on the water, learning how to crawl down from the troop carrier onto the small, almost invisible landing craft.

The psychological indoctrination for the Navajo was a little different from that of the Anglos. We were not a part of the America that had been attacked by the Japanese. We knew nothing about Pearl Harbor. We knew nothing about the ships that had been bombed or the threat from any overseas country. Appeals to our patriotism meant little because we did not have the same sense of country that the white boys had. Instead, the military used psychology that we could understand.

We were told that the Navajo needed to join in the war because the Japanese were coming to our land, our sacred mountains. We had two choices. We could fight with the army overseas, taking the battle to the Japanese wherever they had a stronghold. Or we could wait for the Japanese to come to America, then be forced to fight on our native land, near the sacred mountains, in a last-ditch struggle to save all that we held dear.

Naturally we didn't want to bring the war home to our families. It was better to be a part of the military, to travel across the ocean, to hunt the Japanese away from our land. Thus the white man's war became our war as well.

Finally we were ready to learn code talking. This was one of the great successes of World War II. An alphabet had been developed for the Navajo language so that it could be written. Previously the language had only been spoken. Then the code was developed around this.

The idea had come from the son of a preacher, an Anglo who had grown up on a Navajo reservation. He knew our language, respected our people, and was interested in cryptology. He persuaded the Marines to let him fully develop the code, then gave a demonstration that persuaded the Marine Corps to adopt the system in 1942.

Once a Navajo alphabet existed, each letter was assigned three different words. For example, suppose one letter was "A." In addition to memorizing that letter, we might have to memorize the Navajo words for "apple," "ax," and "ant." Each time we heard any of those Navajo words, we would know that the reference was to the English letter "A." A Japanese who had learned Navajo or even a Navajo soldier who had not been trained in the code would not be able to make sense out of what was being said.

The messages received by the code talkers were already coded. They would be sent in groups of five letters, none of which would make sense until the code was broken. However, because there could be a repetition of the letters, code breakers among the Japanese might be able to figure out some of the messages. For example, suppose the code received was "A . . . A . . . B . . . Y . . . K." The repetition of the "A" would help the Japanese decipher the code. Therefore it was our job to use two different words for "A," such as "apple" (bilasána) and "ant" (wola chee). Although those words, in English, both start with the same letter, the words in Navajo begin with different letters. In order to decipher the code, the Japanese would first have to learn Navajo. Then they would have to break the code in Navajo, and then they would have to break the letter code. It was so complex a process that the Japanese never were able to decipher the messages sent by the code talkers.

The Navajo language was also expanded during this time. We had no words for battalion, regiment, company, squad, and many of the other military terms that were a part of white man's warfare. Those words were created for our language so we would be able to accurately describe the size of troop movements. The newly coined words related to our existing clan system of family identification to make them more familiar.

We also created words for half-tracks (clotl-"frog"), tanks, and other vehicles. For example, the Navajo word for a railroad train (koi-na-albazzsi) translates in English to "fire-driven wagon." But in the Navajo code, we used a word that translates to "turkeys having a rainstorm" (tonzii-bá-nahaltin). Any Navajo listening to us talk on our radios would have thought we were crazy, which was the point of the complexity of the code. Even a captured Navajo would be confused by what he was hearing. Yet the code was actually quite simple, since one of the code words for the letter "T," the first letter in "train," was the Navajo word for turkey. When you add that to the Navajo word for "rain," you have "train." Adding enough words so that the code became "turkeys having a rainstorm" further confused the logic of the approach used.

The training was intense and highly secretive. Some of the Navajo dropped out, either because they couldn't concentrate effectively or because the work was too rigorous for them. We not only had to memorize an elaborate coding system but also had to become fluent in communicating it to one another.

As soon as we had mastered the Navajo code-talking system, we began to study all the other military codes that the armed forces were using. This was the standard course taught to anyone involved in this type of training.

After mastering all the codes, we learned to use the equipment. We had a PBX system, for example, that required hand cranking to generate enough electricity to power the bulky radio. We also learned how to troubleshoot the equipment so we could make field repairs. After mastering the equipment, we were certified as code talkers.

I learned more than codes while in training in the Marines. I discovered facts about myself and my people that had been hidden from me. These had nothing to do with our history, but rather with the way I viewed myself, my friends, and my family.

The BIA schools had drilled one consistent thought into my mind—that I was inferior to others. I was poor, dirty, and ignorant. In truth, I *was* ignorant of the knowledge the teachers gave me and how it could be applied in my daily life.

And so I believed all the negative things I was told about myself and the Diné, who *were* apparently inferior to other people.

While I was in basic training, a tall, good-looking white man came to me and asked me to read a letter from home. He must have been eighteen or nineteen years old, a full-grown man in my fifteen-year-old eyes.

I was certain he was testing me. All white men knew how to read. White men were extremely intelligent. They were the teachers. They had great knowledge. They were all far superior to us Navajo.

I read the letter to him, glancing at his face as I did so. He was listening intently, smiling when the letter was humorous, frowning when it mentioned something more serious. He sometimes glanced at the paper in my hand, but usually looked off into the distance, savoring the words I was certain he really knew how to read himself.

The next day he put me to another test, or so I thought. He asked me to help him write a reply to the letter, which I did.

I was rather annoyed, of course. He didn't seem to be trying to make a fool of me, but I was convinced that I knew all about white people. I was sure that they were born knowing how to read and write. After all, there were no white students in the schools I attended, though there were white people teaching in those schools. Thus I concluded that white people didn't need to go to school. Only the Navajo, the Diné, the Human Beings, did. White people knew everything from birth.

Several weeks later I experienced a shocking revelation: That white boy could not read! He could not write! He told me that he had never been to school. He was raised on a farm in a rural area where no one forced him to get an education. He was illiterate.

I was both shocked and excited. White people *weren't* better than I was. White people had to go to school just like the Navajo. Even more surprising to me was the realization that I actually had skills he did not have, and that knowledge was power.

My knowledge of the English language was limited. I sometimes thought that if a white teenager's knowledge of English could be quantified, it would fill a big cardboard box, while all the words I knew could be crammed into a coffee cup. Yet I was the one reading the white boy's letters. I was the one writing the white boy's replies. He was not God. He was not superhuman. If anything, I knew more than he did.

This truth drastically changed my outlook on the world. Before, I had been ridiculed and belittled to such a degree by the BIA teachers that I felt inferior. We Navajo didn't know how to make planes. We didn't know how to make trains or trucks or even whiskey. Maybe we *were* dumb. Maybe we *were* ignorant. But that guy showed me that there was something wrong with my acceptance of that negative self-image. Once I realized that white people didn't have any more skills than I did unless they got an education, I no longer thought of them as a super race. They were not endowed with all skills, all knowledge. They had to struggle and learn like everyone else.

The second shock came during my code-talker training. We Navajo were not only critical to the war effort, we were learning things that many others had not been able to master, not just because we understood the Navajo language that was being used for the code. The training was extremely difficult, a combination of memorizing and understanding the ciphers, the complex language techniques, and similar matters. Most soldiers could not master it all, and while many Navajo failed the course, most of us who were selected for the training were able to complete it.

For the first time since my initial involvement with Anglos I realized that I was not inferior, I was more than a filthy savage with no future. I did not know where I was headed or what I might do with the rest of my life. I just knew that I had more choices than I had ever imagined.

There was a library available to us, and I decided to take advantage of it. I began studying do-it-yourself mathematics and English books. I wanted to learn more, to be able to do something, because I finally realized that I could.

The training period was not all work. Each weekend, if we had money, we'd get passes and go into Los Angeles. We'd leave on Friday night and stay until the last train to Oceanside returned us to the train station at four or five on Monday morning. We would hop on a bus at the train station and make it back to the base before the six o'clock roll call.

When we didn't have money, we took advantage of the area in which the base was located. Camp Pendleton was a vast federal reservation with a lot of ranch land all around. When we couldn't afford to go into town, we would go to the ranches and break wild horses for the owners. We'd round the horses up, put them in corrals, saddle them, and ride them until they adjusted to having someone on their backs. Usually we weren't paid anything; we were just having fun.

The Los Angeles adventures were a little wilder. The corner of Sixth Street and Main in downtown Los Angeles was the gathering place for Navajo boys in uniform. We would meet there at a bar called the Ritz. It was always packed with soldiers, sailors, Marines, and pilots, almost all of them Indians. There was drinking, an occasional fight, music, and almost anything else you could imagine—if you were of age.

My buddy and I went in there a couple of times until the staff got wise to the fact that you could join the military as soon as you were seventeen, which was underage to be in a bar. My buddy really was seventeen, and though I had an ID listing the same age, I was younger. We were checked at the door, then banned from going inside. We were forced to spend our time going to the movies, picking up girls, or taking the trolley over to the famous Hollywood Canteen at Hollywood and Vine.

The Hollywood Canteen was a big hall that the USO and various celebrities operated for the enjoyment of servicemen. You could dance there, get soft drinks, coffee, finger sandwiches, and cookies, meet girls, and meet some movie stars. People like Bette Davis, Betty Grable, Jane Russell, Dorothy Lamour, Harry James and his band, and many others would go over there to be with the servicemen. They would perform on a large stage, then stand around talking and signing autographs. It was all free for anyone in uniform. We did not think much about the war during this time. We were training, having fun, seeing the big city. The only hint of what we were to face came from the fact that, while we were on base, we were never allowed to be far from four possessions; a helmet, a rifle, a sea bag, and a backpack.

One afternoon we were told to grab our things and get into the back of one of the trucks in a caravan going south. There were thirty Marines in each truck, and the line of trucks stretched into the distance. We were taken to the San Diego shipyards, where thousands of us boarded a troop carrier that pulled out that night.

By morning there was no question about what was happening. There were no more bright lights and big cities, no more ranches where we could work the horses. There was nothing but blue skies and blue water, the waves rising high, tossing the ship from side to side as it cut through the water.

The sensation of movement was continuous and disorienting. About half of us became sick and spent much of our time leaning over the railing. When we were able to get down to the dining room, we'd take our trays to the table, then spend most of the meal catching them as they slid from side to side. Food fell to the floor when we weren't careful, and it was difficult to balance the tray and eat when we had to be cautious about everything. Very little was consumed, though, and much of that was lost at sea. Fortunately the seasickness lasted only three or four days before we adjusted.

On our third day out, we were told that we were going to Pearl Harbor. This was going to be a great war! We were going to Hawaii. We'd be seeing Bing Crosby, Bob Hope, and Dorothy Lamour making one of their "Road" pictures. There would be palm trees and hula girls, women dancing in grass skirts, and the sound of ukeleles everywhere. At least that's what I thought, having seen Hawaii many times before—in the movies.

When we approached the beach at Pearl Harbor, it was nothing like I expected. There were high-rises in the distance, much like the ones in San Diego. We could also see a munitions block, lots of buildings, and a huge area with nothing but tents.

We had been assigned to ships by draft number, men of all different skills and backgrounds split up, unlike the way we had been in boot camp. There were not more than ten of us together from among the forty or more Navajo with whom I started training. We were still separated when we were in the massive temporary base waiting for departure to the South Pacific.

I was sent to Honolulu with about ten thousand troops waiting to be sent abroad. We had nothing to do in the tent camps except eat in one of the massive mess halls, clean our immediate surroundings, and be ready to ship out.

No one knew when he was going to leave or where he might end up.

Each day a company or battalion was suddenly shipped out, though the orders came without regard for how long any of us had been in the area or what skills we had. There was a logic to it, but wartime secrecy prevented any of us from knowing what it was. We just had to be on the alert.

It was April of 1945. The weather was beautiful, but the area was boring. To keep us happy, we were told that no one would be shipped out after 11:00 A.M. each day. We would wait until 11:00, listening for our numbers, then go into Honolulu to pass the time. There were no women in grass skirts, Dorothy Lamour didn't make an appearance, and there were no luaus with roast pig in the middle of the city. There were only the same diversions that existed in San Diego, though at least we could stay in the city until the 9:00 P.M. curfew on the base.

One day during the last week of the month, after the eleven o'clock call gave me yet another day to spend in Honolulu, I was bored and took off immediately for the city. I had no way of knowing that everything would soon be different.

I stayed in town for only a few hours, and when I returned to the camp at five o'clock, nothing was there. The tent city was deserted. The thousands of men with whom I had been living were gone. There was nothing there. All that remained was a hand-written note pinned against the headquarters building ordering me to report to the next wave of Marines who would be temporarily stationed there. Apparently the orders to ship out had come a few minutes after I left. I had been the first in line to get the one-day liberty pass, and I left the moment it was signed. The officer was probably working on the second pass when the orders came to ship out. Because I had left legitimately, I was not in trouble. They left the note for me and shipped out. The giant camp was deserted except for my sea bag, backpack, helmet, and rifle.

The evening was very lonely, I didn't know when the next wave of Marines would come in, but there were many other troops in different sections of the area. I was in the midst of a couple of hundred empty tents, and my commanding officer was gone, but the mess halls were still functioning for the other men, so at least I could eat.

I thought I might be able to get a liberty pass to go into town, but no one in the other groups knew me, so they couldn't let me leave. I had to wait for the next group, since they would have my records and could take me in.

Four days later a new group from Stateside, including several Navajo, came in. I reported to their commander, explaining the situation, but even that didn't help. My records had apparently gone on with the original troops, so I was told I had to wait until they were shipped back to Honolulu.

I waited in Honolulu throughout April, May, and June. I was allowed to go into town, but I couldn't get paid because my records weren't there. The only money I had came from my family after I wrote home to tell them my troubles.

I probably saw everything there was to see in Honolulu during that time. I did get to a luau, though it was obviously staged for the tourists and GIs. I went to some beach parties, and I took in a few USO shows. I saw Betty Hutton, Bob Hope, and the other entertainers who were part of the traveling shows. But mostly I was alone, writing to my family, wanting to fight like my friends and relatives, several of whom had already been killed. Between their loss and the training I experienced, I reached a point where I truly wanted to kill the Japanese. In my mind, they had become the enemy, the people I had to destroy to avenge the deaths of those with whom I had lived.

At the same time I was a little scared. During the long wait, I went with a few Marines to the military hospital in Pearl Harbor to see if we knew anybody. To my horror, there was one of the guys I had trained with. He had been on Okinawa and was caught by a Japanese machine gunner. Bullets had ripped diagonally across his body, blasting holes from his right shoulder to his left hip. The bullets had missed the vital organs, ensuring he would live, but his spine had been severed and he would be paralyzed for the rest of his life.

My reaction was mixed. I was angry for my friend, yet I was also aware that it could have been me. I might have gone as scheduled and been killed on a strange island far from my home. I think I realized my own mortality right then. I admitted that, as much as I wanted to see action like the others, I did not want to get hurt. I was scared of not going, and maybe a little more scared of going. Yet there was nothing I could do except wait, and the longer I waited, the more I wanted to get it over with, to be shipped out into the war zone and shoot someone.

Hundreds and thousands of men went through the area. They would arrive, spend four or five days in the tent city, then leave. The place would stay empty for another few days, and then the cycle would start over again. No one minded my presence. No one made me stay on the base. But it was a lonely, confusing time.

July passed, then August. The atomic bomb was dropped, and the war was almost over when my records finally arrived. I had spent the war in Hawaii, waiting to be shipped out. By the time I left Pearl Harbor with the Marines, the Japanese were about to surrender. We went to Guam, which had been secured, and I rejoined the Navajo with whom I had trained to be a code talker.

The months of inaction for me had been some of the most intense of the war in the Pacific for the Marines with whom I had trained. The

code talkers had distinguished themselves in action on Saipan, Iwo
Jima, and Okinawa. The fighting had been intense, and they told me
how lucky I was not to have gone through it. What they did not realize
was that I was not as mature as they were. I was still a kid, a young
teenager, who had spent months feeling scared, lonely, and sorry for
myself. I had had no money. The guys who came through Honolulu
always shipped out within a couple of days, abandoning me again. I
was miserable, lost, suffering more, I thought, than if I had seen
action.

Guam seemed like my big chance. My unit was one of those being
readied to assault the main island of Japan. Wave after wave of us were
going to land and fight our way through the cities until we took
complete control.

Between the protection ceremony the medicine man had performed
for me and the actions of Harry Truman, I never did get into battle.
V-J Day came, and everyone celebrated. Then we were shipped on to
northern China, where we would help round up the Japanese who had
been occupying the territory there. We would make certain they
knew that the war was over, move them into camps, then return them
to Japan.

My unit and the Navy Seventh Fleet went to Tsingtao, China,
where the Japanese occupation forces surrendered. I was again with
the Navajo, and we stayed there for a peaceful year.

There was much political activity in China at that time, though I
understood little of it. Mao Tse-tung was leading a revolutionary force,
and there was talk of China becoming a Communist nation. Many
Marines took advantage of their free time to visit the sights, traveling
to Peking, going to see the Great Wall, and generally playing tourists.
All I knew was that I was lonely, in a strange land, wanting to be with
my mother. I did my job and then spent most of my free time being a
homesick teenager, still barely old enough to enlist in the Marines.

Although I did not always take advantage of the opportunities in
China, I did learn there. I met a professor named Sam Yee, who had a
doctorate from Shanghai University, and his ten-year-old son, Mo
Sam Yee. We became close friends, and the professor invited me to
his home.

Dr. Yee had made learning a part of his life. In his home he had a
big English dictionary that he studied all the time in order to increase
his vocabulary. He used to play a game with me, having me open the
dictionary to anywhere I wanted and then give him a word to define.
No matter what word I chose, he always knew what it meant and how
to spell it. He told me that he had spent ten years just studying the
dictionary so he could understand English words.

I used to study Dr. Yee's physical appearance. He wasn't Diné, but he also wasn't blond and blue-eyed. He was different from me, but he was also different from white men. Yet he was smart, he was educated. He had learned things that I realized most people of any race did not know, and he had learned those things by getting an education.

Now I knew that the BIA was wrong. I was not stupid. I was an equal player in the game of life, the game of success. I was on an equal footing with anybody. I had the same opportunity as the Chinese, the whites, and everyone else.

The other awareness I had while in China came from seeing the poverty of the people. This was a nation about to experience a revolution, and the reasons were obvious. The Navajo were poverty-stricken following the livestock reduction, but at least we had shelter and clothing. Some children in China were being raised in the open, their stomachs swollen from malnutrition. Women had shriveled breasts and were barren of the milk they needed to feed their infants. These were people who sometimes seemed to have been born old so that they could die young.

What shocked me most was the number of children without parents. I saw fifteen or twenty of them running in packs. Some were as young as three years old. Others looked to be teenagers. They would stay together all day, roaming the streets and the hillsides, sleeping together wherever they happened to be when night came.

Whenever we went into town, the packs would approach us, tug on our pant legs, and beg for food, money, or anything else they could get. Every other morning, we would find one of the children dead. The pack would move on without them, and the city police or someone else would apparently pick up the corpses. No one seemed to care about these children, and there was inadequate food for them to survive.

On the reservation we did not always have as much as we would have liked, but we did have order. We had our culture, our religion, our families, our clans. There was a structure that enabled us to help one another and endure. Even during our hardest times, in the early 1940s, when we had to ration food, no one was homeless. Seeing those children roaming from one trash pile to another was a horrible shock.

The Chinese adults ignored the packs. They walked by them, seemingly unseeing.

Yet there was some fun for us in China. Some of the local men earned their living pulling rickshaws, small carts in which one or two people would ride. The "driver" would hold two poles that extended from the cart and run through the streets, taking passengers to their destinations. The rickshaws were like old-fashioned horse-drawn taxicabs, except that a human runner took the place of the horse.

Three or four of us would hire rickshaws to take us to the barracks.

We had the drivers race each other, telling them that whoever won would get extra money. Then the men would run as fast as they could, each pulling one of us Marines in the cart.

By the time my year in China was over, I had matured in ways I never expected. I had a purpose in life, a direction. I had gained self-respect and learned of a world apart from everything I had ever been taught. I was excited about the future, proud to be a Navajo, proud to be a man. I was honorably discharged on October 5, 1946.

The military offered me a chance to reenlist, of course, offering many of us the opportunity to stay with Uncle Sam for four more years. But all I wanted was to go home, giving thanks to God for getting me through the war alive, unharmed, strong, and ready for the future. I was eighteen years old and had traveled halfway around the world. Now I was determined to kick back, relax, earn a little money, and see about getting an education. All I had to do was learn about what happened in the past, learn what had been discovered, learn what had been published. Education would make me the equal of anyone.

CHAPTER FOUR

My emotions were in turmoil when I returned home. I had never truly been to war, even though I was trained for one of the most important intelligence missions that took place. I had not been able to avenge the cripplings and deaths of my friends, yet I had survived, avoiding such a fate myself, and I was glad for that.

Making life easier for me was the GI benefit called 52/20. For one full year, I was paid twenty dollars a week unemployment compensation. That was enough money in those days even for guys who lived in the city, but on the Navajo Reservation during a time of poverty and struggle, it was enough to make me feel like a king.

To "earn" your pay, all you had to do was say you were looking for a job. The check came until you found employment, so I spent my time visiting people in Teec Nos Pos and Shiprock, avoiding full-time employment for a while.

The Navajo culture had changed radically. The livestock reduction was now complete. Everyone I knew owned fewer than one hundred sheep, and no one had horses. Most people earned their living doing migrant labor on the railroads and large Anglo farms or holding mining jobs, usually in the uranium mines. Some family farms had been abandoned. Instead of living with the seasons, many men and women were living from paycheck to paycheck, just as in Anglo society.

Looking back, I can see that the war years caused almost as much destruction among the Navajo as the livestock reduction did. Navajo boys gained a new mobility during that period. Before the war, most had known little more than the reservation. The few who moved away from the reservation lived mostly in small communities nearby where there was work in the mines or on the railroads.

The draft changed everything. Suddenly Navajo boys found themselves with large numbers of other youths from big cities and small towns throughout the nation. They met college graduates, high school graduates, and illiterates. They traveled to major cities throughout the world. They encountered new cultures and new ideas. Some were tested in combat. Others served with occupation forces, support services, or stateside duty. But they learned of different religions, history, geography, and entertainment.

The result of this sudden exposure to the world at large was twofold.

Some of our young men felt a sense of hopelessness. The more they saw, the more new things they experienced, the more natural it was for them to look at the limited society of our isolated people and find it wanting. Certainly there were Navajo who, like myself, came to realize that whites were not a super race, that it was education and not some inherent superiority that enabled them to build airplanes, trains, and cars. But there were others for whom experience in the greater society only served to reinforce the BIA's teachings that we were inferior. We had learned to work the land within the range of the sacred mountains. They had learned to fly over the land and travel across the ocean.

It was as though someone had taken a culture that had been carefully nurtured for thousands of years and suddenly labeled it a false promise. Everything the Navajo knew, all the ways we had lived and survived, now seemed like a fraud. We had to find new ways, but we had no way to determine what those might be.

To an outsider able to watch over us, we might have been like a giant anthill where someone had taken a stick, poked it in an entrance hole, then moved it about. The ants are alive. They still know what their world was like. But suddenly everything familiar has been destroyed and they don't know how to rebuild.

There is a perception among whites that Indians have long been alcoholics. Cowboy movies often talk about "firewater," and novels dating from as early as the nineteenth century show Indians drinking whiskey and then going on the warpath. Perhaps some of the myths of drunken Indians have a basis in fact in different parts of the country, but prior to World War II the Navajo seldom if ever drank alcohol. Those who did were very quiet about it, hidden from view because drinking was not acceptable. Certainly they seldom got drunk, and if they did, they drank in such isolation that no one ever learned of their disgrace.

By the time I returned, all of that had changed. Suddenly drinking offered an escape from the sense of hopelessness. I saw alcohol openly consumed during squaw dances and other ceremonies. Navajo were becoming belligerent or depressed from drinking too much. They would sometimes disrupt sacred occasions, a shocking situation to someone like me who had not seen the slow decline of the people. Even worse was the alcohol consumption among the young. Teenagers of fifteen and sixteen were openly drinking.

No one understood the dangers of alcohol, though many of us realized that drinking was wrong. We suffered from a lack of knowledge about the effects of alcohol. No one in the Navajo Nation understood what it meant to drink too much. They didn't understand how to pace themselves, how to avoid suffering many of alcohol's negative effects. People drank until they did not want any more, became sick, or passed out.

Alcohol also posed a problem with which my people are still dealing today. I had been taught to avoid thinking of sex and dating until I was twenty-one, when my maturity could be evaluated by those who arranged marriages. But the BIA encouraged teenagers to think about sex and personal relationships. Arranged marriages were foreign concepts for the white teachers. Physical contact between the sexes was encouraged, and no matter what the psychological restrictions from our upbringing, the biological urges simply took over.

By the time I returned from war, many girls were frequently making their own decisions concerning whom they wanted to date and whom they wished to marry. Many of them were working away from home, in border towns like Flagstaff and Farmington, and in big cities like Albuquerque and Los Angeles. They were gaining new ideas and new desires, and considering different ways. They were having babies at ages that were unthinkable in the past. And they were combining all of these changes with drinking without understanding the repercussions.

Today we know that women cannot safely drink during pregnancy. Alcohol affects the fetus in the womb. Even one drink can cause minor problems, depending upon the stage of the pregnancy during which it is consumed. Regular drinking, especially regular drinking to get drunk, can create serious problems. Sometimes it affects how the fetal brain develops. At other times it creates learning disabilities or minor physical abnormalities. These are often correctable with special education programs that enable the child to grow up, attend college, and succeed in a profession. But you have to understand a problem in order to correct it, and in this the Navajo were at a tremendous disadvantage.

What began during that time resulted in two relatively common problems today—fetal alcohol effect and fetal alcohol syndrome. Each takes its toll on our children, and each was unknown before the war.

I did not understand the potential danger of what I was seeing, of course. It was too new, too much of a shock, too depressing to deal with. But I would eventually become one of the leaders whose task it is to address such issues, which had begun to rend the fabric of the Navajo culture.

At the time, however, all anyone understood was that alcohol was pleasurable, and it had a calming effect, especially for the ex-servicemen, almost all of whom were drinking.

These former soldiers had been halfway around the world. They had had the excitement of war, of strange cultures, of the latest technological advances. They had adjusted to the adrenaline rush of constant stimulation, whether from trying to stay alive on the battlefield or from experiencing wonders they never knew existed.

By contrast, there was no excitement on the reservation. The alcohol seemed to quiet the intense desire these men had to relive the excitement and stimulation they had known during the war.

This was no different from the problems faced by white men who were put in special units during the Vietnam War. The men who were part of assassination teams became so accustomed to living on the edge of danger that when they returned to the United States, they generally took one of three directions; some went into law enforcement or fire fighting, often joining elite units such as SWAT teams. Others turned to a life of crime, finding excitement in burglary and robbery. Still others became alcoholics or drug addicts, suppressing their feelings with chemicals.

There were other World War II veterans with the same problems, of course. But I did not know about them, nor did I see the results of the war for society at large. I only witnessed what was taking place with my people, and I could see that nothing would be the same again.

In addition, the Navajo veterans felt unappreciated by the Navajo community at large. They had been to Normandy, to Iwo Jima, to Guadalcanal, to numerous other places that were once unknown and had become a part of history. Yet when they spoke of what they did, of what they had seen, no one seemed to care. Their immediate families were proud of them, but on their way back to the Navajo Nation from their cities of discharge, they had witnessed numerous parades and celebrations. That was not the Navajo way, yet they still sought recognition and respect, none of which came to them.

Some became so discouraged that they went to the border towns in order to sell their medals and souvenirs. Others tried to join the American Legion and the new Veterans of Foreign Wars. But brown-skinned veterans were not welcome, no matter how heroically they had served. In fact, it wasn't until the late 1950s, more than a decade later, that they began their own veterans' organizations.

So much was new, so much was unfamiliar, that it was an extremely difficult time, no matter what a veteran's maturity.

Perhaps things might have settled into the routine of the past if all of the Navajo had stayed on the land they once knew. Perhaps, over time, they would have adapted to the quiet ways in harmony with nature and not the stimulants of the greater world. But the old ways were destroyed. People had to move from their homes to find work. They did not fit in anywhere, and yet they knew they had to survive. Alcohol helped them cope, or so they thought.

There were other problems for the large percentage of Navajo men who had participated in World War II. The previous world war was one in which so few of our people were involved that their return had little or no impact on the Diné. But the returning soldiers of World War II brought new ideas with them. The Navajo religion did not explain what they had seen and experienced. Scientific knowledge alone—even the fact that the earth is round—was contrary to our religious upbringing.

When I joined the Marines, I too believed that the earth was flat and that the sky came down somewhere and touched the ground. The sky was like a dome, fitting like the lid on a serving tray.

Not that the BIA schools hadn't shown us globes. I was in third or fourth grade when I saw one. But seeing a globe and relating it to our experience were quite different, and I rejected the notion as untrue.

When I traveled across the ocean, however, it became obvious to me that the horizon kept moving away from us. Also, I could understand the relative positions of the earth, the moon, and the sun as the earth revolved around the sun.

These were radical concepts, which I eagerly wanted to share with family, friends, and neighbors among the Navajo. However, when I tried to explain them after my return, an old medicine man who had been listening to me said, "Young man, you should never, ever say that again. Don't ever say the earth is moving, because the day that the earth moves is the day that all of us are going to die. So don't ever say that, don't ever think it, don't ever wish it. That's bad."

We Navajo believed that God created the earth to be still and keep all in peace. When God makes the earth move, all life will be destroyed. An earthquake, which some Navajo had experienced, was believed to be an angry warning. The idea of the entire planet moving was terrifying.

I knew that the medicine man was wrong. I knew that the old teaching was erroneous. But I also learned to say nothing. Some beliefs were too ingrained to be challenged by a teenager just back from war. Besides, had I pursued the matter, I would have been punished, and I didn't want to find out just how.

Some of the older Navajo, however, accepted this new information. They would search for stories from our past that would explain it, then add the new concepts to our culture. But the medicine men and the elders could not accept information that was a direct challenge to what they believed, so they had to deny it. It was as though a Christian died, went to heaven, discovered that Judas was sitting on the right hand of God and Jesus was in hell, and then returned to earth to tell other Christians what he had learned. It was easier to deny the new information than to consider changing the beliefs that had been a part of our culture from earliest times.

Soon the younger people began rejecting the Navajo religion and values. They no longer tried to look objectively at what they had learned. When confronted with a reality that contradicted some of the old teachings, it seemed easiest to abandon all of the traditional ways.

Yet the Navajo religion served a purpose and needed to be maintained. It did not matter whether some of the beliefs were accurate or inaccurate. It did not matter that other religions, such as Christianity, dominated the interest of those young people who wanted spiritual involvement. The stories, the legends, and the history that we had been taught for centuries provided a moral and ethical framework for a society whose members had always lived in peace and harmony. But now the turmoil of the Diné was destroying the good along with those beliefs that probably needed to be changed.

I learned to respect everything in both worlds, even though the Navajo religion was quite different from Christianity. Christians have set times for worship, such as Sunday services and Wednesday Bible studies. The Navajo religion, by contrast, is more of a curative and reactive religion.

Some rituals, for example, had consistent components. When I was growing up, everyone, sick or healthy, was outside at dawn, with ground white corn in hand, praying to the east.

The women prayed at noontime, after cooking the meal and pushing back the ashes of the fire. Then, having eaten, all of us prayed in our own way. For example, one man might say, "Great Spirit, thank you for this meal. I'll be healthy and a good runner, and all the riches will be attracted to me. People will be nice to me."

Another man might scoot back a little bit after eating, his eyes open. Then, taking a little of the grease from the meat he had eaten and rubbing it on his hands, his legs, and his chest, he might say to the Great Spirit, "I am going to be healthy. My children are going to be healthy. And my relatives. I am going to have all the energy I need to get through the day."

There was no set prayer. Each person prayed differently. But we consistently spoke of what would happen to us as a result of having eaten. Instead of asking for something, we attributed that quality to ourselves.

A third prayer time was just after sunset when we prayed to the west, using yellow cornmeal. Again, we did this whether we were sick or healthy. This prayer was not connected with a meal, though, because the Navajo generally ate only two planned meals a day.

In addition to these regular prayers, there were religious rituals for specific concerns. We had ceremonies for those who were in poor health, those who had experienced bad dreams, and those who had encountered something that was taboo.

For example, when I was in the military I began dating non-Navajo girls, a practice I continued after the war was over. Because I was exposed to different experiences at an early age, it seemed natural for me to get into social circumstances I knew were wrong. However, each time I returned home, I would have a cleansing ceremony. I was counting on the action I took to not bring me to harm before I could be properly cleansed.

All Navajo life was spiritual. Our work and play were in harmony with the gods. But this attitude, this spiritually harmonious life, was lost to most young people after the war.

It was in the spring of 1947 that I began to be more responsible. I started doing migrant work, then found a summer job in Mesa Verde, Colorado, near Cortez. In the daytime I worked for the National Park Service, cleaning the roads leading to the parks; at night I danced traditional Navajo dances for the tourists.

Dancing for tourists was something that had already been taking place for a period of time. I had never seen it before, since the Navajo of my generation were raised to see dancing as a solemn part of sacred ceremonies, not as a show.

The dances were familiar, and several of the men who worked with me had been participating for quite some time. It was another change for my people, one which I accepted because it seemed to be what I had to do to keep my job. However, different dress codes enabled me to mentally separate show dancing from religious dancing. For the shows we did not wear full regalia—the masks, makeup, special clothing, and other adornment that we wore during solemn rituals. Instead, we wore velveteen shirts, white pants, and a handkerchief headband.

We sang the traditional songs, but we abbreviated them, omitting certain portions that were always included in our formal ceremonies.

The show we put on was quite similar to what we would do when practicing for an important ceremony. Back on the reservation, several of us would get together before we had to dance for the gods. We would dress much as we did each evening when we were entertaining. We would sing accurate, though abbreviated versions of the sacred songs. And we would perform the traditional dances, mastering the steps so there would be no mistakes when we were properly attired and performing for the gods. Normally we did not do these practice sessions in front of a group of tourists, however.

Our reasons for dancing were all rationalizations, of course. We told ourselves that we were just giving the public a sample of our culture, but we never went so far as to anger the gods. It was wrong for us to be asked to do what we did, and it was wrong of us to do it. Yet by setting artificial limits on our actions, we accepted what was taking place. We felt that we were not violating our religion or beliefs, but merely sharing a small portion of our culture.

We made extra money from dancing as well. There were six of us, and when we were done, we would pass the hat. The Park Service expected us to perform as part of our duties, though it was overtime and they did not pay us extra. Whatever we collected from the tourists was divided equally among us.

The tourists seemed to have a fantasy about us as well. One night, when it was my turn to pass the hat, I walked through the crowd and accidentally stepped on a woman's foot. Normally, after dancing, we did not talk with the audience. But when I stepped on the woman's foot, I said, "Excuse me."

The woman's daughter stared at me in surprise. Then she got all excited, telling her mother what I had said. She was amazed that a savage Indian was both polite and able to speak English. Obviously, though our dancing gave the tourists a tiny taste of our culture, we were not really helping them understand us. We never explained either the dances or our religion. Like the little girl, the tourists had no idea that we spoke English and had the same manners with which they had been raised.

The fact that we were working for the Parks Service, just as other Navajo were working for the mines, the railroads, and the Anglo farmers and ranchers, helped contribute to rapid cultural changes. Many of the Navajo were tired, and trying to maintain a dawn-to-dusk prayer schedule during the summer months could be exhausting when added to the difficult jobs we had.

The Navajo were also seeing how others lived. They ate in restaurants and cofffe shops where they watched different Indians and white people, none of whom prayed as they did. They came to the conclusion that perhaps it was not necessary to keep such an intense prayer schedule.

The young people, mostly those under twenty years of age, were, to some degree, products of the BIA boarding school system. The BIA had a Christian bias. Students did not get up at dawn to pray to the east, and those who had been raised strictly and who tried to continue this prayer schedule were harshly criticized for being pagan savages. Some of the children adopted Christianity. Others went through whatever rituals the BIA demanded, never seriously caring about any religion.

The older Navajo were more likely to cling to at least a portion of the traditional ways. But their numbers were small. Their children and their grandchildren perhaps still relied on the curative ceremonies, but they no longer bothered with morning, noon, and evening prayers. In my immediate family, for example, I had stopped the daily praying entirely, while my mother, sisters and brothers, and step-father followed the prayers on an irregular basis.

In the fall of 1947 I became a migrant worker, then stayed on an uncle's farm during the winter. At the same time, a cousin of mine became a truck driver for the BIA, traveling throughout New Mexico. He stopped by the farm in February and asked if I would travel with him to the small community of Fruitland to load his two-ton truck with hay.

We loaded the truck at a BIA farm, lashing the bales to the bed of the truck with chains. Then we drove to Farmington, where what had been a mild snowstorm became quite intense. It was five o'clock in the evening, growing dark, and we decided to get some wine while waiting out the worst of the storm.

Indians were not allowed to buy liquor in white stores in 1948, but my cousin knew a bootlegger in the Mexican section of town. We bought the wine, then parked the truck and began visiting with old friends.

It was clear that my cousin and the others were planning to do nothing but drink, something I did not want to do. I preferred to see an old girlfriend in Farmington, and the guys dropped me off at her home. I spent the evening there and had supper with her family.

My cousin returned several hours later, quite drunk, with two unopened quarts of wine still in the truck. It was dark, the storm was even more intense, and seven or eight inches of snow had fallen. But my cousin insisted that he was all right, that he could drive.

We had to go to Fort Defiance, Arizona, a two-and-a-half-hour drive, but I tried to persuade him to drive only so far as Shiprock, a short and safer distance. Although my cousin refused to stay in Ship-rock overnight, I got him to agree to stop for coffee when we got there.

I was scared of my cousin's driving, but I was also tired, having spent the previous couple of days visiting friends and getting little sleep. Although the heater was on in the cab, I made the mistake of taking a drink of wine to feel even warmer. The combination put me to sleep immediately.

I awoke spinning in the cab. Everything was rolling, and when I glanced out of what was left of the window, I saw that the headlights were aimed at the sky. I wasn't alert, but I knew we were in trouble.

Apparently the truck had started skidding, and my cousin had hit the brakes. The truck went into a 180-degree spin, flipped, and rolled over and over. The bales of hay were piled so high, however, that the cab never really touched the ground. Then some of the bales broke open, and the vehicle landed upside down.

We were halfway to Fort Defiance when the accident occurred, having passed through Shiprock while I was asleep. My cousin had decided not to stop for coffee as he had agreed. The snow had stopped, the sky was clear, but the temperature was well below zero. We knew we could freeze, and unable to see any nearby home, we made shelter immediately.

We used the unbroken hay bales to build an igloo. Then we split some of the hay to rest on, covering ourselves with the one thin blanket my cousin carried in the truck. We set some of the hay on fire, lay down on the straw, and huddled together under the blanket. Our precautions were barely adequate, though, especially since I was so poorly dressed for the snow and was wearing Oxfords, not boots. We were both quite chilled.

I decided to warm my feet by shifting them toward the fire near the warm coals. I finally felt comfortable, dozing off without thinking of the danger.

Suddenly I awoke in great pain. My feet felt awful, the pain increasing. I was certain I had developed frostbite and tried to ignore the pain since there was nothing I could do to stop it until my feet grew warmer. I awakened my cousin and made him increase the fire to fight the freezing cold. But he kept dozing, so finally I stood up to get some hay to add to the flames. It was then that I saw my mistake.

The pain in my feet was not from the cold. I had caught fire. My shoes were almost destroyed, and my big toe was smoldering. My skin was about to burst into flame as I quickly shoved my feet into the snow. There was a hissing sound as steam rose in front of me.

I was miserable the rest of the night. One shoe was almost destroyed, my toe was badly burned, and we had added most of the hay to the fire before the sun came up. My cousin and I were covered with soot, and we had no idea where to get help.

In the early morning sunlight we spotted a hogan a mile or two in the distance. We arrived as the family was preparing fried potatoes, Navajo tortillas, and coffee, the best meal we had had in years. We were able to get warm, then walked to a day school a few miles away in order to get help. Not a single car passed us, so again we were miserable, but at least we could arrange for the BIA in Fort Defiance to help us.

My cousin was fired on the spot. He was told to leave the truck key at the school. Someone would examine the wreck and see what could be done. We also learned that the previous night had been the coldest on record at that time—fifty degrees below zero. In addition, the highway had been closed all night. Apparently we had gotten far enough along that the highway patrol never spotted us.

The road reopened, and a pickup truck gave us a ride to Gallup,

New Mexico. We had almost no money, no jobs, and no way to get back. Fortunately we found an office called Navajo Assistance, staffed by a white man who asked us what happened. We explained everything. Then he asked if we were veterans. We said we were, and he said, "How would you like to go back to school?"

The man mentioned that Fort Wingate, in Arizona, had a BIA boarding school that a lot of veterans were attending. The Veterans Administration would pay for our room and board, plus seventy-five dollars per month free and clear. He even drove us there, though we had nothing but the dirty, smelly clothing on our bodies.

At Fort Wingate we were accepted into the program, then taken to the trading post where we were given credit to buy clothing. We were placed in a barracks for the veterans, who were older than the other students. The food was good, and I was back in school.

I was a sixth-grade dropout, too uneducated to attend the regular school. They placed me in the vocational section, where I trained to be an electrician. I also took classes in typing, still thinking about being a clerk.

I stayed in school for three months until summer break. Then I took a job in Fort Defiance with the BIA, working as a court clerk.

There would be far more education in my future. I would eventually become an engineer, headed for top management with Hughes Aircraft, a success by any standards. But it was at Fort Defiance that I completed the most important part of my training as a Navajo who would one day walk amid the people of several conflicting worlds.

There is a Navajo tradition of observing in order to gain understanding. Anglos talk of the scientific method, making observations in order to reach new conclusions. The Navajo system of observing is slightly different. The Diné's religious history was so complex that almost anything, when placed within the context of the religion, could be understood.

Nothing frightened my people. There was no reason for fear. God had created everything, and there were spirits in all creatures. Sometimes you took the power of those spirits for your own. Sometimes you recognized an evil spirit and called upon one of the familiar good spirits for protection. But it was important to understand the new, the different, in order to remain in harmony and control.

Centuries earlier, the Spanish had arrived on horseback. My people had never seen horses, nor had they encountered the armor worn by the Spanish soldiers. Even the weapons they carried, the swords and spears, were unfamiliar, made from unknown materials.

Other cultures encountering the Spaniards had been terrified of them or had mistaken them for gods to be worshiped and feared. The

Navajo reacted differently, much to the surprise of the Spaniards. They did not recoil from these strange white men astride previously unseen animals weighing as much as two thousand pounds. Francisco Vásquez de Coronado, the first white man to write about meeting my people, traveled with an army of 336 Spaniards and approximately 1,000 Indians of different tribes, all strangers to the Diné. His writings reflect his surprise at the calm of the Navajo, the way they observed and then adopted such strange, new things as the horse.

This willingness to see, absorb, understand, and adopt had been a part of my traditional upbringing. Even as the world I had known fell apart all around me, a portion of me acted as a dispassionate observer. I was able to step back and absorb all that was taking place, a subconscious action that would prove important when, years later, I had to use the knowledge gained during that period.

I had been born as my people were born for thousands of years. My early life was no different from that experienced by my ancestors for generation upon generation. Then I left, discovering the railroad, the mines, big cities, and for a year, China, often believed to be the world's oldest culture. I learned about Christianity. I saw the damage done to my people by the livestock reduction. I encountered alcoholism, poverty, and despair. I witnessed events and cultural changes that normally are encountered only over several generations.

The effect on me was profound. I felt a reverence and respect for the past and for what might have been our present. I experienced the prejudice that has haunted my people for centuries. And I developed an awareness of the potential for my people through education. Finally, as a court clerk with the BIA, I learned about the highest levels of justice and human respect possible in a society.

The tribal court system, along with the Navajo police, had come under the domination of the Bureau of Indian Affairs, but the methods they used were primarily the old ways of the Navajo. The judges were men of great wisdom, though they lacked a traditional education. Their law books were the moral and ethical rules that had governed our people for centuries. There was a rather simple list of crimes and penalties, but it would be many years before an elaborate penal code was developed, and then it was little more than a photocopy of the white man's laws.

Most of the judges could neither speak nor write English. I could do both, and I could type. As a result, they made me a court clerk, though I was not yet twenty-one years of age.

My job proved to be more involved than I expected. I also had to act as interpreter and jailer and perform other duties that were not directly the responsibility of the judges. It was a one-man support operation.

A Navajo would come in with a complaint. I would then refer to the twenty mimeographed pages of crimes and their penalties. For example, if a Navajo man told me that another Navajo man had hit him, I would tell him that there were laws that applied, then explain what they were. Each charge had a different penalty, such as ten days in jail or a ten-dollar-fine. I would read him the various laws that applied to the offense he described, then ask him which one he thought was most appropriate. Once we resolved the matter, I would type out the complaint, then type out a warrant for the arrest of the person.

The man charged was arrested and brought before me so I could set a court date. This would usually be from Tuesday through Friday as a courtesy to the police, whose cases, usually from arrests made over the weekend for drunk and disorderly conduct, were given Monday court dates. I also took in the evidence, such as cases of beer.

When court was in session, the judges would come in, and I would sit with them during the trials. Assuming the case was Navajo against Navajo, both the plaintiff's family and the defendant's family would sit in the front of the courtroom.

I would swear in each person, having him promise to tell the truth. Then I would read the complaint to the judge.

There were no lawyers present. The judge would question both the plaintiff and the defendant, almost always speaking Navajo. However, if someone spoke only English, I would serve as translator.

The judge was in complete control of everything, sometimes talking with the defendant, sometimes the plaintiff, and sometimes with one or more family members. He would probe carefully, always seeking the truth. And eventually one of them would admit what had happened. The defendant might agree that he had indeed committed the crime. Or the plaintiff might admit that he had not been completely honest about what took place. Once the truth was known, the judge would pass sentence.

In an assault and battery case, he might order a jail sentence, a fine, or a suspended sentence. Whatever he did, it was my job to type up the results, giving one copy to the defendant to sign, usually with a thumbprint, and keeping one copy for the court.

Most cases, except for the drunk and disorderly ones, did not end with a jail sentence or fine. The idea behind Navajo justice was to achieve reconciliation and harmony among all parties. Each person had to decide what was fair. Wrongs had to be righted in a manner that was appropriate for the trouble caused, without either side seeking vengence. The person who did wrong would promise not to do it again. His family would support his statement, agreeing to help him stay out of trouble in the future. His actions had disgraced them. His future actions would reflect upon them. They were all involved, all concerned.

When the trial was over, the plaintiff and the defendant shook hands. They had resolved their differences.

It was this sense of fairness that impressed me about the Navajo courts. White man's justice often stuck me as a means for vengeance. Anglos seemed to want to separate themselves from the person who did wrong, whereas Navajo society recognized that the wrongdoer was still part of the community. There were penalties for crimes, but the concern was not punishment. It was making the person whole again, not creating an outcast who would be discriminated against by others. Restoring the person to a productive role in society, always with the encouragement and involvement of the family, was the goal.

I worked all summer, fascinated by the wisdom of the Navajo judges. These were uneducated men, lacking the schooling and opportunities I had had. Yet they knew how to probe for the truth, to question, to gently prod someone who might be lying, to obtain information in a way that any major city criminal prosecutors might have had trouble doing. And when they were done, they went beyond the code books to work out a solution that would restore a broken relationship.

Among the Navajo judges, the most impressive was Jim Shirley. He was tall and slender and sported a big black mustache and the typical Navajo hat and beads. He was also quite wise.

Sometimes two judges would sit on a case. When they recessed, they would talk about the case, asking each other what they thought. They would explore every possibility before continuing with the hearing. I was just turning nineteen, and it was a marvelous thing to be exposed to.

Perhaps the most important part of those trials was the respect for the truth. No one was afraid of the truth. When someone was honest, the plaintiff would always understand. Once the truth was known, it was only a question of rectifying the matter.

For example, suppose someone stole a cow. When the defendant admitted the theft, he would usually give his reason. He might have been hungry. He might have wanted extra money. Whatever the case, everything would be known.

The plaintiff would acknowledge the defendant's honesty by saying that he understood why the person had stolen the cow. Then he would say what he wanted in return, which was usually to get the animal back, if it was still alive, or to get another one of equal quality. The judge then questioned both parties to be certain that the return of the cow would satisfy them.

If the defendant could return or replace the cow, he would. If not, the judge would enlist the aid of the defendant's relatives, who would provide a cow on his behalf. The family would admit that the thief had embarrassed the clan, and they would promise to keep an eye on him so he would not do it again. The defendant would also promise not to steal in the future.

The judge passed sentence accordingly. The defendant had to give the plaintiff a cow of the same age and quality as the one he had taken. There was no further penalty because a satisfactory solution had been achieved.

The Navajo system had no penalty for perjury—lying under oath— because we thought that the idea of swearing to tell the truth was hypocritical. It is human nature for people to avoid facing responsibility at first. Little children, when they do something wrong, routinely say they are innocent. Then the parent probes a bit and the child will put the blame on someone else—a brother, sister, friend. Finally, as the parent and child continue to talk about the incident, the child tells the truth.

The same is true in court. No one is upset if the defendant tries to avoid telling the truth at first. The judge and the men and women involved discuss what happened until all the facts are known. There is no penalty for doing what people do naturally. And eventually the truth is revealed.

The defendant in one case was the driver of a pickup truck who had hit a horse on the highway, killing the horse, injuring his woman passenger, and wrecking his truck. The plaintiff was the owner of the horse, and he wanted it replaced.

The defendant admitted his guilt. He also admitted that he was driving under the influence of alcohol, but he could not afford to replace the horse. The defendant's family arranged to replace the horse and help pay the injured woman's hospital bills. Everything was resolved in a manner that made everyone happy.

Today the laws have been changed to fit white man's courts. That same case, once handled in a manner satisfactory to everyone, would be quite different now. The driver would serve a mandatory jail term of a year or two and would pay a fine and a lawyer's fee, and he might or might not have to replace the horse. A separate suit would be filed against the horse owner for allowing the animal to cross the road. The insurance company would have to pay for the truck and the woman's injuries. The woman might sue both the driver and the horse owner to be certain she collected from someone, an action that would cost more money and involve more lawyers. By the time the case was resolved, everyone would have suffered, and there would be no assurance that the family would take responsibility in the future. There would be actual damages and punitive damages, and everyone but the lawyers would be the losers. But at that time, the defendant was allowed to make reparations. The penalties were appropriate. There was no need for jail. There were no punitive damages. It was punishment enough to be disgraced in the community.

The cases I saw were varied. There were thefts, assault and battery cases, divorces, illicit cohabitations, and numerous others. But no matter what occurred, all parties had to agree to the solution. It was 180 degrees away from the justice of white man's courts and even from the current Navajo courts.

Although I did not realize it then, my months in the court system truly convinced me of the value of the Navajo culture, the Navajo way. There was something inherently good, gentle, loving, and accepting in the manner in which disputes were handled. Not that there wasn't violence on rare occasions between Navajo. The passions of love and hate can be just as intense among my people as among any other. And Navajo men went to jail, enduring the same penalties as others for their crimes. What was different was the understanding among all parties, the acceptance of human life and actions, the effort to resolve problems in a way that everyone involved agreed was fair to all.

I had gone through many changes and would go through many more. But I suspect it was during that period that I realized my people and my culture were worth preserving at any price. We were not better than others. Given the right circumstances, we could corrupt ourselves in the same manner as wealthier people with greater opportunity to acquire the needless vanities in which those with money can indulge. Yet we came close to following the religious ethic expressed by almost all cultures, an accomplishment not achieved by any other group during this century. The Navajo way was in harmony with many of the teachings of Judaism, Christianity, Islam, Buddhism, and many other faiths. The difference was that, until the forced changes of the Livestock Reduction Act, the war years, and the BIA educational system, we had achieved a society so caring that, at the very least, it deserved to be preserved. At best, it might serve as a beacon of understanding, an example for the more advanced civilizations as we moved into the twenty-first century.

CHAPTER FIVE

The social life at Fort Defiance was quite active for me. Although the region needed additional medical care, it had little to offer doctors and other health care professionals who were interested in establishing private practices in more lucrative areas. Instead, a program was established along the lines of the contemporary VISTA (Volunteers In Service To America) organization. Anglo nursing students were able to work for a period of time in the Fort Defiance area, gaining experience, a small stipend, and help with their education.

The nurses committed themselves to a year on the reservation. It was an adventure for many of them, as well as a chance to work under conditions they might otherwise never experience.

The nurses' quarters were near where I was living. I used to hang around with the other young men, talking with the girls, dating them, and generally enjoying their company.

The nurses were quite special for me. They were dedicated young women, without prejudice, who believed in the potential of everyone. We went to Squaw Dances together. I discussed the culture and history of my people and they helped me master English.

At the end of the summer, a recruiter from a Baptist Indian junior college, Bacone College, came to see me. He had actually been visiting with my cousin, a high school graduate, and the cousin referred him to me as well.

I was a sixth-grade dropout, I explained to him. My only other education was the three months spent learning typing and electrical work. I told him about my current job with the court system, explaining that even that was only temporary.

The recruiter said that, because I was a veteran, I would be allowed to enroll in Bacone College and stay with my cousin in his dormitory, attending the nearby high school until I completed my education there. Then I could stay on at the school, taking college courses.

Bacone College was in Oklahoma, an area I always had wanted to see. I told the recruiter to send me a letter about the possibility, which he did in late August. The letter verified what the recruiter had told me: The GI bill provided that I could go to Bacone, receiving free room and board while finishing my high school education at Bacone High School in the town of Muskogee. I would be able to start in the ninth grade, skipping seventh and eighth despite my limited formal education. Then I would become a freshman at Bacone.

This all sounded reasonable to me, and the nurses I was dating encouraged me to take advantage of the opportunity. But I was having fun with the girls, and I liked working for the court system. I was not thinking about the future. I was enjoying some of the most pleasant days of my life; I did not realize that I was also disappointing the girls who believed in my potential.

September came and went. Then October and the time of the Navajo fair. One of the nurses had a car, so several of us drove to Shiprock to enjoy the events, returning to Fort Defiance four days later. Yet always the young women stressed that I should be in school in Oklahoma, getting an education.

What I did not know was that the nurses had decided that I was going to make something of myself whether I wanted to or not. They drove me to Window Rock and took me to the regional BIA office. I didn't know why, and I was scared. The office was filled with white people, and while white people are not afraid of white people, we Navajo had long ago learned that it was easy to lose battles with the BIA.

Suddenly the nurses were going into and out of offices, shouting things, making demands. "What are you doing?" I asked them, bewildered by their actions.

"We're getting your paycheck," they told me. They had decided among themselves that I was returning to classes whether I felt ready or not. They put in my resignation and got my pay. While some of us were at the office, others had gone to my room back in Fort Defiance to pack my belongings. They used a large suitcase they had purchased for me at the trading post.

We returned to the employees' quarters in Fort Defiance around one o'clock in the afternoon. I was shocked, not knowing what was going on. But the four nurses involved in this plot just told me that I was going back to school.

They then loaded my belongings into the car and told me they were driving me to the bus station at Gallup, New Mexico. They had purchased a one-way ticket to Muskogee, Oklahoma, so I could go to Bacone College.

"Wait a minute!" I said. "I want to go to Teec Nos Pos! I want to see my family!"

They would hear none of it, and I started to rebel. The day before, I had been at work. The day before that, we had all been at the fair, having fun. And now they were trying to make me go to school.

But there was no arguing with them. We all knew that going to school was the right thing to do, and as mad as I was, I couldn't really fight them. We got into the car, drove to Gallup, and I was on the bus that evening. I could have gotten off the bus, but I had too much respect for the nursing students and what they were doing. I also knew that I was committed to Bacone, that a bed was waiting for me, and the school was eager to have me come.

I arrived in Muskogee the next day. My cousin was waiting for me, and I settled down in his room, enrolling in high school the next day. The nurses all wrote me letters apologizing for what they had done, stressing how much they believed in me, and telling me to stay in school.

The training I received was for the General Equivalency Diploma (GED) test, so I did not have to attend regular classes. In May I felt that I knew enough to take the exam, and I passed it on the first try. Now I could go on to Bacone.

That summer I worked on the railroad in Nebraska. I did not go home, nor did I visit the various western cities where I had lived. I just worked with my cousin, then enrolled in Bacone that fall.

Bacone was a two-year college providing either a liberal arts background for those going on to a four-year college or complete training in specialty areas. I took general courses that first year, then spent the following summer working in a uranium mine.

There were several Navajo working the mines, though I was the only one with an easy job. I maintained the compressors and other equipment because I had knowledge of electrical systems and could speak English.

Uranium was mined with extensive hand labor during those years. No one fully understood the danger of radiation exposure or the need for protective clothing, but even if the danger had been known, the need for the ore was so great that mining it would probably still have been considered more important than safety.

The mining began with the placement of dynamite in the area to be worked. Then, after the controlled explosion, the Navajo would enter the mine with picks. They would clear the dirt, rocks, and other debris from the blast area to uncover the ore, then chip at the ore until it was broken up into chunks small enough to handle. Finally they would use their hands to chuck the ore into wheelbarrows and bring it to the surface. It was hot, exhausting, dangerous work, and the men felt that they were overworked and underpaid.

One day the other Navajo asked me to file a complaint for them. They wanted me to speak on their behalf concerning the poor working conditions.

I talked with the foreman about the problems, and we negotiated for a couple of weeks. The foreman kept insisting that the schedule the men had to keep, loading two or three large wheelbarrows and bringing them to the surface every hour, was reasonable. I didn't know who was right, but I figured that the best way was for us to try it ourselves. I asked the foreman to go down into the mines with me to do the same work and see what we could handle.

The foreman agreed to see what would happen. He and I began working as fast as we could, setting a pace that we knew we could not sustain for more than an hour. Yet even at that pace, it was obvious that the requirements were extreme.

Still, the foreman did not want to acknowledge the problem. He was under pressure to get the ore to the smelter and didn't want to challenge the schedule set by his boss. "Look, this is ridiculous," he said. "We shouldn't be doing this. Let the Indians do this kind of work."

I told him that if we couldn't handle it, we had no right to ask anyone else to do it. But he disagreed. He said that he had to keep the trucks loaded and moving on schedule.

I kept arguing, pointing out that both of us were healthy and strong, the type of men who would be hired to do such labor, yet even we could not meet the goals that were demanded. It was not right to make the others do it.

The Navajo miners decided to go on strike. They asked me to go with them to the mine's headquarters in Durango, Colorado, forty-five miles away. They wanted to explain the problem to the general superintendent.

I had to tell the foreman that I could not work that day because I was going to help my people by acting as interpreter. I reminded him that the miners were right, that he and I had not been able to maintain the pace expected by the company.

The foreman warned me that all of us might be fired for such an action, but I did not care. We went to the smelter in Durango, but the superintendent was out.

The foreman at the smelter told the miners that he was going to draw a line on the ground. All the men who crossed the line would get that day off with pay to do anything they wanted, then would be expected to return to work the next day. Those who failed to cross the line would be fired, and word would go out to ban them from working for any mining company on the reservation.

The miners got scared when the foreman reminded them that they had families to feed, and that the company, Vanadium Corporation of America, had operations not only throughout Colorado, but in all areas of the reservation. The pay was good, advancement was possible, and the benefits were excellent. Their families would suffer without the money they were earning.

As I watched, all the miners crossed the line, agreeing to return to work the next day. Then the foreman turned to me and asked what I was going to do.

I was frustrated. I told him that I enjoyed my job and had no interest in taking time off from work. I had come to Durango only because I thought the miners had a legitimate complaint and needed me to interpret for them.

The dilemma for me was that the men did have a legitimate complaint. But the foreman put the fear of God into them, causing them to back down. I had to live with my conscience. I hadn't started the strike. It was not my idea. However, the mine owners were still wrong, and I could not go back to work, so I quit the job. I would learn later in life that people would ask you to put your reputation or your life out in front for them, and that when you did, you might discover that they would not be there with you.

Fortunately it took me only a few days to find construction work in Shiprock, and I worked for the railroad another summer. But the mine incident was the first time in my life that I had to stand alone, to hold on to a principle no matter what happened to me.

I don't know if I recognized the change in myself back then. Somehow I doubt it. It was one of those turning points in life that we usually recognize only in hindsight. I was discovering resources within myself that I never knew existed. To this day I don't believe that I have backed away from anything, no matter what I may have been threatened with.

Other changes were taking place during that period, though they were not as profound. Bacone College was a Southern Baptist college, something I had not known when I enrolled. The students were Indian, but they did not practice traditional religions. Everyone there either was a Christian or was taught to be one. In addition to academic courses, we had to study the history of the Hebrews and become familiar with the Bible, from Genesis through Revelation. We studied the life of Christ and the Gospels. We had to attend daily chapel, and each student was expected to preach at least one sermon before graduation.

The idea of becoming a Baptist was not an unpleasant one for me. The tribal religion had been challenged by my recent experiences outside the Navajo Nation, and I knew that certain doctrines were erroneous. I realized that much of what I had once accepted as history was likely to be myth.

Christianity did not contradict the beliefs I still held. It assumed the existence of a single Creator, and of a First Man and First Woman. Some stories in the Bible were similar to those I had learned growing up. Even the philosophy of the medicine man was not incompatible with the philosophies in the Bible. And I felt that the way the Navajo were taught to relate to one another, the animals, and all of God's creation was compatible with what Jesus wanted for mankind.

Ultimately my life was enriched by understanding both faiths. I embraced monotheism, yet could look upon the spirit concept of the Navajo religion as not all that different from the Christian stories of demons and angels. The morality taught by my family was no different from the lessons of Jesus. And while those who cling exclusively to one religion or the other might criticize me for feeling comfortable with aspects of both, the truth is that none of us will know what is truly right until we die. So long as I could do right by all of God's creation— human beings, the land, and the animals—I felt I was following a moral and spiritual path in harmony with both the Baptist faith and the religion of my family.

These thoughts were reinforced by the other students, the majority of whom were Baptists before they came to the school. They had made a conscious choice to study at Bacone, knowing it was a Baptist school. My involvement occurred by chance, but it did change my life.

For example, I began dating a Comanche, something I would not have done before. She was a Baptist and an Indian. Since I was no longer following the strict Navajo religion, I did not feel the need to marry a Navajo. So long as the woman was an Indian, I was comfortable. As a result, by the end of my two years at Bacone, I believed in the Baptist faith, had been baptized, and had preached my sermon. I married my girlfriend, Ruby Wallace, after my graduation from Bacone Junior College.

Ruby, my first wife, was from the small town of Faxon, Oklahoma. She was a Comanche whose family had adopted the Baptist faith. It was for that reason that the children went both to Christian schools and to regular public schools when we moved about the country.

The only time I rebelled was somewhere around the start of my second year at Bacone. The president of the college, a man named Frank Thompson, asked me if I would go to Independence, Kansas, on behalf of the school. He wanted me to speak at the annual Southern Baptist Convention, since the school was getting substantial support from them. In order for them to continue supporting the college, they needed a student from Bacone to speak at the week-long convention.

During this period I was also studying Indian history. Bacone was more objective than the BIA. We learned about the contributions Indians made in agriculture, medicine, and other fields, something that gave me pride. I was thinking about all this as I wrote my speech. Finally I came up with an opening. I don't remember it exactly, but it was similar to the following:

"A long time ago, we Native Americans lived on this continent with everything provided for us—the Mother Earth, the Father Sky—and everything put on earth for our use—the food, the berries, the fruits, and even the animals, like the buffalo. Then along came the white men. They didn't have anything, so we helped them by teaching them about turkeys, farming, making clothes, and surviving in what, to them, was a strange land.

"Then, in return, the whites gave us tuberculosis. They even brought syphilis and other venereal diseases to our people.

"We had no prisons. They gave us prisons.

"We had no taxes. They gave us taxes.

"We had no gunpowder. They brought us gunpowder. They brought us wars to protect our land, our water, our wives, and everything we had.

"The white men came. Now we're out here, no longer a happy people. We're out here like hungry wolves on the prairie."

That was the general tone of the speech I prepared, never thinking about the reaction. I was just saying what I felt at that time—what I believed. It was the first time I had put my anger and frustration into words, though obviously it was not what was expected.

The president of the college, Frank Thompson, was shocked. He said, "Pete, how in the world can you say this? What's gotten into you? What's happened to you?"

I said, "That's how I feel. I prayed about it, and I feel that we were done in. The Indians were done in. We had all these good things, and you guys brought us this stuff in the name of civilization. We had no prisons. We had no orphanages. You guys brought it all up, and now we have to deal with it. That's what I want to say."

He said, "This is the Southern Baptist Convention. You can't say this. We're going to lose our funding for the college."

The president explained that he wanted me to say we were grateful for what the Southern Baptist Convention was doing to help the college, to help the Indians. I agreed to try.

I went back to my room, trying to think of what to say. Frank Thompson had said that he was certain the whites must have made a lot of good contributions. He said that I had just focused on the bad, the gunpowder and the syphilis. The whites must have made better contributions that that. If I wanted to leave my speech the way it was, he wanted me to add some good contributions as well.

I confided my problem to my new roommate. He was not my cousin, so I figured his perspective would be different from mine. I asked him to think about good contributions the whites had made to the Indians.

The trouble was that everything we tried did not work. We thought of education and religion, but the way they were introduced just wasn't right. Finally, three days later, I went back to President

Thompson and told him that I could not find anything good that white people had contributed to the American Indians. There was nothing that had made us a better people.

President Thompson looked at me and said, "Pete, you can't be serious. How about religion? You're here at Bacone College. Hasn't this enriched your life, the study of the Bible and all? Speaking English? Reading and writing English? Hasn't this improved your life as an Indian?"

I said, "If you really want me to stretch this, I can say yes to that. But what I want to say is that if you guys had left us alone, we'd have been all right. We'd have been better off if you hadn't brought all that stuff with you into our civilization. But now that you have brought us all this stuff, we need the education. We need the prayers. We need to be able to speak to everybody. But it's only because you guys have done us in."

"Well," he said, "say that."

So I went back and added it: "Now that we're on the prairie like lonely, hungry wolves, we need education. We need to speak and write like you. We need the religious education that you provide for us at Bacone."

We went to Independence, Kansas, and I delivered the speech. I did go along with President Thompson a little, toning it down and omitting the comments about syphilis and a few other things that would have upset the Southern Baptists.

I have to give President Thompson credit for letting me say what I wanted. But I'll never forget how nervous he was.

For me, that was the first time I had ever spoken out against what I believed was a terrible injustice perpetrated against the American Indian. It was also the first time I recognized the anger festering just below the surface of my emotions. I began studying Indian history in a way I had never done before. I studied the Wounded Knee massacre, the Trail of Tears, the forced removal of the various Indian tribes from their land. I realized that all Indians had suffered during the last couple of centuries. The history of the Navajo was unique, but that did not mean that other histories were without pain, without suffering. All Indians had endured a nightmare of change as a result of the white men's westward migration.

Then I began studying Anglo history to try to understand what had caused the whites to oppress my people. For years I had been taught that Indians were superstitious, uncivilized savages and that the Anglos were better. If that was so, I wanted to understand their past experiences.

A very different picture of the white race emerged as I began reading Anglo history books. I learned about the belief in witchcraft and the burning of witches in Salem, Massachusetts. I read about the tests that were performed, such as tying a woman to a chair and putting her underwater to see if she lived or died, since they believed a witch would survive and a normal person would not. I read of burning women with hot irons to see how fast they healed, another test for witches.

We had the equivalent of witches in our beliefs, of course. We had people such as the Skin Walkers, whom we feared. But we did not torture and murder a suspected Skin Walker in the name of God, as the whites had done. Yet they called us superstitious.

Then I read about Anglo superstitions: fear of walking under a ladder and of a black cat crossing one's path. White people would throw spilled salt over their shoulders so it would go into the devil's eyes. They would knock on wood to avoid bad luck. There were many superstitions, none of which had ever been mentioned when we were being criticized.

The more I learned, the more I came to believe that whites were goofier than we were. No matter what they accused us of, their history was worse. It was filled with violence, revolution, civil war, torture, mistrust, superstition, and inhumanity. Certainly I was angry, but I also developed an even greater concern about preserving the Indian heritage in general and the Navajo way in particular. In addition, I felt that I would one day need to correct both the misunderstood history and some of the wrongs that had been done to the Indians.

Another experience, during my sophomore year at Bacone College, caused me to reevaluate my thinking about society. I was asked to take an intelligence test during a period when I was earning top grades. I was on the dean's list and would eventually graduate with highest honors, and yet the test showed that I was a moron. My IQ was supposedly so low that I was barely trainable for a repetitive job that would require no thinking and change little from day to day.

The test was administered before the current practice of considering cultural differences in the evaluation of students in an academic setting. For example, the test might include a question about the subway. If I'd lived in New York City or had access to radio and television, I would have known what a subway was. But I had been raised on the reservation, isolated from the experiences of the white men and women who created the tests, and I did not have their knowledge. The same would have been true in reverse had Indians created the intelligence test. A brilliant white man who had not lived on the reservation would have been unable to answer questions about tending sheep, planting crops, making moccasins, and other routine activities among the Navajo, and would have scored as though he were feeble-minded.

Yet such reasoning had not been developed in the early 1950s. There was still the biased attitude that assumed that anyone who did not possess what the test-giver considered "basic knowledge" was of limited intelligence.

Despite being a "moron," I earned grades high enough to enroll in the University of Oklahoma. I had been a sociology major at Bacone but decided to go into engineering when I entered the university. I had been told that engineering was the university's hardest course of study. Still hurting from the results of the intelligence test, I wanted to try the most difficult field available to me.

My adviser, J. Bruce Wiley, asked me what type of engineering I wanted for my major: mechanical, electrical, petroleum, or one of the other types.

I asked which was the toughest field, and he said that, while they were all considered difficult, electrical engineering was generally felt to be the hardest. The problem was that all the courses I had taken at Bacone were unrelated to what I needed to study. That meant that I would have to spend at least five years in school, specializing in engineering.

I didn't care what it took to succeed in the field. I insisted that I would take electrical engineering, explaining to him my feelings about the results of the intelligence test. I told him that I did not believe I was a moron and I couldn't spend five more years in school. I wanted to enter engineering school immediately.

However, I lacked the mathematical training I needed, the courses in solid geometry, trigonometry, and differential and integral calculus, all of which were requirements for entering the engineering school. To complicate matters, I was informed I would have to take solid geometry before I could take trigonometry, and differential calculus before I could study integral calculus, training that would take four semesters at least.

I stubbornly insisted that I would take all four at once. By doing so, I would have only one semester of hard work before entering engineering school. I would also be quite likely to fail them all.

Mr. Wiley said that the university did not permit such an action. However, I insisted that it was my money and my time. I wanted to try. If I failed, that would be my problem, not anyone else's. And if I passed, I would be in engineering school after only one semester.

The school made an exception for me, much to my regret. By the middle of the semester, I was flunking two of the courses, barely holding a D in the third, and earning a C in the fourth.

I went back to Mr. Wiley for help. I admitted that I was having trouble. However, instead of encouraging me to stop, he began tutoring me each evening. He also showed me how to study more effectively so that I could learn the basics of math without spending too much time on any one course.

Gradually I came to understand mathematics. I had been raised in a world where reason reigned. There was order to life, but the wisdom of the Navajo came from complex reasoning. When I recognized that mathematics was pure order, that there were certain laws under which it operated, I had no problem. I learned those laws, then applied them to the four courses. By the time the semester was over, I was exhausted, but my grades ranged from C-minus to C-plus. I had passed everything and was eligible to enroll in electrical engineering.

Bruce Wiley was a professor in the electrical engineering school. He taught one of my first classes and continued to tutor me. At the same time, my first child, a daughter, Linda, was born. My wife was working, and I had to work part-time at such jobs as cleaning Mr. Wiley's windows, to pay for the tutoring.

For the first two years I was in the university, I was on the GI Bill. During that time I worked eight hours a night at the state mental hospital in Norman, Oklahoma. I worked from 11:00 o'clock at night to 6 A.M., studying when the patients weren't noisy or causing trouble. When I got home at 6:00, I would sleep some and then attend classes between 8:00 and 10:00 A.M. At 4:00 P.M., I would take my wife to work and take care of our kids (we also had our son Rocky by then) until 10:30 at night. I'd take the kids to her, and she'd drop me off at work, then go home with the kids.

One other thing I learned there, working among the mentally handicapped people, was that, much to my surprise, the people were not crazy. Of course there were very violent patients who needed to be controlled, but there were also people like you or me. The violent ones were obvious, but the rest looked normal. There was no way to tell if they were mentally ill or well. Appearances meant nothing.

More than half the patients, I learned, had high school and college degrees and spoke intelligently. Yet something was wrong with them mentally. At times, when I was walking around in downtown Norman, I didn't know which of the people I saw belonged in that hospital.

When I ran out of the GI Bill money, neither the tribe nor the BIA would give me a scholarship. In fact, the BIA tried to discourage me from continuing with my studies, preferring that I attend trade school to be a carpenter. Otherwise, they said, they would just give me a five-hundred-dollar loan. Thus, for one full year I worked on that schedule so I would have enough money while maintaining my grades in electrical engineering school. After two years, I had to stop my studies. I moved with my family to the reservation in Gallup, New Mexico. There I was able to get a job with El Paso Natural Gas, which was running a pipeline through the reservation.

I spent two years in New Mexico, where our second child, Peter, Jr., nicknamed Rocky, was born. I was handling the receiving of materials and their distribution to the various points along the pipeline construction from El Paso, Texas, through New Mexico and into California.

By 1955 I was able to combine my savings with a scholarship from the University of Oklahoma in order to complete my studies. Ironically, the scholarship was based on my having passed the four math courses in a single semester. No one had done that before, and the university felt that with such an academic achievement, I deserved a chance to finish my studies.

I suppose the transition from a child who constantly ran away from school to a scholarship student in a field of study must seem strange. However, looking back, I think it happened for several reasons.

First, the Navajo traditions fit nicely with the world of education. We were always taught to be observers of our surroundings. We learned to try to understand, to adapt, and to place what we saw into the belief system we held. Our beliefs may have been scientifically inaccurate at times, yet our approach to observation and categorization was very similar to aspects of the scientific method.

I had never been opposed to learning and had always enjoyed mastering new physical and intellectual skills. My hatred for school came from the way I was treated. I rebelled against the racism and bigotry I encountered. I could not learn in such an environment. Formal education always seemed to be related to being attacked for my race, my heritage, my very existence. Yet I had enjoyed learning during my apprenticeship to my grandfather, while studying to be a code talker, and during the time I spent talking with the professor I met in China. I think that by the time I arrived at Bacone, I understood that the attitude of my teachers had nothing to do with the meaning and value of education. I hungered for learning, and when I got mad at the results of the intelligence test, I decided to rebel by being the best I could.

I was also becoming fascinated by science and math. College was the only way I could further explore these subjects, and I eagerly looked forward to continuing my education.

I received my degree in electrical engineering in 1957. During the early part of that year, graduates were being recruited by major companies. Engineers were in great demand, so I was wooed by several different outfits.

McDonnell Aircraft in Saint Louis flew me to their plant so I could look at their facilities. They showed me where I would work, the type of equipment I would have, and the various residential areas within the price range I would be able to afford.

Douglas Aircraft in Long Beach, California, showed me their operation. North American Aviation took me to their plant in Canoga Park, north of Los Angeles. They explained that I would be a research assistant if I went to work for them. They showed me the projects on which I would be working and introduced me to the people who would be my coworkers.

Lockheed gave me the same type of trip, as did others. The only one that did not show great enthusiasm was Hughes Aircraft, though they, too, went through the motions.

I asked Bruce Wiley what I should do. The companies had begun bidding against one another, one offering three dollars an hour more than the other in an effort to get me. The money was intriguing, and most of us who were graduating were thinking about taking the highest offer.

Bruce Wiley told me not to go for the money. Instead, he said I should go where I would have the best opportunity to rise through the ranks based on my ability. He wanted me to look at the company policy for promotion. Some companies would put me in one department, pay me well, and forget about me. Other companies tended to promote only those workers with a certain type of background, education, and upbringing. And still other companies were designed to reward excellence. Anyone who could handle the challenge in almost any department would have a chance to rise through the ranks to the top. That type of business was the one where I would do best, even if the starting salary was lower.

Hughes Aircraft suddenly seemed the best. Douglas Aviation was family owned at the time, and promotion was due to political chance, not performance. Although Hughes offered me less money, advancement to the top would be based only on my abilities.

I accepted the offer from Hughes, moving my family to Inglewood, California, immediately after graduation. My job was in the manufacturing division of Hughes in El Segundo. I earned a good salary and held the title of junior engineer.

I had been on the job only a month or so when my boss, the senior engineer, went on vacation. I was involved with the testing of new firing control units for the F-106 aircraft that had been created by the research and development (R&D) division of Hughes. The units were being manufactured under contract for the U.S. Air Force, and a certain number of them had to be delivered every month or the company would be penalized.

Every firing control unit had to be tested, and I was finding that most of the units could not pass the test. This was a serious problem because the firing control unit was an electronic servo-control mechanism designed to move the wing-mounted guns so they could constantly follow the target. I was responsible for a simple electronic power supply that provided DC current to the various parts. If that malfunctioned, nothing else would work.

The problem I discovered was visible only under an electronic microscope. When the unit was turned on, electricity sent to the various components created a power surge, or spike. If that surge was too great, as it was during the testing, some of the components would be destroyed.

I had built power supplies in school, so I went back to my textbooks to read up on what to do. I realized that it would be necessary to design a filter that would prevent the strong spiking that was taking place.

The creation of the filters was almost an art. Each had to be uniquely designed for the use for which it was intended, and it had to exactly suit every aspect of the unit. I treated the problem like a lab assignment, designing a new power supply that matched the Air Force specifications. When I completed the unit and found that it tested perfectly, I compared it with the ones I had been rejecting. The only difference was in a single resistor. One incorrect part had been preventing the unit from working. Even worse, that wrong part had been written into the construction of the power supply specifications by the R&D department of Hughes Aircraft.

Now I had a real problem. The R&D engineers were the elite in the company. They were the ones with extensive training, Ph.D.'s, and very high salaries. We were in the manufacturing area, producing a supposedly proven product. A junior engineer was not supposed to challenge the men at the top.

Once I discovered the faulty component, I had the technicians replace it with the correct resistor. However, I could not officially make a change for all units without running that change past the R&D men in Hughes's Culver City operation.

I explained what was happening to the supervisor in charge during my immediate boss's absence, showing him the mistake with the resistor. To my surprise, he told me I must be wrong. The control units had been going through tests for several months. They had been installed in the aircraft well before I came along. Before that, the R&D engineers had spent a year developing the equipment. These were not prototypes. There was no way the problem could exist.

My explanation made no sense to my boss, though I knew my test results were accurate. He told me to find out why the units had been passing tests and now were failing them.

Someone, eight months earlier, had realized that too many of the control units were being rejected. That person had modified the testers by adding an extra component that would cause all the controls to register as good. But that extra component had burned out in one of the testers, making it again record accurately. That was why it began rejecting the control units. The other tester, which I had not been using, still had the functioning extra component that passed the units. Instead of redesigning the equipment that was going into the airplanes, someone had redesigned the test equipment to make bad units look good.

My supervisor was shocked. He went over my calculations, concluded I was right, and together we went to see the R&D people. My supervisor was not pleased, though. He was embarrassed that the problem had not been caught previously, and he was reluctant to tell the senior engineers.

When we arrived in Culver City, he literally pushed me through the door to explain what had happened. I had been there six weeks, a young Indian guy with no engineering work history. The R&D engineers looked at me, then asked my boss who I was and why I was there. When they realized what I was saying and heard that I had stopped the line for two weeks, they did not want to believe me.

Reluctantly the R&D men spent the next five hours with me, going over their calculations until they realized that I was right. At that moment, panic hit. The units had already been installed in several airplanes, and the company was going to have to admit its mistake to the Air Force. Either the units would have to be recalled or a team would have to go to the planes and replace the improper component.

My second day in Culver City, a man came in dressed casually in a suede jacket. The R&D men were quite deferential, telling him what had happened. He looked at me and said, "Well, keep up the good work, Chief." That turned out to be my one and only meeting with Howard Hughes, the legendary founder of the company. However, three weeks later, when my boss came back from vacation, I was promoted to senior engineer, and the former senior engineer was transferred to a different department.

The manufacturing division had its own hierarchy, and apparently its managers were impressed with what had happened. I was brought into the head office and asked to take a two-week vacation.

I had only been on the job two and a half months, so the request surprised me. But then my superior explained that he wanted me to go out and recruit some more Navajo engineers.

"I don't know if I'll find any others," I said.

That was okay with him. The two weeks' vacation was a bonus for correcting the problem. But the department also felt that since a

Navajo engineer had accomplished what their people had not, the sensible thing was to hire some more Navajos. I was to go to the University of Oklahoma and the University of New Mexico, then to my family home in Teec Nos Pos for a real vacation.

It turned out that I was a better engineer than a recruiter. There were no Native American seniors in engineering at the University of Oklahoma, and the few who were in such programs were underclassmen who had yet to prove themselves. I had no better luck in New Mexico, so I looked up former non-Indian classmates who had good records in school and were working for a corporation in the area. Their jobs paid a little better than the ones at Hughes, and the work was easier, so they were content where they were. They had done what I had been warned against, going for the money instead of the ultimate opportunities within the company, and there was no dissuading them.

When I returned after two weeks, my total expenses were approximately $150. I turned them in, then got a chewing out by my boss.

"Mr. MacDonald," he said to me. "When you go recruiting, you're supposed to entertain. You're supposed to take people to nice restaurants, buy tickets for shows and sporting events, spend money on potential employees. . . ."

I thought I was being a good company man. I had taken the men to cheap restaurants and coffee shops. My expenses were for a Coca-Cola for one man, a sandwich and coffee for another. I had kept everything as inexpensive as possible so as not to waste the company's money.

My boss explained that I had to take the people to the best restaurants, to show them a good time. They had to be impressed with Hughes, with its willingness to spend money on them.

"That's how you recruit," he said. "Our competitors are doing these things, and they're stealing engineers away from us, people we should be getting from the universities. We've got to spend money to get these guys to our company, and you didn't do that."

In this way, my boss taught me to make business deals through entertainment, through taking people golfing. Fortunately I had not lost any brilliant young engineers who might otherwise have been interested in Hughes. There was no one available when I went to the two universities. But I realized that, had there been, I might not have been successful in persuading them to come to Hughes. I had to learn the white man's way of business negotiation in order to be able to compete.

Suddenly I was a senior engineer with the mystique of someone with special magic for finding problems in electronics. Everyone seemed to presume that my success was a result of being a Navajo. They thought my people had powers and abilities well beyond those of other mortals.

Next came another problem. This had to do with a malfunctioning computer line in a different department. Their engineers had been working on the trouble for a week with no success when they remembered me. Someone from the department asked me to come over and see if I could help.

When I got there, I found a nightmare. The units they were manufacturing had thousands of wires inside. These were early computers, much larger and more complex in construction than today's models. The problem was that somewhere among the wires something was causing the machine to make an electrical noise, which was unacceptable.

The first question I asked was the objective of the project. They said that it was to make the computer noise free. To do that, they had to start with spotlessly clean wires, which were then carefully shielded in a fine material. But something was wrong, and somehow this noise was being created. They were randomly testing the wires to no avail, a process that had lasted a full week. It was Friday morning when I went there, and the problem had to be solved by Monday, when the computers were to be shipped.

This time the unit that was being tested was fine, but something was wrong with the tester. I again started at the beginning, inspecting everything wire by wire.

I worked Friday morning, all that night and the next day until exhaustion forced me to rest for a couple of hours. I continued in that manner around the clock until, on Sunday, I found that one of the welded wires had come loose. Once that minor problem was corrected with new shielding, the computer functioned properly and no longer made noise.

Again my reputation was enhanced when, on Monday morning, the product passed the test. Two or three weeks later, I was promoted to project engineer in charge of power supplies, the computers, and several new projects that were being prepared for the Defense Department.

To the top people, I was now someone special. Their engineers, all with many years of experience, had been unable to resolve a problem that I had found relatively quickly. What they did not realize was that they had far more knowledge and skill than I did. They knew some of the possible places to look when a problem arose, information I frequently lacked. But this meant that they were making random checks on highly complicated equipment. Frequently they were lucky and solved the problem in a few minutes or a few hours. At other times their approach did not work and they had to keep looking, a situation in which random tests are fruitless.

I was not approaching the breakdowns with vast information. I only felt comfortable starting from the beginning. I went step by step as though building a new unit, a time-consuming process, yet one that prevented an engineer from overlooking anything that might have been causing the malfunction. As a result, I found the problem that had eluded them.

The other engineers assumed I approached the problem in the same manner as they had, but that I had some special knowledge that enabled me to find the problem almost instantly. It was simply the careful, methodical effort of a beginning engineer that made me successful.

The Polaris missile program started a few months after I arrived at Hughes. It was considered the most important defense weapon of the time. Military power was changing. We were in the midst of the Cold War. The Soviets had had nuclear weapons for several years. They had been the first to launch a satellite into space, the forerunner of weapons that could be fired from great distances. The prevention of war was believed to be rooted in a campaign of terror in which both sides needed the most accurate, sophisticated, and unstoppable weapons possible so that neither side would dare to fire a shot.

The Polaris missiles would be placed in submarines, the one seemingly invulnerable offensive and defensive vehicle. It was difficult to track a submarine underwater, even more difficult to destroy it. Having a vessel that could cruise unseen and unheard, for twenty-four hours a day, traveling anywhere in the world, was unnerving enough for the superpowers. But having that same vessel armed with a highly accurate long-range missile—the Polaris—could theoretically prevent our enemies from daring to launch a first strike against us.

Our job was to design and build the guidance system so accurately that a missile could be launched from deep under the ocean, break the surface, fly through the sky, and ultimately land in a pickle barrel a thousand miles away. Our enemies would fear such an accurate weapon, but if it ever had to be used, only carefully selected targets would be destroyed in the escalating violence of the early stages of war.

The Polaris missile had approximately ten thousand components to be manufactured by several different companies. Our job was to prepare a proposal that brought together all the manufacturers involved with the construction of the missile in addition to the guidance system, which was our special design contribution. I had several engineers working under me at that time, and we felt that our presentation for the guidance portion would be successful. We were right. Following the standard procedure of the time, designating more than one manufacturer, the contract went jointly to Hughes and General Electric.

The importance of the guidance system cannot be overemphasized. It was critical for accuracy, and even the name of the missile was based on an aiming device that used measurements taken in relation to the North Star—Polaris.

My first job was to develop accurate testing equipment for the items we were manufacturing. This was the most complex engineering job the United States had ever tackled, and I had demonstrated what was believed to be top expertise in testing procedures.

The tests were unusually critical because of what the missile was expected to do. It was presumed that the submarine firing the Polaris would be in the midst of strong ocean currents, which would cause the vessel to roll when the missile was released. That missile would have to survive the rolling launch, pass through the water, break through the surface into the air, determine its proper course, then travel without failure in any type of weather and wind. Corrections would have to be made for different pressures, buffeting, and other far from ideal circumstances that had never been considered before. Thus the tests had to be very stringent. There was no margin for error.

During this period, I was also attending graduate school at UCLA, studying servomechanisms, the devices used for tracking targets. This was a new field and I needed to know the types of problems that could arise and how to correct them.

I soon learned that the limitations of all servomechanisms, critical for launching missiles, space travel, and similar uses, originated in the measuring devices. The greater the distance something had to travel, the more accurate the launch had to be. Even more difficult was the fact that the testing mechanisms always had to be ten times more accurate than the requirement. Thus if a device had to be accurate to within one degree, the test mechanism had to be accurate to within one-tenth of a degree. The existing test equipment was far less accurate than the demands we had to put on it, meaning that I was constantly concerned with the creation of new testing devices.

Even before my assignment to the Polaris project, I had begun looking ahead to such problems. There had been new developments in the use of light and mirrors for testing, a far more accurate system than analog and digital testing, both of which were routine. I had enrolled at UCLA not only to keep current but also to learn how to resolve future problems. This information suddenly became critical when I was made responsibile for testing the new missile guidance system for the Navy.

The requirements proved to be extremely complex. Movement is measured in degrees. Each degree is broken down into segments called minutes, and each minute is divided into segments called seconds. The Navy needed us to be able to accurately measure one second of movement for the Polaris, a segment so small that it had never before been measured accurately. This would be analogous to standing on the top of the Empire State Building and looking all the way down to the sidewalk where a dime had been balanced on its outer edge. One second of arc movement would be like trying to measure how far your eyeball moved as you scanned the extremely tiny distance across the edge of the dime from your vantage point hundreds of feet above. It was movement so slight that it was imperceptible to the human eye, and yet we had to measure it accurately.

My suggestion was to use extremely pure optics—glass that was almost flawless even when viewed under a microsope—and high-intensity light. The Germans had developed such a glass, which we could use with a special testing laboratory built on a floating pad to counteract the earth's movement. Some aspects of these devices had been developed internationally, but they were not widely known and they had not been combined in the ways I suggested.

Once again I was promoted, this time to the Hughes technical staff. This was an elite team of engineers and scientists who worked on future projects, such as trips to the moon and to other planets, often long before the public was aware of them.

All this success was important to me. I was making more and more money, of course. My family now wanted for nothing despite living in a world where material possessions had far greater importance than on the reservation. But I was also proving that I was not a moron, not inferior to white men. I was born into a family in which, if the whites had not entered our world, I would be herding sheep and farming. My hogan would not be a house with running water, plumbing, electricity, and all manner of appliances. I would be without newspapers, magazines, television, and radio.

During this period, I knew that my advancements at work were due to my own talent and skills. There was no Equal Employment Opportunity for Indians or Navajo Preference law to help me. I was promoted not because of my status as a member of a minority group but because of my abilities as compared with those of the other employees.

My teachers at the BIA schools, who were supposed to prepare us for the world at large, could not have imagined a Navajo making such a leap into the future. I was not just a part of the white culture; I was in the technological forefront of mainstream society in the second half of the twentieth century. The work I was doing would affect the world in the decades to come. This was not the clerk-typist's job I had once envisioned for myself. I had no need for a part-time job driving a dump truck. Instead of hauling materials, I was designing equipment that would require some of the energy resources I had once mined.

I was proud and happy, but I was also troubled. I was a stranger in paradise, making money, gaining respect, but never a part of any world. Many of the management personnel at Hughes still thought my "special" abilities came from my being Navajo. They could not accept that a hardworking young engineer, part innovator, part plodder, like so many others, could be successful even though he wasn't white like them. Moreover, my success separated me from the Navajo with whom I had been raised. Although I had joined a local social club for Navajo living off the reservation, it was still not the same. I was a success in both worlds, and yet I was not truly a part of either one.

My new work made me a jet-setter. The gyro unit for the Polaris was made by Minneapolis Honeywell, and I regularly flew back and forth to Minnesota for conferences. I flew to Massachusetts to work with General Electric, and to Rochester, New York, to work with Bausch & Lomb, all of which were producing parts for the project I was coordinating.

I also developed new ways to cut the cost of manufacturing and shipping the products, for which I won an award from Hughes. I was dealing with budgets, manpower forecasts, future projects, and income. I stopped doing design work and instead became the manager of hundreds of technicians. I had to oversee other engineers. I had to negotiate the best price with vendors, sometimes traveling with lawyers and buyers.

There was only one step higher on the corporate ladder at Hughes, and that was what we called Mahogany Row—top corporate management. There was no question in my mind that I would soon be one of the men running the company. I had moved up rapidly and successfully in only six and a half years, all based on my own merit. I had made no mistakes, cut no corners to get ahead. Because of the way the organization was run, my work history ensured my ultimate success.

Perhaps the biggest shock came when I went to New York to meet with the heads of Otis Elevator. I needed their help in designing a system that would move the testing device. The device, though quite sophisticated, was still little more than an elevator, but the contract would be worth many millions of dollars to Otis.

Several executives had been sent to me, and they were determined to impress me. Although they knew my name and position, they knew nothing else about me. We were to meet in the baggage area of the airport, where several people were obviously trying to find travelers whom they did not know. No one gave me more than a passing glance.

I should have realized what was happening. I should have known that the men from Otis were probably looking for a tall, heavy-set Scot or Irishman, who would answer to the name MacDonald. Whatever their stereotypical fantasy, they were not looking for a Navajo Indian in a three-piece suit.

Finally there was no one left but myself and a couple of men still obviously looking for someone. Uncertain, we approached one another and introduced ourselves. The men from Otis were embarrassed that they had not recognized me earlier.

One man took my suitcase, and they escorted me outside to their limousine. The seats were a soft, rich leather, the hides carefully matched so there were no flaws visible anywhere. The wood trim was carefully polished, the paint layered to such a degree that when you glanced at your reflection in the surface, there seemed to be a depth to it, like looking at your image in a glass-smooth mountain lake.

There was a fully stocked bar inside, fine crystal goblets, and an audio system that turned the soundproof passenger compartment into what sounded like a concert hall. One man was busily talking on the car telephone, an uncommon, expensive item in those days. He wanted to be certain that my greeting at the firm was as elaborate as what had been waiting for me when I got off the plane.

As I sat back in my seat, glancing out the window as the chauffeur maneuvered the lengthy vehicle through traffic, I had to smile to myself. The limousine and my purpose for riding in it were not just miles from my childhood home, but a century or more of time from the world in which I had been raised. Instead of carrying water in my mouth to quench my mother's thirst, I could offer her champagne. Instead of being ridiculed for my "stupidity," I was being cultivated by companies whose top executives knew that my ideas could make them millions of dollars. I had "arrived" in ways I never thought were possible, and I loved every minute of the experience.

It was only later, back at home in California, that I became troubled. I loved engineering. I loved business. I had discovered an ability to grasp complex subjects, then use that knowledge in innovative ways. My pleasure came from experiences I doubted my people could begin to comprehend. Yet I was not completely happy.

My mother was living on the reservation in a hogan. She was older and not well, and she was having trouble with the Indian Health Service and with the Bureau of Indian Affairs. Where once the Navajo had helped one another, they now had become so crippled by change that often they had to rely on the white bureaucracy, and it was failing them. There were periodic food shortages, difficulties getting medical help, and even problems obtaining the money and benefits promised by congressional acts.

I helped my mother financially, of course, and she visited me periodically, but she felt her life was back on the reservation, not in a modern city.

I returned to Teec Nos Pos once a year for a few days. Even as an outsider, I tried to do what I could, but increasingly times were difficult.

For the first time since I enrolled in Bacone College, I took stock of my life. Martin Marietta was recruiting me to head their engineering department in Denver. Hughes was obviously going to move me onto Mahogany Row if I stayed with them much longer. But no matter where I went, no matter what I did, my career as a hands-on engineer was over.

Engineering, at the top, became business. You could plan for the future, and you had to understand what was taking place in the laboratory, but your job was getting the best price for parts, being certain the work flow moved smoothly, supervising, overseeing, planning. The hands-on work that had been both a challenge and a delight was mostly in my past. I was becoming a coordinator, a facilitator, and even if I became the best, this was not the work for which I had trained.

In 1963 I learned that Raymond Nakai had been elected Navajo tribal chairman. He was apparently trying to make a change on the reservation. He wanted to see if the decline into poverty and despair could be reversed. To do this, he was seeking Navajo men and women with skills not normally associated with the tribe. One of the people whose name had arisen during this search was mine. A decision was reached in the Window Rock tribal headquarters to telephone me and see if I would be interested in returning to help my people.

I don't think the appeal of returning to the Navajo reservation was the siren's song luring me to my roots, my history and culture. I also don't think that I had reached a point where I felt I had proven my value as an individual in a world from which the Navajo had once been excluded and thus could return to the soil. I can't even say that I was moved by the war cries of the spirits of ancient warriors crying out for the rights of the Diné.

Perhaps I was tired and in need of a vacation before tackling new projects even more complex than the work I had completed for the Polaris missile. Perhaps I thought that I could help organize the Navajo along business lines, then let others maintain whatever organization I started. I never sat down and came to any carefully reasoned conclusion. Instead, I thought that it would be both fun and challenging to take a year's sabbatical from Hughes, return to the reservation, and work for the tribal government. My children would be able to experience a life that was almost as foreign to them, despite their visits, as the world of the big city had been to me when I first saw Denver those many years ago.

Hughes reluctantly let me have a year off. What I found when I returned to help Raymond Nakai was so shocking, so much a continuation of the injustices of the past, that I would not leave again. I had to radically change the course of my life, my hopes and dreams for the future, in order to do whatever was possible to right the injustices that had become a way of life for the Navajo Nation.

Return to the Diné

(1963–1970)

The 1960s were good times for the white man's Arizona. Although slightly more than 82 percent of the land either was owned by the federal government or belonged to the reservations, the remaining property, much of it uninhabitable, was being sold and resold to investors throughout the nation. Land fraud was big business. Worthless lots in the midst of the wilderness, devoid of water, power, and telephone lines, were marketed for vacation and retirement homes.

A crooked developer might spend no more than a million dollars to buy ten thousand acres of such unwanted land. The land would be divided by laying a grid over a map, creating forty thousand quarter-acre plots that lay sometimes on flat terrain, sometimes on mountainsides. It was possible to build homes on much of this land, but owners would have to pay a fortune to truck or fly in materials and laborers. Water would have to be hauled to the sites because there were no pipes, rivers, canals, or wells. Power was nonexistent, and home builders were forced to bring in portable generators, then drive perhaps a hundred miles or more to buy gasoline to run the equipment. Yet despite all these problems, brilliantly worded advertisements sold "paradise" for a thousand dollars a quarter acre, on the average.

The profit on such a venture, by the time all the costs had been met, was usually a minimum of $20 million. And that was for a legitimate, though overpriced, marketing effort. Many companies found that there was more money to be made by not purchasing anything or by failing to transfer land ownership from the developer to the buyer. Then, before anyone got wise, the company would go bankrupt. The buyers, usually paying on time, would lose their money and not have title to the land they thought they were buying. They became creditors of the bankruptcy proceeding, a risk that can happen to anyone making a time purchase with a company. It was easier to view the loss as a devastating financial blow that could happen to anyone than to think the bankruptcy was a scam. The principals of the company would take their share of the money in high salaries and bonuses before bankrupting the business.

Since the land that was for sale was an asset of the company, it would ultimately be sold in the bankruptcy proceedings. The swindlers would frequently buy it back at the court-ordered auction, start a new company with a new name, and repeat the scam.

These land fraud problems, however, were not as serious as other concerns. Only money was involved in fraudulent land sales, whereas the water problems affected life itself. Water was more precious than gold, though everyone tried to ignore that fact. The city of Tucson was built in the heart of the Sonoran Desert. Phoenix was also constructed mostly on desert land. The varieties of cactus—prickly pear, barrel, cholla, saguaro—substituted for the more familiar vegetation of the North and East, vegetation that thrived on the rainwater Arizona lacked.

Most water came from under the ground, though the Salt River and the Colorado River provided rare natural areas of greenery and the potential for recreation. If you remove too much of the groundwater in an area like this, you experience subsidence, the sudden collapse of a section of the earth that creates a giant sinkhole in the ground. Yet even when subsidence, an unpredictable problem in those days, began to occur, most people failed to heed the warnings. Instead, they often continued to misuse the available water.

Areas such as Phoenix were developed with artificial lakes, massive fountains, swimming pools, and imported grass. Conservation of water was not encouraged because it might discourage development. The problem would be handled by future generations.

In Arizona, political parties did not vie for elective offices. As in most other states, there were Republicans and Democrats, conservatives and liberals, but the real power was concentrated in the hands of the descendants of the white founding families—the Goldwaters and the Babbitts, the Funks, Rosenzweigs, Steigers, DeConcinis, and others—whose money had come from lumber, mining, ranching, merchandising, and, oddly, jewelry. Many of the men from these families had attended the same schools and played sports together. They knew but ignored one another's dirty little secrets.

While the old guard still dominated Arizona politics, new arrivals were making a quiet impact behind the scenes. These individuals were drawn in part by the state's frontier mentality. Anyone could carry a handgun in Arizona provided it was visible. Revolvers and automatics were a common sight among both wealthy businessmen and rowdy bikers riding customized Harley-Davidsons, Hondas, and Yamahas. Rifles and shotguns were equally familiar objects, generally affixed on window racks in the cabs of pickup trucks, the vehicle of choice for many Arizonans, regardless of income or profession. Such casualness about weapons attracted men who used them in pursuit of ill-gotten gains.

Tucson became the home of Joseph Bonanno and Peter Licavoli, Sr., both regularly named as active members of organized crime families. "Soldiers" working for such infamous Mafia families as the Gambinos and the Genoveses were spotted throughout Phoenix. Mob figures from New York, Chicago, Las Vegas, Florida, California, and *elsewhere considered the state open territory, ripe for gambling, safe for meetings with rival factions without risk of violence.*

Not every big-name criminal was "connected," though. There were many independent entrepreneurs, one of the most notorious being Ned Warren, who would ultimately be considered the king of the Arizona land fraud racket. Warren's schemes were endorsed, at one point, by Arizona's conservative U.S. senator Barry Goldwater. The endorsement was in the form of a letter included in Warren's land sale promotion package.

The senator's detractors claimed the endorsement was part of a payoff, probably in the form of an indirect or under-the-table contribution to the senator's reelection campaign. Goldwater's supporters, by contrast, claim that Warren was so sophisticated in his methods that he fooled even a member of one of the state's most prominent families.

The Anglos' Arizona undoubtedly had its problems, but the state's appeal minimized its drawbacks. Arizona has thirty-seven hundred hours of sunlight a year, on the average, and while the temperature can soar above 120 degrees in some parts of the state, air-conditioning is everywhere, and humidity is almost nonexistent. In the wintertime, residents of Tucson and Phoenix seldom have to wear more than heavy sweaters, even when midwesterners are fighting seemingly endless snowstorms. As a result, Arizona became one of the fastest-growing states in the country.

The population of Phoenix was less than 65,000 at the start of World War II. During the first wave of westward migration, from 1950 to 1960, the city swelled to 400,000, and ten years later, the population was close to 600,000. Yet despite the phenomenal growth, mirrored in many other parts of the state, the old guard remained firmly entrenched.

The influence of Arizona politicians exceeded the boundaries of the state. In 1964, following the assassination of John F. Kennedy and the ascension to power of Lyndon Johnson, Goldwater persuaded Republican party leaders to let him be their standard-bearer. He was not only a senator but also a general in the U.S. Air Force Reserve at a time when the Vietnam War was becoming increasingly controversial.

Goldwater was viewed as a hawk, a man who would fight the war more aggressively, escalating the number of casualties. A slogan credited to his campaign—"Extremism in the pursuit of liberty is no vice"—caused many people to fear that he could become a dictator. Ultimately he was defeated more decisively in the popular and electoral vote than any other presidential candidate in decades. He had the full support of his state, however, despite newspaper reports that he had ignored his constituents that year, being present for only 7 percent of the votes held on the Senate floor. Yet his candidacy brought his home state to national attention, generating interest in the land in spite of the disdain the nation's voters had shown for one of Arizona's most powerful native sons.

It was during this period of increasing turmoil and unbridled growth in Arizona that Peter MacDonald made his decision to stay on the Navajo reservation. The Navajo land contained energy and water resources so vast that being able to tap into them inexpensively was considered one of the keys to the state's survival and growth for at least the next half-century. If the Navajo Nation learned to use these resources, it would be a major force in the economic future of Arizona. If the Navajo could be exploited by white power holders and their friends, billions of dollars would ultimately be made by everyone but the Native Americans.

An educated Navajo trained in both science and business would be a formidable adversary of those who wished to exploit the reservation land. He would not be part of the early white history of the young state. He would not be a member of the old boy network that had attended the same schools, played on the same softball teams, and remained friends even as members of opposing political parties. He would be an intruder, a man who would neither know nor accept how things were "supposed" to be done in the state.

So the decision by Peter MacDonald to return to the reservation was one that would forever alter both his future and that of the Navajo Nation. His was the last generation to know the old ways, to see the devastation of the forced changes. He had the kind of education that had been denied to most of his peers, and he knew how to move within the two different worlds in which he found himself. Though not even he knew what he was facing, the Last Warrior had come home.

CHAPTER SIX

Native Americans have always experienced racial bias, whether because of the wars fought when whites tried to take our land or because our ways were different from those of the settlers who migrated from Europe. The United States has a long history of bias against various ethnic groups when they first begin to merge with society at large. First- and second-generation Irish, Italians, Germans, Hungarians, and others experienced some degree of bias before being assimilated into the culture.

In 1963 the blacks were fighting for basic civil rights, especially in the South. Yet that struggle was not without its own internal bias, frequently putting black men before black women. Still, there was a sensitivity to the issue and a concern for change.

It was only toward the Indians that people did not seem uncomfortable with their prejudice. After all, the danger from Indians had been "documented" in countless cowboy pictures in theaters and on television. As a result, whites, blacks, Asians, and others all tended to shun the Indians with whom they worked. Nicknames such as "Chief" were common. There was always great amazement when an Indian proved capable of handling a complex task. And in most businesses, it was unspoken, though understood, that no Indian would ever rise to a management position.

Such attitudes led to loneliness and isolation among the Indians. Marriages broke up. Families became dysfunctional. And many Navajo who had financial success off the reservation decided to return because the emotional pressure was too great.

There was housing discrimination, too. Landlords in the better neighborhoods refused to rent to the Navajo who could afford to live there. They had to move into the ghetto, often into tenement neighborhoods where the streets were not safe. When they tried to buy their own homes—if they could find someone to sell them a home in one of the better neighborhoods—the lending institutions found fault with their applications. These same lending institutions, however, found no grounds for disqualification for the same price house with the same mortgage in an undesirable neighborhood. To the Indians, it seemed better to face welfare, poverty, and sporadic employment than to live with such intense discrimination.

I had experienced these problems when I lived in the Los Angeles area, where I was president of the Navajo Club. Many Navajo had been relocated by the BIA after they were trained for good jobs, but their stories were always the same: They could not experience the freedom and happiness they had known on the reservation.

As members of the Navajo Club of Los Angeles, we made as much effort as we could to keep our culture alive. We obtained lambs, took them into the mountains, and butchered them in the Navajo way. We went to schools and organizations, sharing our culture and history with students and adults. We explained why we considered certain areas and mountains sacred, comparing them to the sacred places of other religions, such as Jerusalem and Mecca. We tried to generate an atmosphere of mutual respect.

I am proud of the impact the Navajo Club had on the reservation land, although it was manifested in a totally unexpected way. We began practicing the traditional dances, using the most authentic forms we knew. Some of these dances were private. Others were demonstrated at clubs and schools in order to share a part of our culture.

We learned some of the dances during our childhood. But others were taught to us by people like Howard Gorman, an elder statesman who had served as a council member since the 1920s. Gorman taught us one ceremonial song and dance that had been performed only once before on the Navajo reservation. The ceremony had been put together by a combination of Navajo and Hopis back in the 1800s and was almost completely forgotten. The song was mostly Navajo, though with Hopi inflections, while the dance was more Hopi than Navajo. When we reintroduced it at the Window Rock fair, it was the number-one hit. And to this day, some of the dancers in schools and other places are still performing the dance thanks to Gorman's assistance.

Eventually our club members traveled to Window Rock, Arizona, the headquarters of the Navajo Nation, for a dance competition. Window Rock was the Navajo equivalent of Washington, D.C., and though it was far from a bustling community by the standards of other capital cities, Navajo from throughout the reservation would often gather there for important events.

Although we had both a men's and a women's group, we did not expect to win. We felt that a Los Angeles club, no matter how dedicated, could not compete effectively with reservation-based dancers who were able to practice daily. Moreover, only the best groups from throughout the reservation made the trip to Window Rock for the competition.

Our first surprise was the attitude of many of the younger Navajo at the dance competition. Whereas the elders revered the sacredness of the dances and appreciated the competitors' efforts to be authentic,

Posing with Wanda before a parade in Cave Creek, Arizona.

My maternal grandfather, Deshna Clah Cheschillige.

My paternal grandfather, Dahgahlani.

My mother, Lucy Ute Bileen, photographed around 1950.

Me and my sister Daisy at our home in Teec Nos Pos, Arizona, probably around 1948.

Wanda's maternal grandfather, Earl Greyeyes, who was about 104 years old at the time of this photograph, and her mother, Mabel J. LeClere.

I was a U.S. Marine when I was 15 years old.

A photo of my friend Tso and me while stationed in Pearl Harbor.

A loom set up in a Navajo hogan.

An example of most reservation roads.

A bad winter day.

At my desk at the ONEO in 1963.

Honoring the 1971 Indian Small Businessman of the Year. Left to right: Secretary of the Interior Rogers C. B. Morton; John Nelson Dee, Navajo Tribal Councilman; Mr. Fleming Begaye, Sr., recipient of the award; me; Paul Parrish, president of the Navajo Businessman's Association; and Commissioner of Indian Affairs Louis R. Bruce. (Courtesy Department of the Interior)

I met with Apollo 15 astronauts (left to right) James Irwin, Richard Gordon, and David Scott when they came to train on the moonlike terrain at the foot of Gray Mountain. It was during this time that a Navajo medicine man recorded a warning for any Navajos who might still be living on the moon. (Courtesy NASA)

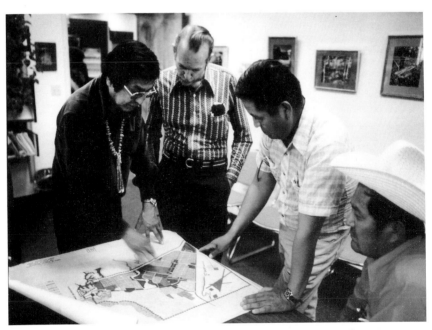

Reviewing plans with Senator Dennis DeConcini and a Navajo Resource Committee member.

Inspecting a coal mining operation on the reservation in 1979.

Enjoying the stupendous growth of the first corn harvest at Navajo Agricultural Products Industries with Resource Committee member Ray Gilmore in 1982.

Arizona Governor Raul Castro (right) and New Mexico Governor Jerry Apodaca at a birthday dinner in my honor at our Window Rock home.

Arizona Governor Bruce Babbitt with me (beginning my role as Cataract sales director), Wanda, and Mel Pervais (Cataract CEO) at the opening of the Cataract sales office in Tempe, Arizona.

My daughter Charity presented a Navajo doll to Great Britain's Princess Margaret at a dinner at the Governor's mansion in Santa Fe. Looking on is Alice King, wife of Governor Bruce King of New Mexico.

the young were drinking heavily, and bootleggers were openly selling alcohol. These young people showed a lack of respect that we had not expected to encounter.

The second surprise was our being awarded first place in the men's and women's competitions. Where other dancers had departed from tradition or failed to master the steps, we in the Los Angeles club had felt so separated from our home that we had taken great pains to present the old dances as flawlessly as possible. Our efforts resulted in our taking the honors.

As a result of our victory, many of the other competitors seemed to sense that if those of us who had taken jobs off the reservation could maintain our heritage, those on the reservation could do much more. The dances were taken more seriously after that, and within a few years the gatherings reflected the reverence and dedication of the early years.

Although I sought the companionship of other Navajo in Los Angeles, I realized that I was somewhat different from many of them because I was quite happy in my profession. Whereas many Navajo took jobs merely to earn more money than they could make on the reservation, not because they were dedicated to their careers, I was driven by the constant challenges of my job. Yet although I worked with other engineers, scientists, and technicians, all of us striving to reach the same goals, had I not been involved with the Navajo Club, I would have had no social life at all. At no time did any Anglo try to get to know me personally. And when I tried to be friendly, I was politely rebuffed. As a result, I have come to feel most at ease only with Navajo.

My wife did not have quite the same problems I did. The Comanche were clannish, with strong family roots, so she was comfortable with other Indians. However, she was also a mother who stayed at home with the children, and this gave her something in common with neighbors in the same circumstances. She was able to socialize during the day because the neighborhood women shared the experience of raising small children who played together. In addition, her family had been Christians for at least two generations, so again there was a common link.

My other concern during this period was with giving my son and daughter a good education. My wife and I had become active in the Baptist church. I was a Sunday school teacher, and both of us felt it was important to provide a good moral upbringing for the children. We felt that a Christian school was more likely to provide both excellent teaching and a moral foundation.

At the same time, I was trying to bring up Rocky, my son, to have as much of the Navajo experience as he could get in the city.

Navajo children are ideally taught by three concepts for which there is no direct translation. One is to gain knowledge. The second is to gain wisdom. The third refers to a combination of physical, mental, and spiritual strength. More than awareness of our gods, spiritual strength means you have to believe in the help that comes through trusting in God, the legends, the songs and the prayers. This gives you the strength you need for living and a respect for others, their dreams, and their visions. Instead of hostility for others, you learn to maintain a harmony and wholeness with all living beings.

While in Los Angeles, there was not very much I could do to expose him to the Navajo culture and tradition, other than to talk and relate some of the stories. At the same time, I tried to spend as much time as possible with him in the evenings and on weekends. We joined an Anglo father-and-son club. Ironically, the purpose of the club was to teach the members about Indian lore and ways. The members met on evenings and weekends to involve themselves with projects related to Native Americans and took Indian names.

Rocky and I were the only real Indian father and son, and that made it fun. On two or three occasions, we went up to the snow-covered Big Bear Mountain where we related some stories and legends about the Navajo and other Indians. It gave me time to be with Rocky and a chance to teach him and the whites what Indians were all about.

Rocky and I became very close during that period. We went to Los Angeles Rams games and got involved with Little League. I bought him a glove and pitched the ball to him.

Since Rocky could not run through the mountains and the forests, I tried to get him into as many athletic activities as possible. He came to enjoy sports, eventually lettering in football, baseball, and basketball in high school. He also made the Yale University freshman football and basketball teams.

It wasn't easy trying to provide the type of education, inner strength, and moral foundation Rocky would need as a Navajo man. He wasn't able to be close to his uncle or grandfather in order to get the extra family discipline that I had experienced.

I also made him run each morning. I didn't want to accompany him. I didn't ever want to run again. I had had my fill of that life when growing up. I was hoping that Rocky would so enjoy it that I would have no trouble getting him to run on his own. I was wrong, though, because he was a city kid.

By the time Rocky was in high school, we were living in Fort Defiance and he was running alone. I would get him up at six every morning and make him run. He would come back around seven o'clock, shower, and get ready for school.

One day I decided that maybe I'd better check up on him. Just before he left for his run, I asked him where he went. He said that he always ran in a circle starting toward the west, then swung around and returned home.

Fifteen minutes after Rocky left, I got in my car and drove much farther east than he could have gone on foot. Then I turned around and went back, again driving farther than he could have gone. Finally I returned to the house. I had not found him.

Eventually I got back into my car and drove to a point where I could see the house and all the routes Rocky might have taken. All of a sudden I saw Rocky come running from a housing development. He ran as fast as he could for the very short distance back to the house.

I drove up behind him and said, "Rocky, what are you doing?"

Rocky told me the path he had taken, the same route I had covered. I then said that he had not done what he claimed. "I saw you coming out of the housing project, and you just made the short run over here. How long have you been doing that?"

"Okay, I'll confess, Father," he replied. "I have a school buddy who lives over there. We just sit and watch television, and after we see several programs, I run back."

I was disappointed in him and explained to him that he wasn't running for me. He wasn't running for his mother. He was running for himself, to be strong, healthy, able to face the challenges of life. I told him that if he wasn't going to run, he should stay home to watch television. He shouldn't sneak over to a friend's house.

Eventually he did run a bit, but it was not the same for him as it had been for me. He did not feel the pressure, the sense of history, the fear of the old people that had motivated us on the reservation.

Our daughter, Linda, was guided by my wife, but her training was quite different. She was not encouraged to run, as were Navajo daughters who were raised on the reservation. And she was taught a mixture of Navajo, Comanche, and Baptist traditions. We tried to share the past, yet we realized that some things could never be the same. We loved both our children and tried to help them find their own way.

Most Navajo and other Native Americans face the same dilemma when educating their children. As a parent, you want your children to know their culture and traditions. Such knowledge gives them the confidence to face the outside world. But to live in the outside world, they need the education and knowledge that will enable them to survive and help them with their people. You can better protect what is yours, your culture and tradition, as you understand the outside world.

Today's Navajo and other Native Americans need to provide educational programs for their children that combine a firm rooting in culture and tradition with the best education possible so they can compete in the world at large. I was very fortunate that my five children were able to have so much of that in a world that had changed so radically from when I was young. My children have become an engineer, a lawyer, an artist . . . so many different careers that once would not have been considered possible for a Navajo. And they are not unusual in their abilities. We Diné know that our children have what it takes to be among the best in the country. They just need guidance and help to master both cultures.

But no matter what we did in Los Angeles, no matter how our children were raised, we Navajo always felt like expatriates when away from the reservation. The reservation was home. The reservation was comfortable. The reservation was familiar. The more pressure we faced in terms of job and housing discrimination, the more willing we were to put up with the hardships of the reservation.

Yet when we returned to the reservation, we found bias there, too. To many of the Navajo on the reservation, city jobs meant progress, money, success, and happiness. Parents and grandparents were happy for the children who had gone off to San Diego, Los Angeles, and elsewhere. Our decision to return to the reservation after giving up a good job was seen as foolish at best, a potential disgrace at worst. The pressure did not end.

My mother was like that. I remember her saying to me, "I don't know what you're doing in Los Angeles, but you're very fortunate to have a job." Of course she was glad to see me and wished I could be with her more often, but she knew there was no job for me on the reservation. She loved me and was pleased that I had a good job and could support myself. This also eased her mind and kept her from worrying about me. She wanted me to succeed, and the job in Los Angeles meant that I was making it on my own. Yet although I wanted her to be happy, I felt called to face the problems the Navajo were encountering back home.

In 1963 the Navajo Nation was dominated by the young, many of whom had been raised without a strong allegiance to their heritage. I'm sure the problem was not unique to my tribe, but we were the largest of the Indian tribes, and due to the almost complete destruction of our people following the Long Walk, the majority of Navajo were young.

Navajo youths preferred not to talk in their parents' native tongue or to admit that they were members of the Navajo Nation. If they were only half Navajo, they would tell people that they were Hispanic, German, Irish, or whatever, perhaps reluctantly adding that they had "some" Navajo or Indian blood. It was as though they had looked around and, seeing the poverty, the bias, and the color problems, had decided that there was no future in being a Navajo. They blamed themselves and their race for the problems caused by outsiders. They developed a crippling self-hatred that made me wonder if their denial of their heritage would ultimately cause the destruction of the Navajo Nation.

Our leadership was in turmoil. The Tribal Council was supposed to represent the people, but its members had come to feel as helpless as everyone else. They were still suffering from the financial reverses that had begun with the livestock reduction and they believed that they were inferior. They had given up, effectively ceding power to the BIA officials and the Anglo lawyer who served as tribal counsel.

This voluntary relinquishing of power affected decisions beyond legal matters. The council members asked the Anglo lawyer his opinions even on social and economic issues outside his area of expertise. His opinions became their decisions. It was not that the lawyer had corrupted them or was seeking personal power. The council members, like all the people, seemed to have lost so much self-confidence that they would not trust themselves to decide anything.

Back in the 1940s, when I left the heart of the Navajo Nation, my people retained hope for the future. They were still left alone to work out their problems on the local level, and they retained the traditional values that had ensured survival and growth over the centuries. They understood the importance of sheep, cattle, and farming. They understood that they had to be self-sufficient in whatever way they could.

Social welfare programs were available in those days, and the majority of the Navajo were so poor that they readily qualified. Yet the acceptance of any sort of assistance was usually considered a disgrace. It also brought shame upon the person's family, because they obviously were not working together in the traditional way.

By the 1960s, however, the belief in self-sufficiency was no longer dominant. The younger people were demanding assistance from the government. They were poor and felt that they deserved government assistance. They wanted welfare and embraced it as a salvation rather than a stopgap measure until they found new ways to be independent. The old ways had been destroyed by the white man, so it seemed only fair to them that their conqueror pay for their survival. If they felt anger about what had happened, it was internalized, creating massive depression. A great nation that had endured every hardship imaginable now seemed to be giving up.

The Navajo of my generation were fighters. We did everything to avoid accepting handouts from our conquerors. The younger generation lacked that attitude, and the results both frightened and angered me.

Although part of my motivation to stay on the reservation and try to change the lives of my people resulted from all that I witnessed, most of it stemmed from my independent study of the history of the Navajo Nation. Until I read scholarly works and journals that were not part of the basic curriculum in the BIA schools, I did not fully understand the effects of the century-old wars against the Navajo. These were a part of what can only be termed the American Holocaust.

When I returned to the reservation after having worked for Hughes, I was shocked, saddened, and angered by what I saw had happened with the young people. I had spent so many years off the reservation, focused on proving myself, focused on a career, my family, the work at Hughes, I did not think about other Navajo being psychologically destroyed. Yet when I looked around, when I saw what had happened as a result of the forced livestock reduction, the disillusionment following the war, the alcoholism, and the lack of jobs, I felt that the holocaust that began during the Fort Sumner years was continuing a century later. But instead of bullets, the destruction of the Navajo Nation was now being accomplished by apathy and despair.

The welfare mentality permeated the reservation. The high point of many people's lives was one or another special work project that became available every six months. Funding was obtained so that a few Navajo men and women could hold makeshift jobs that generally paid minimum wage and lasted just ten days. When such money became available, people would flock to the chapter houses, community centers located throughout the reservation. A table would be set up in front, and fifty or a hundred people in each chapter house would rush to toss their Social Security cards on the table so they would be considered for a job. Usually the work was simple enough so that anyone could handle it, but only ten or fifteen would be lucky enough to get hired. This was often the only work they knew about that was available on the reservation. That the work usually involved only menial tasks, such as moving rocks or painting a building, meant that they were not developing marketable skills or salable products. It was a twice-yearly chance for a little dignity and self-worth, a pathetic situation for a proud people.

Tragically, beyond going from one ten-day work project to another, there was no anticipation of work in the future. The people had no goals other than perhaps to find a way to earn an extra dollar or two to put bread on the table that day. They had no hope because they could not imagine what else might be possible in life. The Navajo survived, of course. Some married. Some did not. Some had children. Others did not. Some drank, often to excess, when they left the reservation. But there was no hope for a better tomorrow, no belief that their actions could alter their fate. The poverty was bad, but the poverty of the soul was far worse.

The BIA was completely in charge of the lives of the Navajo. The Tribal Council looked to them for direction, for employment, for their immediate and future existence. A proud, self-sufficient people had let themselves be robbed of a vision and the self-respect to be willing to pursue any dream that might enable them to lead independent lives.

Officially the BIA was funded to provide employment. The schools had to be maintained. The roads had to be both expanded and re-paired. Appropriations were obtained from Congress. Bureaucratic chores were handled. Yet there was no effort to promote real careers on or off the reservation. I doubted that most of the young people knew what an engineering career was and had no idea that they could enter such a field. There was no tribal clearinghouse for jobs, no thought to where the people would be heading in the years ahead. There was nothing in which anyone could take pride.

The schools did educate the children in their history and culture, though always with an outsider's bias. Although more modern, the curriculum was really not much different from what I experienced in the 1930s. The Navajo children gained basic literacy in a culture they were not able to share.

The end result was that the Navajo teenagers of the late 1950s and early 1960s strove to be as Anglo as they could. Many of them still do not speak Navajo, or don't speak it very well. They saw a future in becoming like white people. Denying their heritage seemed to promise a better future.

What was sad was that Indian children could only be very poor imitation of Anglos. They wore the clothing they saw in Anglo fashion magazines. They coveted the "things" of popular culture, taking pride only in what they could buy, then becoming unhappy when they had whatever they wanted and couldn't afford to buy still more.

The young people were often raised in hogans before going to the cities. They returned to criticize those childhood homes, calling them primitive and filthy. They ridiculed their parents and grandparents for clinging to the old ways. They had no respect for anyone.

The old people were especially upset. They carried the legacy of the survivors of the Long Walk. They had maintained the traditions which provided the values, the knowledge, and the wisdom necessary to live in harmony with the Great Spirit. They had endured the taunts of their BIA teachers. They had worked to assure that the morals and ethics of a spiritual people were preserved.

Now their grandchildren were mocking their heritage, not bothering to learn enough about it to understand that much of it would enhance their lives no matter where and how they lived. The grandparents were embarrassed by the humiliating verbal attacks they endured. They could see what their grandchildren were going to lose by such wholesale rejection, yet they were helpless to reach them. It was almost as sad to them as when our people first faced the armed violence of the Blue Coats in the early nineteenth century.

These children were born after World War II. Their fathers, who went to war with me, were raised in the old ways, were familiar with the tragedy of the livestock reduction era, and were trained for life in a society that was radically altered during their lifetime.

When the men of my generation were sent to San Diego, Chicago, China, Europe, and elsewhere, some of them were able to assimilate what they saw and become a part of it. Others were traumatized, realizing how much more advanced the rest of the world was than the environment in which they were raised. These men came to believe that the knowledge of their grandparents, the religious beliefs that they had held, all that had been so important to them, appeared to be wrong. Truth had become myth. Facts had become misinformation. They had seemingly spent their lives preparing for a fantasy they thought was their future, and now there was no hope for them.

The veterans were also excluded from the old ways because they had missed out on getting permits for raising sheep and were now unable to farm. They were forced to look for eight-to-five jobs—again, something new. This meant that either they had to work on the reservation—perhaps for the BIA schools—or they had to leave the reservation. Frequently they did not live in hogans. They lived in houses with indoor plumbing, electricity, gas, and hot water. They encountered the primitive life-style only when they returned to the reservation to visit their parents and grandparents.

These veterans knew the importance of educating their children, but they had no idea how to raise their children to be responsible. In the past, the sons and daughters worked alongside their parents. From the time they were small, they recognized that they were part of the life of the community. They herded sheep, gathered wood, hauled water, or engaged in other activities that were menial yet crucial to survival. Those children were always responsible. They learned from the adults. There was time to play, but only between periods of work.

Life was not simpler in the past, though it was accepted and embraced. The goals of every Navajo were consistent. We were to fear the Great Spirit, care for the sheep, the horses, and the cattle, farm the land, marry, and be independent. It was rare for anyone to marry before the age of 21, and then it was done only if the person could be self-sufficient. A few of the extreme elderly needed help, but this came from their extended family, not from welfare, and it came only when they could no longer work as they had done all their lives. A parent was proud to be independent of his or her child, yet that child was proud to be able to care for the parent in extreme old age should physical infirmities make that necessary.

The change that occurred was shattering. Working with the land and the animals as appropriate for the seasons was changed to waiting for the arrival of the food commodities truck and the welfare check.

There was a time when the young people would have felt shame if they were not either helping their parents and grandparents or living on their own. Instead, they were marrying at 17 or 18, having babies, and living in the same hogan with their mother or grandmother, living on the older Navajo's welfare check. They did not seek jobs, sometimes because there was no work and sometimes because they had fallen into a life-style that had once been unacceptable for any young, healthy Navajo.

They needed jobs. They needed training. And they needed a separate hogan.

Even those who were working were changing in ways that were destructive to the Navajo. In the old days, a man did not have to make time for parenting. He was always interacting with the children; they were always working together. If a man wanted to spend additional time with his son and daughter, he could. But even a man who tended to ignore a child was still involved, if only because the child could constantly see what he was doing.

Then suddenly everything was different. The man would leave

home, go to work, and come home. His wife might also have a job. Children who did not go to school often had to fend for themselves. They had no role models; they learned from their experiences on the border town streets and their peers. They might have a television set for a companion. They might learn their "wisdom" from slightly older kids in their neighborhood, but they suffered from the lack of opportunities available from the extended family, the close relationship with the seasons and with nature, the constant presence of adult mentors.

There was no way that these children, raised so differently from their parents, could consider themselves part of a continuing society. They either did not know the Navajo religion or looked upon it as a collection of myths and fairy tales they could not imagine anyone believing. Those who knew the Navajo language thought of it as a hindrance in their lives. They wanted to speak perfect English, and when questioned about their background, they often failed to mention that they were Indians.

Yet no matter what they did, nothing worked. There were few meaningful jobs on the reservation, and almost none required or rewarded the education they had obtained. Most Navajo youths went through high school, and many trained for a vocation or received a college education. Still, they were either discriminated against or could not find work, the closest communities to the reservation often being too small to offer many opportunities.

In the late 1950s and through the 1960s, the BIA, funded by Congress, instituted a relocation program in which a young Navajo family, couple, or individual was given one-way bus fare to a major city, such as Los Angeles, Dallas, Denver, or Cleveland. A BIA representative would meet the Navajo in the city, help him find low-rent housing, usually in one of the ghetto areas, and a job. Where needed, the Navajo would also receive some financial assistance for training.

Eventually tens of thousands were relocated under this program, yet only one in four was successful. The others fell victim to predictable crises. Many felt unprepared and lost, like aliens in a foreign culture. They could not relate to their neighbors, who were black, Hispanic, or members of some other minority. Still others were fired from their jobs because they did not understand exactly what was expected of them, or they were placed in positions that were vulnerable to layoffs during financial crises. Whatever the case, they needed additional counseling, continuing support, and at times, additional educational services, especially during the first year in their new home. Unlike immigrants from foreign lands who would band together their first years in the new area, the Navajo were isolated from other Indians. They did not have the support services traditionally available to foreign-born men and women because they were too scattered.

Some of the Navajo stayed in the cities, eventually losing their apartments and having to take to the streets, a predicament that made them all the more helpless and desperate. Others hitchhiked back to the reservation. It was easier to live on welfare with their family than to be miserable and suffering in some strange town.

The BIA, however, did an excellent job of explaining the various government welfare programs that would supply them with subsistence money, and this lost generation of children, as well as their disillusioned parents, decided to accept these handouts. Some had lost their pride, their self-respect. Others never knew what it was to believe in themselves or in their people.

Yet always there was a fire inside the bellies of many of the Navajo. There was a spirit that had not been fully destroyed. Some men and women had the courage to continue to hope in a hopeless situation. They would take a course in auto mechanics, then find that there were no jobs available. So they would swallow their disappointment, hear about jobs in the building trades, and go back to school to learn welding. When welding jobs did not appear, they might become carpenters or electricians. They were like the medicine men, always learning a new skill. But unlike the medicine men, these Navajo never had the opportunity to utilize what they were learning.

The statistics for this time were shocking. Despite the deliberate destruction of the Navajo during the Long Walk, by 1900 the Navajo had achieved 90 percent self-sufficiency. There was no Social Security. There was no welfare. The ten percent who needed BIA assistance did not need it regularly, nor was their use of such assistance respected. Their extended families helped them, and they all worked for the day when the BIA would be unnecessary for their survival.

Just before the forced livestock reduction of my childhood, the number of independent Navajo had risen very close to 100 percent. There were between 5,000 and 6,000 Navajo living in Teec Nos Pos, and there were only four or five who needed occasional assistance. The community worked with them to try and limit their needs, and they were the objects of great pity. They were also so rare that everyone knew them.

Not that we were rich by white man's standards. But the typical Navajo could go from birth through old age and death with meaningful work, enough to eat, adequate clothing and shelter, living in harmony with the Great Spirit, having and nurturing the next generation of children. There was peace and laughter, an existence that was richer than one dependent upon material goods which were purchased for status.

Today there are probably no more than ten percent of the Navajo who are self-sufficient. The BIA has become the controlling force, and the BIA is so entrenched that the employees have more to gain by trying to extinguish the drive for independence of the spirit than by helping the people return to the old ways.

A few Navajo did manage to attain success during this period, however. These were ambitious men and women who left the reservation, left the nearby towns and cities, and journeyed to Chicago, Cleveland, Dallas, Houston, Los Angeles, and elsewhere. They found jobs in the building trades. They spoke the same language as their neighbors. Yet though their work, their possessions, even their English slang was the same as others, they were still different. They were still nonwhite in a period of extreme bias.

These feelings of isolation, helplessness, and hopelessness struck me as the greatest wrongs that had occurred. They needed to be corrected, though at first I did not know how. I knew only that I needed to help restore both the economy and the pride of my people, who were a part of a nation whose history was rapidly being forgotten.

I arrived alone in April of 1963 knowing that my consulting work would be a periodic arrangement for a while. My family stayed in California while I commuted to tribal headquarters.

The work became permanent in June, although my family stayed in Los Angeles for the summer. My wife had to sell our house and get the children ready for the move. But by September we were all living on the reservation together.

I thought I would need a year to help the tribe. My mother, brothers, and sisters had been complaining to me about the difficulties they were having obtaining the various government services that were offered, and it was my intention to help them deal with the bureaucracy. At first I thought this was a minor problem. I was shocked to discover how extremely dependent upon the government they had become.

Years earlier, my mother had given birth in a tent while walking from Utah to Arizona. She had been a single parent for several years, handling not only women's chores but also many of those that my father would have performed had he not been killed. This was a woman of strength, courage, love, and wisdom, a woman who had physically and emotionally survived circumstances that most people could not tolerate.

After the forced livestock reduction, she had worked at the uranium mine sites, washing clothes for the mine workers, and had taken other physically demanding jobs. She had always done whatever she had to do to be independent.

Now in her early sixties, she was still working. She kept the house, chopped wood, hauled water, herded the few sheep she was allowed to raise, and did weaving and other hard work. Yet she had changed. She saw the financial assistance the government was giving to others, and she decided that, if she was eligible, she wanted her share. She wanted commodity assistance and welfare checks, supplements she once would have spurned as demeaning.

I would have understood this if her need had been greater than it was in the past, if she had no longer been capable of surviving without assistance. But my mother's desire to accept government aid had nothing to do with survival. The government had brought a new ethic to our community—jealous greed. Rather sheepishly, my mother pointed to a family that was getting welfare checks and had been able to buy a new pickup truck. She wanted the same opportunity, even though her needs and activities were quite different.

My mother had not had this attitude during the worst of times on the reservation. This was something new, evidence to me of the gradual corruption of the Navajo. To see my mother letting herself reach a level where she wanted to be dependent upon outside sources was extremely painful. I did not want to allow this situation to continue if I could help her and others return to self-sufficiency.

My mother saw some of her neighbors utilizing the social services and being able to afford new pickup trucks. She said that if she would take advantage of the programs, she could have one as well.

Fortunately my mother did not yield to the pressures. I helped her financially, as Navajo adult children had helped their parents for generations. In addition, she continued her weaving and shepherding. She sold wool and the lambs born to her sheep. She eventually got her truck, and she did it through means that did not require her to look outside her own resources and those of her family.

I thought that during that first year I might become part of the Navajo Nation government and find out how to help the people. I had no illusions about the ability of the Navajo to return to the old ways in just twelve months. I certainly did not think I would be instituting self-help programs that would radically change their lives. But I did feel that there would be a way to consolidate what was taking place in such a manner that people could know their rights, obtain what was due them, and somehow begin to stabilize the economic situation for themselves. In addition, I wanted to know what the BIA was doing with the Navajo people, to try to understand the bureaucracy, and to see if favoritism was involved in rendering assistance to people.

There were vast sums of money authorized to be given to the Navajo, yet there was no evidence that the money had reached the Diné. I wanted a cost accounting. I wanted to understand how it was spent because the sums officially authorized seemed to exceed the needs of the people, a fact that made me suspect that waste and bureaucracy accounted for most of the money before the Navajo saw a single cent.

This would not have been a new phenomenon. In the time following the Long Walk, there was extensive theft of what should have been Navajo support. Special rations specifically earmarked for the Navajo were regularly sent to Fort Sumner and Fort Defiance. My people were told to gather there for their shares, yet when they did, sometimes nothing arrived, sometimes there was too little to feed everyone, and sometimes all that was available was a partial ration for each person.

There were also rations that were sent from Albuquerque to Gallup to the reservation land, and again these frequently did not arrive as promised. Years later it was admitted that the rations were routinely siphoned off. Sometimes the military took them to supplement the food for the soldiers. Sometimes they were stolen by traders who profited from their resale. It was similar to modern-day food-truck hijacking by organized crime members who then move the stolen food through mob-influenced supermarket chains and massive discount house operations. The difference is that contemporary theft of truck shipments seldom means people will die. The original shipments were barely adequate back then, so any loss meant fatalities.

Today, if one hundred million dollars is authorized by Congress specifically for the Navajo, most of it will be used by the bureaucracy, which in some areas involves one government employee for every five Indians, and waste. There is no accountability, and often no effort to be certain that the money is spent both for essentials and in a manner that gets the most value for the money.

My sense of history also caused me to be concerned about what was happening. The Navajo were a treaty tribe, not a part of the U.S. government. Back in 1868, the Navajo had signed a treaty that established their relationship with Washington as an independent nation. The Navajo Nation was not to be considered a part of the United States, even though the Navajo people would be American citizens. Despite this "dual citizenship," the Navajo Nation has never officially become a part of the United States, either as a portion of Arizona or as a territory or state.

There were similar treaties before 1868, though they were always broken by force. What is important is that no new treaties changing the status of the Navajo Nation have been signed since.

Nevertheless, I knew that the realities of the law did not matter, and I observed the two forms of regulations—de jure and de facto. The de jure regulations were carefully codified and agreed upon through legislation. The de facto rules came about because no one challenged illegal activities or actions that had nothing to do with the written law. The BIA seemed to be trying to assimilate the Navajo through de facto activities.

This occurred in many ways. For example, the tribal courts were forced to use English, not Navajo, the native tongue of the people for whom the courts were established. The Navajo system of law was being ignored; cases were being decided by U.S. case law and precedents set in Anglo courts. This implied that there was nothing unique about the Navajo courts, despite the well-known history of Navajo decision making, which was quite different from what was taking place.

Part of the problem came from the Navajo Justice Department, which often brought in do-good, liberal "hippie" lawyers who were anxious to show their support for the poor, downtrodden Indians. They were filled with self-importance, determined that they knew how to best protect our rights. Yet they never tried to learn our ways, our system of justice, or what we needed.

All laws are created based on the moral values of a society. This is true for every nation in the world. In the extreme, they may reflect the morality of a dictator who wants everyone to follow his will and has taken absolute control of a country. In the vast majority of cases they take into account the morals, ethics, and historic needs of the people who are to be ruled by them. White man's laws in the United States are based on property because the acquisition of possessions is the key to status for most Americans. Navajo law is based on the individual, and while possessions are enjoyed, it is considered proper to give away anything you own that you feel someone else might enjoy. Such giving to a special person is a sign of respect, of love, and of courtesy, and it is rude for the recipient to feel the need to reciprocate. This is why you cannot bribe a traditional Navajo. It is why the traditional Navajo understands the need for such religious laws as the Ten Commandments in the Bible as a reflection of how far Anglos deviated from the harmonious ways of the Great Spirit.

The new Navajo regulations created by these outsiders were based wholesale on state and federal laws. They photocopied sections of those law books, then changed them just enough so they stated that they were the laws of the Navajo Nation. The lawyers created regulations that were so confusing that a Navajo who acted in the manner in which our people had been raised for centuries would be in violation.

For example, a Navajo might be subpoenaed to serve on a jury. The first confusion comes with the idea of a jury. Navajo discuss a legal problem with all the people involved, the judge asking questions, listening, and probing for truth. Once everyone agrees upon what happened, and this includes the victim or a member of the victim's family, then appropriate restitution is decided. The person who did wrong may not like having to meet the terms of the penalty, but he or she will agree that the penalty is fair, whatever it may be. But never does one Navajo judge another. There is no jury, and the idea of acting in the manner of a jury member is considered to be rude at best.

The traditional Navajo will ignore the jury subpoena. Responding as ordered would be a violation of our culture. And when the final warning arrives, that is still ignored.

Suddenly the person who failed to answer the subpoena is arrested and jailed for a charge the Anglo-influence new court system calls "contempt of court." He or she may be sent to jail for a few days as a lesson. But what lesson has been learned? That unless you disgrace your family and your people by acting against our culture, you will go to jail?

The only way for Navajo laws to reflect Navajo culture would be to throw all the outside lawyers off the reservation, something the Chairman can order. Then the Tribal Chairman must go to each chapter house and give the people a list of questions about problems that occur among the Navajo. The people will then gather in their chapter houses and discuss how each problem should be handled. They will draw on the experience and wisdom of the elders, on our history and legends, on the values passed on to us by the Great Spirit. Then we will make note of what has been decided, and these will be the laws of the people. They will be fair and just within our society, not the society of a people who view property as more precious than human beings.

Then there were nuisance procedures that forced the Navajo to become more dependent on the BIA. For example, in the past, when a Navajo wanted to build a home on available land, he or she could just do it. The land belonged to everyone, and so long as there was no intrusion on your neighbor, you could do whatever you could afford that seemed best for your family. But when I returned in 1963, you had to obtain what was known as a homesite lease, a document administered by the BIA.

The BIA created rules and regulations that had no precedent in the Navajo culture. There were homesite and grazing leases issued by the BIA. They controlled the permits, including who should have them, how they should be enforced, and what the penalties should be for violation. Then the Tribal Chairman and Tribal Council were ordered to handle the enforcement.

For example, if the BIA gave a Navajo woman permission for grazing 80 sheep and the woman grazed 150 sheep, which the land could easily handle, the BIA wanted me to stop her. I refused to enforce the law or allow any other Navajo to enforce it when I was Tribal Chairman. The person was doing nothing wrong except violating a regulation the BIA arbitrarily created.

Today the situation is worse and far more sinister in its implications. The Tribal Council has a law in which a person is given a permit for the use of a certain amount of land that has actually been in use by the family for generations. The land is controlled by the BIA and the Tribal Council instead of the community where it is located and the chapter house serving that community, as in the past.

Under the current program, if there is any permit violation, the permit is withdrawn. If the family continues to use the land on which they were born, and on which their ancestors may have been born, they are considered to be trespassing. They will be forcibly removed for their "crime." Even worse, the permit for the land does not have to be given to other Navajo. The section of land can become a controlled wilderness area where Navajo, though officially owning it, may not live, may not grow crops, and may not graze their animals. Instead, if the BIA wants to negotiate with outside interests to create a hazardous waste site, something that has been discussed as a way of bringing jobs to the area, they can do so. The land has been kidnapped and can be violated in isolation without the Navajo people having the right to reclaim what is theirs.

Equally difficult is the fact that when efforts for change are made, the Navajo are subjected to several layers of bureaucratic red tape. Changes desired by the people may take years to implement when, in the Anglo system, the same effort made for private land might take only a few weeks. If the BIA had been in charge of the expansion and development of the United States immediately after the Revolutionary War, today there would only be the original thirteen states.

A way of life that had once been casual and nonthreatening, and that made allowance for self-determination, had suddenly become something quite different. Almost every aspect of Navajo life now required forms, applications, approval procedures, and similar bureaucratic exercises.

The procedures created another new problem for the Navajo—the potential for political favoritism and corruption.

I did not realize the depth of the problem. I thought I could use my business management experience to reorganize the tribal government structure, alter the arrangements with the BIA so there would at least be fairness and consistency in the rules, and then return to my engineering job in California.

My understanding of the extent of the problems on the Navajo reservation came slowly. I acted as I had learned to do, both as an engineer and as a Navajo. I became an observer, attempting to determine where problems existed, what alternatives were available, and what needed to be done. By the time I had been there a couple of months I felt a little like President Kennedy who, upon entering the White House after criticizing the Eisenhower administration, said that his greatest surprise was discovering that the country was in as bad shape as he had been saying it was during the election campaign.

The first shock came when I began encountering the politics of the tribe. There seemed to be several things going on at once, and though I was never to serve as a member of the Tribal Council, I was soon made painfully aware of them.

First, there was a rivalry among factions that should not have been opposing one another. The sole concern of everyone should have been the future of the Navajo people. Certainly all the men running for tribal chairman expressed this concern, the differences among them relating to their education on and off the reservation. Yet that was not the way all Navajo politicians saw the circumstances.

For example, one group of council delegates supported former tribal chairman Paul Jones. These men and women saw themselves as the old guard and looked upon people like me and the new tribal chairman as the new guard. Undoubtedly they felt that they were the keepers of the historical past while we were making brazen changes that defied tradition and did not meet the current needs of the Navajo people. They did not look into our background. They seemed to see us only as intruders in their territory, even though everyone knew that the earlier policies had led to a continuation of the sense of complete defeat among the Navajo. A woman named Annie Wauneka was a member of the Tribal Council. Her father had once been tribal chairman and she considered herself part of the old guard. She had been raised the traditional way, with limited education and isolated from the outside world of business that was becoming so important to the reservation.

I knew little of Annie Wauneka and did not care about her one way or another. I was young, idealistic, well trained, and sensitive to both the old and new ways. All I wanted was what was best for the Navajo Nation, and I had developed the maturity to listen to the needs and wants of others.

I'm not certain what sort of reception I anticipated. I guess I expected the tribal government to function like the hierarchy at Hughes. There might be arguments. There might be lengthy discussions covering everyone's concerns relative to what was being planned. But everyone would be respected, whether it was someone such as myself, who was both young and returning to the reservation after several years of working in Anglo society, or the elders, who lived as our ancestors had for centuries. I did not expect to be attacked.

The incident occurred one afternoon during a council recess. Annie Wauneka came up to me in the chambers, pointed her finger at me and said, "Young man, you go back to Los Angeles. We don't need you. We don't need you at all. You go back to Los Angeles."

I didn't say anything. I just walked away and returned to my office. All I could think of was how foolish and ignorant she was. I had been working for the Navajo Nation for approximately eight months. My pay was considerably lower than what I had been earning at Hughes Aircraft. My future with Hughes was on Mahogany Row. They were anxious for me to return, and several other companies were trying to lure me away with offers of higher salary, benefits, and various options that would ultimately make me large sums of money.

As director of management, methods, and procedures, I was not trying to bring new ideas that would disrupt the people. I was trying to restore pride in being a Navajo. I was giving up success in the white world to help my people.

But I felt that all this woman could see was someone who was assisting Raymond Nakai, part of the new guard. She would rather focus on politics than on the mutual concerns that would benefit her, her children, and her grandchildren.

I also resented her condescending manner. She was limited in her experience, yet she rigidly focused on the fact that I was not a part of her group, choosing to mistrust my intentions rather than to see me as an ally.

I never told her off, of course. I was raised better than that. Yet I will never forget that experience, and the image of her angry face and accusing finger are indelibly etched in my mind.

Perhaps that incident with Annie Wauneka would have passed from my mind had I not encountered her again and again. In the years to come, she would prove to be the enemy of every chairman as he left power. She would attack Raymond Nakai when I took office, charging him with theft and asking me to put him in jail. She would attack me when Peterson Zah ultimately replaced me, and she would attack Zah when I returned to office after a short hiatus. Later, she would speak against me before a Congressional investigating committee.

Annie Wauneka struck me as an antagonist rather than someone with a plan for the future of the people she claimed to love. And while she ultimately did much good from her council position, she also was, in my mind, viciously divisive and needlessly hurtful throughout the years to follow.

I did not make a decision to fight Annie Wauneka and the rest of the old guard, though I knew they were likely to always be on the offensive against me. My job was to fight the real enemy, the poverty and the people who had created and sustained such a condition for the Navajo.

And the people on the reservation seemed hungry for what I had to say. The politicians at Window Rock were engaged in factional disputes and were not responding to the people. The people saw this infighting and were open to alternatives. I told them that we Navajo had great potential as a people. We had tremendous opportunity. We were a people with everything good going for us. All we had to do was take responsibility for ourselves, pull ourselves up by our bootstraps, and show the BIA and the world that we could do it. I was speaking of self-determination of our destiny, and the people agreed that they wanted to try. They did not have the jealousy and enviousness of the politicians in Window Rock, who could do nothing but fight among themselves.

The way the Tribal Council was allowed to hold its meetings was another nightmare. The council chambers belonged to the Navajo Nation. The structure was built with their labor, situated on their land, and existed for their use. Yet the BIA agency superintendent, Glen Landbloom, held the only key. No Navajo could use the chambers without first going to Landbloom's office and requesting the key.

One day I was attending a council meeting at which the members were debating a proposal brought to them by the BIA. Landbloom was upset that it was taking them so long to come to a decision, so he walked up to the lectern, angrily pounded his fist until there was quiet, and then told us we were acting like a bunch of kids. If we continued to act that way, he would throw every one of us out, put a padlock on the council chamber, and not let us back in until we learned to behave like adults.

I was flabbergasted, not only by what he had done and said but also that the council had deferred to him. They were like a group of rowdy second-graders who had been scolded by their teacher. And these were council delegates, including Annie Wauneka, who had been there for years.

Clearly they felt subservient to the BIA. Perhaps that was how they grew up, and they were now unable to talk back. They could complain, but when the BIA strongly insisted on something, they simply went along. Yet they were independent of the BIA. They were independent of the white agency superintendent. They were independent of the white lawyer who was hired to be the tribal counsel. They had simply chosen to give up their power.

No wonder we have problems, I thought to myself. No wonder we have poverty. No wonder we can't move forward.

I came in with an attitude based on my experience and my knowledge of tribal history. The government was not God. Government employees, especially the BIA, were not God. Lawyers were not God. There were good lawyers and bad lawyers. But no one was better than we were, and some were much worse.

It was 1971 before I could reverse our relationship with the BIA officials. I had just been elected tribal chairman. I went to see the BIA area director and demanded the keys to the council chambers, explaining that no meetings would be held until I was in full control of Navajo property. Naturally, I then changed all the locks.

When I opened the first council session in the chambers, the BIA staff entered the room in force. I looked at the area director and said, "These are the Navajo Nation council chambers. What we do here is sacred because here assembled are the elected officials of the Navajo people. And the Navajo people's vote means something. It is sacred to us. It means sovereignty. So I don't want any disrespect whatever here."

Then I related the story of what had occurred those several years earlier when the agency superintendent pounded on the lectern. I said, "I want to address this to you BIA folks and everyone in this room. The first time any BIA folks come up here to the lectern or jump up without getting the floor properly, and start acting up, I'm going to chase every one of you out of these council chambers. And I'm not going to let you back in until you learn to behave like adults."

After that, they moved out. They hired a Navajo man, called him a tribal relations officer, and let him report back to them what was happening. He took notes at every meeting. They never returned themselves.

But that personal triumph was still several years away. Now I was just beginning to understand our problems, and I was constantly discovering how much we had lost by not standing up for what was ours by right of treaties dating back almost a century.

Next I noticed the influence of the general counsel, the Washington, D.C.–based lawyer hired by the Tribal Council to act as an adviser. The lawyer seemed dedicated to the old guard, who held him in great respect. He was an Anglo, because almost no Navajo had law degrees at that time. The nearest Navajo lawyer was Tom Dodge, whose practice was in Scottsdale, Arizona, a suburb of Phoenix. He had no interest in living on the reservation. The Tribal Council had settled on a man who had experience with Congress and was willing to make periodic trips to Window Rock.

After a few dealings with the lawyer the council had hired, I decided to commission a study of the tribal organization to see how it could be restructured to provide the most cost-effective services for the people. I knew of an excellent group of business consultants at Stanford University and arranged to hire them. However, when the consulting contract was prepared, I wanted to make certain that the Navajo were protected against any problems, making sure the terms provided for legal recourse if the contract was not fulfilled properly. It was a simple matter, and I felt comfortable deferring to the lawyer's expertise in reading contracts.

The lawyer looked at me and said, "Young man, you're new here. My suggestion is that you check with me and with the advisory committee of the Tribal Council, and don't do things on your own. You're not familiar with the reservation."

I told the lawyer. "I was hired by the chairman of the Navajo Nation. You're working for the chairman as general counsel. You're a lawyer and I'm an engineer. I'm director of management, methods, and procedures. I'm responsible for that. All I'm coming to you for is this contract with Stanford Research Institute to help me put this study together. All I'm asking is that you check the terms of the contract to see that I'm not giving the reservation away, and I want you to see that we have legal recourse if they don't do the job. That's all I'm asking you.

"I'm not asking you for a judgment call as to whether these guys are competent or not competent, or whether I should go to the advisory committee or anybody else. This is my responsibility. I'm just coming to you for legal advice, and that's all I want from you and nothing else.

"But you're trying to tell me that I should find another company, not Stanford Research Institute. I'm not going to do that because if the job is not done correctly, I'm to blame. I feel I'm responsible." I told him that I was not the type to let someone else make a decision for me so that I could blame him if everything failed. I believed in making the decision myself, then living or dying with that decision. I didn't put responsibility off on someone else when I was at Hughes, and I wasn't going to do it on the reservation.

Yet despite that, the Anglo lawyer continued to chew me out. He explained for the third time that I was new to the reservation and didn't know the Navajo very well. And he said once again that I was to check with him and the advisory committee before making any decisions.

Again, his arrogance amazed me. He was an Anglo who shared no cultural background with the people who hired him, and yet he was telling me, a Navajo who was raised as a sheepherder, that I did not know the Navajo people. That was the last time I bothered to ask for his help with anything.

The general counsel served two valid purposes. The first was to regularly press land claims as our old treaties were challenged. This was an extremely complex job because there was a desire by some U.S. government legislators to further reduce the Navajo land holdings.

Sadly, neither the counsel nor most of the Navajo whose land he was protecting fully understood the importance of that job. The ideal would have been to have someone as counsel who remembered the stories of leaving Fort Sumner, who knew how the herds of sheep and cattle were slowly rebuilt following the Long Walk.

Working without a general counsel, the Navajo had gradually increased their grazing land beyond the 3 million acres officially set aside for them. Then they would go to the president and prove that the livestock needed more land than had been authorized, and there would be an expansion by executive order. By the time the land had been expanded almost sixfold over the treaty of 1868, the livestock had come to have great significance. They were used for food and clothing and in sacred ceremonies. The animals were also viewed as the special protectors of the Navajo heritage, since they helped us regain some of our lost territory and sacred land. Thus the livestock, the land, and the fight to retain what had been so difficult to regain were both legal matters and a sacred trust. The lawyer did not have to understand all this to be effective, but it would have been best if he had.

The other concern of the general counsel was the handling of contracts from companies that wanted to exploit our resources. The Navajo reservation was mineral-rich, and companies regularly sought to obtain rights for mining and other procedures. In addition, the effort to create jobs had led the tribe into tentative lease arrangements with such companies as General Dynamics and Fairchild Corporation. These businesses were thinking of establishing plants, assembly operations, and similar ventures, and a lawyer was needed to make certain that the deals were fair for both parties.

The problem, as I've said before, was that the lawyer lacked any knowledge of Navajo culture and tradition. He was skilled in Anglo law, knew how the state and federal governments operated, and understood the business decisions that had to be made. But he had no awareness of the old Navajo court system or the way my people historically handled difficulties and disputes. And when the council delegates began accepting his advice on matters other than legal concerns, it seemed as though he was wielding enormous power over the lives of the people on the reservation.

Oddly, the most logical solution to the problem with the general counsel proved ultimately to be of no greater value than using white attorneys. Our reforms included working to get Navajo young people to go to college, then take the training needed to be lawyers who could serve the reservation's needs. However, almost thirty years later we have found that this was not as effective as we anticipated.

The teenagers who did go to college and law school were the children of the veterans of World War II. Their disillusioned parents told them to become as much like white people as they could. They did not have a sense of the Navajo culture. They were not fluent in the Navajo language. They did not have the understanding of their history that would have enabled them to communicate the unique needs of a sovereign Navajo Nation in a white man's court. We found that most of them were only as skilled as the Anglo lawyers—and almost as unaware of the uniqueness of their own people—the Diné—as the Anglos.

Fortunately, as I write this there seems to be a growing belief that there is something special about being a Navajo, a uniqueness that should not be lost. While these men and women may not know what that means, many of them are now studying their own culture in an attempt to regain their roots, and this may lead to better legal representation. Unfortunately, there is no way to predict whether they will seek a full understanding of history and tradition or simply wear long hair and headbands along with their three-piece suits. Their appearance may identify them as Navajo, but their hearts may not be rooted in our past.

We have got to remember that our skin will never be white. Our eyes will never be blue. Education is good for the Navajo. We need to know science and law, engineering, aerospace technology, and other subjects of the world at large. But so long as we're not white, blue-eyed blonds, we are going to face discrimination. Only among our own kind will we be able to prosper without prejudice, and that is why we must work to bring the Navajo Nation into competition with the developed world without losing our land, our language, our culture, and our history.

There is no question that our ways have long been morally superior to any world filled with greed for the latest "things." Our people did not need to buy more expensive cars, live in larger homes, own higher-priced jewelry, commit adultery in search of a more attractive partner, or otherwise work against the harmony of the Great Spirit. In fact, 10,000 years ago it is quite possible that Anglos lived as we did before the forced changes brought to the Navajo by the white men beginning a century-and-a-half ago. Their people changed. We cannot make the mistake of thinking that their changes were for the better.

Traditionally we have been people willing to change as well. When the Spaniards arrived, the Navajo studied them closely. They adopted the horses, the sheep, and the cattle they learned about from the Spaniards. But they did not adopt the methods of forced domination, of abuse in the effort to force religious conversion, and the other negatives they saw. They observed, selected what was good, and refused to involve themselves with that which was not in harmony with the Great Spirit. It is a tradition worth maintaining.

As I observed these problems, I weighed many options, including one that is quite popular today. This is the idea that a modern Navajo should take the best of both worlds—the world of the old people and the world of the Anglo.

But the more I thought about that option, the more problems I saw with it. Which aspects of the culture should be preserved, taught, and understood by all Navajo children and adults? Many people said the language should be preserved. Others thought the ceremonies and religion of the Navajo were of primary importance. Still others felt that the handicrafts, such as weaving and silversmithing, should be saved. And there were those who wanted cultural events, such as the Squaw Dance, to be continued. The debate was beginning then and continues to this day.

I looked at the suggestions and found that most of them were valid, and most made sense. I also realized that certain conditions would exist no matter what we tried to do. Our children would continue to lose our language. They would also continue to be extensively exposed to the world of the non-Navajo. This, in turn, would result in a loss of belief in the Navajo religion and ceremonies.

Navajo young people would likely stop believing that Mother Earth is sacred. They would stop believing in the ceremonies that reinforce the idea that we are a people endowed and blessed in a special way.

There was no reason the Navajo language couldn't be expanded like every other language. There was a written version, which could be used in our schools, enabling us to add words appropriate for teaching medicine, biology, chemistry, physics, and other disciplines in the Navajo tongue.

Almost all other languages of the world are living languages. Terms such as "bit," "byte," "floppy disk," "interface," which are a part of the vocabulary of children learning about computers, did not exist in the English language a few years ago. They were coined to denote new ideas and products, something the Navajo could also do. Then the Navajo would be no different from the Mexicans, French, Italians, and people from other countries, mastering the new, then interrelating with the Anglos and others through bilingual education and translators. Our young people would be a part of the space age without having to learn a new language.

I also felt it was important for the Navajo children to be given an education in our history from the perspective of the Navajo. History is always taught from the viewpoint of the conqueror. It also reflects the bias of the people reading it. That's why textbooks written before, during, and after World War II had very different attitudes toward Germany, Japan, and Russia. Likewise, the textbooks written today will reflect a bias different from that of thirty and forty years ago.

In a free country like the United States, it is possible to learn about all people if you search long and hard enough. The contributions of many races and ethnic groups can be discovered with a little digging. But schools tend to teach history from the viewpoint of the white European settlers whose ancestors came to dominate American politics. Slavery and the Civil War might be discussed, but it is difficult for a black child to learn that a black doctor created open-heart surgery, one of the most important advances in medicine, or that a black pilot of the X-15 experimental rocket plane was the first pioneer astronaut to be killed in America's space program.

My state, Arizona, had concentration camps for West Coast Japanese-Americans, some of whom had been citizens for many generations, because of the fear that they would join with our enemies in World War II. Yet the truth was that there were more problems from the Germans in the United States, including the landing of a German submarine on America's East Coast. But the Germans were white and did not hold land that was critical to industrial development. Thus the truth about loyal Japanese families, whose sons often were heroic fighters during World War II and who sometimes lost their homes so that their land could be used to build aircraft factories, was buried until recent times.

Throughout history, certain truths have been avoided. Most people were not comfortable with the fact that men like George Washington, Thomas Jefferson, and Ben Franklin were rebellious radicals with no respect for the authority of the British. Their antiestablishment ways were played down in history books, all their actions considered heroic simply because they won the war.

This one-sided telling is normal, and there was no reason our children should not learn the Navajo perspective of history, even if it was taught alongside traditional Anglo courses. The information had to be given to our children in schools because parents and grandparents were no longer providing it at home.

I now believe that before Navajo children can pick the best of both worlds they must first accept the Navajo world. From there they can reach out and select the best of the outside Anglo world.

Our children have to learn to be totally Navajo, accepting both the good and the bad in our culture. They should then supplement our ways with the best aspects of the outside world. Not only will they have a firm grounding in their culture and history, they will also avoid a common mistake. Too often people discard an essential aspect of their heritage because, at the time they learn about it, they do not understand how it fits into their existence. They end up rejecting something valuable.

The debate on what should be preserved continues. Yet while we debate, our children are growing up, losing time and opportunities our children should have to gain the knowledge and wisdom for which they hunger.

By the end of that first year on the reservation, I was no longer motivated by a desire to help the Nakai administration in order to help my family. I now realized that there were fundamental problems that had to be addressed, and I felt that I could provide substantive assistance. Having completed the Polaris missile project before I left Hughes, and having fulfilled one level of responsibility, I could entertain the idea of returning to Hughes without committing myself to at least a five- to ten-year stay.

I was not yet involved in politics, even though I worked for the tribal chairman. But I was comfortable in the world of political maneuvering.

I had heard about politics over the years, though this was the first time I had actually participated in the tribal government. In fact, I voted in a tribal election for the first time in 1962, and I voted for one of Nakai's opponents, a man with a master's degree in education. I thought he would better understand both the Navajo and the white world. It was only years later that I realized there was more to a man than his schooling. I had met uneducated people with great wisdom and others who were educated fools.

There were six hundred employees of the Navajo Nation in the early 1960s, compared with approximately five thousand on the payroll today. From the viewpoint of a corporate administrator concerned with the bottom line, government employees seldom generate income. It is hard to hold them accountable for their actions because it can be difficult to define the value of their work. Yet if you look upon the bureaucracy as the key to handling the necessary social services, providing for the needs of the elderly, the disabled, and others in trouble, then you are always understaffed. Either way, in those early days we were a small organization in the process of development.

At first we worked on restructuring the tribal government, developing job descriptions so that we could evaluate the work of every employee. Then we analyzed how best to handle the two quite different aspects of the bureaucracy. One involved the cost-effective distribution of money in a manner that would do the most good for the most people. The other involved business management—oil and gas leases, farming and ranching, sawmills, the operation of electric utilities, and similar tribal enterprises.

The two were quite different. This meant that many of the people in charge had to have dual responsibilities. Others had to be limited because of their expertise. I became director, ultimately responsible for the equivalent of a conglomerate, a combination service enterprise and profit-producing business concern.

There was extensive hostility during the transition we were creating. Tribal business enterprises had existed before I joined the government. Some were run quite effectively. Others became too labor-intensive. Whoever was in charge did not want to offend anyone. If five good workers were needed and the first workers hired were ineffective, they would be kept on and more would be added. It was not unusual to have a three-to-one ratio of ineffective employees to good workers, all of whom were getting the same pay.

We started to clamp down on the enterprises run by the tribe in the same way I had done at Hughes. A worker who failed to do a satisfactory job was fired. And if tribal funds were being used to supplement a business that was not making an effort to make a profit, we cut off money to that business.

Back in the late 1950s and early 1960s, the BIA decided to pursue economic development work for the tribe and encouraged the tribe to start and run businesses. They opened a restaurant and motel in Window Rock called Window Rock Lodge.

The BIA helped manage the facility, but their bureaucratic logic eventually ran it into the ground. The number of employees far exceeded the needs of the business, and there was no overall business plan or method of weighing expenses against costs.

The BIA officials were upset when the Tribal Council arranged for the motel to be closed. Ultimately we built the Window Rock Motor Inn and then leased it to professional motel managers who staffed and ran it properly.

Years later, during my administration as Navajo chairman, this type of decision making got me in trouble. The Navajo Nation underwrote the budget for a newspaper, the *Navajo Times*. Several other newspapers covered the Navajo Nation because their readership was concerned with the land. The *Flagstaff Times*, the *Flagstaff Daily Sun*, the *NavaHopi Journal*, the *Arizona Republic*, and other newspapers in New Mexico, Utah, and elsewhere all had reporters who covered important Indian affairs. But the *Navajo Times* was to be the journal of record of the Navajo people, reporting only news of concern to the Navajo, whether social, political, or national.

Like any newspaper, the *Navajo Times* was expected to sell ads, find cost-effective ways to print, keep employment to a minimum, and perform other profit-oriented actions. In the 1960s, its circulation potential was double that of the profit-making Flagstaff daily newspaper. The Navajo, though frequently poor, were still heavy consumers of food, clothing, trucks, and other merchandise sold on and off the reservation. Plenty of businesses were eager for a chance to advertise to this market, and an analysis of the newspaper as a business indicated that it, like other papers, should be profitable. Yet the paper consistently lost money.

The trouble began when I applied to the *Navajo Times* the same standards I had used during the Nakai administration. I felt, as a businessman, that the paper was overstaffed. There should not have been a need for tribal government underwriting when advertising potential, circulation, and effective management could have made the paper profitable. So I cut off the funding, essentially shutting down the paper because it could not support itself even though the potential was there.

I was attacked for my action, of course. The newspaper, which had been only one of several independent sources of news and information on the reservation, suddenly became a symbol of freedom of the press. Because the paper's editorial policy had not always supported my administration, I was accused of checkbook censorship, shutting down something that would not print my viewpoint. Yet the truth was that I was just upholding the standards we had established during the early years of the Nakai administration. We could not let poor business management cost the Navajo people income and make us look incompetent in the eyes of outsiders whom we might ultimately desire as business partners.

The *Navajo Times*, like most papers, had a bias based on how it was funded. The paper was being run as a tribal government organ, which meant that the tribal chairman could do whatever he wanted with it. I wanted it to either pay for itself or go independent of tribal government funding, making its money on advertising and newsstand sales like every other daily and weekly newspaper. Instead, the staff forgot that a paper was a business, letting editors and reporters handle the financial side instead of just the news gathering and creative side. My feeling was that they had to get business executives to handle the business side, reporters for the other, and the tribal government could not continue to underwrite their incompetence.

After that first year of turning the Navajo Nation's enterprises into true businesses and establishing controls, such as cost accounting procedures and job descriptions, the U.S. government developed a series of antipoverty programs administered by Sargent Shriver. The

Navajo appeared to be eligible for the program, and since I was accustomed to working with the federal government from my days at Hughes, I made contact with Shriver to learn now we could participate. I did not realize it, but that was my first move into what would eventually become a violent confrontation with representatives of the U.S. government.

Some members of the Bureau of Indian Affairs protested the idea that the Navajo Nation might be given money to administer on its own. They explained that Indians could not handle large sums of money. We did not understand business. We would either misuse the money, steal it, or be tricked out of it. Giving us money would result in disaster.

Sargent Shriver listened to their arguments, then told me to prepare a proposal explaining why we needed the money and what we would do with it. He wanted to see if we could put together a satisfactory business plan, a task that the BIA officials felt would be impossible for us.

We put the plan together, and Shriver approved it. Again the BIA objected, this time asserting that, though we were capable of writing such a plan, we obviously could not carry it out. But Shriver thought differently. He arranged for the funding of a number of programs, some of which, such as a Head Start educational program, are still in operation today.

Several BIA officials were livid, a fact that caused me to take a close look at the men and women in that organization. What I found showed me the reason for many of our problems.

The BIA has long been composed of several types of individuals. The best BIA employees are those who feel that they should be working themselves out of a job. They understand that the idea of primarily white people administering an Indian nation is paternalism at its worst. The paternalistic whites, on the other hand, believe that Indians are incompetent and will always be incompetent, that they are incapable of administering their own affairs and incapable of being trained to administer those affairs. Only outsiders can keep them alive.

The good employees—and they are few—recognize that there is nothing inherently inferior about the Navajo or the other Indian tribes. These people are willing to help us achieve self-sufficiency while preserving our culture. They have no preconceived notions about what might be "best" for our well-being. They simply want the assistance programs available to enable us to find our own way. We are to determine our own destiny, and they are to provide a decreasing level of support until we have no further need of their help.

The second group of BIA employees are the paternalists, the do-gooders. Many of these men and women see Indians as quaint people whose culture should be preserved. They like the idea that we make pottery, weave baskets, craft jewelry, and sell our handiworks by the side of the road. They would likely argue against our having indoor plumbing because it works against the rustic simplicity of our people. The do-gooders are naive and a little foolish, though sometimes, with a little maturity, they can become much like the best of the BIA employees.

A third type of BIA employee, far more numerous than the first two, are the true bureaucrats. This is a job requiring little effort. There are handbooks of rules and regulations applicable to all situations that might arise. These employees simply take in money as authorized, disperse it as authorized, and mediate disputes, all according to the book. Innovative projects are shot down because they have not been done before. These employees may or may not be bigots who think Indians are inferior, but they always insist that everyone play by their rules, no matter how archaic or unrealistic.

In addition, the BIA includes a small number of power-hungry incompetents. These are men and women who started their careers in the most menial jobs, then gradually earned more and more influence through promotions. Each new job brought them greater authority over others, giving them a sense of power they regularly abused. Then, after fifteen or twenty years on the job, they reached a level where they could approve or disapprove actions by the Indian tribes they were supposed to be serving. Now they wielded their power in ways that were meant to keep us submissive. This was only a continuation of the way they had behaved their entire career, but instead of hurting the BIA underlings, they were now adversely affecting the lives of thousands of Navajo men, women, and children.

During one of the tribal leaders' annual trips to Washington to appear before the congressional appropriations committees, one of the congressmen complained that year after year for the last century the Indians have been seeking money for their tribes' needs for additional funds. Just what, he asked, was the BIA doing with the money that was appropriated?

The answer the congressman was given was that when General Custer was leaving the fort to do battle at Little Bighorn, he stopped by the BIA office and told the men there, "Don't you guys do anything until I get back." The BIA hasn't done anything because they're still waiting for Custer to come back.

Clearly, the BIA has not been concerned with timeliness. But the nation is underdeveloped, poor, and in need of immediate help. The BIA's inaction is one of the big stumbling blocks to Native American progress.

For example, in 1988 I convinced General Dynamics to build three plants on the Navajo Nation, each to employ 250 people. When the first plant was being built, we had a well-trained Navajo archaeologist check the land before it was cleared, something we both believe in and are required to do. He was a man as well educated as anyone working for the BIA, but he understood the urgency of the work. He went out immediately, spent long hours analyzing the impact of the construction on all aspects of the archaeology, then gave a report confirming that there was no problem with clearance. This we did.

The BIA Area Director became irate. He sent me a letter telling me that he was going to disallow the General Dynamics construction because the BIA's archaeologist, neither better trained nor more experienced than ours, had not checked the land. I thought this was a simple misunderstanding, yet when I explained that we had handled the task, I was informed that the BIA was going to shut down the site. They were going to send their police to halt the workers. They were going to refuse the authorization of training money previously allocated to educate the potential workers for the jobs to be filled.

Eventually we sat down together. I learned that there was nothing wrong with the work our archaeologist had done. There was nothing wrong with the construction of the plant, the work to be done, or the hiring procedures that led up to it. What mattered was that we did not do things the BIA way, and while the work was going to be completed months ahead of what the BIA could have scheduled, that was not good enough.

Finally Wilson Barber, speaking for the BIA, met with the Tribal Council. When pressured on the problem, he admitted that the BIA was not in charge and the tribal chairman was not in charge. Only the Tribal Council, which at my suggestion immediately passed a resolution approving what had been done, was in charge. He saved a little face. Everything went well. But because of what the BIA had pulled, General Dynamics refused to build the two other plants. They were satisfied with the quality of work at the first one, and it proved competitive for their needs. They did not want to fight with the BIA to finish a task that could be handled anywhere else in the world without BIA stupidity.

I could find no way to reason with most of the BIA employees. All bureaucracies harbor automatons who hide behind rule books and parrot policies without sensitivity or creativity. But the BIA seemed worse than most, perhaps because it so directly affected my people.

I knew I could not turn away from the conflict with the BIA and others who were hurting the Navajo. In theory, I could easily turn my back on the politics and social confusion. I had the skills and the reputation to return to the outside world and make an unusually good income, but that would have meant abandoning the people in whom I believed, turning my back on my family and my nation. I also realized that I had unique skills among my people, having been both an engineer and a businessman in charge of several hundred million dollars in product essential for the nation's success. Not only was I driven to begin to fight, I also had the background in both worlds that would make me uniquely qualified to challenge the system.

Having made the decision to stay on the reservation, I turned my thoughts back to the earliest teachings of my people as I sought the strength to fight the new enemies of the Navajo—the BIA and hostile government leaders.

As I thought about what I was facing, I remembered how, from the Navajo perspective, the world was created. There were all types of monsters and enemies of the Navajo throughout the new land. The gods of the Navajo gave birth to twins—the monster slayer and the child of water. These twins were crafty fighters of the enemies who endangered the Navajo. They did not make direct attacks where they might be defeated. Instead, they studied the monsters and other enemies. They analyzed their strengths and weaknesses, then proceeded to attack only their weakness. With such an approach, it did not matter how big, how strong, or how ferocious the monster might be. The twins always triumphed, slaughtering their enemies through the exploitation of their weaknesses.

Navajo history and legend are full of stories of battles against both men and monsters, all of them teaching the same lesson: Stop, analyze, find the weakness, and attack at that point. Do not confront overwhelming force, because you cannot win. Just locate where that force is vulnerable, for there is always a susceptible point, and use your strength to attack there.

I decided to adopt the attitude that I was always going to be in a state of war. No matter how great my enemy, I would always step back and analyze what I was facing, fearing nothing yet respecting both the strengths and weaknesses I encountered. My guide would not be some successful general's autobiography. It would be the history and legends of the Navajo people, from the stories of the monster slayers to the wars that led to the Long Walk. All of these taught that nothing was impossible for the Navajo who understood the lessons of the past.

I also discovered another aspect of my character at that time, one that would soon lead me into politics and the battle for leadership of the Navajo Nation. I realized that I did not care what happened to me if I believed I was right. To this day, occasionally someone will threaten to charge me with a crime if I do not agree to actions I feel are wrong. There have been attempts on my life. I have been told I might lose my job or become party to lawsuits that would cost me everything

I own and everything I might ever own. Yet the truth is that I don't care. I am ready to die, to sit in jail, or to face financial ruin for what I believe.

This attitude came from the training I received as a youth, which taught me never to be intimidated, never to compromise my principles.

Perhaps my attitude also stems from the anger I felt at seeing the hopelessness that overwhelmed so many of the Navajo people during the livestock reduction. I have seen people beaten into the ground because of the greed, bigotry, or stupidity of others. And I have seen people endure with nothing, then gradually rebuild their lives and those of their families.

All I know is that I can live with myself only if I fight to my last dying breath. It was in 1964, following the confrontation with the BIA over the issue of being allowed to administer funds for antipoverty programs, that I knew I would be a warrior, sometimes in velveteen shirt and turquoise necklace, sometimes in a three-piece suit. I did not understand the journey I would soon be taking. I did not know the consequences. Yet I did not care. I had made a transition in life, which I still do not regret.

CHAPTER EIGHT

Once I made the commitment to work for my people, I felt myself change in a way that shocked me. When I first started working at Hughes, I resented the payroll deduction for Social Security. I registered to vote as a Republican and was extremely conservative in my viewpoint. I felt that all welfare was wrong. If someone was too lazy or too dumb to find a way to support himself, then he should not be supported by society at large.

I applied the same thinking to old age. My friends used to argue with me that the elderly needed help surviving since they were likely to be sick or infirm and unable to work. But I said that if I did not have the sense to prepare for my old age, then I should be allowed to die. People had to face the consequences of their actions, no matter what that might mean.

After I returned to the Navajo reservation, however, I realized the need for financial assistance for the unemployed. I was aware how important it was to take care of the elderly. I supported food programs for people who were starving or undernourished. And when I reflected on my change of attitude, I saw the reasons for it.

I still believed that welfare was wrong for people who, by their own actions, had caused themselves to be in great financial trouble. But the Navajo had been systematically denied the opportunity to help themselves.

My people had changed over the centuries. The Navajo had taken advantage of the sheep, horses, and cattle introduced by the Spaniards around the sixteenth century. They went from being an agricultural people to a life-style that combined livestock with farming. They nurtured the animals, increasing their herds until thousands of animals provided great wealth for the Diné.

The herds were slaughtered by Carson and his men as they tried to destroy our people and our culture. By the time the Navajo left Fort Sumner, few animals were left. However, over the next few decades, the herds were restored to the numbers that had sustained the Diné from the time the Spanish introduced them to us.

The suffering was repeated with the livestock reduction of 1934, which eliminated the bulk of food and wealth for most of the people. The failure to educate the people for jobs and to show them how and where to find work had prevented them from earning money in new ways. More important was the federal government's failure to establish a new economic base on the reservation to replace the livestock economy. They had been tied hand and foot by regulations that were not of their making, and these same regulations now prevented them from creating a new system that might restore the economy. Just as we needed to fight, we also needed to help the victims among the Navajo people to rebuild their lives enough to reach a position where they could again determine their own destiny.

Ironically, despite the suffering, had the American government followed the 1868 treaty, we would be self-sufficient today instead of being forced to be a puppet of the BIA. Educational requirements under the treaty assured one teacher for every thirty students, a far better ratio than we have today. Food and housing were assured until we could survive on our own, something we had achieved before the forced livestock reduction. In exchange, the Navajo agreed to lay down their arms, not bother white settlers as they moved across the land to new homes in the West, and not attack the railroad builders whose track was linking the nation. Essentially we were assured of being a sovereign people, and we agreed to give the white men safe passage across our land. It was only when the white men began coveting our land for their homes and our minerals to fuel their increasingly industrialized society that they decided again to destroy us, breaking the treaty that the Navajo always honored.

Like my ancestors, I took that treaty seriously. I realized that the U.S. government had not met its obligations as stated in that document. Even worse, it continued to violate the Indian lands, the water rights, and mineral resources and to damage the existing educational system.

My people needed massive assistance. They weren't poor and unemployed because they were lazy or unable to fend for themselves. They were more like political prisoners or the Hebrews in Egypt at the time of Moses. They were in confinement, in need of an Exodus to the Promised Land. I felt justified in going to Washington and pointing out that the government had yet to meet its obligations as agreed in 1868. Even worse, the government's policies had nearly broken the back of the Navajo. The money I was seeking rightly belonged to the Navajo. It was not an additional welfare program, it was simply the fulfillment of the treaty obligation that had for too long been ignored.

I was not just seeking money, though. An equal need was to have the flexibility to do whatever was necessary with that money, not be locked into programs created or administered by Anglo bureaucrats or the BIA.

What we needed were new programs that were outside the control of politics and the BIA. Over the years the BIA kept going to Congress, requesting and usually getting more money for new programs created by them to make us self-sufficient. But self-sufficiency was always against the best interests of the BIA. They wanted our hands and feet tied with rules, restrictions, and all the red tape that assured the continuation of their bureaucracy.

We recognized the problem and tried to show that it made no sense for the BIA to give an Indian tribe the money needed for a program, then retain its current staff and add additional personnel as overseers, to be paid from the grant that should have gone to the Navajo. If we needed a million dollars for a program, a million dollars would be authorized but we would have to return most of the money in the form of payment for the supervisors. Then we would fail and everyone would say we were incompetent.

The Bureau of Indian Affairs controls more than five thousand jobs in the Navajo Nation alone. There is no way that they are going to voluntarily allow programs that will reduce employment in any meaningful way. That means that before the Navajo can do anything (and the same problem exists for the other tribes, where there may be as many as one BIA employee for every three Indians), most of the money has to be spent on the bureaucracy.

The more I learned about tribal government, the more I realized that the best help I could provide would be to establish new programs outside the jurisdiction of politicians. No matter what anyone may have felt for my people, there were endless special interest groups made up of non-Navajo politicians and businessmen who either put themselves above others or were fighting to stay in power.

For example, I learned that the impetus for establishing the Tribal Council back in 1921 had come from people at Standard Oil Company. Standard Oil's petroleum engineers discovered that the arid lands on which the Navajo were dumped included extensive oil fields. They worked with the Bureau of Indian Affairs to find five chiefs who would sign oil-drilling leases and to declare these chiefs members of the first Tribal Council. From then on, it was in the interest of outside business groups to make sure that all Tribal Council members were sympathetic to what the oil companies wanted to do. It was also in the oilmen's interest to support council members who could be manipulated into, in effect, working against their own people. Sometimes this manipulation was deliberate, but usually it was an easy result of the council members' ignorance of their alternatives.

The Bureau of Indian Affairs, because of corruption or stupidity, frequently involved the Tribal Council in bad agreements. For example, at a time when the standard royalty paid to owners of land from which coal was mined was at least $1.50 a ton, the BIA-arranged leases called for royalties of between 15.0 cents and 37.5 cents a ton. Even worse, there were no escalator clauses, no chance for renegotiation. In this way, generations of Navajo were systematically robbed of their wealth.

In addition to all the other pressures, I needed to find a way to change such matters. We needed the right to tax the coal companies and others using our land and minerals. We had to fight the BIA agreement that had given them unlimited use of our water without paying us. Ultimately I was able to triumph, but the fight was long and hard, and we were often accused of going back on our word. No one wanted to admit that the Navajo, not the BIA, were the ones who were concerned with the best interests of the Diné and had to stand against improper agreements.

I realized that the best way to help my people was to create within the Navajo Nation an independent organization that would obtain funds specifically for the Navajo people. The money would not go through the BIA. Bureaucratic entanglements would be kept to a minimum so that the money would not be siphoned off for high operating costs but would instead pass directly to the people.

The timing of my return to the reservation was lucky. My desires for change occurred at a time when Lyndon Johnson was developing his War on Poverty programs. Some of that work had started under President Kennedy, but the massive attempts to help low-income citizens were made under President Johnson. For the first time in many years, government officials were establishing self-help programs, not the paternalistic handouts that the Navajo and other Indian tribes had previously experienced.

Sargent Shriver was the first powerful government official to examine the conditions in the Navajo Nation, and he supported my people's efforts at self-determination. Oddly, I was a Republican who, in 1964, had supported Barry Goldwater in his presidential campaign against Lyndon Johnson. Shriver was a Democrat, the brother-in-law of the late president Kennedy, and a man who politically should have been against me. But Shriver had the maturity to journey to the Navajo Nation and spend several days talking with us, seeing our special needs. When he understood what was taking place, he was willing to make all manner of waivers in the various poverty programs so that the money we received went neither to the Tribal Council nor to the BIA.

I created a program called Office of Navajo Economic Opportunity (ONEO) that was independent of the old guard, the new guard, and the BIA. This was an umbrella program under which the Navajo people could do anything they wanted for their own benefit. The

Tribal Council agreed to let me establish this organization, I suspect because they did not realize exactly what I was doing.

This was a major breakthrough for me. The organization was completely independent and yet was approved by the Tribal Council. The council was comfortable with this because, so far as they could see, there was no money involved. They did not realize that the money that would come from Washington, D.C., would ultimately be substantial enough to make a difference in people's lives.

ONEO had two other advantages: The organization was structured so that no one could obtain kickbacks or skim money for personal use. Also, the people would be using the money to help themselves, and they would not feel beholden to one faction or another. The politicians could continue to fight among themselves while the Navajo benefited despite them.

The first proposal I made was for $900,000, enough to fund several initial projects I thought would be beneficial for my people.

I had visited the chapter houses to learn what the Navajo felt they needed. I then translated their ideas into a proposal so that I could represent the people in a way acceptable to Congress. That was the method by which I worked with the people, starting with this first ONEO proposal.

One project was a home improvement program. Navajo would be trained in the construction skills needed to improve their homes and those of others. While they were learning a trade, they would be enhancing the living conditions of the people. The Navajo way was primitive, but poverty had brought living conditions for many to such a bare subsistence level that they were dying much too young. There was also a lack of hope, a sense that life would never get better and that, in fact, it could only get worse. Making home improvements would give people hope, and encourage them to work toward an even better life.

The shared $900,000 meant more than just the dollar figure. For the first time, the people were told something was going to happen and it did. Perhaps it was just a simple, inexpensive home improvement measure, necessary but previously beyond a family's financial means. Their friends and neighbors were given the money and materials they needed, the repairs, additions, and upgrades (such as indoor plumbing) were made, and they could all take pride in their achievements. They recognized that they had value as people. Given a minimum level of support, together they could accomplish anything.

For the first time there was a sense that the Navajo were not hopeless. They might still be hobbled by red tape, but even with one hand free, they were able to help themselves and one another. That brief glimmer of hope helped erase much of the destructive, negative teaching in the BIA schools over the previous century.

The next effort was a physical fitness program. The older Navajo had long been in good health because, having followed the traditional Navajo life-style, they exercised regularly. But the generation born after the Livestock Reduction Act and World War II had been left on their own. Many of them were undernourished. They drank too much, sat around, and were overweight, out of shape, susceptible to health problems that had once been almost unknown on the reservation. A physical fitness program would solve the idleness problem by providing new opportunities for recreation. Until this time, most Navajo population centers lacked even a baseball diamond where the young people could play.

The third program was Head Start, the preschool training that would enable our children to compete in the greater society. This included teaching them basic English-language skills. Although the Navajo children were culturally different, they were just as bright and just as skilled in their own way of life as Anglo children from urban areas. But education was geared for children growing up in cities. We needed to give our children a much better understanding of the world outside the reservation than they were gaining on their own.

Fourth, I wanted to start a Navajo Cultural Center. This would be a source of history, education, and pride for the Navajo people. My plan was to arm men and women with tape recorders and notebooks and send them to even the most remote corners of the reservation to locate and interview the elders. The old people would tell the history, legends, myths, religious beliefs, and prayers of the culture, which they had learned from their parents and grandparents. Songs of joy and songs connected with worship ceremonies would be recorded. The elders would tell all that they knew, had lived, and had heard, preserving our oral history, which people had ignored in recent years.

The recordings, their transcriptions, artifacts, and other aspects of the Navajo culture could then be preserved in a compound on the reservation. The Navajo, Anglos, and people from other Indian tribes could come here to learn the truth about the Diné. The cultural center would preserve and perpetuate the history of the Navajo Nation.

Finally, there was a Community Action Program. This was actually the backbone of what I wanted to do. Every chapter house would establish a committee of local people to decide what they wanted to do to better themselves. They would develop various programs and organize committees to accomplish their goals. Everyone would be involved, from the grandparents to the young children, much as they had worked together in the old days.

The Community Action Program would give the Navajo hope and

enable them to feel in charge of their own destiny. It would also reduce costs because the people would work together, using all the available resources instead of waiting for someone to come in and provide the services.

The idea of sharing was in our tradition and worked well. People used to farm together, sharing the chores and working on everyone's plot of land in order to ensure that each family had a chance to succeed.

When we asked for the $900,000—a small amount of money for all these programs, yet still a substantial grant—the BIA became suspicious. If we could get such a sum, perhaps we could get more, cutting them out of their territory. They interfered once again, explaining that they should be asking for the grant money on our behalf. If the money was approved, it would go through their organization and be dispersed as they saw fit among the programs the government approved.

Sargent Shriver was shrewd enough to realize that the idea of ONEO being forced to work through the BIA was inexcusable. We had a right to determine our future. We had a right to succeed on our own. We also had a right to fail, at which time Shriver's Office of Economic Opportunity could reevaluate its decision. But first we had to be given a chance to show what we could do.

I had planned the ONEO program, had written the proposals, and had obtained the money, so the board of directors asked me if I would run it. This was something I had not expected, yet both my anger against the Anglo ways of the past and my desire to see improvement in the lives of my people led me to agree to act as director. There would be no more Hughes Aircraft, no more corporate life-style, no more working for Raymond Nakai. I would be on my own, responsible only to the people of the Navajo Nation and the leaders of Washington's OEO project. I responded to this new opportunity as I had to the Polaris project, throwing myself wholeheartedly into the work in order to use the skills I had gained in recent years.

During this same period my personal life rapidly changed. My wife had married me when I was a very different man. I was young, of course, and hard working. I had scholarships, jobs, and then a career as an engineer moving into the highest levels of business management.

Certainly as Native Americans we were strangers in a familiar land when I worked for Hughes, yet being Native Americans also gave us the advantage of being different. Sometimes there was bias from both Anglos and Hispanics. At other times there was greater acceptance than was experienced by the more numerous minorities in the area. My wife was finding that the life of an upwardly mobile corporate executive could be very enjoyable, even though my work pressures kept us separated more than either of us liked. There was also some limit to our social life in the community because of our ethnic heritage, though the bias was not intense. And she also seemed to tolerate, perhaps even to enjoy to a degree, my work with the Navajo Club of Los Angeles.

Abandoning the world of Hughes and the pace of Los Angeles in order to move onto the reservation had been a difficult adjustment for both of us, but at first we thought it would be temporary. Our children, Rocky and Linda, were tossed into a radically different environment without having a say in what was happening. Yet they had spent enough time on the reservation so that we hoped the move would seem like an adventure to them, something they could tell their friends about when they returned to California.

I did not think that with the move, nothing would ever be the same again. The sights, the sounds, and the smells of Los Angeles were but a memory. There were no massive highways crammed with cars, no skyscrapers, none of the unique city rhythms that came from the constant blend of languages, blaring radios, and honking horns so familiar in what was then becoming the nation's third-largest city.

In their place were the mountains and the flat lands, agriculture and farm animals, the hunting of wild creatures to supplement a diet often determined by the region's growing seasons. There were places to buy food, clothing, and other goods, of course, but they were either in relative isolation, like the trading posts, or off reservation in communities such as Flagstaff. Mostly there were sights, sounds, and smells that would have been as familiar to a Navajo family living centuries before our births as they were to me. I had come home. My wife had not, nor was she comfortable with the pace that was as soothing for my soul as when I was growing in my mother's womb.

Had she at least been Navajo, she might have put aside her love for a different life-style in order to make what would, for her, have been a sacrifice for her people. But she was a Comanche who had been raised a Christian. It was easier for me, raised to be a medicine man, a witness to many different cultures during the war, and a convert to the Baptist faith, to accept both the old and the new ways which both clashed and coexisted on the reservation.

It was also obvious that I was not going to use the knowledge I had gained as an engineer and management expert in the "normal" business world again. Instead I planned to apply it to my growing concept of the Navajo Nation, an independent nation within the United States. The reservation that had once been a nice place for her and the kids to visit had suddenly become a permanent home that none of them were sure they wanted. To make matters even worse, I was constantly traveling throughout the reservation, talking with people, discussing the programs and possibilities. She was seeing far less of me than in the past, forced to endure conditions she did not enjoy, and lacking in the potential for support from me. Increasingly we became intimate strangers, as alien in our relationship as she was to my land.

The result was a breakdown in our marriage. My wife and I became like two friends who were together only because we shared a house. I loved my kids, yet the nature of my work was such that my wife was doing most of the child-rearing. I was quite separate from their world, as they were separate from mine, no matter what we all wanted in our hearts.

At the same time, I had an assistant, a woman named Wanda LeClere, with whom I was spending an increasing amount of time. She was single, and it was her job to help me implement all the programs with which I was involved. But there was more to her than just someone filling a job in the chairman's office.

Wanda had quite different experiences from my own. She was half Navajo, on her mother's side, with a father who was a mix of Potawatamie and Sioux. Her father was an iron worker, moving the family from city to city as he completed one high-rise construction project and then was hired for another. Her mother worked to teach her the traditional ways and knowledge of the Navajo, but her education was in Catholic parochial schools, where she mastered English. She also experienced the prejudice that comes both from being the only Indian in an Anglo classroom and from constantly being the "new kid on the block," switching schools every few months for the first fifteen years of her life. Fortunately, her parents had met in the BIA schools where prejudice, albeit more subtle, also existed, and they were able to provide her with comfort and emotional stability.

Wanda was totally dedicated to the improvement of the lives of the Navajo people. She worked nights and weekends without complaint. She traveled wherever I needed her to go, and we often worked together on strategies for dealing with the state and federal governments.

I quickly realized that I could have no better assistant. I had lived the traditional Navajo life-style throughout my formative years. The Navajo language was where I was fluent. I had the skills my people had been taught for centuries. Yet I also spoke English, understood business management, science, and engineering.

By contrast, Wanda understood the daily life of the white man's world, English being her primary language. She was steeped in the culture and religion of whites, yet her mother saw to it that she knew Navajo, that she learned the religion, the traditions, and the skills of our people. Her grandfather, a medicine man, was also concerned, adding to her education. When she had an idea for a program that would benefit the Navajo but would have to be funded by others, together we shared an understanding of how this could be achieved. We walked together in all worlds, each of us a master of skills in which the other was deficient. We shared a vision, and when we traveled together on reservation business, we often talked all night, each stimulating the other so, together, we were more effective than either of us had been alone.

Wanda understood the combination of skills necessary to both retain the Navajo history and culture and be part of the modern world. It was Wanda who developed programs that would involve the medicine men and others whose work was no longer familiar to many of the children growing up. She later created the Navajoland Festival of the Arts, which brought together the great artists among our people. Some, such as R. C. Gorman, are avidly collected throughout the world and have become quite rich from their work. Others, such as some of the potters and weavers, have work that is as brilliant as anything produced by the European Old Masters. Yet because of where they live and create their work, only those who live near them were familiar with the quality.

Wanda and others who were well traveled understood their importance, but the Navajo we were trying to reach either lived elsewhere or were off the reservation. Even worse, the BIA schools did not give the students an understanding of the full range of the arts. They taught the children to appreciate the genius behind Picasso, whose work is very much outside the mainstream, or Degas, Rodin, or some other artist. But they did not show the skills needed to create pottery, weavings, Navajo style paintings, and the like, nor how to tell the geniuses among our people. Most art has to be explained to be appreciated, and when the effort was not made for the Navajo artists, their work was dismissed as unimportant.

It was Wanda who found ways to provide the Navajo with appreciation for their unique genius. In fact, it was only following her efforts to broaden the understanding that art book publishers began producing books about some of the Navajo artists in order to introduce them to Americans and Europeans who have begun to respect what is happening in our isolated regions.

Wanda helped me understand that, being a Navajo, I and others had a tendency growing up to underestimate our abilities. The programs she envisioned and helped me develop, along with the programs created through the chapter houses, were meant to show the people that we believed in them. We worked to give the Navajo the self-respect traditionally taken from them in the BIA schools, where they were treated as "primitive." She was a tremendous influence on our success with the antipoverty programs under ONEO.

Yet Wanda never lost sight of the fact that because of the continued violations of the 1868 treaty, the Navajo were a people under continual attack by outsiders seeking our land, water, and minerals. She also knew that we had to contend with those who would take our resources and compete with those in conflicting businesses. It took her until 1987, but she was eventually able to begin a special training program (a Native American prep school) for gifted Navajo children. The education for them would be as good as that of any prep school in the country. They would be prepared for an Ivy League education and leadership in any field they chose to enter. She had the sense of the great leaders who always taught us to have the same knowledge as the people we are fighting. Without such knowledge, it is impossible to stop or master the enemy. The Anglo world would always be ahead of us if we did not understand their world and goals as well as we understand our own.

As a result of what Wanda achieved, we had some Navajo seventh-graders reading with the skills of Anglo tenth-graders within the state of Arizona.

Wanda was constantly by my side, as enthusiastic about my vision as I was. She could think of little other than helping the Navajo regain self-respect as they solved the problems of poverty, the constraints of the BIA, and other difficulties. She was a perfect assistant when I needed her to expedite matters, yet she was also an innovator who spoke her mind so effectively that I frequently learned from her.

Wanda was also physically attractive to me. I don't know if the loneliness and the time away from home would otherwise have led to an affair. I do know that I recognized how close we were emotionally, spiritually, and psychologically.

Eventually Ruby and I divorced and I married Wanda, by whom I ultimately had three daughters: Hope, Faith, and Charity. Ruby remained supportive of my work just as she had done while I was in college. I tried to remain close to Linda and Rocky, but I knew they were angry with me. They felt that I had abandoned them for my work and for Wanda. Not until they were adults could they understand what had taken place, though even now some hard feelings probably remain. However, whatever their feelings might be, I love them and want the best for them, including a good education and an understanding and love for the Navajo way.

Ironically, Linda followed me into the field of engineering. Rocky ultimately became a lawyer. They both gained understanding of their father, and though I have had my problems with Rocky, I am pleased that they achieved professional careers.

Hope, Faith, and Charity suffered most for my career choices. Had I not returned to the reservation, all three would have had an easy future. They are extremely intelligent and gifted young women. Faith's field is business marketing. Hope loves teaching psychology. And Charity is a gifted artist who has studied at the Rhode Island School of Design. Yet none of the girls finished their education, and while all of them are doing so now, they are paying their own way. My finances are in such a shambles that there is no way I will ever be able to help them again.

My daughters also suffered in that they had to lead what were often childhoods filled with great boredom. They journeyed with me to the chapter houses, sitting on the podium or in the front row, listening to English and Navajo spoken for four to eight hours at a time. The meetings held no interest for them, and while they were allowed to use crayons, read, and do other quiet activities in their seats, they did not want to be there. They knew I needed their mother, Wanda, by my side, and that I loved them too much to allow anyone else to care for them while we traveled. But it was difficult for small children, and they developed the patience to know when business had to be conducted, and when we were winding up the meetings, the talk becoming unimportant. At that point they would often take a piece of paper and use a crayon to make a sign reading, "Daddy, stop now!" They would quietly hold it just high enough so I would notice, but no one else would understand what was happening. And usually they were right.

Yet the children, especially Hope, gained an appreciation for what was taking place. They accepted the fact that everyone would watch their behavior, holding them to higher standards than other children. They also accepted the fact that occasionally they would be courted by young men who were interested in them as the chairman's daughters, not because they were intrigued by the individual.

In fact, today, as I complete this book from within a jail cell, Hope is doing everything necessary to try to perpetuate an understanding of what the government is doing. She had told me that she fears the future generation of Navajo leaders will give away their heritage because of what has happened to me. She senses that if you face the destruction of all that you personally value each time you stand up for what is right in society, eventually only mediocre individuals will seek leadership. Some will fail to fight for what is right because they are afraid to speak out. Others will sell out, deciding that personal power is more important than principles affecting the Diné. She knows that I may be the last warrior because I am the last leader to come from the old ways. More than clearing my name, Hope wants to end the problems that may inhibit the chance for future sovereignty and the triumph of true justice.

Despite my personal problems, I was excited by my work on the reservation. I was establishing programs, giving employment to Navajos, developing the procedures necessary to monitor the money coming in, and evaluating the results of the programs.

While the projects were being developed, many Navajo people tested me and my commitment. They were used to being told that they could not do what they wanted to do to try to get ahead.

At every community planning meeting, I encountered critics. These were usually old guard supporters who wanted to see if I was serious about letting them determine their own destinies within the scope of the programs.

For example, one group wanted to make pottery and sell it. Another wanted to make baskets, and a third wanted to weave blankets. These were all traditional Navajo skills that had been almost lost in postwar times. The people who were challenging me told me that they wanted to practice these skills, teach them to their children and grandchildren, and make money from the sale of the items they produced.

"Fine," I told them. "Do it."

Then a challenger would remind me that the law did not specifically allow people to weave and sell baskets or to offer handmade pottery in the marketplace. Such effort would require special approval if they were to receive antipoverty money.

I told them that the law was not written for the Navajo. The law did not know the history of the Navajo, their skills, or their ways. Poverty was more than a lack of money. There was a poverty of the soul that could be more crippling than being without income. If practicing traditional skills made some people happy, then this would counter the poverty of the spirit. The people would also be able to make more money than they had in the past.

This obviously was not the ultimate answer to unemployment and poverty, but for those who wanted to practice such traditional skills, it was a start that would give them hope. Later, when these wishes were conveyed to Sargent Shriver, he authorized the funding.

Shriver recognized, as we all did, that programs for improving housing, early education, and similar matters were more important for the long term than reviving traditional handicrafts. Yet if adding the handicraft programs brought results, that was all that mattered. Each time I went to Washington, he gave us a waiver from the normal funding criteria in order to ensure that our programs would continue.

Within six months to a year after the program started, the sense of hopelessness had changed to a feeling of hope. The Navajo people were ecstatic. They were finally willing to dream, and to work for their dreams. Some project ideas they created were small and immediately practical. Others, such as rerouting the San Juan River to provide irrigation and drinking water, could be achieved only with a lot of time and money. But all of the ideas were possible. None of the critics could persuade us to abandon them.

Equally exciting was the effort to help. There were volunteers within the community who came forward with ways to stretch our budget even further. For example, some said that if we would buy the lumber for an approved project, they would bring their own nails, saws, hammers, and other tools. They would do whatever was necessary to make it all work.

Yet the attacks against us were constant. The BIA had buildings suitable for use as preschools, but they refused to give us the unused space. Their attitude was that if we were going to cut them out of funding, they were going to deny us their support. It did not matter that the only ones who would be hurt were the children. The officials with whom I had to work were being petty, in my estimation, and I had no intention of letting them win.

Instead, we cleared rooms in the chapter houses and established the preschools there. We knew that the BIA had hundreds of chairs in storage, so we asked to use them. Again we were turned down. Finally the men dug up tree stumps, smoothed the surfaces, and made them into stools for the children.

Our teachers were volunteers. Our only requirements were that they be able to read and write English, know the Navajo language, and teach small children. We did not care if they were state-certified teachers. We cared only that they were intelligent, competent, caring, and able to communicate with the very young.

Then some representatives of the Indian Health Service, another Anglo bureaucratic agency, informed us that they were going to close down the preschool food program. They said that our volunteer cooks were not preparing food in ways that met their standards. Our cooks, they said, would have to use special equipment that we couldn't afford and that our grant wouldn't pay for.

Again we fought back. I informed them that the cooks were volunteers from among the mothers of the children. These were the same women who fed the children at home before they went to the preschool and who would be feeding them at night when they returned. Their standards were no different in the schools than they were at home. If the children were healthy going to school, they would be healthy eating at the schools.

I explained that my volunteers would be happy to wear rubber gloves, cook with special utensils, and do whatever else these people thought was important—provided the Indian Health Service supplied them at their expense. If that was not good enough, then we would go to the media. We would say that the Indian Health Service did not want the Navajo feeding their poor, hungry children. The publicity would be devastating for every bureaucrat involved.

Suddenly our program was acceptable.

Another ONEO program was the Home Improvement and Training Program, which combined classroom instruction on carpentry, painting, electrical work, and other home construction skills with practical field work. The students would spend each morning in the classroom and each afternoon at the homes of elderly Navajo, doing whatever work was necessary within the scope of what they had learned.

The students used whatever materials they could find among their families and others. And although they had to use whatever was available, it didn't matter. Someone got a home who needed one, and the workers gained training. It was a self-help program that, more than providing experience, created a feeling of being needed. The people, who were in desperate need of help, came out with tears in their eyes, put their arms around the students, and said, "My sons, my sons. Thank you, thank you."

The gratitude the students received was worth more than any money they might have been paid. There was a lot of celebration, even when just a roof was repaired or a floor put in an old house. Sheep would be butchered, and meals served to the community. The communal experience recalled the old days. It was good to see it coming through again.

The housing program grew rapidly. Soon we had crews in every section of the reservation. They were not only rehabilitating existing homes, they were building new ones. The crews often worked six days a week, earning little more than a stipend during the six-month training program. They did not care, though, because they had earned nothing before and now were becoming proficient in the building trades.

Once the men had developed their construction skills, they went on their own. A few began working off the reservation, but most stayed on our land, combining cash payment and barter to support their families as they built or remodeled homes for their neighbors. As each area crew comprised ten Navajo who studied and worked for six months, it followed that large numbers of our young people were becoming self-sufficient in trades that were marketable anywhere in the United States.

I have never held a more challenging position than the executive directorship of ONEO. The source of our financing was independent of politics. The federal government's rules, which worked for urban America and, to a degree, for rural white America, were unrealistic for the Navajo. They were constantly waived for my people, but we did not deviate from the high standards of the program. Sargent Shriver demanded results. But as we proved ourselves a success in all that we tried, our grants increased. After starting from that first year's grant of $900,000.00, ONEO was working with $12 million per year by 1970.

Our success generated fear in both the old guard and the new guard. There were funds available to the tribe quite apart from those for ONEO. Those funds were administered through the tribal council. And there were BIA projects with their own funding. The problem was that none of the other projects worked very effectively. The ONEO program, by contrast, was succeeding.

Suddenly I was a threat to the various political leaders. Some feared a loss of control, others wanted a piece of the financial action, and still others feared change. Where once the BIA had offered secure positions, now those very jobs were in jeopardy. It was like a welfare office. Once people have the sense of self-worth to demand control of their destiny, and once they are given the tools to achieve that destiny, they no longer need organizations like the welfare office or the BIA. This means that either the government employees have to work themselves out of their jobs, or they have to prevent self-determination.

At the time, I did not understand why the hostility existed, since all of us were supposedly concerned with the future of the Navajo Nation. I also did not see the need to keep fighting. I had established an organization that could continue functioning no matter who was in power, an organization that was improving the lives of the Navajo.

I felt that part of my job was to locate new programs whose potential had not been used on the reservation. For example, we learned that in addition to conventional housing loans, which most of the Navajo could not afford, there was a program called Mutual Help. Under this program the Navajo who had been trained in carpentry, electrical work, painting, and other construction skills would be able to apply sweat equity to the purchase of a new house.

The Navajo Nation was filled with low-income substandard housing because few of my people could afford a down payment on a new home. However, under Mutual Help, the Navajo could use their building trade skills to construct a new home. Their labor—the sweat equity—would be used in place of a down payment. Then they would be charged a monthly mortgage fee based on their ability to pay. The mortgage would last as long as it took to pay for the rest of the home. Then, after twenty to thirty years, the Navajo would assume full ownership. Everyone's life was improved, including that of the next generation, who would inherit their parents' property.

Suddenly we were in the big time with a program that the tribe did not control. As a result, my handling of the money and my personal integrity became campaign issues in the 1966 election when Raymond Nakai declared that the housing program was no good, that the money was improperly used, and that there was favoritism among those who benefited. All of the charges were untrue. The program was then bringing $7 million a year onto the reservation, and it included the first and largest Indian legal aid program in the area. In addition, the funds were monitored in a manner that prevented any improper use.

I think that our biggest drawback was not the politics but a problem we encountered with the legal aid program. I wanted to have a Navajo lawyer head the legal services, but by then I had discovered that there were no Navajo lawyers available. In fact, I could not find a Navajo in any law school in the country. This was most likely the result of the way Navajo students evaluated career possibilities, much in the same way I had done when I went to college. Being a lawyer was never a career option in my mind. Lawyers had blond hair and blue eyes. Law was an Anglo profession in which Indians were not welcome. No one ever told us that, but we were also never recruited by the law schools. For now, our legal matters would have to be handled by an Anglo lawyer, Ted Mitchell, and a Cherokee, Woody Sneed. They were both good men, but certainly not were needed for self-determination.

By April of 1966, the pressure had become so strong that I considered getting out. I had learned how to fight the BIA, the Indian Health Service, and other outside government agencies. I had spent three years trying to improve the lives of my people and had created a program that was doing all that we had hoped it would do. But I never expected to be attacked by my own people. I did not know how to fight them, nor did I want to do so. We Navajo should have been working together, and yet I sensed divisiveness. Since ONEO would continue without me, this seemed to be a good time to change my career. Not surprisingly, I decided to go to law school.

I have never felt myself to be particularly smart, though the more I watched the lawyers at work around the reservation, the more I felt that they were dumber than I was. I inquired about different law schools and learned that all applicants had to go through a screening process before they would be considered. I passed that test the first time and applied to several law schools—UCLA, University of New Mexico, University of Arizona, University of Oklahoma, and others. When I was accepted at the first three, I applied for scholarship assistance.

My annual ONEO salary at the time was around fifteen thousand dollars. That was much less than I had earned at Hughes, but I did not want to lose it. I tried to find a school that would provide financial assistance that would at least bring my family income close to that amount. Ultimately that proved to be the University of Arizona in Tucson, where I was offered room, board, tuition, and books, plus a stipend for work as a consultant to the law school professors. I would have a part-time job teaching them about Navajo culture and various legal concerns on and off the reservation—an important subject to a state where so much land was reserved for Native Americans—and the consulting salary was a good one.

I was looking forward to the chance to prove that a Navajo sheepherder, who grew up with every kind of disadvantage on the reservation, could get into law school and get a law degree. Then I could say to the rest of the Navajo students that if I could make it into law school, then they, coming from a better background, could enter any school, including Harvard or Yale.

I began school in September, a time when reservation political conflicts were at their peak. I took a thirty-day vacation from my job at ONEO. I had the time accumulated and felt it would give me a chance to evaluate the experience. I put my deputy, Tony Lincoln, in charge after swearing him to secrecy about what I was going to do. I explained that I might return in thirty days or I might take a leave of absence and get my degree.

It was strange living in a dormitory with the bathroom down the hall, everyone carrying soap, towels, and shaving kit. It was like being in the army, and I never was able to get used to it, though I was determined to stick it out.

The class work was just as strange. My week alternated between classes and lunch meetings with the law professors to whom I was lecturing. I also checked in with Tony each day, spending thirty to forty-five minutes in a phone booth in the student lounge.

It is odd the way problems can arise in unexpected places. After several days of calling Tony, I found a note attached to the booth asking that calls be limited to three minutes. I did not know who had placed it there. No one had complained directly to me, nor had I seen anyone waiting outside the booth while I was using the telephone. There were other telephones scattered about the area, so I just ignored the note.

Next, someone came up and pointed at the note. I waved him away. Then the dean approached me to explain that a complaint had been lodged against me in some sort of student grievance proceeding. The upperclassmen had developed this organization to create rules and regulations for new students to follow. They had their own system of hearings and discipline, none of which interested me. This was part of a program to train the students in ethics, but I was concerned only with getting my law degree.

I had no intention of going along with something as silly as a grievance concerning my use of one of several pay telephones. I had worked seven years in private industry. I had been involved on the reservation. There was no way I was going to play games.

The next day I was on the telephone again when several students came by. I was thirty-eight. They were twenty-one and twenty-two. They handed me their version of a subpoena, asking me to come to a hearing before their board. They informed me that I was in violation of their ethics for disregarding the sign they had placed in the telephone booth.

I had a long argument with those kids. I explained a little of my background, trying to show them that I knew more about ethics and business than they were likely to learn in the next fifteen years. I also pointed out that the telephone was a public one, the reason I was using it instead of one designated for special needs. No matter what signs they might put up, the telephone was meant for anyone who paid to use it. I was doing nothing wrong, and because there were unused telephones available, I was not preventing anyone else from making a call.

The situation was so foolish that I went to the dean and asked him to get the kids off my back. I explained that I was there to learn, not to go before any of the silly boards that the kids had created.

The dean felt he was in a very difficult position. The students had developed various programs and regulations that served a purpose for the young and inexperienced but were out of place with an adult who had been working successfully in the world at large. He did not want to demean what the young people were doing, nor did he want to alienate me.

In hindsight I realize that what I sometimes felt was prejudice against an Indian probably had nothing to do with the incident. These young students were not really aware of my skin color or history. They just saw an "old man" among them, and their bias against me had to do with that, nothing more. It was still foolish and I still resented it.

I thought that would be the end of my problems. I did not realize that there was a Navajo youth attending the University of Arizona who had seen me at the law school. He told his father, and word got back to the advisory committee of the Tribal Council. They checked, found that I was enrolled in law school, decided to declare me AWOL, and passed a resolution firing me from my position. They also sent a copy of the resolution to Washington.

Tony Lincoln alerted me to what was taking place. I could not understand how the council could fire me, since I reported to the ONEO board of directors, not the advisory committee of the council. Yet the action had taken place and no one had challenged the council's right to do it.

There seemed to be nothing I could do. I told Tony that he was in charge. I would continue with law school if I were truly fired.

I received a telephone call from Washington the next day. It was from the third in command of the OEO, and it was one of the nicest telephone calls I've ever received.

President Johnson was having trouble with Congress at that time. He was working to get continued funding for his self-determination programs for low-income individuals and areas. The Office of Navajo Economic Opportunity had proven to be the most successful of all the programs. More people were helped at less administrative cost than in any of the other projects, and he wanted to use it as his model when lobbying Congress to renew the funding. But it was felt that ONEO worked because of me. The president did not want me to accept the council's dismissal. I was told that if I would quit law school and return to Fort Defiance, the members of the administrative staff were fairly certain they could get my job back. They felt that they could apply the necessary political pressure, especially since I had done nothing wrong.

The decision was a difficult one. Sargent Shriver wanted me to testify before Congress concerning the difference the OEO program had made on the Navajo Reservation. At the same time the dean wanted me to be the first Navajo ever to graduate from the University of Arizona's law school.

The dean called the staff of OEO. He was told that the national community action program hung in the balance, depending on what I did. They needed me to testify, and I could not do that unless I returned to being director of ONEO. The dean reluctantly said that he felt I should return.

I was still hesitant. I had put together a series of scholarships and grants, all of which I would lose if I left, and I might never have another chance to go to law school.

We finally worked out a compromise. I agreed to return to Fort Defiance to take charge of ONEO, assuming that the OEO staff could arrange matters with the people who had fired me. There were two conditions, however. One was that I could obtain assistance from the government if I wanted to return to law school. The second, a far more important one, was that the OEO would consider a proposal for funding a special program that would allow the University of Arizona to help Native Americans go to law school. This program would encourage members of all tribes, not just the Navajo, to enter the legal profession.

Everything worked out almost as planned. Tony Lincoln called me within a day or two, informing me that the advisory committee of the Tribal Council had passed a resolution reinstating me. It turned out that Raymond Nakai had been told that if the resolution firing Peter MacDonald was not rescinded, the OEO's most recent grant of $7 million would be canceled. The grant would be available in the future if a new director was appointed, but the OEO would have to approve that person before the funding would be restored. The government officials explained that they had been comfortable with my leadership, so any replacement would have to be as good as they felt I had been.

Nakai obviously did not want the funds to go on hold. Elections were coming up in November, and the chairman did not want to be seen as the man who had cost the tribe $7 million, even if the delay in getting the money would only be a few weeks.

Although I was able to return to my previous position, not everything worked out quite the way we had anticipated. The OEO had no intention of favoring one university's law school over another. Instead, it sent out an RFP—a request for proposals. This meant that every law school in the country was able to apply for funds to help educate Native Americans in the law. These proposals were evaluated, and the OEO felt that the best was the one sent by the University of New Mexico. As a result, they received the money to start a program, which proved quite successful.

I gained something important from this experience. I learned that you didn't have to be a blond, blue-eyed Anglo to be a lawyer. The work was not all that difficult. There was certainly no reason we Navajo couldn't develop our own lawyers, especially with the financial assistance we would be receiving. In fact, the law center that was developed at the University of New Mexico has now helped approximately twenty Navajo youths become lawyers. I was not one, though. I never returned to complete my degree.

Raymond Nakai was reelected in 1966, though, sadly, the two of us were estranged over the law school incident. I returned to the reservation with a sense of the harshness of Navajo politics.

CHAPTER NINE

The time as head of ONEO moved quickly. The programs were effecting measurable changes in the lives of the Navajo people. They now had a sense that they could achieve whatever they desired, and many credited me with the new, more positive feelings on the reservation. They also suggested that I run for tribal chairman, a request that was flattering but not in my plans.

I was apparently impressing others at this time, as well. In 1968 I received a letter asking me if I wanted to work for the federal government. I replied that I would be interested in the possibility of serving and, curious about how I had been selected, I asked who had recommended me.

The reply I got surprised me. The New York–based transition team was using the reference book *Who's Who in America,* first making a list of just the Republicans and then further refining the list by separating the names into areas of expertise, such as economics, law, medicine, scientific research, and so forth. Finally they used this second list to make initial contacts. The same letter was probably sent to ten to fifteen thousand others. The real work would come after they received the affirmative replies. From this shorter list the selections would begin to be made.

The follow-up I received was an application form on which I provided a detailed description of my work and personal history. This form was used to eliminate a large percentage of the applicants. Then I received a third form, which required still more information.

I received a long questionnaire after more applicants were eliminated. Again I survived, this time receiving a much more specific form meant to reveal more about my character. I remember one of the questions: "What, in your mind, is the greatest thing you've done in your life up to now?" The next question asked me why I thought that achievement was so great.

By the time I completed this form, the transition team had moved to Washington, D.C. It was shortly before the presidential inauguration of January 1969, and the new government officials were eager to begin announcing their appointments for the various administrative positions. Having already decided who would fill the top cabinet posts, they were now looking for numerous deputies and assistants.

To my surprise, I survived all the rounds of elimination and received a letter informing me that I had been accepted by the administration. All that remained to be determined was what department I wanted to work in and in what capacity.

There were numerous choices. My preference was to be assistant secretary for economic or business development in the Department of Commerce. I thought that since I had a general understanding of the needs of Native Americans, this would be a good area.

I traveled to Washington to meet with the transition team officials. I was told that one of the available positions was that of assistant secretary working with minority business programs in a national program with a budget of approximately $20 million a year, serving blacks, Hispanics, Chinese, and Indians.

My response was that the minority population was too great to have a substantive program with just $20 million to spend. On the reservation we were receiving a third of that amount, and it was barely adequate.

I was correct to be concerned. The position involved little more than providing brochures and general information to people concerning how to start and run small businesses. I explained that I did not want something so meaningless, and I left Washington with my decision respected and with good contacts within the administration. Men like John Ehrlichman, Leonard Garment, Brad Patterson, and others kept in contact with me, seeking my advice concerning government policy toward Indians.

A second opportunity arose during this time. Walter Hickel, Nixon's first secretary of the interior, offered me the position of commissioner of Indian affairs. I would have worked under him in the Department of the Interior, a situation that left me with mixed feelings. I respected Walter Hickel and his vision, but at the same time, the Department of the Interior had always been considered an enemy of all Indians. The Bureau of Indian Affairs was part of that department, and some of its people were so deeply entrenched that I did not expect them to be willing to adopt new ideas. The job sounded like an honor, and I think it was offered with respect. But I thought it would offer far less opportunity for change than working within the Commerce Department, where projects could be nurtured and funded without BIA interference.

Word got out concerning what was taking place while Walter Hickel and I were still having discussions. The press began talking about it, and I received telephone calls from Arizona congressman Sam Steiger, Senator Barry Goldwater, and others. They were enthusiastic about the nomination and told me they would try to see that it went smoothly through the various approval hearings. They also mentioned some favors they would like from me—the start of the political games I would encounter in the years ahead.

Then I received a visit from Raymond Nakai and his lawyer. They told me how pleased they were about the nomination. They thought it would be a great idea if I took the position, though we all knew that their encouragement had more to do with getting me out of Navajo politics than with their pleasure over my opportunity.

I returned to Washington and met with Walter Hickel for an entire day. We discussed his thoughts about Native Americans and his plans for the future. I explained that I had seen other commissioners appointed with great plans for the future, then watched as they ended up serving only the needs and goals of the Interior Department and the BIA and not meeting the needs and goals of the Indians.

I also told Hickel that the political pressure had already begun. Some congressmen and senators wanted to be certain that I would allow certain pet projects of theirs to go forth on the reservation or that I would ensure that projects be given to their campaign contributors or constituents. I even had a call from Senator Goldwater telling me that when I was appointed commissioner I should choose a Hopi as my deputy. The politicians were trying to pick my staff for me.

I said that I didn't need the job. I didn't need to work from Washington. I had no intention of bowing to all the pressure that was being put on me. I would take the job only if I could do something for the Navajo and for Native Americans in general. But I saw no use in taking a job if a senator was going to tell me to give a certain construction company a job on a particular reservation.

I explained to Walter Hickel that I was my own person. I wanted to be able to hire my own staff, develop my own programs. I explained that if he believed that Indians should have self-determination of their future, then he would have to back me up or I would be fired within three to six months. I said that if Senator Goldwater or anyone else told me to place a certain person on my staff, I would tell him to go fly a kite. If someone told me to give a road construction job on the Rosebud Reservation in South Dakota to the XYZ Construction Company, I would refuse to do it. Such actions would serve only the Anglo friends of politicians. I knew that the congressmen would be upset with me for not playing the game the way they wanted, and that was going to reflect back on Walter Hickel, who would be in the midst of it all.

Hickel responded that he didn't have to be in office either. He was receiving forty-five thousand dollars a year as secretary of the interior but before entering government service, he had paid more than that as income tax on his holdings in Alaska.

I appreciated his position, but I kept pushing the problems he was asking me to face. I said that I might have to fight with his forestry department or his water department. I might have to fight with the

Bureau of Land Management. I was concerned not with being a team player but with helping the Indians.

Hickel was comfortable with all my statements. He said I could have everything I wanted. Then he asked if I had any other requests, and I did. I wanted to be sworn in at the White House with Hickel and President Nixon present. Normally the ceremony was held in the BIA building, which was demeaning. If the ceremony were held in the White House, the impression would be one of top-level support. It would give me respect and an implied power that would otherwise be nonexistent.

The interior secretary agreed to talk with President Nixon, who granted my request. A routine FBI background check was started, and everything was to be concluded in three or four weeks.

Paul Harvey, the Chicago-based newscaster, broke the story that I would soon be appointed commissioner of Indian affairs. I got calls from representatives and senators who were on the Interior Committee and wanted to establish their power. However, I had Walter Hickel tell the committee members to leave me alone, that I would be my own man.

Finally the appointment was only a week away. I was waiting for a call telling me when to report, but the call never came. It turned out that there were problems with the Senate's confirmation. The senators who had reservation land in their states were not interested in meeting my conditions. The commissioner had always been someone they could count on to give out jobs as they directed, to act in a manner that would benefit their constituents. They knew I would fight their interests.

Walter Hickel also proved to be a rebel. He also went against the politicians and was fired in 1970. He was replaced by Rogers C. B. Morton, a man Congress thought would be more amenable to their notion of how the political power game should be played.

After Hickel was fired, he wrote a book, *Who Owns America*, in which he discussed the infighting among politicians that has caused so many problems for the country. He mentioned the difficulties that arose because of his efforts on behalf of all Indians and his attempt to appoint me to office. He explained that the Senate's official excuse for not approving my appointment was that Wanda and I had had a child before we were officially married, a fact that I had never concealed. I supported our daughter financially and openly before marrying Wanda, so this meant challenging me on "moral" grounds was easier for the politicians than admitting that I was not acceptable because the most powerful senators and representatives could not manipulate me.

Nixon was important during this period because he was the first president to be seriously concerned with providing self-determination for the Indians, and my relationship with his staff was a good one. Although Walter Hickel was especially critical of the methods of bureaucracies, a stance that would later cost him his job, Nixon, like every other successful politician, would go only so far in making his opinions known. He backed off from fights that could hurt him, and that was the reason he and his staff would not fully support my nomination.

Nixon's attitude worried many of us. Years earlier, when he was with Eisenhower, the Republican position on Indian affairs had been one known as "termination." Eisenhower wanted to move the Indians into the mainstream of American society. There would be no trustee relationship. The Indians would be subject to essentially the same circumstances as the rest of the population. Reservation land could be taken and sold to private interests. Maintaining traditional life-styles would probably be impossible. And there would be no future support for the survival of the various cultures of the true American native.

But Nixon proved to feel quite differently, as he made clear in an important address to Congress on July 8, 1970. He stated in part:

"The story of the Indian in America is something more than the record of the white man's frequent aggression, broken agreements, intermittent remorse, and prolonged failure. It is also a record of endurance, of survival, adaptation, and creativity in the face of over-whelming obstacles. It is a record of enormous contributions to the country—to its art and culture, to its strength and spirit, to its sense of history and its sense of purpose.

"It is long past time that the Indian policies of the federal government began to recognize and build upon the capacities and insights of the Indian people. Both as a matter of justice and as a matter of enlightened social policy, we must begin to act on the basis of what the Indians themselves have long been telling us. The time has come to break decisively with the past and to create the conditions for a new era in which the Indian future is determined by Indian acts and Indian decisions."

Under Hickel's brief leadership there were many changes. For example, in Ramah, New Mexico, the Navajo signed a three-year contract with the BIA to run their own high school. This meant that the Navajo were in charge of the curriculum, the operations, and everything else that related to the education of their children. Before this, the high school students had always been sent to BIA boarding schools in three different states.

However, despite such support under the presidential umbrella, men like Senator Goldwater and Representative Steiger were determined to change the land-holding arrangements of the Navajo and Hopi in a power play that would cause ten thousand Navajo to lose their homes.

Finally everything was clear to me. Arizona was expanding. Anglos coveted the Navajo land for its great mineral wealth, but the Navajo were unwilling to let the land be exploited. The Hopi, however, had given the impression that they were amenable to working with the politicians. They were expected to sell mineral rights cheap, perhaps below market value, or to allow their land to be exploited in some other way. Had I become commissioner of Indian affairs, with a Hopi deputy, as Senator Goldwater suggested, I would not have been a threat to anyone. The Navajo tribal chairmanship would have gone to someone who, through naiveté or in exchange for favors, would not have fought this devastating new danger. Suddenly I was glad that I was still in the political arena in Arizona.

Perhaps the greatest foolishness when it came to the relocation effort was the fact that the cost of relocation, originally thought to be just $25 million to $30 million, has now exceeded a half-billion dollars. Just the fencing of areas that were once open land has cost almost double the original allocation. Had the two tribes signed a treaty agreeing to work out their own disputes, then split the money spent to date, they would be independent of the BIA and the handouts from Congress. But such rational thinking was not a part of the decision-making process, and the money continues to be unwisely mis-appropriated to this day.

By 1970 I was ready to fight for Navajo political office. Once the Washington power structure had shifted and new funding no longer seemed to hinge on my position in the tribe, Raymond Nakai and the Tribal Council worked to get me fired from my job as ONEO director. I had become too popular with the people and too independent of the tribal government. They did not realize that for the first time, I had the leisure to seriously consider the chairmanship of the Navajo Nation. I saw this opportunity as yet another challenge in my life and agreed to run.

The Navajo do not have political parties as white men do. We are far more democratic. Anyone who wished to run for election could do so. That meant that there were usually several candidates, each with his own ideas of what he wanted to do in the chairman's office.

The primary election whittled down the candidates. Then the top vote getters ran in the general election. In theory, a strong lead in the primary assured victory in the general election. However, there was no certainty.

To my surprise, in the September 1970 primary, in which there were twelve candidates on the ballot, I won approximately 78 percent of the votes, the greatest landslide ever.

Our general election lasted two days so that traditional families caring for livestock would have time to vote. Half the family would go to vote on the first day, while the remaining members stayed home and cared for the animals. Those who had voted would return home the first night, and the next day the rest of the family would go to the polls and vote.

I had rented a small single-engine plane for my campaign on the reservation and used it through the second day of the voting. When the polls closed, I was flown back to Window Rock with my two campaign aides, Wilbur Atcitty and John Nelson Dee. The sun was setting, and I knew that the results would be announced the next day. All that remained was the tabulation.

Suddenly I felt very uncomfortable. I turned to my aides and said, "Suppose we win. Did it ever occur to you that we might win? If so, what are we going to do?" I realized that I might become chairman, but I didn't know what to do as chairman. My aides didn't know what I would do as chairman. I knew how to work for the tribe and for the people. I had learned how to campaign. But I had never really thought about the possibility of winning, and suddenly it was too late to back out.

The men laughed at me. They said not to worry, that maybe we wouldn't win.

"I'm not worried about losing," I told them. "But if we *do* win, we'll have a tremendous responsibility here."

That night I was scared. I had entered the election because I saw it as a challenge. I had said what I believed, and I had demonstrated my skills as head of ONEO. But that was different from winning.

I would be happy if I won, of course. I had fought hard for a victory. But this was a bigger responsibility than being head of ONEO, even though that job had involved me with Congress and the White House. As head of the Navajo Nation, I would be responsible for every Navajo and for all our tribal assets, including the land.

I would also be expected to solve the tribe's problems, the growing land dispute between the Navajo and the Hopi, concerns about water rights, mining arrangements, and mineral rights. I realized that perhaps I had taken on a project that was way bigger than my capabilities. I did not think I would ever be able to sleep. I felt I would be working seven days a week just to keep up. If I won, how would I get a handle on the responsibilities and the details of the job? How would I be chairman?

The only comfort I could find that night came by recognizing my past accomplishments. As chairman, I could do even more, so I made an outline, establishing three goals I wanted to attain for the Navajo.

My first goal was the continuation of the enthusiasm the nation had developed for helping itself. I wanted the people to develop pride, and this meant starting with bread-and-butter programs. People needed to see more food on the table, to experience more than merely subsistence. I needed a program that would allow people to see results.

My second goal was the protection of the Navajo Nation's resources. Coal, uranium, water, and the various minerals belonging to our people had to be conserved and developed. This was our real wealth. Such development, fairly and properly handled, would ensure the tribal income necessary for people to become self-sufficient, to determine their own future. The money would pay for home improvements, education, roads, and whatever else was needed to give the people a future.

The third goal was an offensive effort against our enemies—those who wanted to control us, to take our land, to determine our destiny. Some were bureaucrats in agencies such as the Bureau of Indian Affairs. Some were in Congress. And some were connected with major utility companies seeking cheap fuel and cheap labor for massive profits. Moreover, the legislators of the states surrounding the reservation, as well as adjoining county officials, had been enjoying the benefits of the Navajo Nation's resources without sharing them with the Navajo people.

There were also several fly-by-night promoters trying to sell whatever they could to the tribe. Many were self-styled "consultants" whose concern was for their fees, not for the Navajo Nation. I knew that I would have to discern the difference, using those who could benefit my people and banning those who wanted only to take advantage of them.

Next I tried to reinforce my sense of self. I remembered my achievements and realized that if I won the chairmanship, I would simply face four years that would build on the skills I had been developing. The responsibility was a big one, yet I felt that my past indicated I could handle it with little difficulty.

Still, I experienced a fitful night. And by morning, that fateful November 1970, my greatest hopes and worst nightmares were confirmed. I had won the election to tribal chairman with 65 percent of the vote. It was a major victory, though I wondered if I deserved the support I had been given. I vowed to prove that I did.

Chairman of the Navajo Nation

(1970–1983)

CHAPTER TEN

I knew that much would be expected of me when I took office. I represented change to the Navajo Nation, and that meant that even my supporters would be nervously watching me. The Diné were a people with beliefs and traditions dating back to First Man (Atse Hastin) and First Woman (Aste Asdzian), and although many of the old ways were lost forever, our history, culture, triumphs, and tragedies still affected our thoughts and actions. I would have to walk a fine line in order to maintain the support of as many Navajo as possible while doing what I believed was best for the future.

We had accomplished so much from 1965 through 1970 that the people wanted this momentum, this enthusiasm, this awakening of the Navajo Nation to continue. In the ten years that followed we would come to be recognized as the greatest Indian nation in the United States because the people took their future into their own hands. The administration I brought in helped to push back the obstacles and impediments that kept us bound to the past, in misery, and unable to tackle our own problems.

The first break from the old ways came with my selection of vice-chairman, a position not unlike that of the vice-president of the United States. The vice-chairman's power is determined by the wishes of the chairman, just as the strength of the vice-president is determined by how much authority the president allows him. Much of the time his duties are relatively unimportant. He might be an adviser or he might be a gofer who does what no one else wishes to be bothered doing. Yet the vice-chairman is watched closely following the primary election among the Navajo. His background can indicate the bias of the candidate for chairman.

According to tribal law, the person who wins the primary election has five days in which to select a running mate. Although I came away from the primary with 78 percent of the vote and a good chance of winning the general election, I had had no indication of such popularity when I entered the primary and had given no thought to the selection of the man who would run as my vice-chairman. However, I sought to reunite all the Navajo, and so I chose as my running mate a man named Wilson C. Skeet—a choice that would be heavily criticized by my opponents.

After the establishment of the position of chairman, some unwritten laws concerning the governing of the Navajo Nation came into being and were followed as though they were requirements. One of these was the selection of the vice-chairman from among those Navajo who lived within the original reservation boundaries of the trust land area. Those who lived in the Eastern Navajo area, the descendants of the "Enemy" Navajo (Diné Anaih), who had made a peace with the Spaniards back in 1818, were excluded from consideration—the price they paid for the actions of their ancestors.

Yet nothing in the law specified that the Eastern Navajo should be excluded. Officially they were as much a part of the Navajo Nation as those of us in Arizona or that portion of New Mexico that was considered trust land. The Eastern Navajo sent delegates to the Tribal Council and had full voting powers. But they were a minority among the Navajo, hated for a past over which they had no control, and all the top politicians avoided being connected with them in any way.

During my years at ONEO I had gotten to know all the Navajo, including those in the eastern region. I had come to understand that the problems and concerns of one Navajo chapter were shared by all, and I saw reasons all Navajo should work together. I realized that there were good people everywhere, that the discrimination against the Eastern Navajo (Diné Anaih) was based not on the actions of those who were living but on the deeds of those who lived long ago.

I believed that if I was to help my people achieve self-determination and remain sovereign under the treaties still in effect, I could not allow this discrimination to continue. I went to the Eastern Navajo council and requested the names of four or five people who could represent them as vice-chairman. Among those selected was a council delegate named Wilson Skeet. He and I had been Marines together, though he was a few years older and had been drafted.

Skeet seemed ideal for several reasons. One, he had political experience that I lacked. As a member of the Tribal Council, he understood how it operated while I had always been independent of such offices. He was also, as I said, a few years older and more mature, which I thought would appeal to voters who looked on me as relatively young (forty-two years old) compared with leaders of the past. Having served in the Marines with him, I knew he would handle himself well under pressure, and his knowledge of the Eastern Navajo land issues and land status was invaluable. He understood the multiple jurisdictions of state land, trust land, and the Bureau of Land Management holdings in the Eastern Navajo area. He seemed the ideal man to help me unite my people.

However, the hatred toward him and the other Eastern Navajo was so intense that Raymond Nakai and his followers were quick to use his appointment against me. They pointed out his ancestry, intimating that my choice of vice-chairman was an illegal act, which it wasn't.

I don't know if the majority of the Navajo people elected me despite my running mate or if they realized it was time to begin working together. All that was certain was that when we won with 65 percent of the votes, I felt that we were at last heading in the right direction— toward unity. The vote was of historic significance for the new Navajo Nation, and I felt that I had a mandate to move forward as planned.

The inauguration occurred on January 5, 1971, a clear, beautiful, cloudless day, and the coldest inauguration day on record. Although it was warm throughout southern Arizona, the temperature in the mountains of northern Arizona fell to almost 50 degrees below zero the night before, and by morning it had climbed to only 20 degrees above zero. Yet despite the cold, a massive crowd turned out for the event, including the United States Marine Corps Band, sent by President Nixon from Washington, D.C.

The Marines were shocked by the cold. They did not realize that only a portion of Arizona is desert, and they wore lightweight clothing that would have been ideal for Phoenix or Tucson. They encountered a temperature so frigid that moisture condensed, then froze inside many of their instruments.

My mother was among those present. She had been fearful of what the election might do to me, yet she was beaming proudly. I think she wanted to keep me safe, yet she also wanted me to never abandon my past. On her deathbed, she told me to take care of myself, but also to never desert my people—the traditional Navajo people—because, she said, they needed me. They believed in me. My heart was thrilled to know that she approved the decision I had made even though she had ached for the pain it would bring to me during the political struggles.

The inauguration was held on the tribal fairgrounds at Window Rock, where the wind whipped across the land. There were television crews from several cities, almost all of them suffering the same fate as the band members. Their cameras either slowed or stopped in the intense cold. The only exception was a crew from Denver, Colorado. Those people knew all about high-altitude winters; they had brought along special warming equipment for cameras and tape recorders.

All together as many as 25,000 people were present for the event. Congressmen, senators, governors, and other dignitaries attended. It was an extremely impressive start, and yet, almost immediately after I took office, I discovered that there was an effort in Congress to take land away from the Navajo.

No one can truly keep up with the various bills our representatives bring before Congress. Proposals are made, committee hearings are held to analyze them, and eventually the bills are presented on the floor of the House and the Senate. Some are of great importance to all the American people. Others are of concern to just a small segment of society. Yet few of the bills are mentioned by the news media, who cover only those stories they feel are of enough importance to interest the majority of their viewers and readers. In most cases, information affecting the Navajo and the Hopi is given low priority.

Because of this, it was only through a telephone call I received within months of taking office, a call from Frank Carlucci of the Office of Management and Budget, that I learned about the Navajo-Hopi land exchange. Frank was Sargent Shriver's successor in the Office of Economic Opportunity, and we had become friends. He had learned not only of the proposed bill to shift ownership of some 1.8 million acres of land to the Hopi Indians, but also of a letter from Rogers C. B. Morton, the secretary of the interior who succeeded Walter Hickel. The letter indicated what would pass as the official White House position on the issue. Morton, writing for the Nixon administration, endorsed the bill that would result in the displacement of some ten thousand Navajo. The political deal making I had feared seemed to be taking place.

Morton epitomized the way in which the Interior Department was politicized. He may have been extremely competent, but as treasurer for the Republican party, his loyalties were with the party. He would do nothing to alienate the leaders, including such prominent Republicans as Senator Goldwater. He was expected to endorse the special interests of his party's politicians and their major contributors. I was not supposed to see Morton's letter, but Carlucci wanted to help me protect the Navajo.

The bill had been introduced on July 26, 1972, by Congressman Sam Steiger, with Senator Barry Goldwater's support. Their victory in the House of Representatives resulted in legislation that would end what was known as the Joint Use Area, the 1.8-million-acre parcel of land used equally by the Navajo and the Hopi. Under the terms of the bill, ten thousand Navajo would ultimately be relocated from their homes, with the government underwriting $16 million of the cost.

The Joint Use Area concept dated back to 1882, when President Chester A. Arthur's staff had designated 2.4 million acres of northern Arizona desert as worthless land and ordered that it be given to the Hopi and "such other Indians" as the secretary of the interior felt should have it. This was the period when Indians from all tribes were being resettled onto land the whites didn't want during their westward migration and settlement. The whites were to be given the good land and water that had previously been controlled by the "savages."

The Hopi were a relatively sedentary people whose life-style revolved around permanent villages where they raised crops. Although in the one hundred years following President Arthur's Joint Use Area designation the Hopi doubled their population to 8,000 people, the gain was insignificant, and the Hopi seldom strayed from the small areas they were using.

The Navajo, by contrast, increased to approximately twenty times their numbers, to 200,000 people, following the Long Walk. They had a growing need for land because of their seminomadic life-style (the result of sheepherding on poor quality grazing land). My people dominated much of the Joint Use Area by default. Our relationship with the Hopi was not antagonistic, however. The Hopi cared little about the land outside their villages.

Matters first changed in 1962. A few Hopi, aware of the constantly growing prosperity of the Navajo, added livestock to their way of life. They, too, began to roam the land in search of the best grazing areas, and eventually they came into conflict with the Navajo and their herds.

The original law had been vague. No one had bothered to decide which tribes constituted the "other Indians" mentioned in the executive order of 1882. As a result, the Hopi maintained that the Navajo had no right to the land. They said that since the Navajo had a designated reservation area far larger than that of the Hopi, they had no right to any of the Hopi's 2.4 million acres of the 1882 executive order land.

My people protested. For more than a century we had used the land that the Hopi were suddenly claiming as exclusively theirs. The federal government had provided all manner of services to the Navajo living there, never disputing our right to settle and use the territory. Moreover, many Navajo from the area known as Big Mountain still possessed a document they had received in 1960, issued by the Bureau of Indian Affairs and stamped with a gold seal bearing the words "by the authority of the secretary of the interior," guaranteeing their right to remain on their ancestral land. And since the land use had been established by the federal government, we felt that we were validated in our actions.

I and many Navajo believe very strongly that the Hopi never made use of any land in the Joint Use Area other than the land on which they were living now (on the mesas within the District 6 area). Traditional Navajos have always wondered why the white man is using the Hopis to take away our ancestral land, the land within the four sacred mountains (Sis nájin to the East, Tsó dzil to the South, Dook Oslid to the West, and Debí-Ntsa to the North) that was created by God for use by His people.

A federal court decided to resolve the matter by designating 650,000 acres surrounding what, in 1962, was known as Grazing

District Six as exclusively Hopi land. This area encompassed their primary villages as well as extensive land that they used mainly for hunting and for the gathering of firewood. All other land designated in the original 1882 grant would be the official Joint Use Area.

Most people other than both the Navajo and the Hopi understood that the volume of land was not a lot for the Navajo. When you divided the 18 million acres by the total number in the population, this was an average of 100 acres per Navajo. This was also true for the acreage per capita for the Hopi. Each Hopi also had 100 acres in 1970.

Once the Hopi were given their additional one million acres, they averaged 200 acres per person. Yet with the Navajo population growth, each Navajo was essentially reduced to 80 acres. Yet the Navajo, traditionally being herders, needed more land than the Hopi. The Hopi stay concentrated in villages, adding to the obviously disproportionate nature of what was taking place.

Not much changed at first. We Navajo still dominated the Joint Use Area because it served as range land for some of our sheep. And most of the Hopi did not complain because they had little or no interest in that land.

When an end to the Joint Use Area was proposed, there were many reasons for both maintaining and ending their territorial rights then in effect. These included religious concerns, since the area was sacred to some degree to both tribes.

The main issue everyone in favor of the change tried to avoid mentioning was that of mineral rights. The massive known deposits of coal and oil on Navajo land, included in sections of the Joint Use Area that were to be given to the Hopi, were worth an estimated 1 trillion dollars at that time. Today they are worth far more.

The Hopi were perceived as being far more willing to sell mineral rights to big business than were the Navajo. It was also believed that they were willing to settle for leases that provided royalty payments well below the rate of payment in other parts of the United States. Thus the biggest concern of the originators and the proponents of the bill seemed to be finding a way to maintain cheap access to the minerals at a time when we Navajo were demanding fair treatment concerning our holdings.

Our concerns were not just the political, religious, and historical factors inherent in any change in land ownership. We felt we were about to be cheated out of great wealth by having resources taken from us to ensure below-market availability to economic interests opposed to those of the Navajo Nation.

We did not realize all the power games taking place at the time, though later these became clear. The Navajo and Hopi were very different people in their historical, cultural, and religious beliefs.

They were also quite different in their political history, the Navajo being the tribe that remained a sovereign nation within United States land. Because the Hopi felt themselves a part of the United States, and because they wanted their special needs met in the same manner as exists for urban poor in white man's America, they were willing to make concessions. They were comfortable providing inexpensive mineral and water access, feeling that they would ultimately benefit from good relations with the rest of their country.

Much of this was because the Hopi never used or lived on the disputed land. Because they lived in concentrated communities in Grazing District Six, and because the disputed land was outside Grazing District Six, this was not much of a concern for them.

The Navajo of my generation were demoralized, but they did understand that the mineral rights were like money in the bank. If we were paid what other land owners are paid for fair use, we could meet the needs of our people. We could be self-sufficient. We could stop having to be dependent upon the U.S. government and the BIA. And when the land we were being asked to give up, land we had used for centuries, happened to be where the known mineral wealth was located, it was obvious what was happening. Tragically, as in the days of Kit Carson, efforts were made to assure we would not settle the matter among ourselves. If the Hopi and Navajo were kept divided as in the past, we would have a difficult or impossible time obtaining fairness. Even worse, had we been able to continue working together, perhaps both tribes could have benefited from the resources that were just under the surface of the land.

Although I was angry about Morton's letter, I felt that perhaps I could go over his head to change the official administration position. Often cabinet-level personnel were allowed to act on their own, speaking for leaders with whom they had not discussed bills of this type. The president and his closest advisers felt that the people in those power positions would reflect the known interests of the party. And in the case of the redistribution of the land, the cost would be so minimal that most people would never know what had taken place. The Indians were not perceived as an important voting constituency.

I contacted some of President Nixon's aides, such as Leonard Garment and John Ehrlichman. I explained that Morton had drafted a letter endorsing the Steiger-Goldwater legislation, a letter he was about to take to Capitol Hill. I told the men that I wanted them to say that the administration did *not* endorse the bill. I said they should make that statement based on the fact that it did not reflect an Indian solution to Indian problems. Such a comment would fit with Nixon's publicly expressed interest in Indian self-determination. I was sure that the president would support the refusal.

Ehrlichman and Garment agreed with me. The Republican position, as stated by the White House, was to give Indians the freedom to settle their own boundary concerns. The Steiger-Goldwater bill ran directly counter to that position. Presidential opposition was appropriate.

A week later, when I was in Albuquerque, Leonard Garment and John Ehrlichman called me to read a one-page letter that they were going to ask President Nixon to approve. They wanted my reaction before sending it to both Nixon and the secretary of the interior. The latter would sign it and send it on to Congress.

The letter was perfect. It reiterated the president's support for Indian solutions to Indian problems and made clear that Indian self-determination was the official policy of the Nixon administration. It said that Congress should recognize that it was time to stop the hardships for the Indian people that this bill would perpetuate.

I expressed my pleasure, and they said they would take the letter to New York where both the president and Rogers C. B. Morton were staying. They felt that the approval and appropriate signatures would be obtained within forty-eight hours. Then the letter would be sent to Capitol Hill, a copy being forwarded to me.

I was delighted when I hung up. I was visiting my mother in the hospital where she was being treated for a heart valve problem. Both of us felt that finally things were being turned around for our people.

The next week I received a telephone call from Leonard Garment. This time the news was bad. Rogers C. B. Morton was irate about the letter. Morton stated that he would not sign it and would resign as secretary of the interior if ordered to endorse it. He also said that he would resign as treasurer of the Republican party.

Garment explained that Morton had placed the president in an untenable position. Nixon needed Morton as treasurer of the Republican party. Morton was raising the money for Nixon's re-election. No matter what the president wanted to do for the Navajo and other Native Americans—and I'm convinced of his sincerity on that issue—he wanted to retain power more. He would stand up to Senator Goldwater, who, in essence, had kept him off the ballot in 1964, when Lyndon Johnson's landslide resulted in Goldwater carrying only a single state. But he would not stand up to a fund-raiser. The Navajo could not help him raise money for re-election. Rogers C. B. Morton could, and the Navajo would be sacrificed on this issue to retain him.

A compromise of sorts was worked out. Morton's letter, several pages in length, went out as written, though the president arranged for the insertion of an additional paragraph stating, in effect, that while the bill was all right as written, another solution would be to let the two Indian tribes resolve the issue themselves.

Eventually many of the traditional Hopi also protested the change in the Joint Use Area. They understood the meaningless, severe hardships that such a change would cause, as well as the threat to the land's religious significance. They also wanted to be allowed self-determination. But respect for religion, and compassion for people who would be forced to move from homes that were as much a part of their physical and spiritual lives as they were shelter from the elements, all were deemed less important than having Anglos benefit from the land. Even President Nixon, sympathetic to the plight of both tribes, would not try to overrule a Congress determined to keep Indians dependent and subservient.

The incident was quite a letdown for me, but through it I developed an intense understanding of how politics works on the national level. I had already discovered how to manage local politics, and now I knew that I had to do the same on the national front. This meant ignoring party lines and seeking help wherever it might be available. In the case of the land dispute, I decided to seek the support of Democrats as well as Republicans.

I met with the Tribal Council, and we decided to lobby as many people as we could, as quickly as possible. The only way to handle such an undertaking was for me, the entire Tribal Council, and some of the Navajo living in the Joint Use Area to go to Washington, D.C. We chartered a converted four-engine, propeller-driven World War II cargo plane to fly us from Albuquerque to Washington. The plane was too big to land near the tribe's headquarters at Window Rock, Arizona, so approximately one hundred of us drove in a caravan to New Mexico to meet it, and from there we flew to the nation's capital.

We flew all night, landing at National Airport about 8:00 A.M. Then we divided ourselves into groups of four to six, depending upon how many interpreters were needed for those who did not speak English or did not speak it well. We obtained the roster of all the members of the House of Representatives, then assigned each small group to several congressional representatives.

We spent the first day lobbying, and passed the night wherever we could. Some of our people knew residents of the area who were willing to make their homes available. A church opened its doors and allowed some of us to use its facilities. A few of us were able to stay in hotel rooms.

The hearing was held the following morning. We were shocked to see Barry Goldwater testify on behalf of the Hopi. Since he was a senator and the bill was on the floor of the House of Representatives, the politics of the measure became clear. For the first time I realized that the senator might have a special interest in his dealings with the Indians of his state.

I was saddened by the discovery. The senator was a man who seemed to care about the culture and history of the Navajo, Hopi, Pima, Apache, and other tribes of one size or another that lived in Arizona. For him to be insensitive to the religious issues, the cultural concerns, and the potential for us to work among ourselves to settle the land dispute was a shock.

We were all standing in the gallery, looking down on what was taking place when the vote went against us. The loss was extremely upsetting. We had done all we could in a short period of time, but it had not been enough. We gathered at a hotel, then went over to the Department of the Interior to gather in space provided for us.

I explained that we could not be disheartened. Only the House had voted against us. The awareness of what was taking place had come to us quickly, and we had not had time to effectively lobby the people who voted. Now it was time to work on the Senate. If we could stop the bill there, we could stop it for good.

We returned home, sad but determined. We had several months to plan before the scheduled Senate hearings, and we used the time to build our arguments.

Later several of us went back to Washington and met with major Democratic leaders, including Senators George McGovern, Ted Kennedy, and Walter Mondale—men who were powerful within their party and were considered logical candidates for the presidency. In addition, I met with organized labor and spoke to the leaders of the AFL-CIO.

I explained our problems to the senators, and they were interested in helping. It was a good issue, self-determination for a people who had once been almost completely destroyed. And the fact that the opposition came from men such as Republican Barry Goldwater provided further encouragement. The Democrats would gain newspaper and magazine publicity for their actions. They would appear to be the "good guys" without alienating any special interest groups in their home states.

My office provided the senators with all the information we could gather on the Navajo and Hopi. We also used the AFL-CIO to begin a voter registration drive on the Navajo reservation. The Navajo, although potentially a large voting bloc, had never participated in the voting process. By registering eligible Navajo citizens, we hoped that we could defeat Senator Goldwater in his upcoming bid for re-election. If we couldn't, we could at least show that his power was no longer as great as it had been.

The Senate Subcommittee on Indian Affairs, headed by George McGovern, was appointed to study the Steiger bill after it was passed by the House. McGovern's committee could either pass on the House bill as written so it could be voted on by the Senate; modify the bill and pass it on, killing it in committee; or simply withhold action for a time.

I talked with McGovern and the others, explaining the problems the Navajo relocation would cause for people who felt the territory was sacred. My son, Rocky, a Yale student working as an intern in D.C., was very helpful. It would be a tragedy that would further erode the Navajo life-style and culture. And it would be a hardship for the people who would have to move from land they had considered their home for many years. This program, I told them, should not be allowed to move forward into law.

The committee fight was obviously partisan, Goldwater and Arizona senator Paul Fannin debating Senators Mondale, Kennedy, and McGovern, who used our information.

The debate was thoroughly one-sided. The Arizona senators had only a general knowledge of the Navajo. Barry Goldwater had enjoyed the land and the people, but it became obvious that he had never immersed himself in the culture, the history, the religion, the life-style, and the meaning of the Joint Use Area to the Navajo. He also did not realize that he might need such an awareness in relation to this bill. Since the area was not considered to be of national importance, he and Fannin seemed to assume that the others would accept whatever they wanted to do within their own state, just as they would support senators from other states under similar circumstances.

To their horror, the opposition was ready for them. The Democratic senators had a humanitarian issue they could exploit to make themselves look good and make the two Arizona Republicans look bad. I don't know how much they cared about the Navajo or how much they enjoyed embarrassing their rivals in the Senate. Whatever the case, they had facts and figures that proved devastating. No one hearing what they had to say was likely to vote for the bill. To our delight, we won.

McGovern was sympathetic to the Navajo concerns. He decided to give the two tribes a chance to work out their own arrangement without referring the Steiger bill to the Senate. This effectively killed the bill, though it could be reintroduced in both houses at a later time. Naturally, we were jubilant over our victory.

I had no idea what attacking Barry Goldwater might mean. The senator had long been involved with the Navajo reservation. He was a skilled photographer who had recorded the land and our people over the years. He even owned a trading post in Navajo Mountain at one time. The trading post, called Rainbow Lodge, had been a Christmas present from his wife in 1942. Nine years later it was destroyed in a fire and was never rebuilt. Goldwater apparently lost interest in pursuing that business.

For many years Goldwater worked to obtain federal funds for Indian schools and hospitals. He seemed to act without bias in this regard, though there were frequent rumors that he was pro-Hopi, perhaps due to his acquisition, through gifts and purchases, of one of the largest and most valuable collections of Hopi Kachinas in the nation. The hand-carved Kachinas are considered gods by the Hopi. They are important in religious ceremonies, and though there is a collector market in the dolls, they are sacred items, difficult to obtain. The Navajo wood carvers also make Kachina dolls, and they are far more elaborate than those of the Hopi. But the Navajo artists are making dolls, not gods, because of the difference in the two religions, and the Navajo work is meant for collectors. The Hopi Kachinas given to Senator Goldwater represented an important religious offering normally not possible for a non-Hopi to obtain.

Despite this, Goldwater had long shown strong fondness for the Navajo. During his 1964 presidential campaign, he often spoke the Navajo language. He named his plane *Yei Bi Kin* (House of the Yeis) and his train *Baa Hozhnilne* (To Win Them Over). Even his Phoenix home, located on Camelback Mountain, was called *Be Nun I Kin* (House on the Hill).

Most outside observers had previously viewed Goldwater as a man who tried to keep a middle ground between the Navajo and the Hopi. He seemed even-handed in providing personal and federal support for both tribes. Despite the probable greed and corruption that motivated others in the decision to change the Joint Use Area, it was believed that Goldwater probably did not see the change as hurting the Navajo or helping the Hopi—at least not when Congressman Sam Steiger first proposed his bill in the House. Critics claim that, if anything, Goldwater was concerned with the possibility of benefiting friends who might eventually come onto the reservation to exploit the mineral resources of the land. Regardless of his motivation, Goldwater's actions implied that he was becoming insensitive to problems where he had once been thought to be understanding. Certainly Goldwater did not expect me to mount serious opposition.

By 1972 the Republicans believed it was important for them to show a different aspect of the party at that year's Republican National Convention. One thought was to stress minority involvement, and it was toward this end that Barry Goldwater suggested that I give the speech introducing Richard Nixon as the party candidate for re-election to the presidency. Naturally I agreed. However, it was not to be.

The compromise on the joint land dispute we achieved through lobbying seemed fair to some, but infuriated others. It threatened the availability of natural resources to outside special interests who had supported the Joint Use Area change in the hope that the Hopi would provide better leases. Yet to those more concerned with the important moral and spiritual issues, giving us a few months to negotiate on our own seemed the best way to handle the crisis.

"If there has been no satisfactory agreement reached before next January 1973, I will propose comprehensive new legislation designed to resolve the problem in such a way that no family is needlessly expelled from its home land. Any such legislation must provide for maximum utilization of the joint use land in question and must be fully deliberated in both houses of Congress after all the facts are known," said McGovern in a letter to me. I was so pleased that I willingly gave an interview to the *Washington Post* in which I said that I might have to support George McGovern's campaign for president. I said that unless the Republicans changed their position toward the Navajo, I would give the Democrats my vote. Naturally I was no longer welcome to give the speech introducing Richard Nixon at the 1972 Republican National Convention.

Support from the AFL-CIO was ours for several reasons. One was the organization's bias against Barry Goldwater, who was viewed as antiunion. The AFL-CIO was happy to register voters who were likely to be hostile toward the senator.

There were other benefits to be gained, such as the hiring of Navajo workers for various labor projects. Previously, when an outside company wanted to work on the reservation, we arranged contracts that stressed Navajo preference in hiring. But very few Navajo were actually hired.

For example, in Page, Arizona, the Bechtel Corporation was building a generating station on Navajo land. The construction also affected the Salt River Project, which provided water throughout the state, allowing for growth in previously underused desert areas.

In general, we would make a deal with one business, but they would make a deal with another company, which had different procedures. Thus we might have a contract with the Salt River Project that specified Navajo preference in hiring, but the work would be subcontracted to the Bechtel Corporation, which had its own rules and procedures. Although Bechtel worked with the union, the Navajo preference issue was not their concern. Our contract was with the Salt River Project. There were no pass-on requirements for the subcontractors.

Additionally, when a Navajo applied for a job with the Salt River

Project, the union representatives there would send him to the union's regional headquarters in Flagstaff, Arizona. There he would be asked if he was an apprentice or a journeyman. If he wasn't a journeyman, he couldn't work on the site. Moreover, each journeyman was rated Class A, Class B, or Class C, a distinction that reflected the number of years he had been in the union and determined whether the journeyman would get the job. The newer union members, including almost all of the Navajo men and women seeking work, were Class C members. However, the company was interested in hiring only Class A and Class B members.

To counter this problem, we negotiated with the AFL-CIO to establish a union apprenticeship program on the reservation. The Labor Department was willing to fund the program, so it would not cost the union any money. Thus everyone would benefit. However, in exchange, the AFL-CIO had to agree to a contract stipulating that every Navajo who successfully completed the apprenticeship program would secure a job on the Navajo Reservation. This meant that there would be a Navajo working at the Four Corners Project, the Salt River Project, and all the other union projects. Since the skills of the Navajo men and women would be known to the union leaders, the Navajo hiring preference would be valid.

The AFL-CIO was quite happy to agree to this. It would gain extra members, which meant more income from dues. The companies would have skilled laborers, so the quality of their work would not suffer. And we would have a massive training program to be held on the Navajo fairgrounds, whose building could accommodate both classes and hands-on work.

Oddly, the only opposition we encountered was from the small union locals in Phoenix, Tucson, Albuquerque, and other cities, which accused us of taking jobs away from their members. They did not understand that we had worked out the training and membership programs with the heads of their unions. They began to picket us at job sites, and soon there was danger of violent confrontations. As a result, we traveled to Washington and held a high-level meeting with the top national union officials. The misunderstanding with the locals was cleared up, and the end result was an overall increase in employment opportunities for everyone.

The economic results of the training program were extremely good. When we started, no more than 10 percent of the workers on the reservation's building projects were Navajo. Within three years, 60 percent to 80 percent were Navajo. There was still plenty of work for others because the state was growing so rapidly that it could accommodate everyone's employment needs. But Navajo men and women who had previously been without skills and substantive employment were now holding good jobs and were usually able to stay near their families while they worked.

Not that everything went smoothly all the time. "Games" were played to try to keep the number of hired Navajo workers lower than was warranted, and this caused some battles. Still, the program did at least as well as we had hoped.

Turning to a labor union for assistance would not have been an unusual course of action in other parts of the country. However, *our* doing so was significant. In addition to the self-determination issue, the union realized that there were minerals, especially coal and uranium, on Navajo land. Thousands of energy-related construction jobs were expected in the next few years, and the union wanted to control the hiring process. An agreement with the Navajo not only would give the tribe the political clout it needed to work against Steiger and Goldwater, but also would give the union a voice in an area where previously it had little influence. Our political gains were furthered by the AFL-CIO's sponsorship of COPE (Committee on Political Education), whose purpose was to support prounion political candidates.

However, bringing the union to the reservation was soon to be used against me by Raymond Nakai in his 1974 bid to regain the chairmanship. Although, back in the 1950s, the Teamsters and other unions had tried to sign up members from the Navajo Nation, the unions at that time were dominated by organized crime figures, and there was great violence, even against the members. The unions almost all worked against minorities and were often considered little more than extortion rackets. You did not work unless you paid them money, and even then you might be deliberately discharged from your job. The union leadership often cared only that you had paid the membership fee.

This image, sometimes deserved, sometimes not, constituted a problem that was eventually eliminated by changes in union leadership in the following years. Many of the old union leaders either retired or were imprisoned. Although there was still corruption by the time I was dealing with unions, the new leaders had learned that they benefited the most by seriously aiding the workers. Nakai was playing to old fears, not the current reality.

The voter registration drive proved a success in 1974. Where once the Navajo had ignored the white man's elections, suddenly they were turning out in record numbers in all parts of the reservation. In Hard Rock, part of the Joint Use Area, only one Navajo had bothered to vote in 1970, but following the efforts of COPE and my supporters, 360 Navajo turned out to vote in 1974.

Conventional wisdom indicated that a Republican would take the governorship of Arizona, a foregone conclusion in years past. But after the voter registration drive, 9,006 Navajo voted for Democrat Raul Castro. When the 549,000 votes from all parts of the state were counted, Castro had won by 4,113 votes. The Navajo voters had swung the election for the Democratic candidate! Even more surprising was the fact that Senator Goldwater, often called a "national monument" by the Democrats, did not win his traditional landslide election in the state. For the first time he lost two counties—Apache and Navajo—all because of the massive voter turnout by the Navajo. The Navajo Nation had changed Arizona politics in ways that were to have unexpected repercussions.

Chapter Eleven

Senator Barry Goldwater had two reputations in Arizona. One was as a man who believed in keeping his word: Whether they viewed him as honest or dishonest, most people agreed that he would do what he said. The second reputation was as a man who made accusations in the heat of anger that usually proved to be unsubstantiated. Sometimes he was right. Sometimes he was wrong. But the fact that he frequently erred in judgment and accuracy when emotionally upset made many people uncomfortable with him.

The senator was very upset following the election. He could not admit that he had ignored the new Navajo voters, and by supporting the changes in the Joint Use Area, alienated those who had previously respected him. Among these were the residents of the area known as Big Mountain. Perhaps the least educated of all the Navajo, they had been raised in the traditional manner, the "old way." They did not think about politics or political activism. Although their extended family leaders were still powerful, they were mostly illiterate. They came out to vote for the first time because they were so upset with the Navajo and Hopi Land Settlement Act.

The Big Mountain people were not concerned with the cost of relocation or the physical burden of moving. For them the idea of leaving sacred land was incomprehensible. When a few anthropologists took a belated look at Big Mountain, they discovered that the area is a prominent sacred site, an intricate part of the creation story taught to our people for centuries. Many Navajo go to Big Mountain to partake in ceremonies and to gather medicinal herbs. Those who live there and follow the traditional ways believe that the Navajo have been there since the time of First Man and First Woman. An essential focus of our religion, the mountain contains fifteen separate areas that relate to traditional practices.

Although we could have gone to them and said, "It's written here; the Congress says it," or, "The courts say it," they would have had no appreciation of anything on paper. The only law they recognized was the law that had been handed down in the legends and the traditions of the culture in which they live.

Typical of the feelings of the old people of Big Mountain were those expressed by Ashikie Bitsie, who filed a document with the Department of the Interior. Concerned that the legislators understand the feelings of our people, she wrote: "Let the federal government know that Big Mountain is a sacred place to my forefathers and me. This mountain is a home to all living things, and it is a religious shrine to the Navajo people. Ashikie's father told me and my children never to leave or let go of the Big Mountain area."

Eventually Senator Goldwater gained the courage to visit the Big Mountain area, where the old women, traditionally responsible for family land holdings, greeted him. But his visit did not come until August of 1978, after the 1974 Navajo and Hopi Land Settlement Act ordered the partition of the Joint Use Area. By then there had been many confrontations between my people and the men who were erecting fences and ordering livestock reduction.

During this time, the people were desperately trying to get Senator Goldwater's attention. They were pointing out to him, "Mr. Goldwater, there is this so-called relocation law you are making in Washington. We have no word for relocation. The word that comes closest in our language is 'death' or 'to be no more where you were.' So why are you telling us to exist no more where we were for hundreds of years—in effect, telling us to die?" Goldwater could not answer.

At Big Mountain, Goldwater started by claiming, "I have a very, very full understanding of the sacredness of this area to you." But when confronted by the angry old people, especially the women, some of whom had previously gone to see him in Washington, he became flustered. He started talking about the fence, mentioning that he wasn't sure if it was to keep the Hopi out. He said he knew that there were some problems with "access to water or something." Then he fled as quickly as possible.

The senator had told some of the women that he would spend three days in the Big Mountain area, eating Navajo food and sleeping on sheepskins. Instead, he left after a few hours. Just as he was boarding his helicopter, he made another of his angry, unthinking remarks. "I've lived here fifty years," he said, "and I probably know this land better than most of these Navajo." At that moment my people knew that their shaky friendship with Goldwater was over.

Instead of admitting his mistakes, Goldwater went on the attack. Although there was no difference between the COPE voter registration drive for the Navajo and other drives held in other parts of the country by other groups, he falsely accused the AFL-CIO voter registration workers of using coupons that could be exchanged for beer off the reservation and special travel pay to lure the Navajo to the polls.

Everyone was outraged by the charge, which, if true, was extremely serious. The Justice Department immediately investigated what appeared to be a criminal conspiracy. They found no evidence of truth to any of Goldwater's allegations.

Peter MacDonald was hurt by Goldwater's charges. He did not want to fight the Republicans. He was a firm believer in many of the platforms of the more conservative members of the party. But he would not tolerate the Steiger bill or Goldwater's support of it. He referred to the Arizona senator as "Kit Goldwater," a vicious comment linking the politician with the deadly actions of the man who had been responsible for killing and rounding up Navajo for the Long Walk to Fort Sumner. "Perhaps he is not big enough to admit the shortcomings of the Republican party," MacDonald told an interviewer.

The interview outraged Senator Goldwater. Although MacDonald was convinced that the senator was working against the Navajo from the moment the change in the Joint Use Area was suggested, others felt that the situation was somewhat different, that Goldwater had shown no pro-Hopi bias until MacDonald declared support for the Democrats. Whatever the circumstances, the two were enemies from that day forward, each feeling betrayed by the other.

Tragically it was impossible for the two men to reconcile or find a way to work together. Peter MacDonald had been raised with the story of the Long Walk. He had seen his people demeaned by the BIA. He felt that, as chairman, he had to provide the leadership of someone who was personally responsible for the survival of a proud people nearly destroyed through hate, greed, fear, and covetousness.

The senator undoubtedly saw MacDonald as just another political enemy. He did not realize the intensity of the chairman's concerns. Peter MacDonald might have been able to compromise if he felt a dispute was personal. But where Barry Goldwater was thinking in terms of a personal problem between two powerful men, MacDonald was the last warrior, the man on whose shoulders rested the future of a proud nation. MacDonald, the chairman of the Navajo, dared not consider what MacDonald, the man, might have been willing to do if only his own life was involved. Yet because of the failure to understand this crucial difference, ultimately MacDonald would be forced to literally fight for his physical and emotional survival while striving to keep the Diné from being destroyed with him.

The change in the Joint Use status of the land was fought by Barry Goldwater in the Senate, though not for the reasons MacDonald had hoped. Goldwater was against the Steiger bill but in favor of partitioning the Joint Use Area. What bothered the senator about the Steiger bill was primarily the cost. He stated, "I don't think we have to pay money to relocate Indians when, in the case of the Navajo, they have 16 million acres." He added that the Navajo had "literally tens of thousands of acres that are not being used."

Goldwater was correct in his assessment, but he failed to understand the meaning of the land to men like Peter MacDonald. In the *young chairman's eyes, this was another attack against his people. The land had historical, religious, and cultural importance, and retaining it would enable the Navajo to stand against those whites who had so often chipped away at the original Navajo land holdings, both before and after the Long Walk.*

Goldwater used his political connections to force the legislation that MacDonald so detested, first in the House in late 1973, with Congressman Sam Steiger acting as the sponsor, and then in the Senate. It is impossible to know if the men could have worked through their differences had they not had the political struggle. But once the Navajo took a stand at the polls, Goldwater was determined to have revenge.

That revenge seemed to come, at least in part, from the passage of the 1974 Navajo and Hopi Land Settlement Act (Public Law 93-531), which ordered an Arizona federal district court to partition the Joint Use Area between the two tribes. Although relocation funds were greatly increased to $37 million, almost double what was originally planned, the emotional upheaval the passage caused remained unchanged.

Goldwater and others opposed to the Navajo had done their homework for the new bill. It was presented differently and was introduced by a Democrat, Wayne Owens of Utah. Apparently a number of trade-offs had been arranged between the time the bill was defeated by the McGovern committee and the time the new bill was proposed. Whatever the case, this time there was no way to stop it. MacDonald's opponents had put together a large enough coalition of Republicans and Democrats to overcome all objections.

The full range of influence was not mentioned at the time. Barry Goldwater was a friend of a lawyer named John S. Boyden, who worked for the Hopi Tribal Council. It was that relationship, perhaps more than other factors, that led to Goldwater's aggressiveness.

In addition to relocation, the bill contained other measures that were extremely punitive for the Navajo. For example, under the guise of proper land management, all Navajo herding livestock were ordered to drastically reduce the number of animals they owned. In addition, the reduced herds were to be controlled by the fencing of land into limited grazing areas.

Initially, fifty-six hundred Navajo would be removed from the land, though no more than one hundred Hopi were required to relocate. And always there was the memory of the slaughter of the livestock and the Navajo by Kit Carson, the forced relocation to Fort Sumner, and the additional livestock reduction of the 1930s.

Goldwater, who once seemed to have such deep understanding of the sensitivities, culture, and history of the Navajo, instantly raised fear of a new period of mass starvation and death. Typical of the comments were those of one traditional Navajo who was quoted as saying, "They tell us to get rid of our stock, and after that they will get rid of us." While no one in the U.S. government had such plans, the man's historical perspective made it impossible to ease his fears.

Ironically there was a victory of sorts for MacDonald when the Navajo and Hopi Land Settlement Act was passed. The act included an amendment, which had appeared in the original bill, granting an additional 250,000 acres outside the Joint Use Area to the Hopi. This land was near an area known as Moencopi, and the amendment seemed an obvious return to the days when white leaders systematically took away territory from the Navajo. Again MacDonald lobbied successfully, this time converting not only Democrats but also seven Republicans, enough of whom voted against the amendment to defeat it 37–35.

Once more Goldwater was irate. He wrote to the Senate Republican leader, Hugh Scott, saying: "It pained me to find Republicans voting for an amendment that had absolutely nothing to do with any state in the nation but Arizona."

The implication was clear. Goldwater was Arizona. Goldwater's desires should dominate. And he was determined to do what he could to stop his enemies, whether that meant refusing to campaign for the seven Republicans who had voted against his wishes or teaming up with MacDonald's opponents, people like Annie Wauneka, who had opposed MacDonald from the moment he returned to the reservation.

It was easy for the politicians to blame my concerns about the land division on the traditional enmity between the Navajo and the Hopi. We had been enemies over the years. But times changed, as did the people.

The Hopi had not endured the Long Walk to Fort Sumner. They were never viewed with the same hatred as the Navajo. Perhaps most important was the fact that the Hopi were more willing to accept changes in their culture, becoming an Indian Reorganization Act (IRA) tribe in the 1930s and continuing to work with whites in recent years. Today they are part of the Indian Reorganization Act with a constitution accepted by the secretary of the interior.

More open with their culture and less isolated than the Navajo, the Hopi were willing to compromise. Certainly they became popular with white politicians, whether it was through the sharing of cultural and religious treasures, political support, or even paying the expenses of journalists willing to take guided tours of their land. Whereas the Navajo wanted to be left alone to live as they had lived for centuries, the Hopi were willing to embrace change, even if that meant compromising their traditional values. At least that was how I saw it, and I came to feel that some of the politicians, such as Congressman Morris Udall, a one-time presidential contender, might be called Hopi lovers.

Moreover, the Hopi did not need the land in the Joint Use Area as much as the Navajo did. The Hopi population was smaller than the Navajo, most living quite far from the land in question. There was often a thirty-mile stretch between Joint Use Area land and Hopi settlements. And the Hopi were relatively sedentary farmers, livestock ownership being quite limited.

The Hopi also seemed to be less concerned about the money received for mineral rights. This was due to several factors. First, the Hopi leadership did not realize the true value of the minerals they might come to control. Although this was also true of most Navajo, there were enough exceptions among the Navajo leaders to give the energy and construction companies a tougher fight when developing new contracts.

But even if the Hopi did have a sense of the value of the minerals, they had lived for many years without access to those minerals and their economy did not rely on the exploitation of that land. Thus the royalties they would earn from control of the joint use land, even if less than market value, would be a windfall profit for them, and they would have less incentive to fight for the best possible contract.

We Navajo, on the other hand, experienced many bad deals, and had learned to be tough fighters. Whereas the Navajo were a known factor to the gas, mineral, and water companies, the Hopi were an unknown, and there was reason to believe that they would be much easier to handle.

Beyond the mineral rights, there was no reason for the Hopi to be given the land where Navajo had long been living. They did not need it. Few even considered moving to the areas the Navajo had been force to leave.

The size of our land holdings had also led to a "hate Navajo" attitude in Arizona and parts of New Mexico, despite the fact that they are far smaller than they were before the whites took our land from us. More than 80 percent of Arizona land is either wilderness or Indian reservation land, and the Navajo have the largest holdings, a territory about the size of the state of West Virginia.

The Anglo residents also did not understand the sacred importance of the territory within the mountains. All they saw was that our land was far less densely populated than the land that comprised the white cities and towns. They felt we had no right to complain when some of our acreage was given to the Hopi. After all, they were Indians, too. What were we complaining about?

The white residents who coveted our uranium, coal, oil, gas, and water saw no reason we shouldn't feel that these resources belonged to the state and the region. They felt that they should have access to these resources just as they would if the oil or coal or gas were located in any other part of the state. Their lack of understanding of the history, the treaties, and the legalities involved led to needless anger as well as a lack of support for the Navajo in general, and for me in particular.

The fact is that the independence of the Navajo Nation, if the treaties were respected, could, in a sense, make portions of the Southwest hostage to my people. Studies have shown that the electricity, uranium, oil, and gas that can be shipped from the Navajo Nation in one year will meet the energy requirements of Arizona for thirty years. Currently, what is taken from the Navajo Nation affects Arizona, Nevada, New Mexico, California, Utah, and parts of Texas. This has led to a tremendous interest in not being dependent upon the Navajo, much as the United States has tried to avoid being dependent upon the OPEC nations of the Middle East.

Peter MacDonald failed to recognize the danger he was facing. The special interest groups concerned with using the resources of the Navajo Nation were determined to silence him, no matter how long it took, and no matter what the cost.

The mining of Navajo coal, alone, involved vast sums of money. The Peabody Coal Company, for example, which was mining extensively on the Navajo Reservation, routinely paid royalties to the owners of the land under which the minerals had been found. But in this case, the Bureau of Indian Affairs had worked with the Tribal Council to arrange for a payment of fifteen cents a ton for the coal taken from the mine—10 percent, or less, of what Peabody and other companies paid for coal taken from private lands unrelated to Indian holdings. Even worse, the royalty could not be increased at any time, though the company's other contracts were either for very short terms or had escalator clauses for royalties geared to the changing market value of coal.

At the time the contract with Peabody was signed, coal royalties off reservation were also far greater than pension fund contributions for mine workers. Yet the typical pension fund contribution was sixty-five cents a ton, more than four times the royalty paid to the Navajo. The company saved so much money from its sweetheart deal with the BIA and the Navajo Tribal Council that the Black Mesa Power Station was able to subsidize two-thirds of the electricity bills of the residents in both New Mexico and Arizona. And all of this was done at the expense of the Navajo people.

But coal was only one of the land's resources. There were other minerals, including uranium. And there was water, the lifeblood of the primarily desert state of Arizona. The men who ran the various utilities, mining interests, road construction crews, trucking companies, and other businesses that would profit from the exploitation of Navajo land at lowest initial cost saw billions of dollars in gross income to be made, with millions of dollars in profits. How many succumbed to the temptation to bribe government officials, corrupt bureaucrats, and support those changes in the law that would ensure the maximum benefit for themselves and their companies?

Sometimes politicians recognized that their cooperation with these businesses would gain them some under-the-table benefits. At other times their desires were less tangible, but equally intense. The men in power liked their positions and wanted to keep them. They needed campaign contributions. They needed transportation. If nothing else, they needed to be certain that their opponents did not achieve the same benefits.

Peter MacDonald was expendable. Although many saw him as an honest man, dedicated to his people, there were those who felt that he would take money if they offered it. There were those who felt that he would accept the use of a private airplane to cover the vast expanses of the Navajo Nation. And there were many who, over the years, would ply him with gifts. Yet they all quickly learned that they could not persuade him to work against his own people. They could not turn him from actions that would be fair to the Navajo, and he continued to work to greatly reduce the profits and campaign contributions of the businesses desiring to exploit the Indians.

Ultimately it would take sixteen years to stop Peter MacDonald, if only for the short term. It would take the subtle erosion of his support through lies, innuendo, and exaggeration of his weaknesses. It would require the misrepresentation of his position, implying that the leader of a sovereign nation had to obey the laws and ethical constraints of someone working for the U.S. government. He lived under Navajo law but would be brought down by those who could only try him under laws in violation of long-established, seemingly legally binding treaties that had never been changed.

CHAPTER TWELVE

The efforts to destroy the tribal leaders advocating a continuing Navajo independence were becoming increasingly obvious to me. Starting in 1974 and continuing for three fiscal years, the General Accounting Office and other U.S. government, state, and private agencies began auditing how we Navajo spent the money we were receiving. The money in question came to an estimated $800 million, so an analysis of what was happening to it was certainly in order. However, the audits were not designed to ensure the proper spending of the money involved in order to protect the taxpayers. They were meant to remove me from office, along with anyone else in authority who was insisting upon autonomy for the Navajo people.

My comments may sound like self-serving denials, but even the national newspapers were aware of what was happening. In February 1977, the *Wall Street Journal* ran an editorial criticizing the government's scrutiny of me. At that time I was accused of using the mail to defraud the Tucson Gas & Electric Company of $7,916, and of filing a fraudulent income tax return for 1973. My alleged "crimes" related to the supposed submission of false travel vouchers for charter flights taken by Navajo officials for the benefit of TG&E. My share of the money was supposed to have been $4,520.

Attempts to discredit me actually began in 1972 after the Navajo Fair at the tribal fairgrounds in Window Rock. Each year lumber is used to make shelves and tables for exhibits. Then, when the fair is over, the lumber is broken down and stored. At the end of this fair, the young man who handled such arrangements took some of the lumber home with him. It was a petty theft of Navajo property, but the federal government moved in on the case, apparently using their connection with the BIA as their authority. Although the total dollar amount was small, the crime probably constituting a petty theft, if you include other possible charges, the matter can look quite serious. I don't know whether the government threatened the young man with a charge of theft of government property, but the youth was terrified. Instead of seeing himself facing a first offense resulting most likely in restitution, a fine, and probation, he was certain he would go to jail for a long time and agreed to turn in someone higher up to avoid his horrible fate.

As it turned out, my chief of staff had also taken some of the lumber, using approximately three hundred dollars worth of scrap to build an overhang to shade the front of his house.

Although both men were wrong in their actions, neither had done anything particularly serious. Unfortunately, after my chief of staff was indicted, he was taken before a grand jury and made the mistake of claiming he was innocent.

One of the FBI men involved in the case befriended my chief of staff and took him to lunch after his grand jury appearance. Pretending to commiserate with him, the agent said that he didn't understand why the government was making such a big deal out of a petty theft. In his "opinion," even if my chief of staff was guilty, it was such a minor offense that there was no sense putting someone through all that hell.

The sympathetic ear was all my chief of staff needed. He admitted that he had taken the lumber, expressing his concern that things had gotten out of hand. The lunch ended cordially, but the FBI had what it needed—an admission by my chief of staff that he had lied to the grand jury. What had formerly been a misdemeanor was now compounded by the felony of perjury, which could carry a five-year sentence.

Now the pressure was on. According to my chief of staff, the FBI told him that he would go to jail for five years for perjury unless he revealed some incriminating information about Peter MacDonald.

Before I ran for tribal office, my understanding of how the FBI functioned was quite limited. My image of the organization was based on a television show from the late 1960s, "The FBI," in which agents worked for truth, justice, and all the other values we Americans hold dear. As an ex-Marine and a man who loved the United States, I believed that the FBI was the top law-enforcement agency in the country, that its agents worked without prejudice and without compromise, that the FBI was independent of everyone, determined to fight crime wherever it occurred. Never realizing that this image did not match real life, I was soon to be educated in ways I neither wanted nor expected.

My first awareness of the rather unpleasant truth had come during my first campaign for tribal chairman against Raymond Nakai. Far more politically aware than I, he and his staff had learned that an FBI investigation can be used to discredit someone, even if that person is innocent of any wrongdoing. I also discovered that there were times when, instead of conducting a thorough investigation, agents would question the acts of only one person, find evidence to support only one side, and not attempt to uncover all the facts. This meant that a person making a valid challenge could be the focus of a criminal probe and that guilty parties could escape. If an investigation was not conducted objectively, reputations could be damaged or destroyed.

Raymond Nakai's people understood this, and told the FBI that I was misusing the funds for the Office of Navajo Economic Opportunity. Because it was federal money, the FBI had to investigate.

I was delighted when two FBI agents showed up at my office. They were my heroes, and I would do anything to help them.

The agents wanted information about the ONEO program and the disbursement of funds. We talked extensively, and I gave them everything they requested.

A couple of months later the same two agents returned. This time they told me that I was a target for the FBI.

"What does that mean?" I asked them.

They said that you became a target when someone accused you of wrongdoing related to federal crimes. Either Raymond Nakai, his lawyer Harold Mott, or someone else in the Nakai administration had told the FBI that I was not running ONEO according to the federal guidelines, that I was building houses for my friends and family rather than for those most qualified for the home improvement program.

I was surprised at the charges and denied them. The agents explained that I didn't have to talk with them, and that I could have a lawyer with me if I wanted. But I knew I had done nothing wrong and felt I did not need a lawyer. I gave them more paperwork than they requested, and they left my office.

Neither I nor ONEO had legal representation, but I knew a lawyer and I told him what had happened. He said that when the FBI tells you that you're a target, that means they are going after you.

I said I had done nothing wrong and had cooperated with the agents. But the lawyer advised me to be careful because the FBI was tricky. He asked me if one of the agents was friendly and the other tough. I was surprised to hear him ask that because that was exactly the way the agents had behaved. He explained the trick, that one agent would try to scare me while the other became my friend in the hope that I would confide in him. The lawyer suggested I protect myself by having a lawyer present each time agents came by.

I explained that I couldn't afford to do that, so he said that the next best thing was to have someone present in the room as a witness or to make a tape recording of the meeting. He said that agents did not always act properly and would sometimes say things that were not true in order to trap people. Moreover, agents always worked in pairs, each backing up the other, and meeting with me alone would give them the advantage. Having a witness, a tape recorder, or a lawyer present would protect me.

I still resisted thinking that my heroes could do something like this, but I decided to take the lawyer's advice. When the agents returned, my secretary was out, so I asked the agents if they would mind my tape recording our conversation. I told them that I would be happy to make a copy of the tape for them to take with them so that all of us would have an accurate record of what was said. I explained that until I had talked with my lawyer friend, I really hadn't understood what they meant when they said I was a target. The tape recording would be best for all of us.

The agents refused. They said they couldn't talk with me if I was going to tape record the conversation. I didn't understand, but they said they just didn't work that way. If I insisted upon a tape recorder, they would not talk.

The men left immediately. I was very upset. For the first time I seriously questioned the FBI. These were representatives of the U.S. government. They supposedly had a great deal of integrity. I couldn't understand why they wouldn't talk with me simply because I wanted to use a tape recorder.

The agents came back one more time, and again refused to allow our conversation to be recorded. After that, however, they never returned again, and the election proceeded as it should have done. I had learned that people in high office could use the FBI to discredit their opponents, and I had become a little suspicious of my heroes.

The tactic used on my chief of staff in the lumber theft affair was one I was to see again and again in many cases throughout the United States. The FBI would find someone guilty of a low-level crime, and promise to grant immunity from prosecution, give probation, or let the person off easily if he or she would disclose information that would allow them to indict someone more important. They would then use that information to intimidate this more important individual and then make the same deal with him so that they could move higher still. Sometimes they had an ultimate target in mind, and in the case of the lumber thefts, I was that ultimate target.

But the FBI had a problem with my chief of staff. He insisted that I had done nothing wrong, and he refused to make something up. He was indicted for perjury and given a last chance to provide incriminating information. However, he explained that there was nothing he could tell them that would help incriminate me. He eventually went to court, receiving five years' probation. It is unlikely that he would have faced such a punishment had the government not been trying to find a way to hurt me.

Had the Navajo been allowed to use our own legal methods, the man would simply have returned the original lumber or provided new lumber equal in amount and quality. The case would have ended there.

The *Wall Street Journal* reporters were well aware of how ridiculous the situation had become. The editorial noted that in the previous three years there had been 176 audits and financial reviews of the money the Navajo had received from the various federal and state sources. None of those audits found any form of fiscal mismanagement or theft. The number of audits in so short a time—one audit every six days on average—was far beyond normal. More important, the people and the agencies involved were so diverse that it would have been impossible to influence all of them to clear me had I been guilty of any wrongdoing. And when allegations were finally made, the dollar amount was so small, my history so clean, and the cost of the 176 audits so enormous that the real theft of taxpayers' dollars came from the continued vendetta.

The public thought that there might be some truth to these allegations when, as mentioned earlier, I was indicted at the end of 1976 by a federal grand jury for filing false travel vouchers in connection with an agreement with Tucson Gas & Electric to erect power lines on sections of the Navajo Nation. I had to go to the expense of hiring a criminal defense lawyer who was able to prove that the charges—that I had received $7,916 for falsified travel vouchers—were meaningless. In fact, the federal judge found so little evidence that he issued a directed verdict of acquittal. And Ken Fields, one of the prosecutors, later told the *New York Times* that he thought that he and the other prosecutors had probably been political dupes.

The FBI agents investigating the charges against me admitted on the stand that they had checked my bank accounts and could not find any deposits indicating I had taken any money. They also admitted that they did not check the accounts of others named in the case. Such investigative actions are routine following allegations of criminal activity: Not executing them was evidence that the FBI was using its power to discredit me rather than to determine the truth.

Moreover, the other men involved in the case, who were receiving money from TG&E and not reporting their income to the IRS, were given immunity to testify against me.

Many reporters have claimed that MacDonald is the most corrupt chairman the Navajo have ever had. This sentiment has been echoed by some of the Navajo people, though many others defend him. However, when anyone is asked what his crimes might be, most feel that he learned to live well and to take advantage of the perquisites of the office without compromising his integrity.

Interviews with critics generally produce the same comments. For example, MacDonald took advantage of his position to obtain the use of limousines, airplanes, and gifts, including money. Why were these items given to him? To buy influence, come the replies. And did they buy influence? No, but we hoped they would.

Yet during these same periods, Anglo politicians were involved with land deals from which they made extensive profits. These same senators and congressmen hid campaign contributions from special interest groups by taking the money in the form of exorbitant speaking fees. Others used political action committee funds and even seemingly simple items such as Senator Goldwater's growing collection of Hopi Kachina dolls, which was worth an estimated $500,000 when it was donated to a museum. It was easier to attack MacDonald than to disclose what his U.S. government challengers were doing.

Eventually MacDonald's enemies stooped to pettiness. For example, the aggressive Arizona State University special collections division in Tempe attempted to obtain the personal papers of Peter MacDonald for its collection. This would be the most important collection of written records from the leader of the largest Indian nation in the United States. Regardless of MacDonald's honesty or dishonesty, the papers would provide documented insight into a man whose life and work had great influence on the American Southwest.

Senator Barry Goldwater had previously endowed a chair at Arizona State University and had arranged for his papers to go to a historical center whose archives were housed at the school. When he learned that MacDonald's work would also be there, he was enraged. Goldwater allegedly told officials that if MacDonald's papers were there, he would not continue the endowment. There was also an indication that Goldwater might withdraw his papers from the historical association to which he had donated them. The association was not part of the university, but its storage facilities were on the university grounds.

Thus this was an extremely critical period for everyone, though no one knew what the outcome of the feuds would be. Like a man marked by a Mafia contract, Peter MacDonald, by his actions, had condemned himself to destruction—personally, professionally, physically. Yet the drama that was beginning now would not play itself out for almost sixteen years.

CHAPTER THIRTEEN

W e had good relations with Congress in spite of all these problems. Our efforts to improve the lives of our people often gained sympathy.

During my first term in office, for example, our work on the Navajo Community College began. This two-year school provided three different types of opportunity for Navajo. The first was an education beyond high school, the same as that offered by any other junior college in the country. The second was specialized training in fields requiring two years of intensive study. The third was higher education for Navajo youths who would transfer to colleges and universities to finish their four-year degrees. This type of facility was quite common in communities throughout the United States but had been lacking on the Navajo Reservation despite its large population.

The government agreed to provide continuing funding for the school, allowing us to plan an institution that would serve many generations. The alternative, short-term grants that would have to be renewed, would have prevented us from attracting skilled teachers. The passage of that funding, through what was known as the Navajo Community College Bill, was an obvious victory, of which we were proud.

The evaluation of our energy resources also revealed concerns related to the federal government. Yet, to my amazement, neither the past Navajo leaders nor our "protectors" in the BIA had ever conducted an energy survey.

The obstacles to such an evaluation were twofold. First, there was no inventory of the oil wells on reservation land, the volume of the reserves, or the volume being removed, and no one had determined whether proper payments were being made. The energy companies would send a statement to the United States Geological Survey (USGS) reporting the extraction of a certain number of barrels of oil. Then, three to six months later, the companies would send a royalty check for the oil to the BIA. The government administrator would compare the check to the company's statement and, if it matched, forward the money to the tribe. No effort was made to see if the amount of oil the company reported having taken from the well actually matched the amount removed. Any inaccuracies could be indications of fraud.

The second problem was that no one knew the amount of reserves the reservation actually possessed or how best to conserve them. No one knew if a coal mine could be depleted in one year or if it would last a hundred years. And there was no planning for the removal of the coal to ensure the best income for the Navajo Nation. If the mine had a million tons of coal, it might be in the best interest of the tribe to mine all of the coal in a single year and take the money that could be made from its sale. Or it might be best to ration the coal removal to 100,000 tons a year for the next ten years. Only an inventory of our reserves would allow for this type of economic planning.

It seemed as though no one had cared about the economic future of the Navajo Nation. Energy resources were available for the taking, with no thought for how best to exploit them. This was bad for the country as well, because knowledge of our reserves helps the government to plan strategically by determining the degree of U.S. reliance on foreign energy resources in times of crisis.

For the future of the Navajo Nation itself, the energy inventory was critical. If we were to determine our ability to help finance our move toward self-sufficiency and self-determination, we had to know what resources we had and what we would have in the future. In addition, we needed to be certain that we were not losing money and minerals through fraud. We needed field checks, which the BIA was not providing.

Equally harmful was the practice of delaying the passthrough of funds. Money earmarked for the Navajo was coming six months to a year after it could have been available. This meant that we were losing interest on money that should have been immediately available.

Outraged by these circumstances, I began complaining to the BIA officials and the White House. Simultaneously, an energy crisis was occurring which forced the United States to look more closely at domestic supplies. The Navajo Nation was soon flooded with proposals from energy companies that wanted to use our resources. Exxon Corporation, for example, wanted to lease some Navajo Reservation land to look for uranium.

Again I insisted on a change from the old ways. Exxon acted as energy companies had acted in the past. The officials went to the BIA to plan their lease arrangement, then came to us and told us what they were going to do, expecting the Tribal Council and me to rubber-stamp the agreement. We refused.

I told Exxon that the times were changing. I explained that they would have to go directly to the Navajo leadership if they wanted to do business with the Navajo. If they went to the BIA first, we weren't going to talk with them. But no one had ever had to deal with the Navajo as an independent nation before, and Exxon did not take us seriously at first. Their officials talked with officials of other companies who were doing business on the reservation, but those companies only knew how things had been done in the past when the BIA represented us.

The next time Exxon approached us, the company hired two Navajo men to see us first. These men barely had a high school education and were unable to negotiate for the company. Perhaps Exxon thought we'd be pleased to see Navajo instead of white personnel, but as a trained engineer who had advanced into the ranks of management at Hughes Aircraft and who had consulted with professionals, I was even more insulted than when the company had first approached the BIA.

I told Exxon, then passed the word to the other energy companies, that we wouldn't do business through the BIA anymore, and that we wouldn't begin negotiations with token Navajo Indians. If the companies wanted to see the chairman of the Navajo Nation or the advisory committee of the Tribal Council, they would have to bring in their top people—their president, chairman of the board, or whichever corporate officers they used for such meetings—just as they do when negotiating for mineral rights in other countries. Only the word of such individuals ultimately matters; talks with underlings, especially token Navajo employees, mean nothing without top approval.

After that, Exxon and the other companies began sending their top people. It took us a year to develop what we felt was a favorable lease arrangement.

These changes were not unusual on a global scale, but they were firsts for any Indian land in the United States. Traditionally the energy companies were given the land and allowed to do whatever they wanted with it. Often this meant nothing. They would pay a small fee for all rights to the land and then do no exploration unless energy prices rose significantly. Such speculation tied up the land and was of no value to the tribes.

To counter this, we granted finite leases with specific requirements. For example, a company might be granted the right to look for uranium on a set acreage for five years. The first year the company would be allowed to explore the total acreage. The second year, a set percentage of that acreage would be withdrawn from them and they could only search a smaller area. Additional reductions took place the third year and so forth.

In addition to the acreage reduction, the company was required by contract to spend so many millions of dollars on exploration each year. This assured us that there would be no speculation at the expense of the Navajo Nation. The company was leasing only the land it would truly try to use.

Finally, any mining projects that ensued after exploration would be handled as joint ventures between the energy company and the Navajo Nation. The energy company would take 51 percent of the profits, and the Navajo Nation 49 percent. The arrangement was fair when compared with leases in other parts of the United States and throughout the world. But it also provided a much higher profit for the Navajo than we had been given under the arrangements made in the past by the Bureau of Indian Affairs.

We were proud of the contract we negotiated with Exxon. The moment both parties signed, Exxon would immediately place $6 million in an escrow account. However, there was one snag. Under the federal law, the contract had to be approved by the BIA. The law did not require the BIA to negotiate it, although the organization had taken that power for itself in the past. But the energy companies could not begin operating on the Navajo land unless the BIA reviewed the contract.

Although the BIA officials saw what we had done and recognized it as the best deal any Indian tribe had ever achieved, they were determined to punish us for economic self-determination. They held on to that lease for three years before ultimately approving the contract.

I went to Washington and spoke to the president, to congressmen and senators, to the secretary of the interior, and to others, but nothing was done. And then, when the BIA finally granted approval, not one word of the agreement had been changed. The BIA officials had managed to keep us from getting the $6 million and the interest that money would have earned during those three years.

In the meantime, a consortium of major energy companies formed a joint venture to build a billion-dollar coal gasification plant on the reservation. The companies went the same initial route as Exxon and met with the same response, eventually bringing their top people to meet directly with us.

In order to negotiate with the consortium, we had to hire geologists and other experts to advise us about highly specialized technical matters for which we did not have trained personnel. The talks lasted on and off for two years, but the power companies refused to yield to our demand for a joint venture.

The companies were shocked by our action. In the past, the BIA had negotiated for a front bonus and straight royalty that would not fluctuate with changes in inflation or in prices. But we were looking to the future and changing energy demands. The project would affect Arizona and California, at the very least, two rapidly growing states with increasing energy demands. Prices were likely to increase, and if they did, the profits would escalate rapidly. A joint venture would give everyone a fair piece of the action, even if prices changed.

Although the consortium was not expecting such demands, we saw no reason to yield since what we requested was fair. The joint venture itself meant that we would share some of the financial risk, so none of our contingencies were really out of line.

The companies were not looking at the unique situation of the Navajo Nation. First, we had to operate as a government. The royalty and bonus were not different from what would be paid to any other government, whether in that manner or in the form of taxes. However, since the land was jointly owned by all the Navajo people, we also had to look at this as a business venture that would affect our financial future. We had to negotiate from the dual position of government and business people, making a deal that would be beneficial for all concerned.

The companies were angry because they had spent between $25 million and $30 million on the project. This included special research, tests, lobbying in Washington, lobbying among the Navajo, and many other activities. They felt that after they had spent so much money, an agreement should have been ensured.

It was an odd position for the consortium to take, because such expenditures were the price of doing business. The companies apparently agreed because, six months later, they came back to us, willing to talk joint venture for the first time.

We had also been busy during that six-month period. We were initially trying to develop a fair business arrangement to take to the Tribal Council. But without the pressure of getting the best deal, we'd had time to look at side issues that had yet to be considered. One such issue was the environmental impact of a coal gasification plant. We discovered that the pollution would be so bad that we could not allow such a project. When the companies returned with a fair business offer, we were forced to turn them away because of the other problems it would cause the Navajo people and their land.

My feeling throughout my first term as chairman was that we should not jump into any of the schemes we were offered, regardless of the money. There were too many factors to be weighed, too many unknowns caused by years of lack of oversight. We needed to know what we had, what we could do, and the real by-products of these projects, such as pollution, long-term damage to the land, and disruption of the life-style of the Navajo people. As a result, we concentrated our primary efforts on the inventory of resources and a ten-year plan for the advancement of the Navajo Nation.

One of the goals of the ten-year plan was to change the way we had been operating in the past. We had reacted to every crisis instead of looking ahead in the areas of social, economic, resource, and political development. In 1972 I brought in several top people as consultants, headed by Wilbur Atcitty, to help us determine where we were in relation to these developments in the United States as a whole. This evaluation would show us our problems and our needs.

The results were shocking. Unemployment in Arizona and New Mexico ranged from a low of 5.5 percent to a high of 8 percent, but unemployment in the Navajo Nation exceeded 60 percent—ten times greater than the rate in most of the surrounding communities. Likewise our per capita income was much lower than that of other parts of the country, including the so-called Rust Belt, where the economy was on a decline due to foreign competition in the steel and automobile industries.

Our ten-year plan could not bring us up to the economic level of the nation as a whole, but we felt that we could reduce unemployment to at least 30 percent on the reservation, with 20 percent a preferable target. While that figure would still be high, it would mark a major turnaround in both the job market and the vocational education of our people.

Likewise we wanted to increase the life span of the Navajo. In many parts of the reservation life expectancies were ten to twenty years less than in the rest of the United States. Medical care was limited or nonexistent. Illnesses that were considered minor in other parts of the country due to vaccines and antibiotics were still killing Navajo at a rate similar to what existed at the turn of the century. We did not need new technology; we needed to bring existing medical knowledge to people who had been isolated from such advances.

We were able to put together an exhaustive analysis of what we needed and what we would need in the next decade as the population increased. We looked at the cost, as well as the ways in which our financial needs could realistically be broken down among federal programs, state aid, and money from the Navajo Nation's existing resources. While providing an understanding of what we needed to do to make our people equal to those living outside the reservation, the analysis also showed us how badly our people had been affected by the lack of adequate federal assistance.

Even our ability to travel within the Navajo Nation was hindered by years of neglect. Over four thousand miles of roads had been constructed, yet less than a quarter of them were paved. Transportation was hampered during much of the year by rain and snow, which turned those roads into impassable bogs. Bringing trucks, cranes, and other necessary equipment for the construction of new homes, hospitals, and other facilities was pointless without road improvements.

As a result of these discoveries, I had to do some soul searching. I had been talking about self-determination. I had been talking about being an independent nation within the United States. Yet here I was facing the need to look to the U.S. government for massive support.

I decided that our history had shown that we were deliberately kept in social and economic isolation by the policies of the U.S. government following our release from the Fort Sumner area. We had not failed because we were incompetent or had made wrong decisions about our future. Our problems were caused by outsiders, and there was no reason we should not seek a massive infusion of capital to help us achieve self-reliance. We would use any help available to us to advance our people.

The Tribal Council approved our ten-year plan, which I then took to Washington. I met with Vice-President Spiro Agnew, who arranged for me to meet with Nixon's cabinet in the Treaty Room of the old executive wing of the White House. This unusual high-level conference reinforced the interest Nixon had in the Indian people.

The amount of money we needed was enormous—approximately $4 billion (between $400 million and $500 million per year spread over the next decade). Our experts had also put together the potential cost of delays, based on inflation, and I was able to show that if there were delays in moving forward with the plan, the same results would cost significantly more.

All of those at the meeting understood and pledged their help. The media, in fact, referred to me as a Nixon Republican. It was partly because of this understanding that I was eventually asked to introduce Nixon at the Republican National Convention, before my run-in with Senator Goldwater.

The one thing that did come out of that meeting was a change in the 1972 Republican platform. I may have been hated by Senator Goldwater and his supporters, but Nixon's interest in Indian self-determination resulted in what seemed a subtle change to everyone other than those in the know.

The Republican platform called for all Indian tribes to submit to Congress a plan for economic recovery or economic survival, depending on the condition they were in at the time. Each plan would be analyzed by the administration and Congress. If the plans were realistic, the administration and Congress would fund them. This would bypass the BIA and the Department of the Interior and allow for self-determination. Some tribes would get more money than in the past. Others would get less money, but it would be appropriately designated.

Of course, I had ulterior motives in suggesting all this. There was no way the government could help only the Navajo. Any such program had to be one that would help all the tribes. But since we Navajo had put together a ten-year program just before this change in the Republican platform, we would be the first tribe to receive money.

The convention delegates were quite sympathetic to what I proposed. Despite my feud with Goldwater, my lobbying efforts on the convention floor resulted in the change, the only change anyone succeeded in making in the platform. That success made me quite proud.

Ultimately the course of history worked against us. The Watergate scandal brought down the Nixon administration, ending both its good and its bad policies. Without such intense support, we were never able to gain the full federal assistance we had anticipated. Yet even with limited funding, we followed the plan we had developed, because we felt that even a partial success would mean great advances for the Navajo people.

We looked at other areas for change during this period. For example, the tribal courts were still being run the way they had been in the 1940s and 1950s when I had been involved. The method of settling cases may have been good, but the system was so primitive that it was impossible to establish precedents and a legal system.

We began recording the proceedings for the first time, arranging for transcripts of all cases. We also established a full range of criminal laws and procedures for handling criminal cases. Before this time, the cases were either of a civil nature or related to such offenses as drunken driving and domestic violence. These actions allowed the tribal courts to be recognized off the reservation as true courts.

One of the most enjoyable moments of my chairmanship came in 1971 when I was contacted by the scientists at the National Aeronautics and Space Administration in Houston. The two new astronauts they were preparing to land on the moon, as part of the Apollo 15 mission—Jim Irwin and David Scott—were inexperienced, and NASA wanted to test both the men and the equipment on terrain identical to the landing site selected on the moon.

NASA had found that the Gray Mountain area near Cameron, Arizona, was the right locale. This was a section of Navajo Nation land, and the scientists wanted our permission to bring their men and equipment to the area for the test. Naturally we were delighted to cooperate.

The men and equipment were flown and trucked to the Gray Mountain site. For two days I watched what was taking place. The gravitational pull of the earth was far stronger than that on the moon, of course, so special tires were placed on the moon buggy, the golf cart–like vehicle they would drive on the moon.

A mock-up of the lunar landing module was placed on the ground. Then the astronauts, wearing the same space suits they would wear on the moon, had to climb out of the craft, set up the moon buggy, get on it, and drive around, carefully identifying the terrain and taking soil samples, just as they would on the moon. These men were not geologists, but they had been trained to identify what they saw so that the experts could learn from their observations. The Gray Mountain area was well known to the scientists, so this was like a final exam for the men. In addition, they would test the radio equipment, because, though the support team was right there with them, all conversations would go through Houston, just as would happen on the real flight. They would also have to practice their timing, since the life-support system of the suits would work for only a limited time. The greatest difference between this terrain and the moon, aside from the gravitational pull, was that if the men made a mistake or if they found they could not psychologically adapt to working in the confines of their equipment, the problem would not be life-threatening.

As the astronauts worked, a medicine man came over to the site. He was herding his sheep and became curious about what was happening. Speaking in Navajo, he asked me, "What are those funny-looking fellows doing?"

I explained that the two men were going to the moon and that they were practicing for that trip. The medicine man did not believe me, so I explained the technical aspects of what he was seeing and how they would travel. This got him interested, and he was still watching with me when the scientists took a lunch break, gathering at a giant trailer where a cook had prepared food for everyone.

I took the medicine man over to meet the astronauts, acting as interpreter for the three of them. They talked for a while, and then the medicine man asked if he could send a message with the astronauts.

The medicine man explained that, according to Navajo legend, there were Navajo who stopped at the moon on their way to the sun. There was a chance that a few of the Navajo were still there, and if they were, and if the astronauts ran into them, he wanted to send them a message.

The astronauts laughed, but humored the medicine man by agreeing to take his message. They asked him to write it out, but upon learning that the Navajo language was not a written one, they offered him a tape recorder.

I turned on the tape recorder for the medicine man, then returned to watching the training exercise. The medicine man handed me the recorder when he was through and left to go back to his sheep, which had wandered off just far enough so that he had to herd them together and continue with his work.

When the astronauts were finished for the day, they asked about the medicine man. I explained that he had recorded a message for them to take with them. They turned on the machine, playing it for me so I could interpret it for them.

I immediately started laughing. The medicine man had said, "Beware of these two fellows. They will want to make a treaty with you."

CHAPTER FOURTEEN

Not everything was going well during this period, though. The Indian Self-Determination Act had been passed in 1972, stipulating, among other provisions, that Indians could contract to take over programs previously handled by the BIA. However, the BIA was able to control the terms of the contracts in a manner that ensured failure.

For example, money to run the tribal police traditionally was channeled through the BIA, which then established the tribal police department, set all rules and regulations, and paid the bills. Indians manned all positions within the police, but they essentially worked for the BIA.

The tribe had originally contracted with the BIA to run the police department in the late 1950s and 1960s. During my administration, we applied to make the contract more realistic under the Indian Self-Determination Act. This meant putting together a plan for the organization and receiving the money from the BIA. Although the end result was supposedly determined by the Navajo, the BIA could control the amount of funds we received, and the contract was subject to their restrictions.

The BIA officials used what amounted to a loophole in the Indian Self-Determination Act to ensure our failure. First they established the rules and regulations the tribal police would have to follow when operating under contract to the Navajo Nation. These were far more involved than the rules and regulations the Navajo police followed when the BIA ran the organization.

The additional paperwork and restrictions would not have been such a problem had it not been for the funding. Instead of providing the full amount of money requested, which would have ensured the success of the program, the BIA limited the funding received, providing just enough money for operations and no money for administration. This meant that the tribe would have to either underwrite the administrative costs, which should have come from federally authorized funds, or transfer them from the money meant for operations, which would have reduced the department's effectiveness. Either way there was a good chance of failure, which would allow the BIA to tell Congress that the Indians were too stupid to do on their own what the BIA had administered successfully in the past.

The BIA justified its actions by saying that it had to monitor what was being done with the money provided to the Navajo. If ten or fifteen BIA officials had once worked in a position that was now being contracted by the Navajo, the BIA would hold back enough money to continue paying their salaries. They then would claim that this was their way of being certain the money was being properly spent by the Navajo. They were simply wasting money, creating needless jobs within their own bureaucracy, and ensuring our failure in ways that would not have occurred had they followed the intent of the law.

Ultimately the Indian Self-Determination Act proved to be a fraud. The law was worded in such a way that many restrictions could be placed on the Indians and almost all programs were deliberately underfunded, ensuring their failure. The plans all looked good on paper because, with the money requested, they would have succeeded. The Indian programs were like any business requiring an established minimum amount of capital to succeed. Yet, with this reduction in funds, there was no way the Indians could prove their ability. Even worse, an outside analysis of the plans that had been approved would show that anyone with any intelligence could make a go of them. Since almost no one noticed that money was deliberately being withheld, we Indians appeared to be incompetent.

The final result was that few of the contracted programs survived more than two or three years. The Indians were forced to drop the underfunded programs and allow the BIA to take them back under its jurisdiction. The BIA would then restore the full, necessary operating budget, make the programs successful again, and "prove" that Indians need a paternalistic bureaucracy to survive.

Tragically this was not exclusively a Navajo Nation problem. Had it been, we would have been irate, but the number of people hurt would have been relatively small. But every Indian tribe in the nation faced this problem, from the Navajo, who were the largest, to the smallest tribes struggling to survive. Racist stereotypes were reinforced because of the loopholes in the Self-Determination Act, which actually set back the advancement of the people it was designed to help. The BIA grew larger and larger at a time when we thought it should go out of business.

Despite such problems, we were ultimately able to control far more of the services affecting our people. During Raymond Nakai's last year in office, when BIA service contract arrangements did not exist, his budget had included $30 million in tribal funds and $100,000 in government funds. By 1976, the annual tribal budget was over $60 million, and we had over $100 million in funds from the profitable government contracts. We could not end the frauds, but our successes were on such a large scale that they constituted an obvious challenge to those who believed we were incompetent.

Federal money also enabled us to make many improvements. In 1970, for example, the BIA gave us a budget of $1 million to maintain approximately 4,000 miles of existing roads and to construct new roads. By 1973, we had approximately 4,000 additional miles of roads and our funding had been raised to $18 million per year.

We established the Crownpoint Manpower Center for job training with a $3 million grant. And we increased BIA-backed scholarship funding from $2 million a year to $6 million a year. To meet the educational needs of all the low-income Navajo students who had proved themselves capable of high scholastic achievement, we actually needed $8 million when we started, but we did succeed in tripling the money available from a program that originally no one had expected to grow, and that was quite a triumph for us. Even so, we are still in need of an additional $14 million of scholarship assistance if we are to fully meet the needs of today's students.

We also began looking for land where we could build a new capital, including our own buildings, schools, and an airstrip. When I took office, the Navajo Nation offices were housed in rented BIA buildings. Having our own, from which we would rent space to the BIA, would go a long way to making clear that we were autonomous and would help eliminate the notion that we could operate only with the approval of the BIA.

Our one failure—though I would call it a success in light of what has happened in the industry since—was with the American Indian Bank of Washington, D.C. We thought it would be a good idea to establish a bank, run by American Indians, that would serve the needs of Indians. We were able to obtain top personnel, including Barney Old Coyote, a well-educated Crow Indian who served as the bank's first president. And we were able to borrow a million dollars for initial funding, a loan that we paid back the first year. I was on the board of directors until 1982, and the bank went out of business a couple of years after that, all assets being sold in 1987.

The idea was a good one. Our bank would be quite similar to the independent banks that once were a part of rural America, serving the needs of agricultural communities in which incomes varied from year to year and a knowledge of local business conditions, including boom and bust cycles, could help long-term planning. The needs of the people in such areas were so different from those in urban areas that large banks accustomed to working in major cities lacked personnel who could tell the good loans from the bad.

We faced a few problems: We made some bad loans, and we had to deal with restrictions against certain types of expansion that would have aided our people. But overall we did better than we realized. At the time we went out of business, the bank had made a small profit for everyone involved without going bankrupt and without needing the federal government to bail out depositors. We simply lacked the immense capital necessary for growth and could not stay as we were without ultimately getting into trouble. Rather than create problems, the business was closed, a sound management decision that kept anyone from being hurt and that taught us that the establishment of such a bank had been premature. However, in light of the eventual failure of many Anglo savings and loans, we were a success even when we closed.

Yet I could never escape the frustration and sadness of our circumstances. The problems were evident to everyone who studied the report we had prepared on reservation conditions and needs. There was no question that what we were seeking to do was necessary to benefit the people of the Navajo Nation. There was no question that our conditions matched those of a Third World nation, although we lived in the most advanced country in the world. Yet our isolation from mainstream America, the lack of interest by the national news media, and the uncaring bureaucratic mentality of many BIA administrators made every day a new fight. People expressed sympathy with our plight when we showed them the facts. But with so blatant a problem and so clear a plan for change, we should not have been constantly at war to achieve what was right. I could not help but wonder just how much progress we had really made in the last century.

The changes that were coming all too slowly to the Navajo Nation began at least to occur throughout the United States. We had the people, the expertise, and the dedication to return often to Washington to bring attention to our problems. Congress looked at what we were saying, agreed with our position, then considered ways to help the Navajo. But although we were the largest tribe, Congress could not make an exception for us. Each funding effort was coupled with new funds for all the Indian tribes. As a result we soon found that we were in a leadership position for all Indians.

It was not that we wanted to take on such a role. We were not altruistic. Instead, we believed that we would have a better life only if all Indians had a better life. We soon became spokespeople for other tribes as well as consultants, answering their leaders' question about how to better their conditions. This led to yet another confrontation when I decided to bring the knowledge we had gained about maximizing the nation's resources to all Indians whose land included needed energy resources.

I was a little naive about what I would face when I made this decision. Although I had already challenged Senator Goldwater and his friends, I did not fully understand the trouble I was creating for other members of the federal government. But my insistence upon the Navajo taking advantage of their energy resources as a way of becoming independent was a message touching other rebellious hearts. To this day, though our cultures are different and we have often been at odds in the past, unity among the tribes when dealing with shared economic issues has increased all our incomes. We have made millions of dollars more than we would have had we acted alone, allowing the BIA to speak for us.

My re-election to the position of chairman in 1974 went smoothly. I had my supporters and I had my enemies, but everyone knew we were moving in a positive direction. Changes were taking place that were making conditions better than in the past. While many Navajo, especially the elders, did not want to see changes, most recognized that, since they were inevitable, it was better to have them managed by a Navajo than by the BIA.

The land dispute was now taking place on two fronts. In 1973 we became involved in a legal dispute with the Ute concerning two sections of land along the New Mexico and Colorado state lines. Neither area was particularly large, but both contained a lot of oil and gas, and it was important to resolve the ownership issue.

Back in the 1800s the government had conducted a bad survey that created overlapping boundaries. Although Raymond Nakai's administration had considered settling for half of the land and half of the oil, an agreement had not been reached by the time I became chairman. I felt that there were adequate records to determine the true owner of the land, and my legal advisers assured me that their research indicated the Navajo actually owned both parcels. I decided to fight because we needed all the land that belonged to us. By the time of the re-election, the court had ruled in our favor. We were given title to the land, and we were also given all the money that had been placed in escrow as a result of oil and gas leases in effect in the area.

By 1975 the BIA's actions concerning our dispute over the Joint Use Area were becoming quite intense. BIA agents were impounding any Navajo livestock they found grazing on land designated for the Hopi. The Navajo tribe had to pay a daily fine for the livestock, as well as more money to have them released, or the animals were sold at auction.

The Navajo people living in Arizona, where the impounding was occurring, were angry. Some of their animals had wandered onto Hopi designated land, and some were deliberately grazed there, since the land had previously been available for Navajo use. But we were also receiving reports from both sides indicating that in a number of instances, BIA workers were herding livestock grazing in properly assigned locations, moving them onto Hopi land, and then impounding them. Apparently this was being done to create a confrontation that would make the Navajo look bad.

The BIA got their confrontation, but it was not quite what they wanted. My people could not tolerate the impounding of the animals. The animals were doing no harm, and there would have been no problem had it not been for the tensions arising out of the dispute over the disposition of the Joint Use Area. We had to stop the impounding before there was bloodshed.

I arranged a meeting at the Navajo chapter house in Jeddito, Arizona, and there we decided to march five miles to Keams Canyon, part of Hopi land. We alerted Washington to what we were going to do and demanded to meet with BIA officials from both regional headquarters in Phoenix and Keams Canyon. I explained to the officials that unless they met with us to resolve the problem, there would be bloodshed that none of us desired.

Between one thousand and fifteen hundred Navajo gathered on the day of the march. We were angry but controlled. We were still at the stage where we truly wanted to talk, and our members included Tribal Council delegates and other officials who were able to speak for large numbers of our people.

But the Hopi and BIA officials had other plans. They had flown and trucked in approximately fifty heavily armed BIA policemen, all equipped with assault gear. They looked a little like the lines of armed resistance used to stop rioters, and their presence was as much of a surprise as the barbed-wire fencing placed across the highway on the way into Keams Canyon.

At first we were informed that we would not be allowed to talk with anyone, that the men were there to stop us from setting foot on Hopi land.

I explained who I was and said that unless we had a meeting with BIA officials, people were going to get hurt. It was time to talk, and we were not going to leave until a conference could be arranged. After a few tense minutes, it was agreed that several Tribal Council delegates and I could come through the barriers to speak with the BIA superintendent from Keams Canyon and the regional director from Phoenix. The rest of our people were allowed to mill about on the road, waving signs protesting the BIA and the relocation act.

After the meeting, we arranged for a call to be placed to Washington, D.C., requesting a formal order putting a moratorium on the impoundment. Our cattle could graze as they had in the past without our people fearing that they would be taken.

Some of the problems we had seem almost humorous in hindsight. Before Public Law 93-531 went into effect, the Navajo and Hopi were given six months to negotiate a land settlement on their own. Hopi chairman Abbott Sekaquaptewa had a negotiation team, and I had a negotiation team for the Navajo. We went to Salt Lake City for a meeting, then to Albuquerque, Phoenix, Window Rock, Flagstaff, and several other cities. The negotiating teams came up with a workable plan that was then turned over to the lawyers, who vetoed it. We tried again, and again the lawyers went against it. Finally we were united— against the lawyers. We threw them out and began working together. Twice we reached a good understanding of how we could resolve the land dispute, with each side gaining something.

The problem was that the two tribes approached the negotiations with different bureaucratic mandates. I had seen too many instances in which negotiators lacked authority, so I worked with the Tribal Council to find men whose word would be ratified automatically. Whatever our negotiating team decided would be binding for all of us.

The Hopi viewed matters differently. Their negotiators were only the first step in a rather lengthy process. They always had to go back to their Tribal Council for approval. Usually this meant running an agreement past their lawyers as well.

Two or three times everything seemed perfect. We'd have an intense negotiating session and end with both sides feeling that the best possible arrangement had been made. The papers were drafted and a meeting to sign was scheduled for three or four weeks in the future. Then we'd sit down again, and their negotiators would explain that the agreement had been vetoed either by the lawyers or by their Tribal Council, or both.

Finally the two negotiating teams realized that their efforts were meaningless. We were all negotiating in good faith, but the Hopi lacked the authority to truly handle the matter. Even worse, they kept coming back with the same message: The Hopi had a nonnegotiable right to half the land, and that they would only agree to negotiate the other half. In our minds, fairness was lacking, though even if it hadn't been, it was futile to talk with people who could not make a final decision.

During this period Wanda was becoming involved with personal projects. Concerned that we were ignoring the arts in our efforts to develop economically, she wanted to provide cultural experiences that would give the Navajo exposure to the arts as they were known in the world at large, not just in the traditional Navajo skills. Even the latter were missing from the lives of some of the young people whose parents had drifted away from such activities.

Wanda's answer was the creation of the Navajoland Festival of the Arts, a special summer program involving many people from the arts. The idea was to bring major names in acting, painting, sculpture, pottery making, weaving, and other fields to different areas of the reservation. The men and women who participated would spend a day or two in each location where the children, from age five through high school, were gathered, then move on to a different area. They would contribute much of their time and visit many locations.

Some of the participants were famous only within the Navajo Nation—highly skilled weavers, potters, and jewelry makers who taught the children the basics of what they did. The weavers, for example, would teach the children every aspect of their skill. Then the kids would go out and shear sheep, card and dye the wool, spin the wool, erect a loom, and weave a rug. They were given an education in both an art form and a part of their history that otherwise would have been lost to them. At the least, they gained an appreciation of the old ways. At best, some of them might become inspired to continue their education in such crafts, ultimately making such work either their profession or their avocation. Either way the skill would be preserved for the next generation.

Other participants were major names in the entertainment field. We had Clint Eastwood, Lorne Greene, Dale Robertson, Dennis Weaver, and other actors of their stature. We had opera singers, ballerinas, and painters, including R. C. Gorman, whose work was well known both to his fellow Indians and to Americans throughout the United States.

My whole focus during those first two terms, beyond reacting to the energy, housing, water, and land problems, was to advance the education of the Navajo people. I was determined to help them learn their history and understand the world at large. We needed to develop medicine men and doctors of medicine, artists, computer operators, financial experts, historians, lawyers—people with all the skills needed to be a part of late-twentieth-century America—without losing our heritage. When I was not reacting to a crisis or fighting to preserve our resources, my energy was devoted to such ends.

The energy issue remained a primary concern, of course, for the Navajo Nation and other tribes. On January 31, 1975, Comanche LaDonna Harris of Americans for Indian Opportunity organized a conference in Billings, Montana, that brought together a number of tribal leaders. One of the meeting's purposes was to explore what energy resources truly meant to the U.S. government. For the first time, many tribal leaders learned the prices charged for energy by Third World nations such as Kuwait and Iraq. They also gained new respect for their own energy resources, because the "worthless" land that had been given to the tribes was now known to contain 70 billion tons of coal, half the nation's uranium, and possibly the largest oil fields remaining in the continental United States.

I decided to organize several tribes into a coalition I liked to call the Native American OPEC. The coalition came about during a trip to Washington, D.C., where we attempted to seek support for our efforts to evaluate our energy resources. Following our first meeting with the president's special assistant in the Department of Energy, we were told to organize ourselves in order to gain White House backing. This we did in a room assigned to us in the D.O.E. We discussed our concerns, trying to come up with a name for our group. We agreed on all the issues we were facing except this one. It was after midnight, we were tired, and the name continued to elude us. Fighting hunger and exhaustion, I reached into my pocket and removed a package of Certs breath mints. I glanced at the wrapper just before slipping one of the mints into my mouth. Then, joking, I said, "Why don't we call ourselves CERT?" No one realized I was referring to the mints in my hand, so they asked me what the initials stood for. Thinking for a moment, I replied, "Council of Energy Resource Tribes." We adopted the name. We were finally able to adjourn and get some sleep. I was grateful that I had not been carrying Tic-Tacs or Life Savers, for had I been, we might have spent more hours trying to find a name.

I was elected chairman of CERT, and we were able to gain initial funding for the inventory, which eventually showed that among other resources, we Indian tribes controlled approximately one-third of all the coal and uranium reserves known to be available within the United States. The next step was to gain additional financial assistance to develop them.

During this period President Jimmy Carter called a Camp David summit on the energy crisis. Those who mattered in the field—top oil company executives, national political leaders, and others—were there, along with a few, such as the Reverend Jesse Jackson, who had no connection with energy production. The Indians, however, were excluded.

I was shocked. We controlled a third of the energy sources in coal and uranium, as well as large supplies of oil, natural gas, and other essential resources. We had completed a study proving what we had. We had formed a coalition. Yet no one paid any attention to us.

I never did ask the government why we were excluded, but my personal feeling was that we tribal leaders simply did not matter. All Native Americans were supposed to go along with the decisions of the

Department of the Interior and the Bureau of Indian Affairs. That was the way things had worked in the past, and there was no reason to think that our efforts had changed anything.

We decided to use the same tactic that John Wayne used. We circled the wagons or, in our case, the tribes, and said, "By golly, if you're going to get the coal, you're not going to deal just with the Crow or just with the Navajo or just with the Cheyenne. You've got to deal with all of us."

My people had mixed feelings about what I was trying to do. The old people were bitter that their traditional way of life was being so relentlessly challenged. The young people were angry over the lack of jobs, the difficult present, and the bleak future. And both young and old had seen the worst excesses of the exploitation of our mineral wealth.

The actions of the Four Corners Power Plant near Fruitland, New Mexico, were typical. The plant was on the northern rim of the Navajo reservation land and was an essential provider of electricity to a multistate region. It was also a polluter of the land, its lack of adequate scrubbers and other antipollution equipment rendering the immediate surroundings an ugly brown. The Navajo who had their hogans in the adjacent area had to live with the pollution, but did not benefit from the electricity produced. They had neither electricity nor running water.

The coal for the plant came from a 31,000-acre strip mine. General Electric's subsidiary, Utah International, worked with the Bureau of Indian Affairs to develop a lease arrangement for the land. Not only was strip mining the most scarring method possible for obtaining coal, but nothing meaningful had been done to restore the land when it was no longer needed—despite the fact that successful restoration projects had resulted in thriving plant life in former strip mine sites in Ohio, Kentucky, and elsewhere.

My people felt like helpless witnesses to repeated rape. The first rape was the violation of Mother Earth. Strip mining is a perversion to the traditional Navajo. The second rape was financial. According to the Bureau of Indian Affairs, the Navajo were too "stupid" to negotiate a proper lease for the coal fields. Thus we were raped by their "wisdom" and were paid a royalty of only fifteen cents a ton for all the coal used, regardless of the number of years the company operated the mine. If the BIA had negotiated the standard lease for land owned by white men, we would have received $1.50 a ton for the coal used, and if the price of coal increased, so would our royalty.

CERT was a dangerous coalition in the minds of BIA officials and congressmen whose friends were reaping the benefits of cheap power and resources. The divide-and-conquer mentality would not work.

Should one tribe weaken and not want to fight, other tribes would encourage their resistance until our resources were purchased for fair market value. We would also be able to use the victory of any one tribe over an energy exploiter as a precedent for the others. As a result, we were unable to receive any financial support from the federal government for this phase of our self-determination efforts.

I thought long and hard about what to do. We qualified for federal government assistance under a number of different programs. We needed the money to fight the old contracts that had proven financially destructive. Yet we were the victims of prejudice, fear, and backroom deals. The only answer seemed to be to do something outrageous enough to attract attention, yet practical enough to ensure that we would be taken seriously. I contacted the Arabs.

There was little difference between OPEC and CERT. Like the Arab nations, CERT members put on a united front, but our histories were quite different, and our past relationships had not always been cordial. On a personal level, we Navajo were often at odds with the Hopi. Other tribes had long-term, often violent conflicts with one another. Yet we knew that only by uniting for a common good—the effective use of our resources—could we survive.

I don't know how much help OPEC would have provided. We were not seeking to become connected with the Arab states. We simply wanted advice from their experts on how to develop our reservation holdings most profitably.

I wrote to the secretary of the interior in my position as head of CERT. I explained that since we had been ignored, we would like permission to go outside the United States for help in developing our reserves. I explained that we wanted to contact OPEC for advice, and the assistant secretary of the interior wrote back, giving us permission.

We hired Ahmand Kooros, who had been Iran's energy minister and who had worked for the shah when his government was supported by the United States. Kooros helped us send CERT officials to OPEC countries to learn their bargaining techniques.

The moment my action became public, there were many objections. Many people feared we were traitors to our country. I was called the "Shah of the Navajo." Yet we had acted with the full awareness of the White House.

The federal government was so embarrassed that it almost instantly awarded CERT a $200,000 grant to conduct an energy resources inventory. This was followed by a second federal grant of $2 million, along with other funding that ultimately reached $20 million. We also were finally able to meet with the governors of Colorado, Utah, Arizona, and New Mexico, who, until then, had seemed to assume that they could take the mineral resources of the Indians in their states for granted.

Some critics said our efforts amounted to blackmail. But they overlooked the fact that we qualified for such economic assistance right from the start. We had been turned down only because CERT's actions conflicted with the self-interest of businesses whose executives had given money to congressmen, either directly or through political action committees.

The one reaction that hurts and angers me to this day was the charge that I was being unpatriotic. All the leaders of CERT were seen, by some, as enemies of the United States. Yet nothing could have been further from the truth. Many of us were veterans who would again serve our country in time of need. We did not want to hurt anyone. We simply wanted to get fair market value for our energy supplies. I never could understand how white men leasing their coal fields for royalties equal to $1.50 a ton of coal were more patriotic than Indians who were receiving only fifteen cents a ton and who wanted fair treatment.

CERT's efforts began paying off. Coal, which was selling for $6.00 a ton when the BIA negotiated contracts for the various tribes, had risen to between $15.00 and $20.00 a ton. The CERT contracts resulted in fair market value that would change as the price of coal fluctuated over the years.

Whereas the BIA's leases had essentially given the power companies all rights to the land, CERT negotiated joint venture agreements that let the Navajo and other tribes participate fully in the development of our resources.

This was not a perfect arrangement by any means. Although Gulf Oil developed a strip mine near Window Rock, paying 160 Navajo workers $9.00 to $12.00 an hour, the per capita income throughout the reservation was only $1,000 a year at the time, so the high pay did not make much of a dent. Yet those 160 high-wage employees would have had no jobs in the past. Presently, Gulf Oil at Pittsburgh Midway Mine is now employing over 450 Navajo workers representing 90 percent of the work force.

There were detractors among my people as well. Even with Navajo joint venture participation, they felt strip mining would still continue and the existing power plants would still belch smoke.

One comment I often heard was that in one generation the resources would all be played out and the land would be forever scarred. My critics claimed that we were playing into the hands of whites and government officials who were willing to sacrifice the western lands for energy. They felt that few people would benefit on the reservations. They also said that it was wrong for the Native Americans to think that they would get rich from the costly heating and cooling bills of the whites.

Our detractors also ignored how the money was being spent. We were developing programs that would educate young Native Americans, not only as miners but also as finance capitalists skilled in economics and as engineers, technicians, and technologists. They would have abilities that would help their people on the reservations and that could be used anywhere in the world.

Two of my critics were Russell Means and Dennis Banks, cofounders of the American Indian Movement (AIM). Means felt that I was being taken advantage of by both the multinational oil companies and the U.S. government.

Dennis Banks was more direct. "We oppose any form of destruction of Mother Earth," he stated when questioned about CERT's plans to exploit the resources for the good of the various tribes. "The elements are put there by the Great Spirit for the health of the people."

My goal as chairman during this period was both to build the Navajo Nation and to help other Indian nations. The AIM movement, which had its own agenda and purpose, was founded about this time. Its members were critical of tribal government establishments, often accusing tribal leaders of incompetence, selling out, or being taken advantage of.

At one point AIM, under Means's leadership, went to Washington to take over the BIA building. When they brought women, children, and the elderly, among others, into the building, the government did not know what to do. Officials of the Department of the Interior and the White House solicited comments from various Native American leaders and tribal chiefs. Most who came to Washington said they did not support AIM because they were rebels and activists and advised the government to kick the rebels out of the BIA building, using force if necessary.

I was approached by CBS's "Face the Nation" program and asked to comment. "Those are my people," I said. "Yes, they call themselves AIM. But they are Native Americans, and more than likely they have Navajo among them. And though they're being criticized for what they have done, I don't think the White House should go in and force them out or shoot them out. They have a message. Native Americans have been hurt. Native Americans have been cheated. They're not there to hurt the BIA or the building." I said that I was sympathetic to them.

Although I disagreed with AIM's tactics, what makes them angry is what makes me angry. It is only in our methods that we differ.

I appealed to the White House and Department of the Interior officials to meet with the people, learn their list of grievances, and address their needs. I suggested that they work out some arrangement, maybe take some money in there and pay the people's way back home.

The next morning I went to the White House and the Department of the Interior. I told the officials that I didn't want them going in with force, that they were dealing with my people, some of whom hitchhiked and drove all the way to Washington.

The next day, $60,000 in petty cash was brought over to the BIA building and issued to the people so that they could return home after discussing their grievances. From that day forward, Russell Means has been in my corner. He responded to future attacks on me by reminding them that I was the only tribal leader to come to their aid during the BIA incident. He has since come into the Navajo Nation and become a strong defender of Navajo rights and treaties. He married a Navajo wife and has two Navajo kids.

In the summer of 1990, Means broke into the BIA office and tried to make a citizen's arrest of the BIA area director. He was thrown into Crownpoint jail. Three or four months later, the director resigned and retired. I congratulated Means for having the courage to do what many of us felt should have been done.

AIM went even further with its criticism of the Navajo Nation at that time. The Tribal Council was created through the effort of Standard Oil, as previously mentioned. But where I am willing to tolerate the system that exists, no matter how wrong its creation may have been, many AIM leaders feel that the system has no legitimacy. They refuse to work with what they feel is an Anglo-imposed leadership organization that violates the long history of local democracy and consensus government.

Other criticism came from families in areas where we gave leases for uranium exploration and mining. These families felt that we had not prepared them for what was to come. They felt that the land would be raped, that the water might be wasted or damaged, and that there would be extensive health hazards.

It is hard to know if there was a communication problem between CERT and the people affected by some of CERT's activities. Some families with no prior political interests became political activists against me when they learned that uranium mining would be conducted near their homes. They sometimes worked together and succeeded in stopping an occasional project. Yet there were others facing similar circumstances who applauded the action as one that might lift them out of poverty and give their families a future.

There was no easy answer. The traditional ways of life had been shattered. The "protective" BIA had cheated us of our rightful income.

We were under pressure from all sides, and eventually it became difficult to separate valid criticism and concern from fear of change, political special interests, and other self-centered motives that were far removed from tribal concerns. What mattered in my mind was that we did something, that we took control of our lives, our resources, and our future.

Yet even nationally there was a price to be paid. It was estimated that congressional representatives felt a growing resentment toward Native Americans. They were beginning to believe that it might be easiest to just sell off the reservation land, end the tribal governments and tribal rights, and announce that all Indians would be mainstreamed into the society at large.

Such a change might not matter to some. Certainly there were Indians of all tribes who lived in major cities and did not care about their culture, their history, or their tribe's future. They saw themselves as Americans, cosmopolitan members of the American society at large.

But this new approach threatened to destroy our culture and ultimately keep our young people from knowing our traditional lifestyle, religion, and history. Such an action would accomplish what the Long Walk and the livestock reduction had not. And the only way to achieve this goal in the minds of many was to get rid of me and those who thought as I did, replacing us with others who would concede to the whites and allow the stripping of our resources at prices that would guarantee continued poverty.

This is not to say that I always made the best decisions during my three terms in office, a record among Navajo chairmen. In the mid-1970s a group of Indian militants, including some Navajo, took control of the Fairchild Camera & Instrument Corporation's Shiprock, New Mexico, plant. It was up to me to remove them from the plant, to order the police force under my command to oust them. However, I chose to let the occupation continue, to not risk the extreme violence that could result from such a confrontation. The plant finally closed, resulting in the loss of 1,200 jobs.

I don't know if my decision was the best one that could have been made. Had I ordered the police to move swiftly, lives would have been lost, enough so that people would probably have said that even 1,200 jobs were not worth Navajo men spilling each other's blood. I would have become the chairman who killed his own people instead of the chairman who allowed Navajo to lose their jobs.

The one consistent discovery I made during my first terms in office was that we Native Americans had given the impression that we did not know how to deal with outside interests. This was due partly to our subjugation under the BIA and partly to the fact that many of our previous leaders, without experience in the outside world, did not know how to find the technical expertise they needed.

For example, the Navajo Nation had certain water rights by treaties that were inviolable. We had every right to use the water for crop irrigation, for livestock, for drinking, and for other purposes before it went anywhere else. Yet in the years following the signing of the treaties, when the population of previously desolate areas within various states started expanding, water was needed for growth, and the government decided to take back these rights.

In 1971, the state of New Mexico wanted to take control of much of the San Juan River. In the past, the state probably would have been able to achieve its goal. But because of my engineering background, and with others in positions of leadership who also had technical backgrounds, the efforts were defeated. To accomplish this, we hired outside experts in law, geology, and other fields. The tribe used almost a million dollars to hire the Williams Brothers of Tulsa, Oklahoma, to conduct a complete water study in the Four Corners region of the Navajo Nation. They were commissioned to look into the San Juan River and the upper and lower Colorado River Basin and all the waters that belonged to the Navajo.

We acquired voluminous legal documentation dating back to the 1600s. We found even the most obscure treaties, along with the various state and federal laws that had evolved over the years. Eventually we acquired everything that had to do with water. Then we sent drilling crews throughout the entire area to spot drill in order to establish the existence of water tables and to determine the amount of water remaining. We were able to learn the scope of our resources, the annual rainfall in good and bad years, and all the other technical details we needed to be effective in court.

By the time the hearing on the issue was held in Aztec, New Mexico, a year and a half later, we were experts in the entire water issue. Our lawyers—from a New York firm that had previously settled a major water dispute among Nevada, California, and Arizona—were more than knowledgeable. They were armed with all the existing technical information that we provided.

I'll never forget the looks on the faces of the lawyers for the state of New Mexico. Our documentation easily filled a space the size of a four-car garage. The portion that was brought into the courtroom for exhibit purposes alone was so enormous that it was apparent to the opposition that they could not fight us. In fact, their lawyers had only a single volume of documents to use against us, an amount of material that, in the past, would have been sufficient.

I was happy to see their reaction. They took one look at what we had, then asked for a continuance. That was in 1973. At the time of this writing, the state of New Mexico has still not requested a new court date. But we continue to keep our records up to date, just waiting for the next battle, which, because of our preparedness, will probably never come.

This success reflects one of the important lessons I learned at Hughes Aircraft: Whoever has the most information will win a lawsuit.

Such information is of two types. The first is information related to the case. The more you know, the better you can prepare your arguments and anticipate any counterarguments you may have to deflect.

The second is information concerning your opponents. Sometimes a court system has individuals who are biased against one side or the other, and it may be best to wait to file a suit until the makeup of the court is different. Or it may be that although one tribe has a better case than another, whoever files the suit will set a precedent. Under such circumstances it is best for one tribe to help the other so that the precedent that is set is one that reflects your interests.

I approached court fights according to the old Navajo tradition of studying one's enemies, waiting, and not attacking until one could bring all of one's strengths against the enemy's weakest point. Information was always the best weapon available to everyone. Information brought power.

CHAPTER FIFTEEN

It was 1978 and I had known power. I had been chairman of the Navajo Nation for two terms—eight years. My time in office was as long as that of any American president with the exception of Franklin Roosevelt. I had been wined and dined, feted, praised, and hailed as someone greater than a mere mortal though somewhat less than a god. I had also been cursed, reviled, accused of heinous crimes, and called a destroyer of traditions.

Yet while others saw me in terms of black and white, all good or all bad, they didn't know my heart, my mind, and my soul. I had come to understand the Oriental saying that you should be careful what you ask for because you might receive it. I had learned the limits of power, and I had learned them in a manner that was shockingly harsh.

I never thought much about my mother when I was running for chairman of the Navajo Nation. I loved her, of course. I respected how she had lived, what she had accomplished, how she had triumphed over conditions that others would have been praised for merely surviving. But we had rarely talked about my life, her feelings concerning my work, or my decision to enter politics. That conversation did not take place until we were alone together following my first inauguration.

My mother was pleased not only by the level of success I had achieved but also by the fact that I had shown I could make something of myself. I was shocked as she began to explain the pressure she had been under from the time I was a child, the criticism she had received from family and friends because of me.

I had always thought that my mother was the best mother anyone could have. She had a difficult time raising her family after my father was killed when I was two years old. She worked hard and never had many material possessions. Even when she did, her love for others was such that she gave away almost everything of value, being happier in the giving than in the ownership.

Sometimes, when she was able to sell a sheep or a blanket for more than she needed for survival, she would buy herself a necklace or other piece of jewelry, or perhaps a nice shawl. She would enjoy it for a while, then give it to me, one of her other children, a grandchild, or a friend, saying, "This would look better on you than on me." She had so much love that such actions brought her great happiness.

I had been considered a wild kid when I was growing up, especially because I kept running away from school. My mother had been criticized because she had not kept me under control.

When I went to college, she was again criticized. I was over twenty, an age when a Navajo was expected to have a job and raise a family. Others in my family had "finished school," though to the Navajo that meant that they had completed the eighth grade. Almost no one understood that there could be more to education than learning to speak, understand, and write English. Only a ne'er-do-well could be adult and still be in school. The lack of understanding reached a point where I had to say I was working in Oklahoma rather than admit that I was going to college and studying to be an engineer.

My election to the chairmanship of the Navajo Nation showed that I was at last successful in a way that other Navajo would recognize. My mother's love for me, her belief in my future, and her acceptance of my deviating from the only course in life she fully understood had proven worth the heartache. I had achieved something of great importance.

Along with her pride, however, there was continued pain. Until she died in 1972, my mother would sometimes suggest that I leave my position as chairman and go back to work in Los Angeles. She made these statements in reaction to the criticism she overheard in trading posts and elsewhere on the reservation.

My mother wasn't the type to confront someone or enter into an argument. Upon hearing someone who did not know that she was related to me criticize me, she simply minded her own business. The people were just saying what they say about all politicians, good and bad. Yet she hated the remarks, especially when she felt that I was trying to make life easier for the Navajo. She would tell me that those critics didn't know better, that they were the type who would follow someone else and blindly fall off a cliff after him. She thought that maybe I should let them suffer, maybe I should go back to Los Angeles and just take care of my family.

I did not mind her comments and was pleased that she had witnessed my triumph. But when she became ill in 1972, I became hopelessly aware of what I could and could not change.

My mother had a bad heart valve that, at first, caused her to have an enlarged heart, which led to complications that affected her liver. I took her to specialists in Albuquerque, but she was afraid of the surgery that might have repaired the valve. The doctors were also concerned about operating by the time she was in enough pain to admit to the problem and seek medical help. Her body had deteriorated to such a degree that they were not certain she could survive the trauma of the operating room.

In the end, I could do nothing but watch her die. We got her the care needed to ease her suffering. I spent as much time with her as I could. And she died as she lived, concerned about me, her other children, and her friends.

That was the first time that, as chairman of the Navajo Nation, I had to face the true limitations of power, though it would not be the last. Others who were close to me died in the next few years. My second cousin Wilbur Atcitty, a brilliant, well-educated young man who had been seen as a possible successor, was killed in a car crash. And in 1978, one of my closest friends and advisers, a medicine man named Buck Austin, also died.

Buck's heart was strong, but like my mother, he had an incurable liver disease. My wife, Wanda, and I lovingly called him "Big Thunder" because that was what he was like. He was an older man, knowledgeable in the traditional ways. He performed prayer services for me when I needed spiritual help. He was a confidant, the protector of my family, a teacher, mentor, and someone so close that I called him "older brother," while he called me "younger brother."

Buck's deterioration was slow and painful. I wanted to do something for him, bring him special food, a gift, whatever he desired, whatever he needed. He said that all he wanted was to get well and be healthy again. Yet all I could do was pray and pray and pray, and ultimately he died.

Those deeply felt losses during my first two terms caused me to stop and look at the realities of power. Many people thought I had achieved everything. I was at the pinnacle of success. As chairman of the Navajo Nation I had all the power that accompanies the ruler of a country. People sought political favors from me. People were anxious to do my bidding. I could get someone out of jail or influence a governor to release someone from a state penitentiary. I had access to the president, to senators and representatives. I could travel internationally and be received by heads of state. I was in charge of a police force. I was the executive who oversaw a budget of millions and millions of dollars. I had access to perquisites that made my daily life easy while others struggled in hardship.

Yet when my mother died, and later, when Buck passed on, I felt insignificant. In fact, by the time my "older brother" was suffering through his last days, I, as chairman, had literally moved mountains, fed the poor, built houses, provided water, and established scholarships for previously undereducated youths. And all Buck asked of me was to go on living. The most basic desire of man, and I, like the doctors who treated him, was powerless to reverse his inevitable decline.

I realized that there are things in life we declare to be important. I realized that there are many ways we control our own destiny and that of others. But in the face of life and death of those we love, being chairman, being rich or strong, or powerful . . . none of it ultimately matters. I would enjoy the years of leadership, delight in the battles and the triumphs. Yet these losses helped me keep a perspective concerning what really mattered in life.

By 1978, I had decided that my family meant more to me than power. I felt it was a good time to consider a successor. I had dramatically improved the overall living conditions for many Navajo, setting programs in place that ultimately would help everyone. I was winning concessions from the federal government and changing many of its policies so that a new chairman would have fewer old battles to fight. The intense desire for change that had driven me during my first two elections now no longer burned so brightly. I set about finding someone to take my place who I felt would continue my policies.

At this time the American Indian Movement militants were trying to gain more attention for themselves. I did not have a great deal of respect for some of them because I felt that they had united to oppose important changes in development of the land, the existing government, and the education system. Such opposition was not necessarily wrong. I just felt that true leadership came with a plan for the future. It was not enough to say something was bad. It was necessary to formulate a policy that would bring about something better. This they had not done, nor did they seem interested in doing so. They were protesters without a plan for positive action. However, my next confrontation with AIM was one I was able to turn to the advantage of the Navajo people.

The incident occurred at the Aneth oil field in Utah, part of the San Juan basin, and one of the largest and richest oil reserves on any Indian reservation in the United States. The AIM people hated the oil drilling, especially what it did to the land. They did not like the way the lines crossed important grazing areas. They feared the ecological damage that would be caused by oil spills. They did not like the Anglos who moved into and out of the area and felt that they were disrespectful to burial areas. They were angry with some of the Anglo oil workers who drove their pickup trucks to where young Navajo women were herding sheep and tried to pick them up. Ultimately, with some forty grievances behind them, they staged a takeover of a building that housed monitors and controls for the oil fields. There was no way to tell when a problem might arise and no way to handle a crisis without being inside the structure. With the building controlled by the militants, the oil company executives contacted me and demanded that I order the Navajo police to evict the protesters immediately.

I have always been a pragmatist when it comes to the Native American people. If I could use something to their advantage, even if I was personally against it, I would do so. So it was with the AIM protest. As much as I disagreed with AIM, the takeover provided the perfect opportunity for me to try to back the oil company into a corner regarding its bad lease.

I sought legal counsel to determine whether I could use the takeover to negotiate a new lease. One attorney said I could not. Another attorney said that there might be a way to legally isolate the field, evict all Anglos during the period of the crisis, and then work out an agreement that would include the lease.

I wasn't certain how sound my legal grounds might be, but I really didn't care. I felt that I had as adequate a justification to take control as I was going to get. As a result, I removed all outsiders and then went to see the militants. I told them that I felt we could work together to benefit everyone.

The militants gave me a list of their grievances, the majority of which were quite legitimate. I told the presidents and CEOs of the companies that had complained that I felt they needed to come out and see the problems firsthand.

At first the oil company officials involved did not want to deal with any of the problems. Then they agreed either to come themselves or to send top executives empowered to negotiate on their behalf. We met together, sitting around a long table that reminded me of a treaty room, while the grievances were presented. The officials agreed to exercise more control over their workers, to establish safeguards that should have been created in the first place, and generally to resolve matters in ways that met the general approval of AIM. They also agreed to renegotiate the leases so that they were in line with those currently in effect in oil fields in land owned by Anglos or other nations. We all gained a victory.

It was during this oil field crisis that I decided to not run for reelection. I had a friend, the first Navajo physician to live and work on the reservation, whom I wanted as a successor. Dr. Taylor MacKenzie was bright, concerned about the people, and seemed ideal. I began encouraging him to get involved in politics, seeking the endorsements of various chapter houses.

Dr. MacKenzie was enthusiastic, but his approach was not what we discussed. First he obtained an endorsement from a militant Navajo group known as the Coalition for Navajo Liberation. This group was hostile to me and my administration and was in disfavor with most of the Navajo people. I was hurt that Dr. MacKenzie had accepted support from my enemies, and I felt that he was politically at risk because the group was so widely disliked by most the chapter houses.

Dr. MacKenzie seemed to understand the problem and agreed to seek the support of more respected groups. Unfortunately his next move was to gain the support of Annie Wauneka.

A simple endorsement from Wauneka would have been enough in my eyes, but her support came through my friend's choice of Milton Bluehouse as a running mate. Bluehouse was Annie's son-in-law, a fact that presented me with two problems.

The first problem was obviously with Annie Wauneka. People were getting disenchanted with her and an endorsement by her could have a backlash. But what mattered was that it was inappropriate of him to choose his running mate before the primary election results were announced. It was arrogant for him to act as if he expected to be first or second place in the primaries, and thus be a candidate for election, and it also established a political bias that he could not afford. A smart politician would have waited to see the primary results and learn who his opponent might be. Then he could select a politically advantageous vice-chairman.

I could not support such poor judgment and decided to run for a third term. My opponent again was Raymond Nakai. Frank Paul was my running mate. He was bright, well educated, and had both political and administrative experience.

At this time, I initiated what was to become the largest gathering of tribal leaders in over a century. I held a national Indian convention in Window Rock early in the summer in order to circle the wagons against encroachment on our water rights. We established what came to be known as NATRO—the Native American Treaty Rights Organization. For two days we participated in intense workshops and study groups pertaining to water rights, land ownership, sovereignty issues, court rulings, and pending legislation that would affect not only Indian tribes today but also past treaties. We were determined to understand where we were and what could be done about groups such as the County Coalition for Abolishment of Indian Treaties, which comprised Anglo politicians, ranchers, and others who wanted to take advantage of Indian treaty lands and resources. They felt that if they could abolish past treaties and "mainstream" Indians into American society, they could do as they pleased with our minerals and water.

The convention began a movement toward joint funding of lobbying efforts and the encouragement of Native Americans in politics to help work against our opposition. Unfortunately I could not take too active a role in the work that followed because of the re-election campaign. Other leaders, though agreeing with the ends, were uncertain of the means. Some felt that NATRO should handle everything. Others felt that a different group, such as the National Congress of American Indians or the National Tribal Chairmen Association, should handle the effort. In the end, what could have been a strong coalition was weakened by power struggles.

But despite these nuisance situations, we were moving forward effectively. The Navajo people supported my effort, and I was rewarded with an unprecedented third term as tribal chairman. The only opposition Raymond Nakai could muster was an attack on my success. He claimed that when I ousted the BIA from power over such areas as government and health, I planned to fire Navajo employees of the BIA and replace them with my friends. During the previous election he had claimed that I was selling control of the Navajo Nation to Anglo union leaders. Now his sudden switch to accusing me of doing too much for the Navajo made little sense. Either I was pro-Navajo or I was pro-Anglo, and the changes we had achieved were apparent to everyone. I was easily re-elected.

As was to be expected, many of the issues of my first two terms continued into the third. Education was still a primary worry, though we had learned a great deal about our problems in those eight years.

During the first two terms, I thought that by making education available to the people and by increasing the desire among the young to take advanced training, a concept foreign to their parents and grandparents, I would automatically improve the life of the people. I did not realize that we had a problem with quality and a cultural barrier.

The quality problem resulted from the uncoordinated efforts to teach our young people. It was not until 1975 that we consolidated all instruction so that we could have consistent education in all schools throughout the reservation. But by 1978, we realized that even our best schools were not up to the standards of the public schools throughout the states in which the reservation was located. Students who earned the highest grades in our schools, kids who were bright, well motivated, and of a type who would help our people, would be only average if compared with Anglo children. Our kids had the ability to learn, and their intelligence tests showed that many were extremely bright, some even testing at the genius level. But the quality of the schooling they received was inferior to that offered in non-Navajo schools. They did not take advanced courses in math, science, and other subjects. As a result, they entered college with less basic knowledge than other students. Their grades instantly dropped, or they had to study their college courses and, at the same time, teach themselves the basics that the other students had learned earlier.

The solution to this problem was threefold, though it would take a full twelve years to show results. First, we had to strengthen our curriculum, make it more demanding, and give our kids a thorough grounding in the courses they needed before going to college. Our students had no problem adapting to a tougher curriculum, but the full benefit of the change would not be seen until the youngest ones worked their way through the education system.

Second, we had to help our young people make the emotional transition to the culture they would experience on college and university campuses. These college-bound children were going from a family-oriented rural culture to dormitories in urban areas. It was a radically different world from the one they had known. Many were homesick. Food, music, styles of dress, the slang used by other students, and even the forms of entertainment differed from what they had experienced in the past. They had trouble feeling a part of the college experience and wanted to go home. Often their grandparents, and sometimes their parents, did not discourage them from leaving college. Thus 70 percent to 80 percent of our young people dropped out of college at the end of their first year.

At the same time, our need for young people skilled in computer programming and operation, finance, business administration, and even general office work was growing. Added to this were the types of jobs we were beginning to offer both on and off the reservation, for many of which it was obvious that higher education was critical.

Third, we addressed the problem experienced by those children whose needs were not being met. For many years we had received federal assistance for children who were impoverished, were of lower than average intelligence, or had some form of disability. We had children who were extremely poor as well as those from dysfunctional families, so we had long been getting money from programs ranging from Head Start to special education for kids who were in some way impaired. We were also addressing the needs of the average kids by improving their training so that they would gain job skills and be able to succeed in college or vocational school.

However, the best and brightest among the Navajo were also disadvantaged. These kids often became bored, many of them were disruptive, and some dropped out because school offered them no challenge. Yet these were our future leaders. These were the children who, with the right stimulation, would become doctors, lawyers, engineers, professors, scientists, economists, and other professionals. We needed to stimulate them, to give them as extensive an education as their minds desired.

The answer was the creation of the Navajo Academy, a college preparatory school no different from the private prep schools used to

A visit to the reservation by senators Barry Goldwater (far left) and John McCain (center).

The chairman's in-box is always piled high with paperwork.

In 1983, when I was out of office, Wanda and I visited President Reagan and presented him with this Navajo rug American flag from the Navajo people.

I visited Vice President Bush in the White House with fellow Navajo code-talker James T. Nahkai.

As chairman, I always wanted to be available to listen to whatever was on anyone's mind.

Wanda and I visited with Navajo students at the Brigham Young University campus in Provo, Utah.

Chichiltah, 1982: It must have been something I said ... Navajo humor, the greatest!

On the campaign trail at Teec Nos Pos in November 1982.

Protesting relocation, Navajo veterans marched into Keams Canyon, site of the Hopi BIA Indian Agency.

The government called in Indian police—pitting Indian against Indian—to suppress the march.

Katherine Smith of Big Mountain questioned a BIA official about relocation.

A woman is restrained by a police officer as she attempts to question a BIA official about relocation.

Navajo Nation council members visiting the Big Boquillas Ranch *before* it was purchased.

Harry Reasoner interviews me on the reservation in June 1982.

Wanda, my grandson Bernard Dailleboust, me, and my son Peter Jr. (Rocky) on the occasion of Rocky's becoming a member of the Arizona Bar Association.

Turning the roast at a family reunion on Mount Carrizo, Arizona, in 1991.

Wanda and me with our daughters Hope, Charity, and Faith, in a photo taken probably in 1978.

train many of the brightest minds in the rest of the United States. We could give all our children a chance for higher education by improving our general educational system, and we could send children who showed unusual skills to the Navajo Academy to receive the training that would enable them to compete at Harvard, at Yale, or anywhere else.

Another concern that became apparent while I was running for my third term—and was a major focus for me after my inauguration—was the taxation of the energy companies operating on reservation lands. Back in 1972 and 1973 I had arranged for all treaty laws related to taxation to be researched. I wanted to be able to prove that we had as much legal right to tax businesses operating on leased areas of Navajo lands as state and federal governments had to levy such taxes in other parts of the United States.

Once we had the proof, we decided to prepare for the legal battles we knew would follow our efforts. We assumed that since the energy companies had been functioning for years without this extra expense, they would challenge us in the courts. To be certain we could meet such a challenge, we had our attorneys prepare for every possible type of attack and be ready to counter any action. Only when we were certain that we could win arguments thrown against us did we announce the establishment of new tax laws beginning in 1978.

The day after the taxation began, twenty lawsuits were filed by a broad range of energy companies—Kerr McGee, Phillips Petroleum, Texaco, Exxon, and others. Suits were filed simultaneously in three different district courts, a move we had anticipated.

We met the challenge and won easily in both the Albuquerque and Phoenix federal district courts. Only the decision in Salt Lake City was not to our liking. That decision held that we had every right to tax but only after we obtained the approval of the secretary of the interior.

However, many people saw that third decision as yet another victory. They wondered when I was going to have the secretary of the interior rubber-stamp our taxation, something they were certain he would do.

I agreed that the secretary of the interior would probably uphold our right to tax. But I also knew that the minute I went to him, I would be giving him a power he had no right to have. I had been claiming that we were an independent nation. If I suddenly agreed to have the secretary of the interior approve our action, I would create a situation in reality, even though not in law, that would diminish our sovereignty. We would become no different from the Indian tribes that had developed approved constitutions back in the 1930s. As a result, I vowed to fight.

The election for chairman was held during this time. My stubbornness was expected to cost me some votes, since many people did not want to continue a court battle that could have been avoided by yielding to the stipulations of the judge in Salt Lake City. They also pointed out that we might eventually be held in contempt, facing fines and other legal costs beyond the price of the original litigation. I probably did lose some votes, but I persisted.

There were several different appeals, but the courts in Phoenix and Albuquerque warned the energy companies within their jurisdiction to begin setting aside money to pay their taxes. The funds could be held in an escrow account pending appeals, but the companies were warned that, if they lost, they would have to pay the Navajos from 1978, the time of the original action.

It was interesting to see the reaction. First, approximately half of the companies dropped out of the appeal. They apparently agreed we had the right to tax and did not want to spend any more money, especially since they realized that if the appeal was successful, they would benefit from it.

Second, we appealed the Utah decision in the Ninth Circuit Court of Appeals. That court ruled entirely in our favor in 1982, as my third term was coming to a close.

Ultimately only one company, Kerr McGee, took the matter to the U.S. Supreme Court, which let stand the appeals court rulings. The tax money had to be released. Approximately $200 million was given to the Navajo Nation in 1985 as a result of what we had begun in 1972. I was out of office by then, and although the new chairman attempted to take credit for the money, the people remembered the court battles of my third term and I shared in their joy at the progress we had made.

During my third term in office I finally found a way to end our battle against the Joint Use Area legislation. There was a section of the law that allowed the Navajo to obtain a quantity of federal land equal in acreage to the territory we would lose to the Hopi.

Previously our concern had been with the land we were losing. This was sacred land, part of our religion and history. The loss was like the forced separation from a loved one, a situation so serious that it was easy to overlook all other aspects of what was taking place. But the vast majority in Congress did not understand the sacred nature of the land or how serious the change might be for our people. They saw only the issue of fairness, and in order to ensure that everything was done properly, they ruled that we could claim other land of equal acreage. We had the right to choose from the vast federal lands not assigned to Indian tribes, and that is what we did. Our first selection was the Paragon Resource Ranch in New Mexico.

The federal government owned extensive land that was leased to ranchers and developers, just as we leased portions of our reservation. This meant that power companies were able to use coal and other minerals as long as they paid for the privilege. Likewise, ranchers and farmers throughout the United States often lease government-owned acreage for grazing, raising cattle, and growing crops. The farmers and ranchers are able to use land in a way that earns them a livelihood that would otherwise not be possible. And the payments they make for the privilege help the state or national economy.

We selected the Paragon Resource Ranch for one reason: It contained coal. This was not sacred land. This was not land where my people could point to areas where important events had taken place. This was simply land that had billions of tons of coal. We selected land so valuable that we knew New Mexico would scream. The state government at that time was working with New Mexico Public Services to mine the coal in this area.

Our strategy was to do to white America what was being done to us. We did not want the coal, nor did we need the money that leasing the mining operation would bring. We did not want to take prime grazing and farming land away from Anglo ranchers and farmers. We only wanted to continue living with the Hopi as we had for centuries, without problems. But the only way we could get people's attention was by making them hurt, if only economically, as we were hurting.

Suddenly we had support from the ranchers and government officials who were using the land we were trying to claim. Our action appeared to be legal, and even if there were some way around it, our opponents quickly realized that they had something of value to lose.

We suggested that the simplest solution was for the government to admit that Public Law 93-531 had been a mistake. The law could be repealed, and arrangements could be made for the Navajo and the Hopi to work together to settle the land problem. After all, there was no reason all of this had to be rushed. According to our beliefs, we had shared the land since the time of First Man and First Woman. Some historians said we had been there for two thousand years, while anthropologists dated our dwellings back at least several centuries. Whatever the case, it would not matter if another generation or two lived and died before we worked out our differences, given all the time that had passed.

There were special interests involved, as already noted, but our action had touched the nerves of equally powerful interest groups who were horrified by what we were doing. They put far more pressure on members of Congress to make a change than others had placed on the senators and representatives to get us off the land.

By 1982, near the end of my third term, two champions of our cause had emerged—Senator Pete Domenici of New Mexico and Senator Dennis DeConcini of Arizona. Even Barry Goldwater, now nearing retirement, was looking at the matter more pragmatically.

With legal change in the air, a commission was established to re-evaluate the problem and see if the Navajo and Hopi could work something out among themselves. There was occasional press coverage of what was taking place, though that had less impact than we had hoped. The reporters for the major newspapers often examined the issue thoroughly enough to understand the emotional overtones of what was taking place. A few even had the sense to relate the matter to the holy lands of the Middle East, where land not only has agricultural and strategic value, but also contains sites sacred to three religions— Judaism, Christianity, and Islam. By transferring the sensitivity shown toward the clashes in the Middle East to our land dispute, the reporters truly expressed what was taking place. Unfortunately, the editorial writers felt that their papers should do only so many Indian stories. We were not important enough for continuing coverage even though our story involved vast areas of land within the United States as well as millions of Americans, both Indian and white.

To further bolster our efforts, the Navajo Tribal Council authorized an expenditure of a million dollars to publicize our case. The Hopi were also engaged in a public relations effort, but we felt that a full understanding of what was taking place would cause people to support a cessation of the relocation, if nothing else.

Our plans involved several efforts. We would hire legal specialists for the court battle, of course. We would prepare a book that would explain our view of the dispute and provide all documentation, to be published for general sale and also distributed by hundreds of our young people at colleges and universities around the country. These Navajo representatives would be trained in all aspects of the law and the history of the problem. They would be able to explain to others what was taking place and, we hoped, develop a grass roots movement appealing to congressmen and senators throughout the United States. We would rent an office in Washington, D.C., to serve as headquarters for our lobbying effort, and we would use radio and television as well.

We felt that we would win because we had no plans to attack the Hopi. We didn't want to turn this into an Indian war. Instead we wanted to show that if the law was repealed, negotiations would ensue between the Navajo and the Hopi. There would be no congressionally mandated change. All arrangements would be made by the people directly involved. Our compromise would be opposed only by greedy outsiders seeking to exploit the dispute.

It seemed to us that there could be no problem. The support was such that I felt certain that some time in the early 1980s everything would be resolved. Ultimately, to my horror, I would be proven wrong.

Other needs were also addressed during my third term, many relating to projects already several years old. In other matters, I continued to make important changes.

For example, I worked with the Tribal Council to establish a permanent office of Navajo attorney general. The attorney general would be appointed by the chairman, with a budget for a small staff of attorneys. There would be a central office where all tribal records would be stored. Additional funds would be available for contracting with specialists in areas such as water rights as the need arose. We would appoint lawyers to the position who were dedicated to fighting for the Navajo cause. By 1981, our legal system was becoming as respected as any in the United States. (After I left office in 1982, the attorney general's office was filled with "hippie-type" lawyers who seemed to have no sense of Indian needs or history. They were playing politics instead of fighting for the sovereignty the Navajo Nation must protect in order to exercise self-determination.)

I didn't want to run for a fourth term in 1982. There seemed no way that we could fail to put an end to the Joint Use Area, given Congress's sympathy after my move to take valued land as our part of the exchange. We had already appropriated money for the fight, which I thought any chairman could easily handle.

Even CERT, in which I could no longer participate if I left office, had reached a point where my involvement was not critical. In fact, early in 1982 we gained national attention when we sponsored the Night of the First Americans at the Kennedy Center. This program, which was videotaped and sold to network television as a fund-raiser, involved everyone from the Reagans, George and Barbara Bush, and various members of Congress, to entertainers such as Sammy Davis, Jr., Martin Sheen, Loretta Lynn, Wayne Newton, and Jonathan Winters. It was an evening of comedy, music, pageants, and a salute to all Native Americans.

There was also the first annual CERT fund-raiser dinner, a hundred-dollar-a-plate affair that raises approximately two hundred thousand dollars annually. The Kennedy Center event and the annual dinners have provided extensive scholarship help for Native American youths entering any field that relates to the use of our natural resources.

My accomplishments by now were well established. I had achieved far more than I ever expected when I first returned to the reservation. And my wife and children were tired of my being on call twenty-four hours a day, seven days a week. It was time for us to be a family again.

I had started my third term with the thought that Frank Paul, my vice-chairman, would be the next candidate for chairman. Unfortunately Frank, though an excellent executive, had not established an adequate power base. People did not know him well, and they certainly did not see him as a leader. He might have had no difficulty running the Navajo Nation, but it seemed certain that there was no chance of his being one of the top two primary election vote-getters.

My supporters felt that I should place my name in the primary, something I did halfheartedly. I had no interest in campaigning, though I went along with their wishes. However, when the votes were counted, Peterson Zah and I were facing each other in the general election. My early mentor and longtime opponent, Raymond Nakai, had come in third with 5,000 votes.

My strength and my weakness is that I am a fighter. I had won the primary. I was facing the general election. My heart told me to be with my family, but my fighting instincts said to run against Peterson Zah, a man with whose politics I did not agree. I could use the fourth term to groom a successor and help him get known throughout the Navajo Nation. I could promise my family that the fourth term would be my last. And if I lost the election, I would go down as a warrior, able to sleep at night yet still be involved in the affairs of the Navajo Nation to a lesser degree. Either way, I could not really lose.

This election proved to be quite different from the others. Most of the people on the reservation wanted to continue the programs I had started, but few wanted me as chairman.

The Navajo are a young people. A large number were voting for only the first or second time. From the time they first became aware of politics through the classes they took in school, I had been their chairman. To them I was an old man, and the idea of having someone younger in office was exciting.

Peterson Zah was such a man. Younger than I, he was a dynamic man who had excited the imaginations of the Navajo youth. They did not see that he seemed to have no sense of history. They did not see that he did not couple his attacks against me with positive plans of his own. I felt that he would seek change for the sake of change, not for a plan in which he believed, and such a man seemed wrong for the Navajo Nation. But this was the perspective of someone who had lived through the many changes experienced by the reservation. The young people had no such perspective, and if I tried to educate them, they would still see me as the incumbent fighting for power, not as a challenger.

Although he was not in the race, Raymond Nakai was a concern to both Peterson Zah and me. Nakai's 5,000 votes could swing the election to either of us. If it was possible to gain Nakai's support, along with the support of his followers, winning would be certain. Toward this end, we both approached the former tribal chairman.

Peterson Zah made the first move. He asked Raymond Nakai for his endorsement. They were both long-term opponents of mine, so it seemed logical that Zah would gain the extra votes. That was not to be the case, though.

I then went to see Raymond Nakai for several reasons. The least important was the political one. I wanted the votes of his followers, which could come only from his support. But so much had happened between us since I first ran for chairman in 1970 that such an appeal would not have been successful. I did not want to compromise my principles for his support, and he did not want to back someone with whom he had been fighting for twelve years. Political motivations were simply not enough to create a bond between us.

I think I went to Raymond Nakai mainly because I remembered 1963. I remembered being a young man on the fast track at Hughes Aircraft, appalled by the way the Navajo people were being treated by the U.S. government and the Bureau of Indian Affairs. I remembered being approached by Raymond Nakai, listening to his plans, and being moved that what he was seeking truly seemed best for the Navajo people.

Raymond Nakai was an aggressive politician, a gut fighter, a man of determination, skill, and ambition. Yet he had let me establish ONEO, an organization independent of his control. He had listened to what I was trying to do for the Navajo people, recognizing that, if it worked, it would be a good thing, and he had given me my head. Looking back, I could see that he and I had always had the same goals in mind for our people. Only our methods differed. We had become political opponents, yet I still admired him and I still respected what he had done and what he tried to do. I wanted to rekindle that friendship, to let him know of that respect.

I also recognized that Peterson Zah's politics were not appreciated by either of us, because his were the politics of militancy, which can destroy rather than build. Nakai and I may have had our differences, but we both were looking to the future. When we got angry at something, we developed a counterplan that would be productive, whereas Zah seemed to be comfortable with defeating an opponent rather than moving forward.

Ultimately, Raymond Nakai and I agreed to work together. We held a rally near his home at which he pledged his support to me and my campaign.

I cannot honestly say that Nakai's backing was beneficial; there is even the chance that it helped cost me the election.

To the young people, Raymond Nakai and Peter MacDonald were two old men. Nakai had been in politics before many of them were born, and I was the same age as or older than their parents. Peterson Zah, many years our junior, had greater appeal.

The media were also against me by then. Approximately 80 percent of the newspapers and radio and television stations had endorsed my first campaign in 1970. Perhaps 60 percent had endorsed my second, and maybe 40 percent my third. It is probably not much of an exaggeration to say that I would have been surprised if I retained 1 percent by the fourth campaign. It was not what I had accomplished that was being attacked. The people simply wanted a change in leadership. The MacDonald name was "shopworn." People wanted someone new.

Losing the election was not really a surprise, though I went down fighting and the returns were fairly close. It was time for a change for everyone, and I felt certain that I was leaving a positive legacy for my successor.

Although I had never been in prison, I felt like a man who had just been released from twelve years in a penitentiary. I was standing outside the gate, suitcase in hand, aware that the whole world was at my feet. I could return to law school. I could go back to engineering. I could sit at home for a while, take a job in a totally different field, move to some other part of the United States. Anything I wanted to do, anywhere I wanted to go.

But what would I do first? Where should I start? I had everything, yet I felt as lost as I had on the night before that first election a dozen years earlier, when my greatest fear had not been losing, it had been winning and starting a life for which I felt totally unprepared.

The Last Battleground

CHAPTER SIXTEEN

I t was 1983, and little was certain. I couldn't predict what might take place in the Navajo Nation during the next four years. Peterson Zah, the new tribal chairman, had gone to school with the Hopi tribal chairman, Ivan Sidney, and they had pledged to cooperate. They had also agreed to build a road to the Peabody coal mine together and to work with Congress.

Both men seemed well intentioned. Peterson Zah's primary concern, he said, was education. He felt that education was the key to the future for the Navajo people. Yet there was also the issue of growing unemployment, and I felt that he did not have the background to tackle it.

As I left office, I knew that the Navajo would never again live the way they once had, though I believed some things should not have to change. There were still old people who wanted to lead the seminomadic life of shepherding and cattle raising. Many of them lived in the Big Mountain area and were devastated by the consequences of the relocation issue. The changes that did not directly affect their livelihood, such as the introduction of roads that made travel easier, still affected the land. They believed that the spirits were being abused, that change was wrong.

There were also the young people who, through television, had been exposed to a new way of life. As many as half of them did not speak any Navajo. They knew little about our history and religion, except as seen through the eyes of our conquerors. They wanted stereo systems, VCRs, fast cars, and other toys of contemporary urban society. They did not care about the land, laughed at what they perceived to be the ignorance of the medicine men, and wanted to find a way to get into the American fast lane.

Then there were the men and women in between, who wanted good jobs on the reservation. They had a fondness for the past, but often no desire to return to the old ways. They also enjoyed aspects of the present. They were willing to work in the mines, to do hard physical labor, or to go to school to learn high-tech job skills. But they preferred to work on the reservation, to live where they had always lived. Most spoke at least a little Navajo, and all had heard some of the stories of our past as told by their parents and grandparents.

Still, I had great anger against anyone who would not take our cultural heritage into consideration. I also was frustrated by the Hopi land settlement and the relocation of so many of our people. Naturally I disliked Peterson Zah's politics, though no more so than any other politician at odds with a strong member of an opposing party. I also was suspicious of his growing connection with the Hopi, believing that he should fight for the retention of the land.

I did not realize that Peterson Zah was so hostile to me. I knew that many of his fellow AIM members were extremists, and that, like adolescents first becoming aware of the world, they seemed to think in terms of black and white, forgetting that life almost always falls into shades of gray. The young fail to see that people are not all good or all bad, that problems and solutions are often not clear-cut, and that they affect different individuals in very different ways. They are shocked to see an evil person perform an act of kindness, or to see someone they feel is good behave in a reprehensible manner.

Although Peterson Zah opposed some of my policies, I thought that upon evaluating the efforts I had made on behalf of the Navajo, he would agree with some, disagree with others, and wish to modify still others. It was obvious that he was going to continue several of the programs I had originated, that both of us agreed the results were good for the Navajo people. Yet when he took office, he seemed to focus only on the aspects of my work that he opposed, and his hostility extended to me.

I got my first indication of his hostility when I was evicted from my home. The tribal chairman is provided a home in Window Rock, as are governors and the president. When a new chairman is elected, the former chairman is given sufficient time following his successor's inauguration in which to move. That period provides plenty of time to pack, find a new home, and relocate.

I had been in office for twelve years when Zah was elected. One of my daughters was in the last half of her junior year in Window Rock High School. Another was finishing her freshman year at nearby Rehoboth Mission School. Though we thought we might ultimately leave Window Rock for a while, we did want to stay at least long enough for the older of the two girls to graduate with her friends. Ideally both girls would complete their high school education there, though that would depend upon the work I chose to do as a "civilian."

Wanda and I decided to build a home in Window Rock, and asked the Tribal Council to provide us with a site. The tribe owns all the land on the reservation. Hogans and larger homes are built at the expense of the Navajo living in them, but the land on which they are built is never the property of the homeowner. The land is "borrowed," in a sense, though once the Tribal Council has approved a site, the builder can stay there all his life, then pass the home from generation to generation. This allows for family continuity on the land without that land ever being owned by any individual Navajo. My request was granted, I made preliminary arrangements for a construction loan, and then I began preparing for my new home.

In December, not long after the election but before the official transition of power, Peterson Zah filed a lawsuit in the tribal court to prevent me from keeping the approved lease site in Window Rock. He maneuvered to the point where suddenly, in January, I was given a forty-eight-hour eviction notice to be enforced by the tribal police. We were in the midst of a blizzard, our home filled with twelve years' worth of possessions. We had rented nothing because of our plans to build, and the forty-five-days rule approved by the advisory committee was still the law.

Zah's tactics guaranteed I would have a problem. I could appeal his action in tribal court, and I was certain to win. But until the court ruled, Zah's orders would be in force. This meant that I'd have to leave the chairman's home, find a place to stay, go to court, then be allowed to return to the chairman's home long enough to plan the next move. There was nothing to do but obey in order to prevent the tribal police from forcibly evicting my family.

Fortunately we found a vacant double-width trailer that was barely adequate. We borrowed a truck, got relatives to help us, and managed the move at 1:00 A.M. on the last day we were permitted by Zah to be in the chairman's house.

Next, Peterson Zah's staff confiscated all of my personal records. I had made copies of everything I had done from the time I entered office in 1971 through 1982, when I lost the election. These were not originals because the originals belonged to the tribe. These were copies, considered personal papers, which I planned to use to write my memoirs. I had been storing them in a friend's trading post in Fort Defiance, but Zah's people took them all. They justified the action by claiming that I was trying to steal tribal records. Had that been the case, their action would have been justified. Had they taken the papers, gone through them to see if there were any originals, and retained only those that belonged to the tribe, that would have been valid. But even after there had been time to check to see what I was doing, they retained them, ultimately forcing me into a two-year court battle to regain them, a battle I eventually won.

I had to laugh a little when they finally opened, under the lens of a TV camera, the boxes that had been confiscated. I had placed more personal things in there than I remembered. Copies of my papers were there, of course, but so were such personal items as Christmas cards Wanda and I had received—and even some old socks.

Despite the hostility toward me, I did not feel that there would be problems for the Navajo Nation. I left office with a solid infrastructure for new business in place. The people were doing better, and groundwork had been laid for important projects, such as the completion of six shopping centers being built throughout the Navajo Nation.

The centers were especially important because basic businesses, such as supermarkets, had previously not been available to most of the people, some of whom had to drive to a major city to buy groceries. A cost analysis of the expense of such travel in the average pickup truck owned by the Navajo living in one of the six locations showed that, between gas and wear and tear on their vehicles, they spent fifty dollars beyond the cost of the groceries. The shopping centers not only offered the Navajo convenience, but enabled them to get ahead financially.

There were other projects as well, most of which have already been mentioned, but the important point is that I now felt I could think about myself rather than the Navajo Nation. It was time to get into new fields and achieve the American dream, which was eluding me and the nation I had been representing.

One of the businesses in which I had been involved since the early 1970s was Denay, Inc., an insurance company I owned in partnership with Bob Jackson of Phoenix. I owned 70 percent of the company, and Bob owned 30 percent. He also ran his own separate insurance company, which he had owned for many years.

My decision to enter the insurance business was a calculated one. Back in the days when I was running ONEO, I became aware of a variety of insurance companies owned by major politicians, such as Clinton Anderson Insurance, owned by New Mexico senator Clinton Anderson, and Manuel Lujan Insurance, owned by New Mexico representative Lujan.

I wanted to have a side business in the event I left politics. So many politicians seemed to be involved in insurance that I decided it must be a good field for someone in politics. I entered into partnership with Bob Jackson, an expert in commercial property and casualty insurance underwriting, both of which were among the easier fields for an outsider. We were close friends, and I knew that I could trust him to run the business.

Bob's own firm out of Phoenix was also involved with property and casualty insurance, however, and there seemed to be several conflicts of interest. Both companies were capable of bidding for business involving the Navajo Nation and Navajo entrepreneurs. In addition, Denay was equipped to handle all types of commercial property and casualty, so any business Bob Jackson sought for his firm could also be handled by Denay.

We finally settled on several approaches. First, Bob Jackson's personal firm would concentrate on non-Navajo business, as it had always done. But when he sold for Denay, he would stay almost exclusively with business related to the Navajo.

Second, I would not sell insurance. I took the training and the state exam only after I left office in 1983. Obviously I profited from the company, and obviously a selling point was the fact that I was a partner, but I was not licensed to do any myself. That was all handled by Bob.

Third, I would establish ethical procedures for myself, which I continued to refine during my twelve years in office. These procedures have led to controversy, and yet they are actually quite simple to understand.

The Navajo Nation did not comply with any federal or state laws when it came to ethics. In fact, until 1950, the idea of this was foreign to the Navajo because there was no corruption.

Bribery and implied (oral) contracts are a creation of the white world. They stem primarily from the European tradition of exchanging money for favors. Sometimes there is an implied contract with such a relationship, such as someone saying, "Here's one thousand dollars. I want you to vote for my construction company when you and your board of directors decide to build that new headquarters building." If you take the money, it is understood that you will do what the person asks. A bribe has been offered, and it is understood that you have accepted it.

Certainly there is no binding contract. A white man can just as easily take the $1,000 and vote his conscience. But even if that decision is made, the man is likely to feel guilty. He will feel he has been involved in a dishonest proceeding, that he either should not have accepted the money or should have done what was requested. it is an uncomfortable situation.

Such arrangements appear even in the Bible. As a result, there are extensive ethics rules in the various American and European governments.

By contrast, before 1950, the Navajo had no graft. Bribery was unheard of, and there was no way to be corrupt. Remember that for centuries the Navajo had no central leader. We had nothing but extended families, each operating according to the decisions of that family.

Standard Oil's actions leading to the creation of the Tribal Council and tribal chairmanship really changed nothing. Other than those individuals, there was no power. The Navajo Nation had no employees. Everything was handled by the BIA. It was only in 1950 that the first employee was hired by the Navajo Nation. And it is only in the last forty years that the number of employees and their responsibilities have grown to the level where it is possible to bribe people.

Yet even with the change, before 1983 there were no ethics rules. Instead, everyone behaved as Navajo people had always behaved.

For example, if a man came to your hogan and wanted to give you a horse, you would take it. You might know that the man was trying to ingratiate himself with you, that he wanted some favor. But he was not asking for a favor. He was not asking for a promise. He gave you the horse. You took the horse. And then you did as you pleased, even when that went against the man's wishes.

Navajo people realized this and were not foolish. They did not try to bribe anyone because there was no way they could do so. They would only be wasting their valuables, because the person with whom they were dealing would do whatever he or she wanted regardless of any gifts that might be exchanged. The Navajo consider gifts as expressions of love and respect, nothing more. There were no tribal laws governing the giving of gifts.

The Navajo people had experienced many examples of ruthless business tactics. Before we instituted sound business procedures, we were sometimes ripped off by fly-by-night operations, some of whose personnel were crooks, and some of whom were semihonest. They came to the reservation, painting a glowing picture of new business they would bring us, telling us they would employ Navajo people, and gaining investment money from the tribe.

Sometimes the company did not even exist. For example, a man came to see us with an investment offer and arranged to fly our leaders to an exclusive business address in Beverly Hills. There they showed the leaders an elaborate office, took them to an expensive restaurant, and put them up in fine hotels. They spent perhaps several thousand dollars or more for the business. No one was worried because they had seen the offices. Unfortunately, no one had done any thorough checking. Had they done so, they would have discovered that the luxury office was being rented by the day or week. There was no business, and there were no plans to start one. The con artists made many times their "investment" to get tribal money, then disappeared with the funds.

Other companies were quasi-legitimate. A tennis shoe manufacturing firm was established before I first took office. They leased a building and filled it with sewing machines and other equipment needed for production. They hired Navajo women to work, trained them, and brought them materials. Everyone was happy—until they left in the middle of the night, sneaking out with the equipment and not paying anyone.

Whether this was all part of an elaborate con from the beginning, or whether they simply got into trouble and abandoned us, we never knew. When I came into office, I simply had our lawyers go after them and take them to court to regain the money they owed.

My approach to ethics was based on the unique government that we had. The American system has a complex infrastructure that not only divides power among the executive, judicial, and legislative branches but supposedly also maintains careful checks and balances among all three. The Navajo Nation is quite different. The chairman has to distribute federal funds to various projects, deal with tribal funds being used for various projects, and act as the CEO of various corporations, in addition to recruiting businesses.

Working with federal money is easy. The federal government has guidelines that everyone must follow concerning how the money is to be spent and how it is to be recorded. There are both civil and criminal penalties for failing to account for everything.

Dealing with tribal funds follows almost the same pattern. There are no guidelines, but there are unofficial ways to handle and account for the money, ways that were established by previous tribal chairmen. I had their examples as well as my own business training. Again, there was no problem for anyone.

The third "hat" the tribal chairman wears, the hat of businessman, is the area of concern.

The Navajo Nation owns businesses, including sawmills and a power distribution facility. These are independent businesses, just like any business off the reservation. However, the profits benefit the Navajo people.

These businesses require supplies, and companies seeking to sell to us come to the chairman or to Tribal Council members. They talk about their services, and sometimes wine and dine us. These are acceptable business transactions, for sales representatives and others have always used expense accounts to help solicit business.

There are also companies that provide services, such as insurance. Again there may be wining and dining, though with services, the issues are clear-cut. All parties must meet certain specifications. Once they agree to that, the contract is offered to the lowest bidder. As long as everyone who wishes to do business on the reservation has an equal opportunity to do so, and as long as the companies have a track record that shows they can supply the service, price is the only criterion.

In addition, the Navajo leaders try to bring companies to the reservation. This might be for joint ventures, such as new power plants or mining operations. Or it might be an effort to provide employment for our people. Sometimes such companies come to us, especially when we are perceived to have the resources. At other times we compete, like other cities and countries—providing tours of the area, wining and dining the people, entertaining them, and generally doing what all businesses do to gain more business.

Before 1950 the BIA handled most of these efforts. These people received gifts, were wooed, and cultivated the business owners. But since 1950, the Navajo have handled more and more of this themselves, my administration being the first to demand direct involvement without the BIA acting as middleman.

Although no guidelines existed for creating ethical standards for handling business, I made the decision to act as I would if I were still at Hughes. I learned in my early recruiting days that you do not spare money to get the people to the reservation, taking them to dinner, and doing whatever else was necessary to attract their business, within the limitations recognized by all corporate heads.

Likewise I was comfortable being wooed, whether that meant being flown somewhere to see a facility, being taken to play golf, or even being given a gift. I knew that the businesses were spending their money to influence me, and I didn't care. I felt that so long as I evaluated every business on the basis of what it could do, how it could benefit us, and how much it would cost, nothing else mattered. I was not being bribed. I was not selling out. I was not seducing anyone, nor was I being seduced.

These were the ethical procedures I established as Bob Jackson bid for Navajo Nation insurance business for Denay, Inc. There is no question that Jackson and I knew that many people would consider Denay because I was part owner, talking with Bob to win my favor. And he would have doors opened to him that might otherwise be shut. Furthermore, if the tribe bought insurance from Denay, as part owner of the company, ultimately I would profit.

Under federal ethics laws, as well as those of many states and cities, it would have been improper or illegal for Denay to get involved with the Navajo Nation during my administration. It would have constituted a conflict of interest. To avoid this, many government leaders with extensive investment holdings use blind trusts for those holdings while in office. But my actions as chairman did not fall under any other jurisdiction, and nothing I did was wrong under the traditions or laws of the Navajo Nation.

Our approach was simple. First, I would not vote or in any way try to influence the decision of the Tribal Council or anyone else involved in the decision-making process. Second, the requirements for insurance would be set by others without any input from me. In that way, if Denay could not handle Navajo needs, there would be no bid from our company. And, third, all insurance companies bidding would have to prove they could meet the needs outlined by the reservation.

The contract would ultimately be given to whichever company came in with the lowest price.

Denay, Inc., won some Navajo Nation business, and I did profit in my capacity as part owner. But the terms were identical to those offered by the other companies, as outlined by the tribe, and our price was the lowest of all the bids. I did not vote or try to influence the decision, and because the business went to the lowest bidder, the Navajo people got the best deal from among the companies seeking to underwrite their insurance needs.

Under no circumstances did I do anything wrong. I was not involved in the day-to-day insurance transactions. I did not know when bidding took place. I simply received a profit and loss statement at the end of each year, along with my share of the income. However, if the president of the United States was the part owner of an insurance company, he would have to sell his share of the business before the company could make the bid. He would be in violation of American government ethics laws by bidding. Any outsider looking at the Navajo Nation's legal concerns would have judged us by his own laws, not those that applied to the Navajo. Consequently, the perception of impropriety existed where there had been no impropriety. And while this may seem like splitting hairs, the actions that were taken against me would make these distinctions critical.

I had long been at odds with Annie Wauneka and her old guard followers. She had resented me when I went to work for Raymond Nakai, but later, when I took office as chairman, she seemed to mellow. She came to me on friendly terms and asked me to send Nakai to jail.

I asked Annie Wauneka why I should do that, and she listed what she felt were his crimes. To me these "crimes" were minor, including taking some leave money he may or may not have been entitled to and taking furniture that had been in the home provided for him by the tribe.

I didn't know that any crime had been committed. The allegations at worst seemed rather petty. However, this was at a time when I was filled with anger over the attacks on and the abuse of the Navajo people by BIA members and other outsiders. I was not about to create divisiveness among the Navajo. My priorities were to help advance my people, to make us independent of the BIA, and to stop outsiders who were coming after us. I explained this to Annie and then told her that if she felt a crime had occurred that warranted prosecution, she had legal recourse to go to the courts herself.

I don't know exactly what happened, but shortly after I left office, I was told that some of the people in the Zah administration wanted to destroy me politically. They felt I was too popular with the people and there was a risk that I might return to office.

Various federal agencies began to explore misuse of funds and possible evasion of income taxes. Their investigations were intense and thorough. They wanted to know if I had received honoraria for speaking engagements over the years. If so, had I reported them on my taxes? Also, I flew at tribal expense to many parts of the reservation and the nation at large. Were these always business flights? If there was any question, could the pilots remember seeing me with a briefcase?

I had taken vendors to lunch or dinner at tribal expense. Had I shown favoritism? Was I receiving kickbacks at the expense of the tribe? They explored any way I could have committed a crime, and except for leaks from friends involved with the investigation, they conducted it in secret.

Many people on the reservation undoubtedly would have applauded Zah's actions against me had they been publicized. Nevertheless, many months later one of Zah's lawyers angrily stated that he felt the investigations were a waste of time. He had been through enough documents to feel that I had done nothing wrong. He also felt that the obsession to "get MacDonald" was keeping him and others from working for issues of greater importance to the tribe.

In the meantime, in 1983 I bought out Bob Jackson's 30 percent in Denay, Inc., went to insurance school in Phoenix, took the exam for my license, and passed it. But before I could go into the insurance business full-time, a longtime friend, Mel Pervais, an Ojibwa Indian, asked me to join him in business. He was the sole owner of Cataract, Inc., a company doing approximately $20 million per year in the energy business.

Mel's work excited me for many reasons. The first was that he was an Indian entrepreneur, a full-blooded Ojibwa Indian who did not use Indian Preference or the so-called federal "buy Indian act" laws to get business. Moreover, he was the owner of a thriving business. Mel was doing what I wanted my people to do. It was exciting to see. His was a Horatio Alger story among the Native Americans. So few Native Americans from any of the tribes had gone into business that I found it exciting to use my expertise to help his company.

Another reason for my excitement was the actual work he did—the repair and maintenance of many of the controls and monitors used by nuclear power plants and coal-operated plants. The company also overhauled generators and turbines. There were several locations around the country, though the company was based just outside Philadelphia. I would be working from the Phoenix office, where I would be in charge of sales and marketing. However, because Wanda hated the Phoenix heat, we built a home in a new subdivision of Flagstaff, approximately 140 miles to the north.

I was also delighted to be able to use my engineering skills, testing gauges and writing procedures, in a field that related to my work at Hughes. And because I was working in sales, I had seemingly unlimited income potential. In addition, I worked out an arrangement whereby Mel let me do consulting work on my own when there was time, either under the Cataract business or under the Denay, Inc., name.

Our efforts in outbidding Bechtel, GE, and Westinghouse made us so successful that I worked myself out of a job. In just eighteen months, we were a $49 million per year business. Mel was offered $25 million in cash for his company, and since he was the sole owner, he decided to sell. Most of us stayed on to help with the transition, but after a year, I was involved with other activities.

The consulting work took me into new fields, and I also explored other sales ventures. For example, through Denay, Inc., which I had turned into a consulting business rather than an insurance company, I began representing a British-American bingo company. This is one of those big businesses that most people do not realize can earn millions of dollars a year.

Rural areas frequently consider new ways to improve their economic position. One is bringing in manufacturing plants of one type or another, but this is not always realistic. Usually the rural areas have little to offer manufacturers outside of cheap land, tax breaks, and a work force. The company may plan on relocating employees from an expensive urban area, but many executives will not move to isolated locations that offer only a limited social life. People who enjoy going to symphonies, ballets, rock concerts, and the like do not want to move to a town where there may be, if they are lucky, a single movie theater and a jukebox in the corner bar.

Another method, which is more successful when allowed by state law or overlooked by local sheriffs, is the introduction of one form of gambling or another. Sometimes this is a totally illegal enterprise such as cock fighting. At other times there may be back rooms with slot machines. One legal approach, especially on Indian reservations, is bingo.

Bingo may seem to be the domain of little old ladies and some church groups, but it is far more than that. In a rural area a bingo parlor is both a way to gamble, often for large sums of money, and a place to socialize. Sometimes families participate. Other times couples go to drink, gamble, and be with friends. It is not unusual for people to spend twenty-five to two hundred dollars or more a night in such places. In some areas, the bingo hall becomes the center of all activity, and people return week after week.

The companies that help set up large-scale bingo games know that there is money to be made. Even more important, this is a cash business, and no one knows when skimming of receipts occurs. Some of the companies trying to gain a hold on the reservation want to take as much of the profits as they can get. Others are completely legitimate, recognizing that they can be fair and honest while still making a lot of money.

The British-American bingo company for which I was working was completely honest. They knew that they could spend large sums of money to entertain the tribes and still make handsome profits over the years.

In addition to my work for the bingo company, I was involved with a variety of other projects under my Denay corporate banner. When the Acoma tribe decided to get into the road-building business, they bid on a road that was approximately a mile and a half long and needed grading and other work. The project should have been bid at $1.5 million, but they bid $1.1 million. They had many problems. They bought special equipment before they had any cash. They needed a bond but could not qualify for it because they had no track record. Finally, their tribal money was frozen by the BIA.

Mel Pervais and I helped the Acoma in several ways. Cataract agreed to bail them out for $60,000, and I got them out of their purchase agreement with Caterpillar Equipment. I also helped them obtain a per-project lease arrangement and renegotiated their contract so they were on a cost-plus basis instead of locked into a bid where they would lose everything.

The entire time I was out of office I was pursuing the American dream, exploring new fields, and having fun. My family and I were enjoying each other. We took trips to the West Coast, saw Disneyland and the ocean. We vacationed on the East Coast, in Jamaica, and elsewhere. Life was good for us, and I was able to be with the people who were most important to me.

Many of the people involved with the promotion of bingo and other forms of sanctioned gambling are known to have been involved with disreputable individuals. Although MacDonald entered the bingo business at a time when many people were seeking to disgrace or destroy him, no one criticized this one venture. He was able to provide help without involving himself, the business, or the tribes he assisted with any hint of dishonesty.

CHAPTER SEVENTEEN

I t was in 1985 when people began coming to me and talking about my re-entering the race for chairman. They mentioned the problems on the reservation, including my greatest concern, the Joint Use Area.

When Peterson Zah first took office, he stressed that he and his longtime friend and schoolmate, Hopi chairman Ivan Sidney, would sit under a piñon tree and work out the Joint Use Area problem. They convinced Senators DeConcini and Domenici that there was no reason to repeal Public Law 93-531, as I had worked so hard to do. In fact, because the new Navajo chairman refused to fight for the repeal of the law, the senators did not even bother trying to get it out of committee. They simply let the matter die, assuming that was what the majority of the Navajo desired.

But Zah and Sidney never sat under the piñon tree. Zah decided that when a law is passed, that law is to be obeyed. He saw no sense in fighting the law, no sense in getting it repealed. I am certain he recognized that there would be hardships, but he seemed to feel that it was better to endure those hardships than to challenge an act passed by the U.S. Congress. He told the people they had to move from their land.

I had worked to develop the support of the white ranchers in the Joint Use Area. Zah also eliminated that leverage. He agreed to not claim the lands I had claimed, lands that were available to us under the law but that no one wanted to give up. Without that valid claim, there was no pressure from either the ranchers or the New Mexican politicians to stop the Joint Use Area proceedings.

Several things happened as a result. In theory, the cost of resettlement was eased by a $68,000 grant to each family building a new home in another location. However, one large group of people moved but didn't get their benefits. Some were able to live with other families. Many were left outdoors, surviving as best they could until someone could help them get their money.

Although I enjoyed my life-style, I would have been content herding sheep all of my life had the forced reduction of livestock not taken place. Even after traveling around the world with the U.S. Marines during World War II, I still would have been comfortable with the old ways. They were not so exciting as the places I had been and the things I had seen, and there were none of the diversions of the big American cities I had visited. But over time, I know that the pace of life in the Navajo Nation would have suited me.

After the Cataract project, I returned to the reservation and happened to visit the Joint Use Area, in which the eviction of many Navajo was in progress. I felt that the situation had deteriorated. It seemed to be easier to deprive people of their homes than to help them achieve a new life.

Perhaps the most common sight created by this legal maneuvering was that of the Navajo man, sometimes with a wife and even children, either sitting by the side of the road or roaming the countryside without purpose. He had his bedroll and a few possessions that enabled him to survive off the land. He had a piece of paper guaranteeing him proper relocation, a job, and a future at least as good as the life he had had before his eviction. But the paper was not being honored. There were no jobs and no hogans set aside to handle the refugees. The people had no recourse when they discovered that the papers they were given were more government lies.

As in the 1930s, during the first years of the Great Depression, mere survival was so difficult that staying alive was a triumph of the spirit. The people I saw with their bedrolls were the Navajo equivalent of the wanderers of the Great Depression. They had the courage to face each new day, the will to live, yet they also felt a sense of hopelessness, as though they suspected that one day they would be shown the futility of trying to live from sunrise to sunrise, and then they would give up and die.

Other problems resulted from the change in the Joint Use Area, especially for those who had yet to be moved. As a result of the regulations administered by Hopi and the U.S. government officials, Navajo residents waiting to relocate were not allowed to alter their homes. If a roof leaked, if a wall deteriorated, if a fire damaged a portion of the property, they were not allowed to make repairs or restorations. The people would ultimately be moved—or so the reasoning seemed to go—and there was no sense in giving them permission to make any changes.

It was easier to live in a deteriorating home than to be homeless. But the people who had to live in these increasingly substandard structures had nothing with which to compare their present plight. Elderly men and women were forced to spend their last days in housing that no longer provided adequate shelter from the elements. Even a broken well, perhaps easily repaired, had to be abandoned, forcing people to walk a long way to the nearest available water. Only the Hopi could continue to maintain their property.

The situation made my anger grow, but I knew that whatever we did as a nation had to be handled carefully. I decided to run for re-election in 1986 shortly after my first grandson, Bernard Peter Dailleboust, was born. I won, but only by 700 of 62,000 votes. There was no mandate. I was considered an unknown by some of the people. Others remembered me but demanded that I prove myself all over again. Even my ardent supporters seemed a little wary about what might happen with my return.

The 1986 election of Peter MacDonald raised questions that remain unanswered. He received a far greater proportion of the votes in the primary, compared to his opponent, Peterson Zah, than he did in the general election.

MacDonald's supporters claim that Zah tried to buy the general election. They say he did little to meet the most critical needs of the Navajo people during his four years as chairman and that when MacDonald made a strong showing against him in the primary, he suddenly provided money to various groups and individuals, correcting problems that had been overlooked throughout his four years in office.

Zah's supporters claim that he acted as he always had, that the voting pattern changed because the incumbent chairman went among the people, reminding them of his achievements. Then, realizing that they truly preferred the incumbent, they switched their votes, though not in enough numbers to restore Zah to office.

I had decided during the time I was away from reservation politics that the future should come from economic development. Although the exploitation of our natural resources was still a controversial issue, it seemed less immediate now than it had when I left office. The problems of nuclear energy use in a society where the technological safeguards had yet to catch up with the potential dangers were becoming a national concern. The construction of some nuclear power plants was canceled, and others were put on hold partway through their construction. Alternative fuels were looked upon as superior, even though they were not as cost-effective. Environmental groups were fighting the mining of uranium, adding another obstacle.

Coal use was down around the country. Since most commercial accounts place orders three years in advance, any changes that affect hiring policies are slow to occur. The nation was in a down cycle at the time, so reliance on the exploitation of our natural resources to restore our economy no longer made as much sense as it had made four years earlier.

My goal instead became finding ways to bring 1,000 new jobs a year to the reservation. We had the natural resources some of the companies would need. With individual businesses, such resources could be used in a manner that would seem less offensive to my people. We had a stable labor force and enough capital for investment where necessary. In addition, we could offer tax incentives. Yet our unemployment rate was currently 40 percent, so even 1,000 new jobs a year would mean a slow recovery. However, if handled properly, the recovery could be permanent, immune to outside problems.

In July 1987 I held the first Navajo Economic Summit, an event that made news literally throughout the world. In addition to the American press, the event was carried by the media in Germany, Japan, and other countries. Among those attending the summit were designer Oleg Cassini, General Dynamics Corporation president Oliver C. Boileau, Marmon Group president Robert Pritzker, and many politicians, including Senators Daniel Inouye of Hawaii, Dennis DeConcini and John McCain of Arizona (Goldwater had retired by then), Jeff Bingaman and Peter Domenici of New Mexico, Ross Swimmer of the Bureau of Indian Affairs, and some governors and other dignitaries. There was even a videotaped message from President Ronald Reagan. Arizona governor Evan Mecham, however, sent his campaign finance manager, Ralph Watkins, in his place. Watkins was one of the members of the federal Hopi-Navajo Relocation Commission, and so was offended when the moderator did not bother introducing him. Mecham later became the first Arizona governor to be impeached; obviously his insensitivity bothered others as well as us.

I tried to explain our feelings to the assembled individuals. "I ask you all to imagine for a moment what it is like for a young Navajo to pick up a newspaper or turn on the evening news," I said. "Or what it is like to drive into Phoenix or Albuquerque. And what it is like to witness this explosive success of the free marketplace and the growth it has created all around us.

"It is the feeling of being America's economic orphan. It is the anger of asking why the forces of risk and reward, which have built the most robust economic engine on earth, have passed us by. It is the despair of fearing to dream great dreams, lest they never come to pass."

We kept the talks private. Neither the press nor the public was allowed to attend. We felt that if we ensured privacy, there would be no need for anyone to be polite or to grandstand for voters. We could obtain honest reactions to our plight, even if they were painful. As it turned out, some of the comments did hurt.

Robert Pritzker, the president and CEO of the Chicago-based Marmon Group, an international complex of approximately sixty corporations employing 27,000 people, expressed shock at the lack of a self-sufficient private sector on the reservation. He also said that what the Navajo Nation had to offer—free worker training, tax breaks, government underwriting of factories, and a large cheap labor pool—was no longer unique. While many of these incentives were not common within the United States itself, they nonetheless could be found in other countries throughout the world. Even worse, in his estimation, was the fact that the current Navajo business structure was primarily a state-operated economy suffering from all the problems of bureaucratic planning.

The political structure of the Navajo Nation was also shown to be problematic. The Seva Development Company of Scottsdale had a $30 million contract to build a resort on Lake Powell, Arizona, which was signed by members of Peterson Zah's administration but then suspended by me when I took office. The concern was not whether I was right or wrong in my action, but that there was no continuity of agreements from one administration to another.

Senator Domenici, a primary proponent of the summit, pointed out that private enterprise was a minority activity in the Navajo Nation. Outside businesses operating on the reservation might have to comply with one set of regulations when they began, but the moment there was a change in administration they might have to conform to radically different policies. They might even find that after four years of effort a thriving business could suddenly be expelled from the reservation because of animosity from a new tribal chairman. The senator wanted to see "a reasonable set of rules in regard to behavior." He also wanted to find "new ways to put the marketplace of ownership into the reservation."

Senator John McCain explained that the federal government was attempting to make business circumstances better. He said that he had proposed a new Indian enterprise bill that would ensure many tax breaks for businesses relocating to Indian reservations. He also wanted the secretary of the interior to serve as the arbiter of disputes. While I was naturally hostile to that provision, all the business people were pleased that the federal government expressed concern.

There were some positive comments during and after the meeting. Oliver Boileau, the president of General Dynamics Corporation, mentioned that his company had already hired 480 Navajo to make circuit boards and wire harnesses under defense contracts. He was quite pleased with the quality of the work, the production, and the relationship his business maintained with our people.

Utah Sewing Operations was also mentioned as a successful venture. This Navajo business supplied the jumpsuits worn by NASA astronauts.

And designer Oleg Cassini expressed his pleasure during an interview with a reporter for the Cable News Network. He said, "They talk the language now that any businessmen talk. They are represented, the people, by skilled, young, aggressive, intelligent people."

New Mexico's governor, Garrey Carruthers, admitted that there was a need for the states to develop economic treaties with the reservations. Such arrangements could work on behalf of all parties.

Ultimately four problems were noted. The first was that the tribal government interfered in the economic arena, preventing business development by both private enterprise and Navajo entrepreneurs.

The second concerned federal involvement. Legislation was needed to provide tax incentives to businesses, to help capitalize Indian entrepreneurs, and to encourage defense contractors to use the Navajo businesses as subcontractors. One of the problems long experienced by Indian entrepreneurs is that they do not own the land on which their homes are built. A home can theoretically be removed or destroyed at the whim of the Tribal Council. Everything is connected with tribal ownership, so those Indians who want to go into business cannot borrow against their homes as people living off the reservation can do.

The third problem was the need for the Navajo government to eliminate the needlessly complex bureaucracy and red tape that surrounded the establishment of new businesses. In the past, our system of families, clans, and tribal concerns required business owners to obtain from 50 to more than 125 separate permits before they could begin operating. This was so time-consuming that moments of opportunity would pass, and start-up capital would be depleted. By simplifying such procedures to approach the way they existed in American society at large, we would ensure faster, safer start-ups.

Finally, the states and the reservations located within their borders needed to develop stronger relationships. Each could benefit the other, but it was necessary to begin with a plan such as that expressed by Governor Carruthers.

I must confess that my return to the chairmanship in 1987, and the experience of the economic summit, gave me a perspective I previously did not have. Although during my first twelve years in office, we Navajo gained at least our share—and probably somewhat more—of the available federal and state funds, I did not really begin to exploit our wealth for our own benefit until my fourth term. I came to realize that we should develop the nation as a business and that the key to our economic future lay in the profitable use of our land. To accomplish this, it would be necessary to borrow from Anglo real estate procedures.

American corporations do not wait to start a project until they have

$50 million or $100 million to spend. They create "paper" money by working out bond sales, collateral arrangements, and similar deals.

For example, suppose we wanted to build a ten-story office building in Phoenix. Following traditional American business practices, we would put up $1 million for the land, then seek tenants for the as-yet-to-be-constructed building. Next we would go to a bank or other lending institution to request a loan to cover the cost of construction. We would use the structure we wanted to build as collateral. The rental agreements would prove to the lender that there would be a steady income from the property to meet the monthly payments.

My plan was to gain money for projects in the same manner as Anglo America. This would be accomplished in several ways.

First, I wanted to begin developing some projects on our own. The resort on Lake Powell, contracted for during Peterson Zah's administration, was a good example of this new thinking. The Seva Development Company had approached the Tribal Council with a proposal to build a marina on Lake Powell, a man-made recreation area in northern Arizona. Although the Del Webb Development Corporation already operated a tourist spot on the lake, the proposed Antelope Point Marina would be located far enough away from it to ensure sufficient tourists at both sites. Such a development made sense.

However, I discovered that the arrangements that had been made and approved by the BIA and the National Parks Service worked against the Navajo Nation. The corporation, which had never built a marina and planned to hire outside expertise, had $1 million to invest, and had arranged to combine this amount with $3 million of Navajo Nation funds, along with certain benefits: The Navajo would give the developers free concession rights along the water, seventeen acres of land for which neither a purchase nor lease payment would take place, and unlimited free water use. In addition, a highway stretching for several miles would be built to the water's edge. In exchange for all this, the marina would be constructed in stages, beginning with a docking area and service station. As other funds became available, the remainder of the development would be built.

In addition, the company agreed to establish a shell corporation for the venture, the Navajo Nation receiving 51 percent. However, for every dollar that was spent by the public, eighty cents would go to the outside corporation and twenty cents would go to the Navajo, for the next thirty years. Since the cash outlay on the part of the Navajo was already three to one at the start, not including the road construction, the land, and the water rights, this deal was outrageous to me.

Naturally I fought this arrangement, and ultimately suspended the contract, but I also came to realize that we could have developed the Antelope Point Marina ourselves. Like Seva, we had no expertise in marina construction, but, like them, we could hire outside experts for design and construction. Yet we had never thought about doing such things ourselves.

Next I looked at existing businesses on the reservation. Our electric power came from a coal-fired generating plant located on reservation land. The plant was owned by the Arizona Public Service Company, which operated it with coal mined from our land. Yet at any time APS chose, it could deny us electricity while still providing power to non-Navajo land in the states it served.

I was aware that APS was in trouble. It had expanded beyond the power industry, buying a resort, a bank, and other unrelated businesses. In addition, it had invested heavily in a nuclear power plant that was far more costly and less efficient to operate than originally planned. The company had been denied rate increases by the Arizona Corporation Commission because its financial problems related to business difficulties unconnected with generating electricity. I thought that perhaps the Navajo Nation could buy the generating plant and operate it ourselves.

But such ventures needed capital, and I decided to put together a plan for bringing new cash to the Navajo people. The money could be earmarked for one project or another without dipping into tribal funds. Ultimately we could use a variety of financing arrangements, but first I wanted to explore bond issues.

I designated one bond issue for the purchase of land primarily in the reservation's Eastern Navajo region. A checkerboard area owned partly by the Navajo, partly by private concerns, and partly by the government, portions of the region had been deemed suitable for purchase by a special committee based on such factors as size, quality, location, and potential for future income. The committee's first choice was the Big Boquillas Ranch land, a 500,000-acre property. It was available for under $70 per acre at a time when other land of equal quality was selling for at least $100 per acre.

There were other development ideas I wanted to put into effect, including the construction of a needed airport in Window Rock, housing projects, and new businesses. Some interest had already been shown by such industries as General Dynamics, which was already operating on reservation land. An infusion of money would help us begin projects, attract outsiders, and most important, increase employment.

I began looking to bond issuers to see what help they could provide. We sent representatives to all the major companies and they all expressed interest. However, they still wanted to do business as it had been done in the past. They wanted us to put up our land, or all our water rights, or some other massive asset as collateral, even though the value of such assets far exceeded the money being obtained.

We wanted a fair deal. We did not want to have to put up more collateral than the money we received. If we obtained $50 million, we wanted to use only the minimum assets needed, not everything we had, to protect the investors.

Ultimately we found our answer. A Japanese bank, the largest in that country, agreed to completely underwrite a bond offering. If we defaulted, the Japanese bank would be responsible to the bond holders.

In exchange, the bank asked us to use only the income from the Peabody Coal Mine in Black Mesa as collateral. The bankers had conducted a study to determine the stability of the coal mine during the time we would be paying them back. They found that the known quantity of coal that was mined in the area, along with the long-term contracts various energy companies held with Peabody, assured more than adequate income for the life of our bond agreement. They would not lose, and we would not risk being robbed of our assets during that period. In the end, they offered us $100 million.

Everything was looking good. When I first took office, tribal unemployment was 80 percent in most of the Navajo Nation, 60 percent in the most economically secure areas. Over the years I had reduced it to 45 percent. In most parts of the United States, 45 percent unemployment would be intolerable, but the Navajo had to overcome two major obstacles: the lack of new jobs and the massive increase in the annual work force. With an annual net increase of approximately 3 percent of our total population, 5,000–6,000 more men and women are seeking jobs every year. Thus, going from 80 percent unemployment down to 45 was a major accomplishment. And, with the new cash infusion, I hoped to bring the unemployment rate down even further, to 10 percent.

My dreams were many. We could develop high-tech research and development with some of the money. The Navajo people would be trained to apply the skills and creativity demonstrated in such traditional work as the extremely intricate and inventive weaving and jewelry to math, science, electronics, engineering, and related disciplines.

Money carefully spent could stimulate Navajo entrepreneurism. We could become as viable a business force as the Japanese, the Koreans, and other Asian nations. However, what I did not expect was that my world was about to change in ways I could not imagine, and that my future would be determined by one single event: the Big Boquillas Ranch purchase.

Land has a different meaning to a Navajo than to an Anglo. Some Anglos see land ownership as a nuisance: The grass must be cut, the leaves must be raked, the snow must be shoveled. For others, it is the source of pleasure through gardening, perhaps raising flowers, vegetables, fruit trees, and other plants. And for still others, land is a place for farming or ranching, a means of earning a livelihood.

The Navajo use their land. They farm. They graze cattle. They eat and sell their produce. These fruits of the land are gifts from their mother, the earth, who nurtures them and whom they lovingly tend in return.

The Navajo treat the land like an aging parent who is almost entirely self-sufficient. Such a mother lives with her children, baking for them, cooking for them, tending to their needs. Yet where once she was fiercely independent, now she needs care, tenderness, and occasional assistance.

And just as no child puts a price on his mother, so the Navajo cannot put a price on their land. How do you value that which gives you life? Certainly land is part of agribusiness, and many Navajo, especially those with business executive experience, such as Peter MacDonald, know that. Yet for the Navajo land remains a commodity without price.

The Big Boquillas Ranch was located in northern Arizona, just south of the Grand Canyon. While it officially comprised 729,000 acres, a portion of that was Arizona land leased to the ranch owners, whose property actually consisted of 491,000 privately owned acres. The leased areas could be passed on to the buyer of the 491,000 acres under the same terms offered to the original owners, but eventually its use would be renegotiated or the land would be returned.

Big Boquillas—or Big Bo, as it was commonly called—was owned by Tenneco West, which at one time had been involved in ranching. The land was used for cattle grazing and mineral exploitation.

Big Bo had been offered for sale in the early 1970s when Tenneco West decided to ease away from ranching. Tenneco was asking for $25 million for the land in 1983. However, either no one was interested or no one was able to consummate a deal.

By 1985, Melvin Jans, who represented Tenneco West, felt that the company would benefit if it could get out from under the holdings for around $18 million. One potential buyer, Karl Solomon Investments of Wichita, Kansas, had offered $17.8 million that year, then decided against the purchase because the owner of the company thought the price was too high.

Other offers came in. E.G.B. Investments offered $25 million in September 1986, but the deal fell through, as did a $25 million offer from the Topango Properties Company the following December.

In 1987, Con Englehorn, a real estate appraiser from Headquarters West in Phoenix, stated that Big Bo was worth no more than $25 million and probably should sell for less. He had appraised sections of the property at one time or another during the previous twenty years. Although he had never evaluated the entire property, he felt that his appraisal was a fairly accurate one. Nevertheless, the ultimate sale price for Big Bo was to prove considerably higher.

In early January 1987, Bud Brown, a friend of Peter MacDonald as well as one of his fund-raisers during the 1986 campaign for chairman, approached Melvin Jans about buying Big Bo. A meeting was set for the seventh of that month with Jans and Tom Tracy, head of such businesses as Tracy Oil and Gas Company, Reppel Steel, and White Eagle Stucco, joining Brown.

The deal was rather complex. Tracy and Brown were partners, but Brown was taking the role of broker. The official purchaser was to be Tracy Oil and Gas, and the corporation put up a $100,000 refundable deposit for the deal on February 14, 1987. The purchase price would be $25 million.

Some time in February, Tom Tracy made a written offer to sell Big Bo to the Navajo Nation for slightly more than $33 million. The property had not been purchased, though it had gone into escrow. The idea was for Tracy and Brown to buy Big Bo, then sell it immediately, making an $8 million profit from the transaction without having to put up much money.

Tracy and Brown used the $100,000 to buy time for themselves. They then requested an extension on the purchase on March 25, at which time they agreed to put down another $250,000 to hold the property until July 9. Along the way they also agreed to pay more for the land, at a price of $26,250,000, which would now include the 491,000 acres and half the mineral rights.

While all this was taking place, Tracy and Brown were negotiating with the Navajo Office of Land Administration, headed by Ninibah Cahn, and the Navajo Nation concerning the purchase of the land. Tentative agreements were reached, with the Navajo putting up $500,000 toward the purchase on May 25.

Several issues became unclear at this point. Edison Woods, the Navajo appraiser who was sent out to evaluate the land, felt that the *property was worth between $50 and $63 per acre. This figure placed a proper purchase, in his opinion, at between $24 million and $31 million. However, the exact offer was $33.4 million, and in order for the deal to go through the Navajo needed an appraisal that matched the agreed-upon purchase price.*

In theory, since Tracy and Brown were not in a position to come up with the money to buy Big Bo without a way to immediately resell the land, the Navajo could have waited out their purchase option. Then they could have gone directly to Tenneco West and consummated the deal on their own for far less money. (See Appendix for copies of pertinent letters and memos.)

Robert Pencall of the Bureau of Indian Affairs said he had been told by Edison Woods that Ninibah Cahn, the director of the land administration office for the Navajo Nation, wanted him to raise the valuation to match what the Navajo were going to pay. But even this allegation does not answer the question of MacDonald's involvement.

It is known for certain that a few days after Peter MacDonald was elected tribal chairman in November 1986, Bud Brown paid to fly the MacDonalds and their daughter Hope to Hawaii. Brown picked up all costs for the trip, which totaled approximately $5,000. MacDonald had been a friend of Brown for several years, and the businessman could well afford the generosity. The government claimed that this was the first stage of a bribe related to Big Bo. Yet MacDonald's actions were no different from those of many U.S. representatives and senators. Ethically, questions could be raised, but legally, there was no wrongdoing.

MacDonald was inaugurated on January 13, 1987. On February 24, a wire transfer of $25,000 was made from Reppel Steel to United Bank of New Mexico to help pay off a portion of the MacDonald loan. In the spring of 1986 the chairman was facing high expenses for his children's education, along with business and personal concerns, and had taken out a 120-day loan for $70,000 from the bank for himself and his son, Rocky.

Unable to repay the money at the time, he gave the bank $10,000 and continued the loan for the remaining amount. The $25,000 from the steel company was put toward that balance. In addition, on January 17, Brown delivered a BMW sedan leased to MacDonald, paying $2,657 down and $813 per month. Brown was also the credit reference for the car. MacDonald signed the lease for the BMW.

It is not certain when the Big Bo purchase by Brown and Tracy was planned, but the arrangements were formalized in an agreement letter dated February 20, 1987 (see Appendix).

The twists and turns of all these deals became rather complex. A tape-recorded discussion between Peter MacDonald and Brown re-

vealed how the finances would be explained to the public. That conversation, on November 22, 1988, preceded the Senate hearings into various aspects of Indian affairs, which were held at the end of January and throughout parts of February 1989.

Ironically, MacDonald had eagerly anticipated the Senate hearings. Advance publicity by the Senate, including statements made by the principals, indicated that the hearing would be an investigation into the Bureau of Indian Affairs. MacDonald was thrilled that the BIA corruption would at last become a national concern and he made available to investigators all the documentation of problems with the BIA that the Navajo had carefully assembled over the years. However, in the end, the BIA's corruption and mismanagement was ignored (at this writing, there is beginning to be concern, so overwhelming has the evidence been against the agency), and most of the committee sessions were spent attacking MacDonald, ensuring that his voice, when fighting for fair treatment relative to water, mineral, and land rights, would not be heard. Instead, the investigators listened only to the November 22 tape. And that conversation marked the beginning of the downfall of Peter MacDonald as a respected leader of the Navajo Nation.

What is ironic is a fact not learned until 1992, long after Peter MacDonald had been publicly disgraced. He was facing prison, and the political opponents among Arizona's state government leaders were stressing the folly of Big Bo. Then a number of Hopi tribal leaders and outside real estate people revealed that the Hopi had also planned to buy Big Bo. They had been using part of the land for recreation purposes and had begun to recognize the vast mineral potential. They saw what MacDonald had seen, and had the Navajo not beaten them to the purchase, they would have owned the land. Much of the pressure from white state government leaders speaking against MacDonald resulted from their knowledge of the Hopi plans and their anger that the Hopi, whom they considered friendlier to their desires, had been thwarted in their efforts. In fact, by 1993, the Navajo administration was discussing the possibility of making partial reparations to the Hopi by giving them land, the ultimate insult to a traditional Navajo.

CHAPTER NINETEEN

In hindsight, I can see that the purchase of the Big Boquillas Ranch was a mistake for my career and my life. In addition to the charges and countercharges that resulted from that transaction, several important issues need to be mentioned.

First, I felt then and I feel now that the purchase of the Big Boquillas Ranch was in the best interest of the Navajo Nation. We gained almost half a million acres of land, including half the leased mineral rights. The long-term value of the land is far greater than what we paid, and this is significant, since the Navajo do not buy land as a short-term, speculative investment the way Anglos do. Many of the elders, in fact, would say that we had merely ransomed our mother from those who illegally took her from us.

Equally important, Bud Brown could not have found enough money to pay the Navajo to *not* buy the ranch once we set foot on the property and evaluated its potential. We saw what it meant for the future of our people, and that was far more valuable than the price we needed to pay to get it.

As far back as 1971, the Navajo Tribal Council considered buying Big Bo. At that time Tenneco Corporation would have sold us the land for $21 million in cash. We did not have the cash then, and we did not have the cash sixteen years later when the land was still available. All we could offer was payment over time, which Tenneco did not want.

The only way we could get adequate credit to buy Big Bo in 1987 was through third-party involvement. Brown and Tracy offered the land on terms that enabled us to make the substantial payments necessary to purchase the land at $33 million.

Friends of mine were involved with the deal, and there is no question that they made enormous profits. They conducted the sale of the land the way many small businesses, such as furniture companies, offer their products for blacks and other minorities in America's ghettos. Such companies know that low-income people do not have the cash to buy furniture. Only through credit purchases can low-income families buy the furniture they need.

Many merchants in inner-city ghettos mark up their stock by as much as 300 percent, then give extremely liberal credit terms to their customers. The purchasers may pay far more than they would in a nonghetto store, but they get the items they want and need immediately.

There is little difference between these ghetto deals and the Navajo Nation's purchase of Big Bo. The land was "flipped," one person buying it on Tenneco's terms and then immediately selling it (the "flip") for a high profit, but in the only manner the new customer, the Navajo Nation, could afford.

Brown and Tracy made almost $8 million in windfall profit by flipping the land sale. And the Navajo Nation obtained land that would otherwise have been impossible to get.

Did I benefit as a result of the two men's actions? There is no question that they were trying to influence my decision. Ultimately I acted in the manner I thought best, even though that meant paying an inflated price for the land. I also received a trip to Hawaii and other benefits. I like to think I would have received them anyway. Certainly, before the sale I was led to believe that Bud Brown was so wealthy, the cost was no different to him than if a normal person took my family out to dinner. Yet ultimately I learned that much of his money was borrowed, and the source of his borrowing was a man who truly did hope to influence me.

I hope I did not receive his friendship because he thought I was in the position to influence the purchase from which he profited. However, to this day I cannot be certain. What is comforting is the fact that even if I was as corrupt as my enemies say, the Tribal Chairman cannot influence a major purchase such as Big Bo. All agreements are the results of the Tribal Council, and those members represent too many different attitudes and beliefs to ever, as a body, deliberately work against the Diné. Besides, tribal lawyers, as well as lawyers retained from outside, reviewed the offer and prepared the sales document for the Tribal Council.

For those of us on the Navajo reservation, 1989 was supposed to be a time of hope. We had been told that the United States Senate was at last going to look into allegations of corruption, mismanagement, and other problems within the BIA. At last there would be a public forum for all of those problems we had been complaining about.

Several Anglo newspaper reporters had also been looking into the problems. In 1987, various publications in Arizona, Utah, New Mexico, and elsewhere had run articles on child molestation by a part-time BIA school teacher. And while such problems have arisen in public and parochial schools around the United States, the reporters found that the BIA officials alerted to the crisis allegedly did nothing about removing the teacher involved.

Other teachers were growing marijuana, then sharing it with their students, according to the investigation. On the Navajo Nation, we learned that some BIA teachers were coercing Navajo children to take off their clothes and pose for sex pictures. Again, when reports were made to the BIA supervisors, there was no indication the teachers were removed from their positions of trust.

There were also some reports about unfair contracts, especially with energy leases, and many of the other concerns we had been expressing over the years. The *Arizona Republic* presented one of the strongest series of articles more than a year earlier, the reporters focusing on such issues as health care and poverty. The reporters discussed the billions of dollars that had been provided to the BIA to administer on behalf of the Indians, and the fact that most of the money was either wasted or spent on the bureaucracy. The bloated BIA management prevented that money from reaching the actual programs it was supposed to fund.

Some of the information detailed complaints we had made for years to no avail. Other information had been hidden so that even we in positions of leadership did not know about it. In all cases, the government did not act until Anglo reporters for some of the state's most powerful papers made the incidents public. Then a committee was established to formally investigate.

The Senate's Indian Affairs Committee established a subcommittee, led by Daniel Inouye of Hawaii and John McCain of Arizona, which included senators from states with large Native American populations. At last it seemed to everyone that Indians would have their day in court. We could end the waste and corruption of the BIA, at last showing that something like 90 cents of every dollar authorized for Indians never reached the Indians. It was spent on the bureaucracy.

My staff and I were very happy about what was happening. We had been alerted a couple of months in advance by some of the people involved so that we could begin documenting the problems with the BIA. This we did, carefully preparing as though we were going into court. We showed how the Indians often received ten cents on the dollar from the appropriations. We showed how as much as $70 million in Indian money was lost through such poor record keeping that no one knew if it was spent, stolen, or sitting in some forgotten account somewhere. And we had found that when some of the tribes gave their money to BIA to manage, just as Anglos might use a banker or investment counselor, their work was not up to the minimum accepted standards in the white man's world. Even worse, no one knew if the losses were through bad management and incompetence or corruption and deliberate theft.

In addition to the concerns mentioned in the newspaper accounts, I had several areas I wanted to emphasize. I wanted to show how we were receiving less money for mineral leases than was normal for private agreements throughout the United States. I wanted to show the mismanagement of our land, as well as the improper loss of acreage. While we should have been maintaining and enlarging our land holdings, the BIA was causing us to lose land. I planned to show the way the educational system prevented the full development of our young people for both of the worlds in which they would be living— Anglo and Navajo. And my biggest concern was the loss of tribal sovereignty. All tribes were being denied their independence, whether the tribe was constitutional or treaty. The BIA was illegally trying to act as tribal government, something that had to be stopped.

What we did not know was that my political enemies were planning to avoid the BIA problems as much as possible. They wanted the hearings to challenge my leadership and to destroy me any way necessary. They knew they could gain the support of BIA officials, since attacking me would reduce the pressure on them. The fact that I had nothing to do with the health service, the education program, and the other issues about which we were challenging them did not matter.

We also had politicians who were trying to take care of their home states. For example, the New Mexico Public Service Company was negotiating with the BIA and others to lease mineral rights in order to mine coal and build another generating station. The coal would come from Navajo lands and the generating plant would be on the reservation. Ultimately the cost of that power—so critical to the state—and the extent of pollution damage to the immediate surroundings (reservation land and the Navajo who lived there) would be determined by negotiations from which everyone was trying to exclude the Navajo. Profits could only be made if the deal was for less than the fair market value. The Navajo assertion of their rights would hurt that deal, as well as similar arrangements with those tribes that also had energy resources on their land.

A good example was the issue of the land known as the Paragon Resource Ranch. There were several billion tons of a highly desirable type of coal in what were known as thirty-foot seams on the property. Most coal seams run five to ten feet. The Paragon Resource Ranch coal would not run out for decades, even with very heavy mining and use. The story began well before the hearings in Washington. It occurred just before and during the time when I was defeated for re-election between my third and fourth terms as chairman. In this case, it was the Navajo and not the BIA who were involved with the negotiations, but the manipulations, the power plays on both sides, and the splits that occurred among all the parties would eventually come back to haunt us almost a decade after the situation began.

The Paragon Resource Ranch issue arose in the late 1970s when Congress was trying to give land back to the Navajo. They had taken land to give to the Hopis, so they felt they should compensate us with land elsewhere. At first they wanted to provide land around Page, Arizona, in an area called Vermillion Cliffs. This was 250,000 acres regularly used by ranchers, hunters, and outdoor enthusiasts. The land provided recreation for Anglos, and enough special interest groups objected to its loss to the Navajo that a new parcel had to be sought.

We would have been able to use the land for settlement and grazing. There would have been no damage to the land, but the recreational users would have had to go elsewhere.

Initially we thought that Congress would not go back on its word. At the end of one session, we were told that the land would be ours despite the opposition. But heavy lobbying made the land issue a priority for the start of the next Congressional session. We were told that a change was being made in the law so that the land would *not* be ours to use.

A new hearing was held. A new law was created that specified we could have 250,000 acres of land, provided it was not more than 15 miles from the existing Navajo reservation. Then the New Mexico officials said that they were concerned about the law because, while Arizona had 250,000 acres of land that could be eligible for transfer, New Mexico, which was also home to a portion of the Navajo Nation, did not. Through their pressure, the Navajo would be given a maximum of 30,000 acres, the remaining 220,000 acres coming from elsewhere.

The truth was somewhat different than the allegations. New Mexico had almost as much available land as Arizona. However, unlike Arizona, the land eligible to be transferred was extremely mineral rich. This was land contiguous to the Four Corners region, and while we were looking at agricultural and homesteading uses in Arizona, New Mexico's land in that area would have given us access to valuable minerals.

It is important to remember that we were not trying to hurt any of the states or their people. We were not trying to steal white people's land to get back at them. The land in question had been part of the Navajo Nation for centuries. It had been stolen from us during the Fort Sumner period, and, ever since, we had tried to get it back. We had fought for three generations to regain the holdings given to us from the time of First Man and First Woman. Yet the Anglos saw only that they had developed the land for their own uses, and they resented our coveting "their" land. They also feared the cost of having to buy from us what we felt they had long ago stolen.

New Mexico was not worried about the loss of land. They were worried about the specific land we were going to take.

Our decision was to extend the eastern part of the reservation to include 30,000 acres of Bureau of Land Management (BLM) territory which our people had been legally using for grazing for many years. It adjoined our existing territory. It was within the limits set by New Mexico. And it was familiar to our people.

The new land, known as the Paragon Resource Ranch, was precisely what New Mexico feared we would take. The state had planned to place a power-generating station on the land and establish mining operations to obtain the coal needed to operate the station. Our actions were about to cost New Mexico a cheap source of electrical power.

Suddenly the government leaders were calling me, trying to get me to accept some sort of deal. I refused, gaining the enmity of New Mexico's senators and governor.

When Peterson Zah took office in my place, the New Mexican officials tried to make a deal with him. They said that the Navajo really did not know how to handle an energy resource like the Paragon property. Instead, the Navajo should pay the state half the royalties from the coal or else these officials would be forced to go to Congress and legally regain the land.

I never worried about such threats. The Navajo had no expertise in managing a resource such as the Paragon property, but there was no reason we couldn't just hire outside experts who would do the work until our people could be trained.

Peterson Zah did not appear to see matters my way. Whether he was afraid of what might happen or thought the change would be beneficial, I neither knew nor cared. I was angry that he gave New Mexico's officials the right to negotiate with New Mexico Public Service and a consortium of related businesses to build a generating station. The Navajo would supply the coal without charge as their financial contribution to this consortium, and in return, the Navajo would receive one-fifth interest in the generating station.

There was more to these issues than stated, however. In fairness, Zah was looking to a Navajo preference in hiring. He saw that our people would be given jobs that currently did not exist. The agreement would reduce unemployment, and this was a good thing. However, jobs would have been created at least to the same degree if we had a better arrangement than the one to which he committed us.

Zah did not take into consideration the problems that were being created. In addition to the loss of revenue from the minerals, the Anglo companies were to be given exclusive rights-of-way through our land. There would be roads built cutting across our acreage, and they were meant to be used by the consortium, not the Navajo. Utility operations involving Utah, Colorado, New Mexico, Nevada, California, Arizona, and elsewhere would have all been tied together so they could create a cheap utility right-of-way for oil, gas, and electricity. The alternative was that they would have to go around the reservation, a very expensive proposition. Any possible control was being denied to us.

Later, when I returned to power, I told the New Mexico officials that the deal was off. I would stop the mining of the coal and fight the generating station unless new contracts were drawn up. The only way we could achieve economic self-sufficiency was to have full control of our land and mineral rights. Then all the states would have to negotiate with the Navajo, assuring our sovereignty and maximum possible legal power. If anyone attempted to improperly work around us, we would be able to turn off the switch, bring down the gates on the waterways, and shut down access to that which was essential for the survival of Anglo cities. There would be no free passage through the reservation, no continued control over what was rightfully ours.

I did not want power and control over the white man. But neither did I want any non-Navajo coming onto our land and dictating how we must live, work, and develop our resources. We had been controlled by outsiders for more than a century. For their benefit, the Anglos had been trying to change our legal system, our economy, and our culture. So far as I was concerned, such abuse of the Navajo would stop with the Paragon Resource Ranch issue. It was obviously not a popular stand.

There were some other considerations I was looking at as well. Anyone could see that the access roads and the mining would effectively cost us most of the value and use of the Paragon Resource Ranch. However, it was during this time that some scientists posited that the magnetic fields given off by power grids are extremely dangerous to live near, so it was possible that many thousands of additional acres would have been lost because of basic ecological problems created by the generation of electrical power.

In addition, once any legal agreement is finalized in state courts, all subsequent conflicts are resolved in state courts. This meant further damage to the Navajo legal system. The Navajo Nation would become no different than any other property holder under state law. Again, our unique status would be lost and there would be no reason to continue with an independent tribal government.

Zah had gone for a deal that offered a few jobs and a certain amount of money. Yet, over time, the actions would have cost the Navajo millions of dollars, thousands of jobs, and the use of thousands of acres of land. Political and economic leverage would be eliminated, and our efforts for sovereignty would have been further eroded.

In addition to the 30,000 acres in New Mexico, I selected 220,000 acres that included choice land south of Winslow and Flagstaff. This was government land, leased by the BLM to ranchers and used by many Arizonans in ways that were quite profitable for them. The land did not have the inherent mineral value of the Paragon Resource Ranch, but its loss would have a more immediate effect on far more people than would the New Mexico property.

Shortly after this, Senators Pete Domenici and Dennis DeConcini introduced legislation to repeal Public Law 93531. This was the Navajo/Hopi relocation act, and the belated opposition resulted from the reaction of irate constituents.

I was delighted. It was early 1982, and with the repeal of the law, the Navajo and the Hopi would be left to settle their differences themselves. True, the land we had selected in Arizona and New Mexico would no longer be ours. The selection would be null and void, something desired by both states. But at the same time, we would regain our sovereignty, our people would not suffer from forced relocation, and everyone would benefit. It was the ideal compromise, and if the change occurred, all crises would have been avoided.

I lost the election in 1982, and neither Peterson Zah nor his staff pursued the matter. I don't know if lobbying and publicity would have made a difference. I just know that it did not happen. Instead, because there was no pressure and little publicity, the proposed repeal bill was allowed to die in committee.

The government then took away a portion of the land that should have gone to the Navajo. The half of the land needed for the generating station and the mining of coal went to the special interest groups in New Mexico. The Navajo would have no opportunity to get the land that had almost been ours. We were in the same situation we had been in a decade earlier when the Navajo/Hopi relocation act was enacted.

I had planned to discuss all of this in the Senate hearing. My staff had been working in the archives to show the documents that proved our case. However, some of the leaders of the investigation into Indian affairs knew that they were being investigated in the Charles Keating scandals related to the savings and loan industries. It seems to me they needed dramatic headlines to call attention away from themselves. Investigating the horrors of the BIA would help my people. However, it would do nothing to get headlines outside of a few states where there were shared concerns about Indian rights and the future of the tribes. Attacking the chairman of the largest Indian Nation in the United States would make headlines everywhere, and it would call attention away from the excesses of the BIA.

I think I would not be so angry if an investigation into my actions had been a separate hearing. I obviously would not have agreed with it, but it would have been my problem and my battle. What hurts so deeply is that the committee knew that there were very serious concerns relative to the BIA. They knew that money was missing. They knew that education was lacking. They knew that some BIA personnel had been living as though they were beyond the law, hurting an unknown number of helpless children. Yet they chose to ignore those important issues to come after me.

Had I been guilty of all the charges made by all the enemies who exist, prosecuting me instead of looking into the BIA would still not have been right. I had been a part of tribal leadership for a little over a dozen years. The BIA had been hurting the Navajo people for decades, and the stories that had come out in the press reinforced that fact. Yet the government realized that if they went after the BIA, the Navajo and other Indian tribes would be in a position to demand fair market value for their water and mineral rights.

To make matters worse, I was not popular on the Navajo Nation at that time. I had won the 1986 election by 700 votes out of a total of 60,000 votes cast. Within a few weeks, a recall petition was begun, and by the Fall of 1987, supposedly 30,000 people had signed it.

I soon learned I could not count on all of the council delegates who previously supported me. There were some who always wanted to be on the side of the winner in any election. They were seemingly close to me during the years when I had massive support among the Navajo, but once my popularity slipped, they began making overtures to the opposition. They did not formally support the others because they feared that I might regain my old position with the people. But if I lost, they would not be tied too closely to me. Their concerns were not with the Navajo but with being connected with people in power. My inability to rely upon them for anything added to my troubles.

I started to worry about all this during the months before the Senate hearing, then realized it was unimportant. I had to be concerned with economic development and exercising sovereignty for the Navajo. Nothing else truly mattered.

The Big Boquillas land purchase was, to me, the most important decision I made at this time. The more than 700,000 acres would be the largest land acquisition the Navajo had made since 1934. More important, approximately 450,000 acres of Big Bo was private land. The rest was state and federal land, which meant that it would be considered trust land. The BIA was responsible for overseeing trust lands, treating the Navajo like children who could not be entrusted with anything of importance. But the private land purchase belonged to the Navajo, and that was far more important than mere ownership.

We learned that there was private investment money available from the Japanese and others that would allow the Navajo Nation to develop whatever projects we desired. However, we needed to own a resource in order to attract the investment. The 450,000 acres could be used as collateral to allow us real autonomy. We would not need BIA approval or involvement. We would be able to seek our own destiny in ways not previously possible.

The land we purchased was also meant to serve as a tactic for even more assured sovereignty. It began at the edge of Interstate 40, which traveled west from Chicago to Los Angeles and extended to the rim of the Grand Canyon.

Prior to the purchase of Big Bo, our western boundary, past Tuba City to Cameron, was the 1934 Fixed Boundary. This was the end of the Navajo Reservation land as permitted by an act of Congress in 1934. With the forced livestock reduction, and with our lack of sophistication in the ways of the white man's world, we were trapped. We did not know about private purchase of land. We did not realize that we might be able to ransom our mother, the earth, regaining what had been rightfully ours before it was stolen during the Long Walk and the period that followed.

Big Bo did not extend our land in relation to the Fixed Boundary. Instead, it put our land adjacent to a stretch of private land that ran 35 or 40 miles, linking the two parcels. This meant that, with the purchase of Big Bo, it would only be a matter of time before we could afford to buy the additional land. And since it was all private, the purchase would give us further holdings that could not be touched by the BIA. Again we would have expanded our sovereignty in ways that had been denied my people for a century.

Ultimately we expected to regain what might be called the aboriginal land. This would run from Grants, New Mexico, past Flagstaff, and into the western part of the reservation. It was the land the Navajo controlled long before white men arrived. In the meantime, we had finance companies willing to help us float bonds because the 450,000 acres gave us the ability to finance our future the same way the rest of the United States was able to do.

The problem arose when it came out that the purchase of Big Bo was a flip deal with Bud Brown, Tom Tracy, and the Navajo tribe. I was implicated, along with some other officials, and this gave the impetus to the recall petitioners to rally against me. My enemies among the Navajo were saying that I was corrupt. They did not look at my plans. They did not consider whether or not the plans were valid, and whether or not there were alternatives. And they were encouraged by outside enemies in the state and federal governments who were concerned by the way I was running the tribal government.

The enemies may have had different motives. They may have had very different ends in mind. However, they all agreed that Peter MacDonald had to leave office, and the fact that the election had been a close one gave them hope they would succeed.

I tried to get my message across to the people. I attended chapter meetings, hoping to explain what and why I was doing what I was doing. I wanted them to understand why I felt the necessity of making the land purchases in any way that could be done. But the people who attended the chapter meetings were mostly the older Navajo, the ones who understood the importance of sovereignty. They hated the BIA. They hated the corruption, the incompetence, and the way a proud people were seemingly held in disdain. They supported me all along.

The media was the voice of the opposition. Their reporters, who lacked a sense of history, looked at the business deal and found it wanting. In one sense, they may have been right. But there was no way to buy the land without the "flip," and there was no way to become self-sufficient without the ownership of the 450,000 acres of private land that formed more than half the Big Bo property.

The anti-MacDonald faction was excited about the change in publicity. Big Bo became a symbol, not a substantive issue. No one wanted to look at the true value of the land or the potential it held for the Navajo. The purchase, which had to be approved by the Tribal Council, a fact conveniently overlooked by most critics, became the point where it was felt that I was vulnerable.

I also found that the media in the Southwest was hostile to me. I had been chairman longer than any Navajo in the history of that position. I had tried to steer the people in directions I felt were best for the Navajo, and I was seen as a tyrant by some of the reporters. In addition, my plans went against the best interests of the Anglos.

For example, since Arizona is essentially a desert, priorities must exist. Water has to be available for agriculture, drinking, and cleaning. Those three necessities keep us alive and healthy. Arizona's population was among the fastest growing in the nation in recent years, but the water was adequate for meeting necessities. The real difficulty came from the developers who created so many artificial lakes and decorative fountains, and whose landscaping used non-native plants. Southern Arizona is desert land, yet vegetation native to Florida and elsewhere is commonly imported for its beauty. The end result is an extraordinary use of water and the rapid depletion of what is available.

Massive water projects such as the Central Arizona Project and the Salt River Project were developed to counter this problem. But much of the water was rightfully controlled by the Navajo and other Indians.

Those of us who were familiar with the treaty arrangement with the United States and who were willing to fight to preserve the provisions wanted payments made for the use of water taken from us. Our needs were for drinking, cleaning, and agriculture. We were not misusing it. We were willing to share, but we wanted to share at a price that would be similar to what would be paid if the water source was on private Anglo land.

In the late 1970s through 1982, we started a project with the U.S. Bureau of Reclamation to divert several hundred thousand acre feet of the San Juan River to make water available for the entire Navajo Reservation. (One acre of water at a depth of one foot equals one acre foot.) The Bureau of Reclamation made an engineering study to see how the water could be diverted to serve all the communities on the eastern and central portions of the reservation. Canals would be created to divert the San Juan River in much the manner of the Central Arizona Project, which was bringing water to Phoenix and other cities. There would also be a second phase to the project, with the water taken from Lake Powell and its environs then made available to all the western part of the reservation.

The Bureau of Reclamation came back with an engineering design that would cost over $300 million for just the project's first phase. Worse, it would not serve all the communities we wanted served. As a result, we hired Williams Brothers of Tulsa, Oklahoma, to make a similar engineering study and design to verify the U.S. Bureau of Reclamation's engineering study.

The Williams's Brothers engineering study and design revealed that for less than $300 million, we could develop the project and serve all the communities of the Navajo Reservation. I don't know how many millions of dollars the Bureau of Reclamation people spent for their design, but the Navajo Nation spent over $1 million for ours. We then took the proposal to Congress.

The congressional people advised us both that the project was too expensive and that there were two different designs—the U.S. Bureau of Reclamation design and the Williams Brothers' design. They wanted us to sit with the U.S. Bureau of Reclamation to see if we could convince them to go along with our less expensive design and engineering plans. Needless to say, the U.S. Bureau of Reclamation acted like a typical bureaucracy and never sat down with us so we could get congressional authorization for a single plan.

When I left my position in 1982, the water project was never followed up. Then, when I returned in 1987, I decided that if Congress did not want to fund the several hundred million dollar water project, we could do it ourselves. The downstream water demand was a minimum of a million acre feet, so I proposed charging $100 per acre foot per year. This came to a fraction of a cent per gallon and seemed quite fair. This would have enabled us to build the project with water assessment money alone.

While this has yet to be done, there is no reason not to do it. The studies would need only slight updating. And by using the assessment procedure for Arizona, Nevada, and California, there would be no need for outside money.

We also wanted more careful use by the desert communities. Water was too scarce to be used unnaturally in Phoenix, Tucson, and the surrounding cities. Yet the perceived unlimited availability of water in the lower half of the state was what kept property values so high. Even the payment of one or two cents a gallon to the rightful tribal owners of the water would have made people aware that Arizona cannot use water as casually as it is used back east. Again, I was creating enemies of issues because of greed and exploitation.

The fight was a losing one. My staff, division directors, and department heads were assigned to reach as many of the young people as possible. Those who were working regularly could not attend the chapter meetings, even if they wanted to do so. And the others, who were unemployed or only employed part-time, had no interest. My time could only be spent at the chapter meetings, since I had so many other responsibilities, and this meant that I was only speaking to the older people, who understood the history of the Navajo. They felt that I was fighting for the best interests of the Diné, but they had even less influence on the younger Navajo than I did. The disillusionment of the Navajo who came back from World War II had effectively cost us the support of their children, the generation that was rightfully seeking to gain power. The failure of the men my age to teach our history and our culture led to a breakdown that could cost our people the future that should have been theirs.

I was not insensitive to the so-called Forty-niners, the younger dissidents who took control of the tribal government. They were simply coming from a position lacking the history that would have given them an understanding of what I was trying to do.

The winter session of the Navajo Tribal Council was scheduled for February 14, 1989. The Senate hearings started on February 2. All my enemies saw the Senate hearings as a way to destroy me, though their motives differed from one another. Some wanted to profit from the use of our land, our water, and our minerals without paying fair price. Some wanted to make a quick profit, not seeing the long-term potential of what might be a prolonged legal battle to re-establish our rights under the 1868 treaty. Some wanted to curry favor with the white politicians within the state. Some thought I was a foolish old man who should admit that we should act like just another ethnic or racial group within the United States. And some thought that I was crooked, that I had misused my power, misappropriated tribal funds, and was concerned only with myself and my family. Often they were in harsh disagreement with one another, yet they were united in wanting to rid the Navajo Nation of my presence.

The Senate committee was aware of this when their hearings started, and it was not difficult to focus more on me than the problems of the Navajo. Lip service would be paid to the BIA excesses, to the child abuse, child molestation, and other problems. But that was more for the press and because it was too outrageous to completely ignore. The most important matter taken up and reported was the attack against me. Yet my corruption, if it existed, was a Navajo problem to be settled in a Navajo tribunal. It had no place taking attention away from the problems resulting from BIA mismanagement, corruption, irresponsibility, and dishonesty. The Senate had a legal mandate to oversee, modify, or eliminate the BIA. It had no legal mandate to attack a lawfully elected tribal leader.

Most Americans assume that United States Senate hearings are honest, thorough, and conducted without influence of partisan politics. People may feel that the conclusions reached may reflect bias, but they believe that the hearings themselves are impartial.

Americans also believe that the transcripts of such hearings published by the U.S. Government Printing Office, the world's largest publisher, are complete. Thus, when the three-volume report entitled Hearings before the Special Committee on Indian Affairs United States Senate One Hundred First Congress *was published it was assumed that the report contained complete copies of documents and transcripts of tapes, including the Brown recording. Nothing was further from the truth.*

The complete transcript of the conversation between Brown and MacDonald was not provided until trials in tribal court. The material published with the Senate report was only a partial transcript. While there was nothing wrong with this, there was no indication that the Senate was not using all the information to achieve its conclusions. Thus the material selected looks completely negative toward MacDonald. And because a Senate hearing is not a court proceeding, the person being attacked has far fewer rights. Even worse, since the story was not a big one nationally, though it was extremely important regionally, the vast majority of reporters made no effort to check that all available materials were used. As a result, a reading of the portion of the published tape transcript released at that time seemingly shows MacDonald as thoroughly dishonest in regard to the Big Bo purchase, even violating the ethical standards by which he lived. It was a tragic ending for a man once honored, and it was done for so small an amount of money that it made him look petty. Even as a "criminal," he seemed to deserve no more respect than a petty sneak thief.

As it was, the additional material, unknown until MacDonald's Navajo trial, shocked everyone who heard it, including the Arizona newspaper reporters who covered the proceedings. It showed quite clearly that MacDonald had acted in an honest manner. He had insisted upon telling the truth at a time when he did not know he was being recorded. And the truth proved that he was not a criminal and did not violate any trust.

The tragedy of the Senate hearings is that they were used as evidence of MacDonald's fall. Whether liked or hated, respected or considered incompetent, MacDonald was attacked for reasons that had no basis in truth. He was being brought down, not because of his actions but because the Senate hearings did not include the full transcript of a tape that proved that allegations against him were fraudulent.

If MacDonald had reached a point in his career where his actions violated the laws and ethics of the Navajo Nation, he deserved to be held accountable. But even his worst enemies realized that he was being attacked for a secret tape recording that, when played in full, actually cleared his name.

The state of Arizona has long been a hotbed of land fraud deals. The scams sometimes involve the sale of worthless, isolated land or the sale of one piece of land to several different buyers, all of whom think they have exclusive ownership. In other instances land is sold without ownership.

Many people, including well-known people in government, have been involved, directly or indirectly, with land fraud schemes. Transactions that are legal and ethical in Arizona often seem questionable to outsiders. Land flipping is one such time-honored practice.

Experts in real estate sales in Tucson and Phoenix maintain that many land, housing, and commercial property sales involve one or more flips. The purchase is made by the first party only after he has arranged for a second party immediately to take it off his hands at a higher price. One real estate broker said, "The flip is so common, we just assume it's happening in a lot of deals. The only time I ever saw anyone raise an eyebrow was when the same piece of land was flipped six times the same week. That's just the way we good old boys play the Arizona real estate game."

In light of this, there are several issues to consider regarding the Big Bo purchase. First, the story of Big Bo did not become a legal concern among most Navajo until the Senate hearings took place. If anyone was upset with the purchase, it was the Hopi who had planned to buy Big Bo themselves. However, that fact was not known by many people outside the Hopi reservation at that time. Second, the Senate investigations were conducted, in part, by men who were trying to play down their own breach of ethics.

The head of the Senate investigating committee was Arizona Senator Dennis DeConcini. The selection of DeConcini as the head of an ethics investigation was ironic. DeConcini had accepted campaign contributions totaling $84,200 from Charles Keating, the head of Lincoln Savings and other businesses. DeConcini was one of five politicians who received money, resulting ultimately in at least some of the politicians' using their influence to delay an investigation of Keating's financial empire. For eighteen months they headed off efforts by various government agencies that would have taken control of Keating's thrift institutions. Instead, loans—many of which were weak at best—continued to be granted in the rapidly collapsing real estate market. By the time the influence of the politicians ran out, no longer able to delay the inevitable, Keating walked away an extremely wealthy man, although his financial businesses were in ruins. The cost to the taxpayers, at this writing, is estimated to be as much as $1.5 billion more than it might have been had there been no delays in the investigation. Keating is now in jail, disgraced. But everyone profited in the short term by having attention called away from what was taking place at the time. In addition, Keating was also found to have profited from the sale to the federal government of land he owned that became part of the Navajo-Hopi relocation effort.

I was accused of personally receiving cash and benefits worth a fraction of what my chief Senate adversary had received. And while my actions might have cost the tribe money it would not have spent had Tenneco been willing to sell Big Bo for multiple payments over time, the tribe came away with valuable land that will profit it in the long term. DeConcini's deliberate or naive actions, along with those of the other four politicians involved with Charles Keating, will cost every taxpayer in this country a minimum of hundreds of dollars. An offer has been made by the Japanese to take the Big Bo land off Navajo hands for $100 million.

But attacking an Indian proved to be a good way to keep the public from focusing too much on the men known in the press as "the Keating Five." Besides, there was no denying that the sale resulted in massive profits for Brown and Tracy, another fact that made for good headlines.

The media were largely against me during this period, though a few reporters noted that I was accused of personally gaining less than

$50,000, which includes several trips paid for by Brown, while Brown and Tracy made millions. Those reporters, and I am obviously biased in their favor, also noted that either I was the cheapest corrupt politician in America or there was more to the story than anyone wanted to admit. Almost no one chose to look too closely at the people bringing charges against me or at the profits that others were making.

I had other concerns, perhaps the greatest being the fact that the senators used my son, Rocky, to testify. It was a difficult time for me, an affront to our culture, and a situation that forced me to be honest about his strengths and weaknesses.

Rocky had taken several years to establish himself in a career. He eventually became a lawyer, a profession whose members are vulnerable to intense pressure.

Ethical standards for lawyers have never been clearly defined, perhaps because their work at times requires them to lie and mislead on behalf of their clients. Americans have an adversary system of justice wherein the jury often has to decide whether the prosecution or the defense is telling the truth. Lawyers can engage in the most outrageous behavior and receive only a reprimand from the Bar Association, or they can make a minor mistake and be disbarred, depending on where they practice and what kind of friendships they have made.

Rocky was vulnerable to pressure. The investigators made clear to him that unless he testified, he would probably be disbarred. His career would be over. All his training would have been for nothing.

Rocky was in a no-win situation. He could be disbarred if he chose not to testify. He could also be disbarred if he did not say what the committee expected to hear. (Ultimately the committee granted him personal immunity from prosecution for any crimes to which he might admit.) He could be disbarred if the truth later proved to be different from his testimony. And he could go to jail for contempt, perhaps also losing his license, if he failed to appear in response to the subpoena.

Many individuals have lied under such circumstances. At best, coerced testimony is considered doubtful in a court of law. The person is perceived as being so afraid of losing something that he or she may not tell the truth under oath. In any case it was a terrible way for any committee to try to learn the truth. For Rocky, who was raised in the Navajo culture, being forced to speak against a member of his family was emotionally shattering.

I encouraged Rocky to tell the truth because I felt we had not done anything wrong, although, in the beginning (late 1987 through early 1988), we thought about trying to have some sort of explanation about the two transactions. We wanted to be able to tell what happened in a logical manner, finally accepting the reality that the truth was not so logical as we would have liked. We ended by just explaining what had taken place. Rocky had absolutely nothing to do with the purchase of the Big Bo land.

What gave rise to my concern was a conversation with Bud Brown in late 1987. I learned that the U.S. Department of the Interior was sending out an agent named Tony Brown to investigate the Big Bo transaction. At the same time we had our own investigator authorized by the Tribal Council, a man named Michael Hawkins.

While this was going on, I was looking for things that the federal government could consider wrongdoing on my part. I have always mistrusted the Feds. I have felt that if a tree is old, rotted, and repeatedly struck by lightning before falling in a forest where a man is hiking, the Feds will try to find a way to blame that man for what happened. They seem to launch investigations where guilt is assumed and they only need to find some reason to place blame. They don't look for innocence, and thus they never see it. They don't accumulate all the facts, then try to evaluate them in an unbiased manner. They just want to be certain that the conclusions reached before their investigations begin are never contradicted by the revelation of truth. And while my generalization is obviously biased as well, anyone who has ever looked at the U.S. government's trail of broken treaties with each and every Indian tribe in America will understand my cynicism.

Back in early 1986, right after the tribal election, I asked Bud Brown for help with payment on a bank loan I shared with my son, Rocky. He could not make any payments, either, just then, and though we were mutually responsible, I knew that the bank would always look to me first because I was the only signator on the note. All I wanted was the interest, which I made clear to Bud. The total amount was something like $3,000 or $4,000. With that money, the loan would have been rolled over for another year. But instead, he paid the interest and a major portion of the principal—$25,000 in all.

I thought Bud Brown was rich at the time. I thought he could well afford to give such help to a friend, but it was far more than I had requested or needed to keep from being in trouble with the bank. I was pleased, of course. I was also quite surprised and a little embarrassed by his generous action. I would have to repay him, though he made clear that I could have the time I needed, a luxury I did not have with the bank at that moment.

Then, sometime in late 1987, when I was reviewing everything that was out of the ordinary in the recent past, I asked Bud why he had paid so much more than I had requested. I also wondered how he did it—by check, wire transfer from his account, or whatever. My questioning of Bud was done after the Big Bo purchase, but the money had been provided before that purchase was made final by the Tribal Council. So far as I was concerned, my request for help had nothing to do with Big Bo.

I learned, to my surprise, that the money Bud used was money that had been owed to him by Tracy. Bud said that he arranged for Tracy to make a wire transfer from his account to my bank, the record then showing that the $25,000 I received came directly from Tracy.

I didn't really know Tracy. He was a business acquaintance whose connection to me was based on the Big Bo sale. This meant that an outsider could easily get the impression that I was heavily involved with the man. After all, if we weren't close in ways not previously known, why would he make such a transfer of funds? There was nothing in either bank's records mentioning Brown, with whom I had a long acquaintance.

This information terrified me. Tom Tracy had the land and the money, and I never approached him for anything. But he's the guy who made the transfer of funds. I knew that anyone looking at all that would come to the conclusion that I had received a payoff.

I was extremely angry with Bud Brown. No matter what his intention in all this, the fact that the money came from Tracy would have made the payment of my interest, all I had requested from Brown, suspicious. But with $25,000 involved, intentions meant nothing. The entire loan was for $60,000, a ninety-day note that expired and was going to be rolled over for another year.

Later, during statements by Tracy's accountant to the various investigators, it turned out that Bud Brown went to Tracy and told him that I needed $25,000 to have my note paid on time. This was back in January or February, though I had made the request of Bud Brown right after the election of November 1986. The two-month delay came because Bud Brown was leading me on. He did not have adequate funds of his own right then even for my interest payment. However, he knew I thought he was quite wealthy, and he did nothing to dispel my belief.

Apparently Bud Brown was telling Tracy either that he owed me some money or that I needed to have all the money that was paid to the bank. From what I learned later, apparently Tracy believed him but did not trust him with cash. Tracy refused to give money to his business partner directly, allegedly out of concern that not all the money would be used as requested. Instead, he checked with my bank to confirm my loan, then arranged to have the wire transfer direct from his account to mine, not going through Brown.

My suspicion in hindsight is that Bud Brown needed approximately $20,000 for personal bills or whatever. He knew that he would be able to pay it back from his share of the land deals being worked, yet he also either had been turned down by Tracy or expected to be turned down by Tracy. He figured that if he borrowed the money for me, he would take the portion I needed to pay my interest and some of the principal, then use the rest for his personal needs. He had agreed to repay Tracy in any case, so he could see no problems.

We only discovered later that the impression of impropriety was worse than we knew. At least one of the trips Wanda and I took with Bud had been paid for by Tracy. We thought we were being treated by a long-time friend, and because he was paying, we had our belief in his financial success reinforced. Instead, the money was coming from a man with whom I was doing business, a man I did not know outside of the business relationship, and thus a man who could be seen as trying to bribe me.

In early 1988, I talked with Bud Brown about the $25,000. I said that I was sure the Feds were going to say that the payment was some kind of bribe. You and I know it isn't, I told him, but there is no way we can show that.

Brown didn't feel that way. He claimed that Tracy owed him the money. He said that it was his money, and all he was doing was loaning it to me. He refused to look at the fact that once the money went directly from Tracy's account to mine, there was no way that anyone was going to think that the money came from Brown.

The situation was bad at best. The appearance of dishonesty would outweigh the facts. We tried to figure a way to change the image of a very bad situation, and we finally considered Rocky. His share of the loan owed to the bank was about $35,000. Rocky was not involved with the Tribal Council or the purchase of Big Bo. If we could consider the $25,000 wire transfer initiated by Bud Brown to be a loan to Rocky, and if we considered the payment to be Rocky's responsibility, the situation would not be so bad.

Bud Brown was enthusiastic about the arrangement. He also knew that Rocky was still struggling financially. He said that since Rocky was a lawyer, and since Bud Brown regularly needed an attorney to help him with his real estate purchases, he could give Rocky work. The normal fees for the legal assistance would be applied to the loan.

Our discussions about how to handle the money lasted two to three weeks. Finally we settled on the concept of Rocky owing Bud Brown. There had been no paperwork generated up to that point, so we planned to create paperwork that would establish Rocky's debt to Bud Brown. We would also arrange to have Rocky's debt to me be reduced by $25,000. I would still have to repay the bank for the remaining principal plus interest. Rocky would owe me $10,000, and he would owe Bud Brown $25,000.

The solution was not perfect, of course. Proof of our intent to act honestly would always be questioned because of Tracy's wire transfer. But it was the best arrangement we could make under the circumstances, knowing that the Feds would look for the worst possible motives.

The other problem came with a BMW automobile I was leasing and which I turned over to Rocky to use. It was a luxury car that we could both afford, but that Rocky wanted. The problem was that Rocky had made a number of mistakes with his personal finances, and he was still fighting to re-establish his personal credit. This was why the bank loan combined my need with his, and why I was primarily responsible, though Rocky was paying me back for his share. This was also why the leased car remained under my name. I was responsible for the lease, no one else.

Again Bud Brown had come through, setting up the lease and making just enough of the $800-a-month payments so that I owed him (and Rocky owed me) approximately $2,800. The arrangements were made because I had been under the impression Bud Brown could easily afford it when he made the offer. Remember that I knew Brown to be rich, we were friends, and the financial arrangements were not unusual given all the circumstances I thought existed. Later, when I had no more need for the car, I thought that it would be easier for me to transfer responsibility to Rocky. Instead, the transfer rules followed the same standards as the original lease agreement, even though so much money had already been paid. Rocky was given the car to use, he was expected to make the payments, but everything was in my name.

Later I learned that apparently Bud Brown had obtained the money from Tracy, accepting what I was told by my lawyer was $4,000 in cash from which he paid the money, keeping the rest for his personal use. He allegedly misrepresented what was taking place to Tracy, though he did not worry about that since he was planning to repay his friend both with what I paid him back and from his own income.

By making all the loans clearly connected to Rocky and not me, we hoped to stop the problem before it got out of hand. We never thought someone would think we were trying to create a conspiracy to hide the truth. We just wanted to free ourselves from as many repercussions from Bud Brown's actions with Tracy and our bank as we could.

With all my anger, I still have to remember that everything apparently stemmed from Bud Brown's pride. He knew the land deals on which he was working would make him rich. He knew that he would be able to repay anyone from whom he borrowed money. And he wanted to be seen as a wealthy big spender who helped his less fortunate friends. His generosity was based on the incomes of others and the promise of his future. The result was a series of deals that looked bad and hurt some of the people he thought he was helping. Yet the fact remained, had Bud Brown been honest with me about his finances from the start, I would have gone elsewhere to borrow the money. I would not have done business with Tracy, who was trying to sell land to the tribe. His failure to tell me the truth about the source of the money he was offering was just what my enemies needed to try to destroy me.

In hindsight, we were probably stupid to do anything. But at the time, we thought what we did made sense. We prepared the paperwork for the loans, making it clear that they were for Rocky. Then a consulting contract was prepared between Rocky and Brown, though Bud Brown never signed it.

Somewhere in the summer of 1988, the Senate investigators decided to wire Bud Brown. He had made a deal with them that obviously we knew nothing about. He would be electronically rigged to tape record a meeting with Rocky and myself that would reveal a so-called coverup.

Once Bud was working undercover for the government, he kept coming back to Rocky and me, asking the same question. He wanted to know how he could explain what happened with the money.

The questioning made no sense, yet it did not worry us either. We had explained what happened, from the actions of Tracy without our knowledge to the arrangement that would reduce or eliminate any backlash against me. I assumed that no one was trying to "get me" when I first learned how foolishly Brown had acted, and I continued to think that way.

Once more I stressed that the money Brown had Tracy pay to the bank was for Rocky's portion of the loan. The BMW money was also between Rocky and Brown. I was off the hook for the cost of what was Rocky's car, and he had his indebtedness to me (though not his personal indebtedness) reduced by $25,000. It was an explanation that should not have been necessary, but it allowed us all to get on with our business.

Bud Brown said that he was scared that Tracy might reveal something about him, another statement that made no sense. I didn't know what problems existed between Brown and Tracy, nor did I care. Rocky was driving the BMW, and the payments were being worked out through the consulting agreement Brown and Rocky had put together. Rocky was capable of handling the business consulting work Brown needed done, so everyone was benefiting honestly and fairly.

Brown returned to Rocky and me again and again, each time with questions apparently created by the lawyer he used for personal work and with the collusion of the Senate investigators. Brown had letters from the lawyer questioning the agreement with Rocky and me. They made no sense to me, though I just assumed he had a lawyer who did not know what he was doing. I did not know that a "sting" operation was taking place.

This situation continued for three or four months. Then Bud, apparently pressured, said that he wanted to know if Rocky and I were going to stick to the same story. It was an odd question, worded differently than before. I didn't think much of it at the time because I was annoyed with the constant complaining. But in hindsight, the slight change in wording could easily have been misconstrued to make it seem that we were lying.

Bud said that he was too old to be going to jail. He said that he feared being cited for perjury. He said that he wanted to make sure we were going to stick to our story. Then, somewhere along the way, Rocky said something like, "Oh, yeah, we've got to stick to our story. We're the Three Musketeers."

I can only imagine the impact some of this must have had on those trying to trap me for something wrong. The implication could easily be that we were attempting to fake something. At the same time, I wondered about Bud Brown.

Then Bud began to talk about how he had an interview with the Senate investigators and he wanted to be certain we kept our story in line with his. And we kept assuring him that there was no problem, always assuming he was telling us the truth.

Finally, toward the end of December or the first part of January, Rocky and I each had lawyers coming in to advise us. We had met with my lawyer, a Denver man, months earlier when we first explored the proper wording for a statement concerning the $25,000. The lawyer felt that what we were saying was proper given the facts in the case. But we returned to the lawyers when we were subpoenaed by the Senate investigators.

Nowhere along the way did any of the lawyers feel we were committing a crime. We were told to just tell the truth, the story that had been related from the start. I was to lay out my going to Brown for help, the $25,000 that came unexpectedly from Tracy, and our decision to try to clear all our names of impropriety.

We were also told to not back up Bud Brown unless he told the entire story as it happened. A partial story or a deviation from the truth would be perjury or misrepresentation of the facts.

Bud Brown was not satisfied. He wanted to meet with Rocky, me, and the lawyers at some restaurant, but the lawyers refused. They told us to meet with Brown and say nothing, just be passive. By then they knew he was acting strange, and there was a question whether he was wired.

My lawyer reminded me that I had committed no crime. However, by changing my story, I would become guilty of perjury.

The dinner went off without incident, apparently a problem for the FBI and other agents who were working with Brown and tape recording Brown's telephone calls with his knowledge. Thus, a couple of days later, Brown called Rocky, who reminded Bud that he and I were just going to tell the truth.

Later I heard a copy of the tape that was made, and there was a silence in response to the statement. Rocky repeated what he said, then noted that Rocky's and my lawyers wanted to talk with Brown and his lawyer, who did nothing about it.

Rocky again called to try to arrange a conference call among the lawyers and Brown. He reminded Bud that we were going to tell the truth. And it was at that point that the heavy surveillance of Brown ended, because it had become obvious that we were going to tell the truth, not perjure ourselves with a false or partial story.

Bud Brown had not yet talked with the Senate under oath. However, he was giving us the impression that he had stated something different from what we had agreed. That was not the case, but it was a sting operation trying to get us both to perjure ourselves and engage in an illegal coverup. Yet none of that happened.

Finally Rocky was scheduled to be interviewed. I told him to tell the truth, that we had done nothing wrong, nothing illegal. Just let them know what happened, and that's what I planned to do with my interview. Instead, his questions and answers were prescribed by the investigators. He was not allowed to deviate from or explain the pre-arranged answers he gave.

I'm not comfortable talking about what happened next. I have a mixture of sadness, anger, and frustration in my heart.

First there was the questioning. Rocky may be physically grown, but for whatever reason, he has always been somewhat too innocent and trusting. All of us reached a point where we were a little paranoid about the government, but no person raised on the reservation ever can trust the white man's approach to the law. And in this case, wiretaps and other investigative tools truly were being used.

Rocky, Bud, and I were just nervous enough about what was taking place that we took one precaution when planning meetings. Going on the assumption that we were being overheard, which it turned out we were, yet not followed, which I assume we weren't, we referred to planned meetings together as "golf balls." It was a rather foolish inside joke since Bud, Rocky, and I are all avid golfers who frequently played together. I'm sure anyone listening and thinking a bit could figure out what we were doing, but at the time it seemed to make sense. The government had their intrigue and we had ours, and none of it in any way hindered the truth from being revealed.

But Rocky and his wife seemed to like the intrigue more than they should have. They decided to speak in code between themselves.

I don't know why. I was too angry, and the actions were too stupid, for me to want to bother to ask them the reason. Maybe they just decided that they were playing a James Bond novel.

Rocky and his wife were living apart while working for a time in two different cities. Their marriage was strong, but with Rocky doing consulting work, he often had to go where the client was, and for a while that meant living away from home. They had their joint bank account where his wife was living, and a second bank account in Phoenix where Rocky was working at the moment. Each time he got paid, and his checks were often for $5,000 or $10,000 at a time, he would deposit the money in the Phoenix bank. And each time the couple needed money, he would transfer whatever was necessary to the bank where his wife had access to the cash.

Rightly suspecting a wiretap on the telephone, Rocky and his wife decided to keep their financial affairs "secret." The truth was that no one cared about their personal business, and it did not matter how much he earned or how much they spent. But Rocky had to be "cute," so he and his wife referred to the money as "golf balls," an idea he "cleverly" got from what he, Bud, and I were saying as our code for "meetings." Under Rocky's code each golf ball represented $1,000. Thus he might transfer seven and a half golf balls to his wife, or deposit five golf balls in his own account, or whatever.

The end result of all this was trouble that came from his formal committee testimony where there shouldn't have been any. First there was a problem because Rocky told the truth without being allowed to explain any of the background. This, at least, was the fault of the committee's procedures. Rocky admitted under oath that the $25,000 loan did not exist originally but was created after the money had been unexpectedly wire transferred by Tracy. However, he was not permitted to explain the rest of the story, in which it would have been clear that the reason for the statement we made was to avoid the problems created by Brown and Tracy. The full story made sense. The partial story hinted at dishonesty. To this day I still owe Bud Brown the money I know was a loan.

Then came questioning about the term "golf balls." The Senate committee wanted to know what it meant to Bud, Rocky, and myself. Instead of answering the question in that way, Rocky explained it in the manner he and his wife were using it. He said that a "golf ball" was $1,000.

Naturally, the press went crazy. Nobody bothered to look at the way the term was used in context in the transcripts of the wiretaps that were made with the help of Bud Brown. If they had, they would have seen that the explanation made no sense. The numbers would not add up in any way that could be interpreted as a connection.

At the same time, I think I would have reacted in the same manner as the media. The situation was outrageous on the surface. If Rocky makes a statement under oath and it seems incriminating, why bother checking to see if there is anything more to the story? Certainly that is good enough to make today's headlines, something I probably would have done if I were in their position.

Even worse, from that moment forward, Rocky had compromised his future. He was viewed by the investigators as someone who could be "turned." Rocky had incriminated himself, although innocent, and that action meant that he could be used. There was a good chance he could be encouraged to give statements against others, and the government knew how to exert pressure a weak, naive young man like that could not handle.

Rocky and I have talked many times since the hearings, and I fully understand what he went through. I do not think that I would have acted as he did, but I was never put in such a terrible position. I do resent the people who caused such pain and who used tactics that have resulted in continuing arguments concerning what is truth and what is not, issues that should have been fully resolved in the hearings.

The hearings resolved little, unfortunately. Most interesting to me were the comments made by Senator DeConcini after testimony given by Annie Wauneka. DeConcini said:

"I think it is worth repeating that tribal officials are duly elected public figures, as Senator McCain, Senator Daschle, and myself are. Their budgets are supported by some of their own funds and by federal funds. Many similarities exist between tribal governments and state and county and other local governments. Unlike federal, state, and local government officials, elected tribal leaders are not covered by the same federal criminal statutes concerning corruption as federal, state, and local officials would be in dealing with federal funds."

[NOTE: The Navajo Tribal Chairman's salary is 100 percent funded by tribal funds. This is money from royalties. No money comes from the state or federal governments.]

"Allegations of corruption among certain tribal leaders and the lack of applicable federal laws have followed committee investigators throughout the country, and we cannot ignore these types of facts and figures and claims that have come to us, and that is why we have pursued this.

"The committee is concerned that the misery and the poverty and the homelessness found on many of the reservations are actually being accentuated by certain elected leaders in the way they manage, mismanage, and actually defraud their people.

"We are examining whether Congress should expand the laws governing such kickbacks and gratuities and bribes, should expand the laws to include tribal leaders."

I recognized a familiar theme: the Indians have to be protected from themselves. Paternalistic whites are needed to deal with reservation problems. Never mind that the senator speaking those words was credited with influencing the delay in the exposure of Lincoln Savings, one of the largest thrift institutions to fail, at tremendous cost to the taxpayers. Never mind that members of the U.S. Congress and Senate had allowed themselves to be influenced by special interest groups whose lobbyists offered lavish inducements in return for favorable legislation. By attacking the Navajo, whose laws, by DeConcini's own admission, were different from those of the U.S. government, the senator diverted public attention from the scandals unfolding in Washington.

Attacking the Navajo also took responsibility away from the BIA. By blaming the poverty on the reservation on corruption among the Navajo leadership, the senator made it easy to ignore the bad energy deals, the poor BIA schools, the lack of meaningful job programs, and other failures of the federal government. The Long Walk was not caused by the Navajo. The livestock reduction laws were not passed by the Navajo. The resettlement act was not passed by the Navajo. Even other issues raised during the hearings, such as the influence of organized crime on some of the reservations and sexual abuse by white employees of the BIA, did not involve participation by the Navajo, who were merely the victims.

During the period following my fourth election as chairman I had one major triumph. Although I call it a triumph, it was actually another sad episode in the life of the Navajo Nation. And this one was so blatant that none of the investigating committees wanted to explore the issues that surrounded the actions I was forced to take. An objective look at what was taking place could only cause embarrassment for the American government.

The story began in 1965, when I was head of the Office of Navajo Economic Opportunity. My relationship with Raymond Nakai was strong at that time, since I had not become politically active enough to be viewed as a threat to him. I was simply a Navajo doing a job and doing it well, at least in Nakai's eyes. Because of this, I occasionally accompanied him to Washington and elsewhere for meetings.

On one occasion, we met with Stewart Udall, a highly respected congressman and environmentalist, who served as secretary of the interior during the Kennedy and Johnson administrations. Udall was widely praised for his integrity, aggressiveness, and sound environmental policies.

The federal and state governments, along with Anglo environmentalists, expressed concern about our tradition of living off the land. We dared not catch too many fish or kill too much game because we would cause problems for the ecology. Or so the whites said.

The truth is that, for centuries, all Indians did what white people only now claim to be trying to do. As caretakers of Mother Earth, stewards toiling to keep life in proper balance, we respected all living things. All Indian tribes had special prayers or other ceremonies to show respect for the spirits of those animals we had to kill for food.

White men destroyed most of the buffalo, shooting them to keep them from grazing on the rails and slowing the passage of trains. Men like William "Buffalo Bill" Cody slaughtered game merely to kill it and let it rot. The meat and skins of those animals could have supported many Indians. Indians fished only for food, not for sport or for the mass exploitation of the waters. They killed deer for food and clothing, not for blood sport or to display, stuffed and mounted, in their dens. And Indians did not throw disposable diapers into the water, destroy the rivers with industrial waste, or pollute the air with massive coal-burning plants.

And yet by 1965 the Department of the Interior seemed to look on Indians as a threat to ecology. There were times I felt as if we were being treated like little children who had been herded together into one safe location where we could not do too much harm to our surroundings. Anything that was good for us would be given to us, provided we were appropriately grateful. And anything that was deemed unhealthful, no matter what the truth of the matter, would be denied.

Having jobs was considered good for us, a belief with which no Indian would disagree. And one company interested in Indian labor, apparently, was the BVD Company.

BVD manufactures undershorts and undershirts, among other products. The company needs workers with manual dexterity and a location that offers inexpensive warehousing facilities and easy access to cities. The work is not water-intensive, and thus a northern Arizona plant made a great deal of sense.

Secretary of the Interior Stewart Udall had been negotiating with BVD to build in a location that, according to him, would benefit the Navajo. This occurred during the period of BIA paternalism, when the BIA decided what was right for the tribes, made all the arrangements, and then brought the project to the Tribal Council for a rubber stamp. It was unusual for the secretary of the interior to handle such a task, but apparently this was Udall's special interest. Whatever the motive, though, he presented Raymond Nakai with an accomplished fact. The BVD Company was going to build a plant in Winslow, Arizona, sponsored by the Navajo Nation. The fact that the Navajo were told nothing about it until after Udall assured BVD that the Indians were giving it their full support means nothing.

The plant's location has little significance to those who live outside of Arizona. Winslow is a small community near the Grand Canyon. At one time it was a layover stop for railroad crews, but changes in the rail system eventually ended that use. The main income came from tourism, so any sort of new business was welcome. However, Winslow was *not* part of the Navajo Reservation.

The Navajo Tribal Council rejected the plans for the Winslow-based BVD plant. Though they would have been happy to help BVD find an equally viable location on tribal land, they would not act as a sponsor for any business built off the reservation.

The Tribal Council's decision was not a rejection of BVD. Stewart Udall had simply created a situation that was unworkable. Supposedly representing the Navajo Nation, he had negotiated without telling us and selected a site that had no connection with us. He had made a mistake, and it was not our responsibility to help him save face.

Udall should have realized that, even under the best of circumstances, there was underlying hostility each time the BIA negotiated business arrangements on behalf of the Navajo. Even in an ideal situation—where the business was a good one, where the contract was fair to all concerned, and where Navajo would be gainfully employed—there was anger. Many of us felt that the BIA was really saying, "Here's a program we developed to help you. We created it. We worked hard to obtain the best possible contract. Now you lazy bums approve it. That's all we ask of you, so be grateful to us." And since we were not allowed to negotiate on our own behalf at that time, the BIA was doing for us what we weren't doing for ourselves. Ignoring the fact that their laws prohibited us from taking the actions we wanted, they used our compliance with these laws as a way to further demean us.

Now the government had gone too far. Stewart Udall had apparently used his reputation and position to bring the BVD plant to Winslow, where the company would work with the Navajo. But this was an arrangement that the Navajo could not endorse. If he had brought BVD onto the reservation, Raymond Nakai and the Tribal Council would have embraced the company. He chose to place it off Indian land, however, so our leaders had to refuse to endorse Udall's plan.

None of the Navajo leaders thought that the rejection was particularly meaningful. The plant was welcomed by the people of Winslow, who regarded BVD as a new employer and were eager for a source of additional tax revenue. The residents of Winslow would not have minded if Indians were employed there along with locals, and some of our people would have been able to make the commute. We simply could not sponsor the project at the site selected.

Apparently Stewart Udall saw matters differently. He seemed to feel personally responsible for what took place, and he took our rejection as a deliberate slap in the face.

In 1965, shortly after the Tribal Council rejected the agreement, Raymond Nakai and I, along with other representatives of the Navajo, met with Udall in Washington, D.C. We discovered that he was livid with us. The proposal for the BVD plant was on his desk, and when we entered his office, he seemed unable to control his rage. He was pacing the floor instead of sitting and talking quietly with us. "You embarrassed me," he told us angrily. "I worked with BVD. I worked with these people very hard, very long, and got them to agree to come to Winslow so they could employ your people, and now you did this to me. You put me on a ledge. You made a liar out of me. Your Tribal Council voted it down."

Raymond Nakai tried to defuse the situation. He pointed out that he had not been made aware of any effort to bring the BVD plant to Winslow or anywhere else. He had not been told about the negotiations. And when he did hear about them, at the same time that the information was given to the Tribal Council, he could not control the men and women who were there.

Udall disagreed. He stressed that Nakai could have controlled the council. He could have told them how to vote. He was the chairman, and he should have exerted strong leadership. He did not understand that the chairman does not always control the council.

The secretary really attacked Nakai. It was shocking, but there was nothing we could do. Although we tried to appease him, the fact was that he had been wrong in the way he had handled the negotiations.

When at last we were able to leave, Udall gave us the final word; "Okay. You guys embarrassed me. You made a fool out of me. With or without the Navajo, I am going to bring the BVD plant to Winslow, but don't come to me for any more favors."

Udall then asked the Hopi to sponsor the BVD plant in Winslow. Remember that Winslow was not on any tribe's reservation land. That part of Arizona was in private hands, and Winslow was as much an Anglo community as the far larger cities of Flagstaff, Phoenix, and Tucson. The Hopi had as little connection with it as the Navajo.

The community of Winslow, anxious for the new employer, made available a parcel of vacant land for the plant. The Hopi sponsored the plant. Everyone was happy. Ironically, the majority of the employees were Navajo, simply because the location was closer to our reservation land than to that of the Hopi.

Less than two months after Udall's "defeat" by the Navajo Tribal Council, Robert L. Bennett, the commissioner of Indian affairs, issued an executive order freezing from further development the 3 million acres of land west of the Joint Use Area. This covered Tuba City, Cameron, Page, and other communities all the way to the Grand Canyon.

This "Bennett Freeze," which I remain convinced to this day was part of Stewart Udall's revenge against the Navajo, dictated that the Navajo and Hopi had to settle all their differences. Until such time, the Navajo living in the designated area, approximately twenty thousand in all, could make no home improvements, could not make additions to their homes, and could not construct new homes or add water lines, power lines, or sewage services without the approval of the Hopi. The only way to describe such an order would be to compare it with Canada telling the United States that, until it settled its disputes with Mexico over immigration, drug trafficking, and oil development, no one in Texas, California, Arizona, and the other border states would be allowed to build residences or make any home improvements.

Perhaps Udall and Bennett thought that the Navajo and Hopi would quickly settle their differences and that no one would suffer from the decision. But the reality was that for the next twenty-five years the Hopi did not approve any Navajo requests concerning the land and the people in the designated area. A hogan in need of repair in 1965 continued to deteriorate for the next quarter of a century. Aging people with minor, easily rectified housing problems in 1965 became elderly, their problems now major. Their housing was substandard, and they had no legal recourse because the Hopi would not approve *any* changes—from simple routine maintenance to the acquisition of modern conveniences.

The Navajo in the Bennett Freeze area were also cut off from proper sanitation. They could not use modern communication systems, including touch-tone telephone lines. Former miners with black lung disease and other work-related problems could not use the electricity necessary to power medical devices critical to their health. These Navajo lived in squalor, and the conditions under which they lived were a direct result of the pettiness of Udall and Bennett. Clearly, people who had the money and the manpower to improve their lives were being denied an essential human right.

The 1965 executive order creating the freeze territory could have been overturned by an executive order from one of the succeeding commissioners. But it wasn't. In 1974 Congress officially turned Bennett's executive order into law. The action became a part of the Navajo and Hopi Land Settlement Act.

It is nice to talk about a peaceful solution with the Hopi. It is nice to talk about Indian unity. It is nice to talk about negotiations. And perhaps one day enough people on enough reservations will suffer in similar ways so that all Indians will rise up together in anger. I doubt it, however. Each tribe has a unique history, religion, and life-style. All tribes have been forced into situations where they must frequently fight with other tribes to obtain land. This creates rivalry where historically there was none. Where once there was peaceful coexistence between the Navajo and the Hopi, or at least boundaries accepted by both tribes, the white man's forced reservations have led to continuing territorial disputes.

The tension between the Navajo and the Hopi was not going to be resolved the way the freeze regulations demanded, and I firmly believe that all parties involved in its creation, as well as the Anglo BIA and Interior Department leaders who have followed, recognized this fact.

When I took a good look at the freeze area, what I saw convinced me that, no matter whose fault this situation might have been, I could not allow it to continue. Hogans that were just large enough for a husband, a wife, and a small child or two now housed three generations. Housing was available in other parts of the reservation, of course, but since our people believe that extended families should live close to one another and since each generation was not allowed to build its own hogan, the families either stayed uncomfortably together or broke with tradition and became separated by many miles. It was not unusual to see ten or fifteen people sharing a single hogan. No one wanted to live in such circumstances.

I quickly saw the full effects of the freeze. There were elderly people whose wells had run dry but who could not legally dig a new well on their own property. There were handicapped people who could not build a wheelchair ramp onto the front of their homes. There were hogans with roofs in disrepair; the water from rainstorms accumulated inside, rotting parts of the ceiling and walls. Mold and mildew created an unpleasant odor that lingered year in and year out.

Adding to my outrage was the fact that the changes and services needed were both affordable and easy to provide. There was adequate money, either within the affected families or from tribal programs for which the people qualified. Because the federal law had been obeyed over the years, the Hopi had refused to give permission for repairs or construction, so they did not occur.

I was angry and ashamed. This situation should not have occurred. It was wrong of Udall and Bennett to establish the freeze. It was wrong of the Hopi to refuse to give the Navajo permission to repair and upgrade their homes. It was wrong of Congress, the Interior Department, the BIA, and others in federal power positions to fail to rectify the injustice. And it was wrong of the Navajo leaders, including me, not to force the issue in whatever way possible.

My solution to the problem, during my fourth term as chairman, was the creation of Project Hope. We created what amounted to an assault on the law, like a military operation. We gathered trucks, materials, and work crews and prepared to move to several areas of the Bennett Freeze territory and into the 1882 Joint Use Area simultaneously. Some of the crews were to build new structures or add on to old buildings; others were to handle repairs. Whatever the people needed and wanted was going to be done.

Although the Anglo press had never been interested in Navajo affairs, I knew that we might be challenged for our actions. We were deliberately breaking the law. Had such an effort been mounted in another part of the nation by some other group, it would have been front-page news. But the plight of the Navajo had never been that important to the media. Our people were isolated, our life-style often somewhat primitive. No reporters were routinely assigned to the location, no still photographers, no television crews. The world was unaware of what was taking place. The few who were at all familiar with the land affected by the freeze had no sense of the squalor and indignities endured by its residents.

Still our militant response might gain media attention. I quickly realized that we needed to reveal the conditions under which the Navajo lived if we wanted to awaken the world to what was taking place. It also became clear that, without media awareness, any retaliation against our actions would go unnoticed by the world at large. The presence of the media might even defuse some violence.

My answer was to have a group of social workers act as the advance guard. They visited the people designated to receive assistance from the Project Hope crews. They photographed conditions in the hogans. They wrote detailed descriptions of the living conditions. These social workers were all professionals, whose observations, we felt certain, along with the photographic record, would hold up in court.

Some of the social workers' reports were horrifying. They had found one Navajo woman who was blind, and whose legs were almost useless. It was, of course, impossible for her to work. She lived in a shack with an outhouse some thirty or forty yards away. In order to find her way to the outhouse, the woman had tied a length of twine from the shack to the outhouse, keeping it low to the ground. Holding on to the string, she had to crawl to the outhouse. She did this summer and winter, always crawling, carefully keeping the string higher than any snow accumulation. Yet running right past her house was a water line that had been in existence before the Bennett Freeze. Had the freeze not taken effect, she would have had indoor plumbing by 1965. And since that time there had been no other serious obstacle to making her life easier, to providing her with comfort and dignity. Because of the freeze, however, it appeared that she would ultimately die in a continual struggle for the basics of life.

Changing the blind, disabled woman's circumstances became a priority. Her home was the first in her area to receive assistance. A Project Hope crew attached the water line and built a bathroom onto her house so that she need not continue to live in so horrible a manner.

The social workers' field reports enabled us to identify those individuals living in each area whose needs were the greatest. Usually these were the elderly and the handicapped. We then readied hundreds of work crews and put them into a position so that they could begin work at dawn. We were determined to do as much work as possible before being faced with armed opposition. We felt certain that some state or federal law-enforcement units would come in and stop us. By having so many crews out there, we hoped to accomplish more work over a longer period, because the government would not be able to concentrate an attack by soldiers or police in a limited area.

And so it began. The workers took great pride in what they were doing, moving swiftly but with care. They took pains to provide long-term help for the people. They were not interested in a symbolic "show" or in making repairs that might fall apart in a few months.

Watching the crews in action was like watching a well-trained, battle-tested army confident of its ability to triumph. The workers knew that there might be violence. They knew that they might be arrested and taken to jail, but they did not care. They were doing something for their people. They were correcting a terrible injustice.

That first day, everyone worked until it grew dark and they became too tired to continue. We waited the entire day for armed resistance from someone, for demands that we cease our repairs. Yet when the day ended, nothing had happened.

The crews were back at work at dawn the next day. Again there was no incident. We worked for ten days before we heard a protest, and by then we had constructed twenty to thirty buildings and made thousands of minor and major repairs.

The protest came in the form of a lawsuit charging us with every crime the Hopi's lawyers could think of. We were in violation of the law. We were in contempt. We were accused of everything short of murder, or so it seemed.

Finally we went to court and presented the judge with the photographs we had taken and the reports we had gathered. We offered no defense for what we had done. We had knowingly broken the law. But we felt that our motivation, as documented by the photographs, justified everything.

"This is America," we told the judge. "How in the world can you do this to somebody? This is their land. They've been here since long before 1965."

Unquestionably we were guilty of violating the conditions of the Bennett Freeze. The judge could have thrown me and my tribe into jail for violating what had become federal law. Instead, he was understanding. He said that no government should allow such a situation to exist. At the same time, he said that the law had to be obeyed.

The judge offered a compromise. He could not change the congressional action. Only the U.S. Supreme Court could do that, by reviewing it and finding it unconstitutional. He ordered us to go to the Hopi with all future requests to make repairs in the freeze area. The Hopi would have ten days to respond. If they refused to allow the repairs or additions, we were to bring our request to the judge, along with photographs and field reports. He would then make the decision.

The law was not changed, but the federal judge in Phoenix had given us an option. Although he ultimately rejected many of our applications, all of which we felt were valid, enough requests were approved so that my people began to hope for a better life.

I have talked about the Joint Use Area from the Navajo perspective. It is easy to understand that the Hopi viewed the issue differently, that they, too, had been hurt by the white man over the years. Yet in 1987, we Navajo had reached a point that almost resulted in violence between the Navajo, the Hopi, and whatever force Washington could have used to stop our efforts to fight the Bennett Freeze.

Eventually the BVD plant, which had started all this trouble, was closed. The land was given to the Hopi, who persuaded a Korean hat-manufacturing company to take over the site.

Twenty-five years of hell. That was the price we paid for failing to buy Stewart Udall's brand of undershorts.

CHAPTER TWENTY

I f the Navajo Nation had had land that was either worthless or of limited agricultural value, Peter MacDonald would never have become known to the American public. The Senate hearings would have focused on BIA problems in areas such as health care, alcoholism counseling, and child molestation. Everyone would have congratulated themselves on taking care of the simple, docile "savages" who owe their existence to the largess of the Great White Father in Washington. Unfortunately for the Navajo, the U.S. government's reservation policy often has the problem of giving the wrong land at the wrong time.

The Black Hills of Dakota were declared Sioux Indian reservation land in one of those poetically worded treaties that usually have phrases about the Indians having rights for so long as the grass shall grow and the rivers flow. Then someone discovered that there was gold in the Black Hills and suddenly the Sioux, who had caused no problems, needed to be removed by General George Armstrong Custer and other military killers. While Custer was destroyed at Little Bighorn, other Blue Coats followed, and the Sioux discovered just how short a time "forever" can be. The grass was still growing and the rivers flowing, but the whites took their land in order to search for gold.

The Navajo Nation has the misfortune of being on mineral- and water-rich land in two states desperately in need of that wealth. Arizona cities have been among the fastest growing in the nation. Both Arizona and New Mexico have vast desert regions. The ability to use cheap coal, cheap water, and other riches can be extremely important to the future of the cities created by and dominated by the Anglos. As a result, any Navajo leader who is challenging the takeover of those resources in any manner that does not include fair compensation is a danger to the desires of the developers. Thus Peter MacDonald's stand on behalf of the Navajo as a sovereign nation has made him the enemy in the eyes of many Arizona and New Mexico business and government leaders, be they white, black, or Hispanic.

Equally frustrating for MacDonald was the rise of a young rebel movement among many tribes of Native Americans. They formed the American Indian Movement (AIM), a rebel organization in its early days, which staged often violent protests and takeovers.

AIM was not an unusual phenomenon on the American landscape when it was formed in 1968, ironically by men who had often been raised off the reservations. They were little different from the Black Panthers and similar radical political and social groups that existed during the 1960s civil rights movement in America. And like the African-American "extremists," the AIM leaders had a mixture of fighters against injustice, men and women seeking complete separation of Indians from the United States, and power-hungry extremists willing to do whatever was necessary to obtain or retain their leadership. They, like many of history's dedicated revolutionaries throughout Europe, South America, the United States, and elsewhere, were zealots who seldom thought further than the next battle against the oppressors. They wanted a change. They wanted to end the patronizing relationship between the BIA and the Indians. They wanted their people to be free to live traditional lives on their own land. They wanted non-Indians off the Indian reservations. And like so many other zealots, they shared neither a vision nor a plan for long-term change.

Peter MacDonald was attacked by rebels such as the AIM leaders with almost the same ferocity as he was challenged by the Anglos. He was trying to strike a balance, to add land, establish greater Navajo sovereignty over all facets of their lives, to bolster pride, and to bring the Diné meaningful jobs. He wanted the relationship between the Navajo and the United States to be somewhat like the relationship between Canada and the United States. This meant, to some in AIM, that he was in bed with the enemy.

MacDonald was worrying about jobs and willing to find a way to bring outside business onto the reservation to employ Navajo without his people being exploited. Some AIM leaders thought that no outside business belonged on the reservation, and if their opposition cost the people employment opportunities, so be it. To them, it was a small price to pay.

Peter MacDonald understood both attitudes. He was sympathetic to many of the statements of the AIM members. He was also angry enough at the BIA and the Anglos oppressing the Navajo through lack of respect for their potential as people so that he could have taken up the gun.

But MacDonald was a mediator, a man who sought compromise where possible as he worked toward bringing the Navajo Nation into the twenty-first century. This meant that he had to deal with repeated acts of violence from as early as 1971. And when, two decades later, the decision was reached to send him to jail so that the outside governments could negotiate with less knowledgeable, less visionary, and thus more pliant younger Navajo leaders, violence became an issue for which he would be brought to trial.

Ironically, had Peter MacDonald wanted to use violence as a tool for reclaiming political power, he could easily have done so. The Navajo are well armed for battle. Unlike urban Americans who delight in purchasing automatic weapons of a type familiar to elite military units, then firing dozens of rounds of ammunition at anything they perceive as a danger, the Navajo hunt for survival. They own rifles, shotguns, and occasionally, handguns meant for bringing down wild game. They are excellent shots and understand that you only aim a weapon when you intend to take a life.

Many of the older men were World War II veterans, combat-hardened, and comfortable with the idea of dying for their beliefs. As Peter was embattled politically, under siege by federal investigators, AIM activists, Peterson Zah, and others, there was growing tension on the reservation.

Ultimately this led to the July 20, 1989, confrontation outside the Navajo Nation headquarters buildings in Window Rock where some of the older Navajo, most MacDonald supporters, stopped a police car driven by an officer named Hawkins. The officer drew his revolver while still in the car and began threatening the demonstrators. They were afraid they would be shot, so several of them tried to grab him and his gun. At the same time, a seventy-year-old man climbed into the back of the police car, put a choke hold on Hawkins, relieved him of the handgun, and enabled the others to tie the officer's hands and feet before moving Hawkins onto the sidewalk where everyone would be safe. Then, as other police gathered, Officer Charlie Smith fired a shot that struck Arnold Begay, who later died from his wound.

Another officer fired three rounds of his shotgun into the air. However, one of the rounds struck a demonstrator in the shoulder, nearly ripping off his arm.

During this same incident, an officer deliberately killed a demonstrator in what he claimed was self-defense. (In all, two demonstrators were killed and two others wounded by the police, though the demonstrators carried only two-by-two sticks of various lengths to use defensively against police batons.) The officer, when interviewed after the shooting, explained that he was running to help a fellow officer, drawing his gun at the same time in case he needed the weapon. Suddenly a shot rang out and he fell, wounded in the leg, at which time a Navajo demonstrator came over to him. Convinced that the demonstrator had a police revolver in his hand, which he planned to use to finish off the officer, the Navajo policeman fired two rounds point blank into the demonstrator's heart, killing him. The fact that no other handgun was found just meant that someone must have taken it.

The credibility of the story was challenged when an investigation into the shooting found that the police officer's gun had fired three rounds, not two. The officer said that he thought he had fired the third round much earlier, perhaps a day or two before, while driving on patrol. It was not until three years later, when questioned once again in preparation for the trial of the demonstrators, that he said he fired the revolver at a coyote threatening a sheep and lamb. The problem with the story was that the officer was required by the force to file a written report of every incident involving firing a bullet regardless of when or why. He filed no such report, nor did he check his weapon to see that it was fully loaded with live rounds before heading into a demonstration that could turn violent. In addition, he had not remembered the story of the sheep, the lamb, and the coyote just a few days after he made his heroic rescue of the animals.

Later, a weapons instructor unofficially trying to re-create the incident from the statements of the police officer and the witnesses suspected that officer pulled his revolver while his finger was on the trigger, accidentally shooting himself in the leg. Then, not realizing that he had wounded himself, the officer, in shock, confused by the injury, the noise, and the adrenaline rush, fired the rounds that killed the Navajo demonstrator. He may have lied when he realized that the man was unarmed, and he may genuinely have been confused enough to think he saw a gun, not a makeshift club or some other object.

The officer's wound was consistent with a close-range injury from the same caliber gun he carried. In fact, it is precisely because such accidents are common that many police weapons instructors teach officers to unholster their guns with their trigger finger pointing straight along the guard, not actually touching the trigger until they are aiming at their target. Yet when Peter went to court, none of the ten attorneys, all public defenders, were familiar enough with police training and handgun injuries on the job to introduce the possibility of an accidental, self-inflicted wound. Even worse, the defense attorneys at the trial, heard in September of 1992, gave questionable advice to their clients.

For example, the defense attorney for the seventy-year-old man who had held Officer Hawkins convinced him to plead guilty to such crimes as burglary (entering the police car and taking the revolver) and assault with a mandatory twenty-seven months in jail with no chance for probation. However, on the stand he explained that he feared that the officer was going to shoot somebody in his panic, and he got involved to try to keep anyone from getting hurt. The man probably would have been declared innocent of the charges, which required intent to do harm for him to be convicted, yet his lawyer convinced him to make a stand that sent him to the federal penitentiary.

During that same period, a woman received a twenty-four-month deferred sentence and a fine for walking into the administrative finance building, then carrying out two cases of pop, which she set on the porch at the request of others. Again she pleaded guilty to a federal burglary charge at the suggestion of her public defender.

MacDonald was not involved, but because the demonstrators supported him, he was eventually charged as if he had been present instead of provably being three miles away. The charges included conspiracy, kidnapping, and several others related to the violence he knew nothing about until after the fact. Ignored by all but the people who were present was the fact that if MacDonald had actually suggested that his supporters use force, there would have been a bloodbath. The men who dislike him want him out of office. The men who support him would kill to protect him. The fact that there has always been almost no violence on his behalf has always been proof to the Navajo that the Last Warrior is a man who wants to see the Diné united, not split by factional fighting.

MacDonald and his lawyers have repeatedly pointed out that the federal government charged MacDonald with "conspiracy," which is not a crime over which the federal government has jursidiction when it comes to Indian tribes.

Federal jurisdiction is established through the Indian Major Crimes Acts (IMCA). These are the laws that enumerate when the federal government may prosecute crimes by Native Americans on their reservations. The laws cover such serious concerns as murder, armed robbery, kidnapping, and the like. Conspiracy is not listed in the IMCA. MacDonald and his lawyer contend that the judge knowingly acted improperly, implying that if he was wrong, the appeals process would correct the problem.

MacDonald felt that the court was making law concerning federal jurisdiction without congressional action. If right, and the point seems valid, then all Native Americans face the risk of a judge making a law without congressional sanction. It is an improper use of the judicial process, and may have unfairly sent MacDonald to jail for a crime he not only did not commit, but for which he should never have been brought to trial.

Tragically, the courts have repeatedly taken facts, put them together out of sequence, then used inaccurate information to create "truth." Yet an examination of the entire range of explosive incidents with which Peter MacDonald was involved over the two decades when he was at the peak of his power reveals information quite different from the public record.

There were moments of violence and near violence during my years in office. Some came from forces dedicated to the disruption and destruction of the Navajo Nation. But others came from among Indian groups such as AIM.

My first crisis encounter with AIM during my term came in 1971 during the Fairchild Plant takeover in Shiprock. The Fairchild Plant was a major employer of Navajo, with approximately a thousand Navajo working there. Some were assembling special harnesses for equipment used by the Defense Department. Others were even more skilled, assembling computer chips from silicon wafers. It was a microscopic operation involving delicate welding and great skill, and it employed three shifts. Many of the workers were women with two or three years of formal education, but because of their skills as weavers and silversmiths, they were able to quickly master the technical needs.

Fairchild had been in business on the reservation for almost two years. The tribe had assisted by constructing between fifty and seventy housing units for Navajo who lived in outlying areas and needed a closer place to stay while working for the plant. Thus it was a cooperative effort that was succeeding for everyone.

The money was good for the workers. Many of them bought cars or mobile trailer homes. They were able to buy furniture. They had credit in nearby big cities such as Farmington, New Mexico.

When the AIM people came over, they claimed that Fairchild was taking advantage of the Navajo labor force, not paying proper wages. Fairchild was paying the people minimum wage, but for the first six months an unskilled employee was on the job, learning the position for which she or he had been hired, the BIA was picking up approximately half the pay. This was because Fairchild needed skilled labor and did not want to pay for people who did not yet know what they were doing. The arrangement struck with the BIA assured the Navajo would get training, and that Fairchild's expenses would be limited until the work force was properly skilled. Fairchild provided full pay, with no supplement from BIA, after the six-month training period.

The AIM members thought there should be more money from the start, and had many other grievances. Rather than trying to find a way to negotiate change, keeping the plant open, working in the manner of union organizers, the AIM members took control of the plant. It happened one night when the AIM members walked into the plant armed with guns, ordered the workers to leave, and locked themselves inside, prepared to fight anyone who tried to remove them. A few went up to the roof with rifles, acting as observers and potential snipers.

The next morning, several hundred people gathered outside Fairchild, standing across the way, building fires to keep warm while trying to learn what was happening. There was the regular shift, of course, as well as observers. No one understood what was happening with AIM, as yet, or why.

Ironically, one of the AIM leaders was Larry Anderson, who is now a council delegate. The rebels of that time moved on to become tribal leaders, fighting politically where previously they had fought physically. Yet at the time they were against the tribal government and wanted nothing to do with anyone who was part of it, calling them "apples"—red on the outside and white on the inside. But their primary targets were oppressive whites and the BIA.

The AIM leaders had the philosophy that the only good people were the nonelected tribal members trying to make a living any way they could. The minute any Indian came into a position of power, even if by popular election, he became suspect at best, no good at worst. It was the same type of people's movement criticism heard among the more radical members of the civil rights movement, though there they were using the term "Oreo"—black on the outside and white on the inside.

The AIM leaders had no program that was expressed at the time. Instead they picked a target, attacked in whatever way they thought appropriate, made a lot of noise, then negotiated some sort of agreement with the whites or government officials involved. After that they picked another target. Yet there was no cohesive plan for anyone or anything. They wanted to right wrongs with no thought to the consequences or the future, or to a vision for the people other than to be free of whatever the leaders defined as oppression.

Obviously I agree with the AIM leaders on many formats. Yes, the poverty was bad, Yes, the BIA was bad. Yes, the whites had been oppressive. And, yes, there were probably some tribal government leaders who were bad. But to go in with high-powered weapons and everything else was foolish.

It took Fairchild three days to decide to close the plant and leave. A thousand jobs ended instantly. And given that usually only one person per five-member (on average) family worked for Fairchild, that meant that the AIM action affected five thousand people without their support or consent.

The morning of the takeover I had an emergency huddle with George Vlassis, tribal counsel, the lawyers, and members of the Tribal Council. What should we do? Did we go there and try to fight it out? Did we try to negotiate?

Everything was a concern. Fairchild had not yet abandoned the plant, though it was obvious that might happen at any moment. I had just won my first election, beating Raymond Nakai, a very popular leader. The wrong decision would turn the people against me more completely than they were against the AIM members keeping them from working. Even worse, most of the people living and working in the area of the Fairchild plant had been Nakai supporters. I was disliked by the people in the building and by the people watching what was taking place.

Finally we decided that five or six of us would go there and see if we could go inside and negotiate. However, the AIM leaders claimed they did not want to meet with anyone inside the plant except the Fairchild leaders. But Fairchild's officials went to Farmington to wait out what was taking place, wanting nothing to do with armed rebels who used violence for their first encounter.

The five or six of us who represented the new government went to Shiprock to try to get into Fairchild. We lacked any protective equipment, deciding that if they were going to shoot us, they would shoot us. Only George Vlassis decided to go armed, placing a pistol inside his briefcase, informing me that he would take his chances if they searched us. He would risk his life for the Navajo, but if shooting started, he wanted the option of getting off a few rounds in self-defense.

Twenty-four hours more had passed by the time we got to Shiprock and managed to talk our way inside. Then they gave us a long list of demands, including that we file no charges against them or their active supporters. We agreed to their request because we wanted to get them out as soon as possible. Fairchild had not yet shut down its operations, but we knew the company's officials were probably looking for an excuse to pull out.

The AIM negotiators, led by Larry Anderson, asked for time to speak with their members. Then we went back to Window Rock to meet with the advisory committee of the Tribal Council to discuss the AIM demands, including not prosecuting them for their occupation. The advisory council agreed to some of the demands, and also agreed to meet with Anderson and a few AIM leaders in Window Rock as we had in the Fairchild plant.

It took three or four more days before the AIM people, comfortable with our agreement, abandoned Fairchild. Then we made a massive effort to get Fairchild to change its mind and return to full operation. However, they had experienced too much. They returned to the plant only long enough to empty it of equipment.

Tragically, the AIM leaders considered their action a victory. They were very young men and women, between the ages of eighteen and twenty-five at the time. They had little sense of Navajo history, for they belonged to a number of different tribes around the country and some had been raised in the cities, not on their reservations. They understood oppression and bigotry. They were upset with those among their parents who were alcoholic, unemployed, and underemployed. But they had no sense of the need for an Indian nation to grow, to have an economic base around which education could spring up, around which jobs and financial prosperity could grow. Among all the AIM members, probably not more than a handful had any sense of the fights our various peoples had led over the centuries.

The next potential for violence was even more deadly. In 1973 and 1974, the federal government decided to put the squeeze on Navajo families living in the area that was part of the Navajo-Hopi land dispute. The BIA, the Hopi police, who actually worked for the BIA, and Hopi range riders were ordered to impound all Navajo sheep that had strayed over the imaginary lines of partition. There were no fences, no signs, no way for a herder to know when his sheep were in approved Navajo territory and when they strayed into an area that was meant for the Hopi. The Hopi were just as confused about the territory, though in an effort to move the Navajo off the shared land that had just been declared to be Hopi, decisions were made that regularly led to the roundup of Navajo livestock.

The Navajo naturally tried to retrieve their sheep. Many Navajo women took their Winchester rifles and went out to both attack any Hopi who tried to take their sheep and regain their livestock. Some of the Navajo were overpowered, arrested, and placed in Hopi jails. We realized that if we, the leaders of the tribal government, failed to do something quickly, we would have a bloody range war that everyone would lose.

We called a meeting in Jeddito, a community near Keams Canyon. A thousand Navajo were there, and we requested that the BIA officials in charge of the Hopi come there to negotiate.

A BIA official, a man named Ragsdale, arrived with a couple of his assistants to talk with us. Unfortunately, the Navajo who had gathered were in no mood to be talked to by an official they knew was not going to give them a positive assurance that things would calm down. The anger over the livestock, over the land dispute, over all the recent problems overwhelmed common sense.

The women who had been hurt the most spoke first. They demanded to know why Ragsdale and the BIA were hurting them. They wanted to know what they had done to cause such problems.

Ragsdale probably was not authorized to say anything. He was not in charge of the congressional decisions that had caused the problem. Yet by showing up, he became the focus for all the frustration. When he began being evasive with his answers, refusing to admit that he was powerless to effect change, one woman became so frustrated, she began slapping him repeatedly until she was restrained by security people. We finally had to tell the BIA representatives to leave for their own safety.

We had a meeting during which we decided to call Washington, speaking with the secretary of the interior's office. We said that we wanted the impoundment stopped immediately, the impounded animals returned, and a moratorium placed on all further impoundment orders. This made sense to them as well, so they telephoned Keams Canyon, where Ragsdale had gone to await further developments.

Keams Canyon was three or four miles from where we had our meeting. The people wanted to make a show of force, so we agreed to march to the BIA offices there.

The BIA was anticipating an assault by the Navajo. The office had been barricaded, and barbed wire was strung across the highway. About thirty BIA police, specially flown in from Indian country in other parts of the nation, were standing in full riot gear, their rifles held at port arms.

I led the people to the fence. I told the police officers that we were going inside to talk with the BIA officials.

The police officers said we couldn't come inside. I tried to reason with them. The men had been deliberately brought from areas where they belonged to different tribes and so would not be personally sensitive to the Navajo-Hopi dispute. But they were Indians and I tried to explain that this was a problem with the white men, that Indians should stand united against the wrongs of the BIA. The Navajo who were with me had been seriously hurt and needed to resolve the problem.

The police refused. They had their orders.

Finally I told the police that they and the BIA officials had fifteen minutes to agree to a meeting. If they refused, we were coming inside without permission. The police would have to shoot, and that meant that Indians would be shooting Indians on behalf of white men, something none of us wanted. Fortunately everyone understood the seriousness and the BIA officials agreed to meet with me and four other leaders to discuss the problem.

The BIA officials fortunately understood that the situation was escalating to a crisis point. It was necessary to pull back or there would be bloodshed. The people could not handle any more pressure than they were already facing with the orders to leave the land they and their ancestors had used for centuries.

Calls were made to the BIA area office in Phoenix. Calls were made to Washington. And in the end, a moratorium was approved. The livestock impoundments would be ended until an appropriate arrangement could be worked out. We avoided what I believe would have been a spontaneous all-out war, against either the BIA or the Hopi.

That moratorium lasted almost a year. Grazing land boundaries, the so-called imaginary lines, were no longer strictly enforced by the BIA and the Hopi rangers.

Then, around 1978, we had another armed takeover by AIM, this time in the Aneth oil field in Aneth, Utah, part of the Four Corners area. It bordered on the Navajo Reservation, and several of the major oil companies share a plant where the gathering lines from the different oil fields are joined. The oil is either trucked from there or sent to the major pipeline that links Texas and California.

The AIM people, again well armed, took control of the station there. Among the oil companies using the facility, each with several hundred pumps, were Standard Oil, Superior, Phillips Petroleum, Arco, Connoco, Gulf, and Mobil. The land was leased from the Navajo, usually with bad leases. Some went back to the 1930s, but most of the lease arrangements go back to the 1950s and 1960s, when there was a major oil boom in that area. This was the period when President Eisenhower believed that all Indians should be assimilated into the United States, all sovereignty ended, all existing treaties that allowed for sovereignty broken. There was no way that the BIA was going to negotiate a lease favorable to the Indians who claimed the reservation land under which the oil was being pumped. There was certainly no way the lease would ever be as good as those which were routinely given to private interests under whose land oil had been discovered.

For instance, most BIA-negotiated leases ranged from 10 percent of the cost of the barrel to 25 percent of the cost of the barrel, with the average BIA lease one barrel for every six pumped. However, private Anglo land had leases based on the quality of the oil and the cost of the pumping, so that easy pumping of what was known as sweet oil would allow for royalties of at least 50 percent or 60 percent for the land holders. Heavier oil, difficult to pump, brought less money for the land owners. But when the Aneth oil field leases were given, neither the BIA nor the Navajo Nation employed engineers capable of analyzing the oil fields to learn what would be fair. All that was certain in hindsight was that, on average, the Navajo were receiving far less money than would have been paid for the same oil fields leased from private, Anglo holdings. Thus there was a scandal in Aneth, though not a new one.

By 1978, when I created CERT, we were in the process of doing the inventories of our lease holdings. We had a scientist from OPEC examining our oil fields, the quality of the oil, and the cost of pumping. He was able to tell us the difficulty of obtaining the oil, the approximate cost of the oil pumped, and what we should be negotiat-

ing as a fair lease. As chairman of CERT, I was referring all the issues
to the scientist to learn how things could be handled in the courts,
something previous leaders had not known to do.

AIM either did not know what was taking place with the CERT
scientist or did not care. Instead, they took over the Aneth field at
night, and by morning I began receiving telephone calls from the New
York offices of all the major oil corporations. I was warned that the
roads had been blocked, that armed men were on the grounds, and
that there could be a crisis. The oil could begin spilling out of the
equipment if not properly monitored and controlled, and that would
result in an ecological disaster.

I flew immediately to Aneth, where the tribal police had gathered,
blocking the area. Again AIM announced its demands, which stated
that the people who lived in the area had complained to the AIM
people that the oil workers were nasty, crude, rude, and disrespectful
of sacred places, including burial grounds. In addition, the Navajo
women herding sheep were chased by the oil workers. The implication was that the attention the women sheepherders received was
more than an attempt to pick them up. It was as if the women had
valid reason to fear they might be raped.

It quickly became obvious to me that the oil companies were not
attempting to work around the sacred areas. It was most cost effective
to lay pipe in as straight a line as possible, and this is what they did.
Yet to be respectful of our culture, they should have laid their pipe so
it would go around the sacred areas. Even worse, the digging brought
up the skeletons of dead ancestors, a physical desecration.

There were several pages of AIM demands, as usual, but the first
points alone outraged me. If the accusations were true, there was no
way I could allow such abuses to continue. The oil companies had to
be stopped, yet they had leases that I was supposed to protect.

I was in a serious bind. It was my job as chairman to make sure that
businesses with valid leases for reservation land could function within
their agreements, which made me protector of the oil company rights.
However, my first duty was to the Navajo, and if our women were
being harassed and assaulted, if our sacred lands were being dis-
turbed, then that took a higher priority. I knew that the oil companies
would begin suing us if we didn't resolve what was taking place, so I
immediately had George Vlassis gather the leases so we could see
everyone's legal obligations.

I also called another attorney, Edgar Cahn, who was in Florida. He
was an activist lawyer with knowledge in leases. I explained to both
George and Edgar that I wanted to side with the AIM members, then
bring the oil company executives to us. I wanted the oil companies to
clean up their act, then improve the leases. This would include not

only the financial side, but also correcting the environmental problems.

I may have been at odds with AIM under normal circumstances, but when it came to the Aneth oil field, AIM was heaven sent. Fortunately, Edgar Cahn found that the law allowed the tribal chairman to establish a quarantine of an area if there were a fire or an emergency. This measure was supposed to be designed for forest fires, though I ordered George Vlassis to help me issue an order quarantining the Aneth oil field, where no fire raged. All non-Navajos were to be removed from the area, an order that effectively stopped the oil companies from sending in an armed security force to retake the gathering buildings.

I immediately began to catch all kinds of hell from the oil companies. Even George was upset with me because he felt I was misusing the authorization. However, I said that there was an emergency in the Aneth area with a tremendous potential for fire, and no one could argue. All that oil was flammable, and someone could have taken a match to it. The fact that I knew there was probably no such risk, at least for the moment, was ignored. The important point in my mind was to bring things to a head quickly, without violent confrontation, and to use the situation for change.

I imagine that if they had taken us to court, we probably would have lost. I didn't care. I just wanted to do anything to beat them to the punch.

Next we got some food into a truck and hauled it to Aneth to feed the AIM people. We had perhaps twenty-five people from AIM and as many as a hundred local residents with them. This local support of the AIM action reinforced my belief that most of the AIM charges were accurate.

The oil people set up headquarters in Cortez, Colorado, approximately seventy miles from the Aneth fields. The AIM people had security guards along the road, and we had tribal police further out so no one could break through for a violent confrontation.

George and I went to the AIM people on the third day of the takeover. This time we were searched and George's revolver was removed from his briefcase.

The AIM people were not overly friendly, but they were pleased that I told them I wanted to help. I agreed with most of their complaints, particularly the way the oil company roughnecks were going after the women herding sheep.

I was troubled about why the complaints by the women never reached Window Rock, where I was headquartered. It appeared that they made the complaints to their local leaders, but the chapter officer or the council delegate never took it any further. The local Navajo members of AIM may have realized this, though no matter what, everyone saw this as a great opportunity for achieving deserved publicity. The problems had been allowed to fester until they became a cause for the local AIM group.

I explained to the AIM leaders that I was not going to fight for all their positions. I was going to narrow the list to four or five of the most important points, then take them to the oil companies.

This was not what AIM wanted. They wanted face-to-face negotiations with oil company authorities, after which an agreement would be signed in everyone's presence. I thought this was fair, and they agreed to let me limit the issues to jobs, environmental controls, respect for the sacred places, leaving the women alone, and better royalties. Those were the most important concerns and not an abuse of power.

I then had the former OPEC scientist working for us analyze the oil field leases. Some were for fresh oil, some were for what was known as a secondary stage of pumping, and some were for a tertiary or third stage. Each had a different value because each had a different cost.

The following day, there were more corporate jets in Window Rock and Cortez than had every been there. Finally George and I, along with several council delegates, went to Cortez to explain the demands.

The oil executives ranted and raved at us, and we let them have their say. Then, when they were calm, we explained that there was nothing to negotiate. Their workers were chasing our women, and there was no way to justify such action. Their methods of transporting the oil were needlessly desecrating sacred places. Their laxness in the pumping was causing spills that destroyed the land, endangered surrounding livestock, and gave off terrible odors. And they could not have a major business in the middle of Navajo territory without giving financial support, including jobs, to the people whose land was being used. The demands were not unfair. And in the case of the oil spills, better quality control would make them more money over time. If anything was out of line, it was the argument against acting in a more professional, businesslike, and humane manner.

Then, after explaining what the people wanted, I said that there was something more desired by those of us who represented the financial interests of the Navajo Nation. We said that we had to receive a fair, competitive price for the leases. We presented them with the figures our scientist had put together, knowing they were valid. The oil company executives made a counter offer, but when all was over, they agreed to fairer prices very close to what we stated.

After the fourth day of the takeover, the oil company executives agreed to come to the Aneth plant to sign the negotiated agreement with the AIM members present. They were frightened of violence, though we assured them that we would protect them.

The AIM members used the time to attack the four or five executives. They talked about how wrong the oil companies were, how racist, and so forth. They said that they were appointing a monitor to receive reports of any new abuses, and if anything valid was reported, the new agreement was to immediately be ended.

We also wrote in the new lease fees. Now we would receive as much as 60 percent to 70 percent instead of the previous 25 percent high. There were lower sums for some of the pumping as well, again depending upon the quality of the oil and the difficulty getting it. In addition, we agreed to have a Navajo-manned office acting as overseer of all aspects of the agreement.

Even our triumph left a bitter taste. A lot of the oil fields had paid for themselves years earlier. They had amortized their costs and were pumping what amounted to pure profit. Traditional long-term lease agreements allowed for all of these considerations, though not the ones the BIA had signed. The oil companies had made what, anywhere else, would have been obscenely high profits, so cutting back to a fair return on their investment was comfortable for them.

AIM may have had a bad name, and I thought they were rash in the ways they did things at times, though I was delighted with what happened in the Aneth oil fields. For once we could take advantage of their tactics.

Later, members of AIM took over my office, and I was not so happy then. Fortunately we negotiated their leaving without bloodshed, though the situation was made more tense with the arrival of the FBI. The FBI wanted to take charge of what was happening, trying to usurp authority from the Navajo tribal police. Not much was resolved with AIM other than their removal from my office. However, we did establish territorial jurisdiction when I ordered the tribal police to shoot any FBI agent who tried to interfere with the tribe's law enforcement. I said this after our police chief, Phillip Meek, said that FBI and federal officers were challenging his authority by telling him that they would shoot him if his police were to try to remove the AIM members. Such an extreme threat against the Navajo Nation police chief had to be countered, and I felt the necessity of using their language in the same manner as they had done.

I made it clear that the FBI did not have the right to involve itself with a legal matter concerning a sovereign nation. The sovereignty of the Navajo tribe had to be defended. However, I don't know if they understood what I meant or were just afraid of being shot. They did back off and stopped trying to interfere. I also related this story at a press conference so the public would be aware of what had happened. Then, a few weeks later, I met in Window Rock with the U.S. Attorneys for Arizona and New Mexico. We worked out a memorandum of understanding whereby the Navajo Tribal Police would have primary jurisdiction on the reservation. If they needed help, and if they requested it, only then could the Federal agents come in, and then they were to assist, not be in charge.

The year 1989 was filled with violence. When the Tribal Council took over the tribal government by putting me on leave on February 16, something they did not have the right to do, the BIA sanctified their action by declaring my signature was no longer valid for official documents. Leonard Haskie's signature was the only one to be valid, a fact that angered many people, including Russell Means of AIM.

Russell Means's attempt, in May or June of 1989, to personally right the wrong by placing BIA area director Jim Stevens under a citizen's arrest seemed almost rational. This effort failed because Means announced what he was going to do before arriving. By the time he reached the office, Stevens was waiting with four armed federal officers, as well as television news crews to record everything that took place.

Means was allowed into Stevens's office, where he brazenly announced that he was arresting the area director and taking him to the U.S. attorney. He said that Stevens could cooperate or not, but he was going to go.

Stevens naturally refused to go, so Means started to use force, trying to restrain the area director's hands behind his back so he could drag him out—all while the cameras were running. Then the federal officers jumped Means while the area director began fighting viciously, biting Means's hand, pulling on Means's braid, and kicking him in the shin.

Finally Means was subdued and thrown on the floor, all the while being taped for television.

Nothing surprised me except for Means's support. Zah supporters had been trying to get me recalled since I took office in 1987. Recall petitions had been circulating for months, though they were thrown away after the Senate hearings. Those hearings became the excuse for an anti-MacDonald movement among members of the Tribal Council that led to forty-nine opponents uniting, with enough power to push me out. I had been careful to introduce issues where close votes were unlikely, most of the voting going heavily in my favor. Only the Big Bo purchase had been close. But the Senate hearings gave my opponents a reason to emotionally strong-arm those who were sometimes with me, sometimes against me. I instantly learned who my fair-weather friends were and who truly supported me.

I entered the opening of the 1989 winter session of the Tribal Council on February 14 knowing that there would be a major confrontation. The Senate hearings had made me international news. What normally was a political meeting of interest only to the Navajo had become major news. Waiting to record the events were television and radio crews, as well as print journalists, from all three major television networks, from Phoenix, Albuquerque, and Denver, from the Cable News Network (CNN), and from several international publications.

We knew that the dissidents were going to use the opening of the winter session to try to take control of the government. I explained to my staff that all we knew was that there was an allegation against me and nothing against the vice-chairman.

According to tribal law, there is no provision for the chairman to be impeached or thrown out unless he is insane, uses alcohol to excess, has been convicted of a felony, or has gone several months without attending Tribal Council meetings. If one of those four situations existed, two-thirds of the council had to then vote to throw me out. I knew that whatever was being tried against me was not legal, and we had to stick with the law when fighting it.

We entered the council chambers as if it were a normal session. There was a normal agenda prepared for the opening meeting.

I told my staff that I wanted those who were undecided to be lobbied so we could get as many supporters as possible. Since the chairman recognized the speakers on the floor when someone raised a hand to be recognized, I wanted my supporters to plan on raising their hands as quickly and as often as possible so I could have my supporters monopolize the floor. Everyone was allowed to speak, but only in the order in which they raised their hands. I couldn't stop anyone from speaking, but I could have my people monopolize the time early in the meeting.

The council chambers were packed, television camera lights blazing. Outside were trucks with satellite uplinks ready.

The session started with an invocation, then I discussed the procedures. We handed out the proposed agenda as prepared by the advisory committee for the eighty-eight council delegates.

One of my men raised his hand and requested the approval of the agenda, and another supporter seconded it. Then the opposition made a countermotion that the tribe adopt their different agenda, which included the appointment of a chairman and vice-chairman pro tempore for this session. Then the chairman and vice-chairman were to be put on administrative leave with pay, after which an interim chairman and vice-chairman would be appointed. This would take the place of the prepared agenda.

The debate was noisy, each side cheering its own resolutions and booing the others. Most of the day was spent with the arguments, and by recess it was obvious how intense the opposition was going to be.

During the lunch break I met with my staff and the floor leaders in my conference room. It was obvious that people were very angry with one another, and my supporters thought that we had enough votes to beat the opposition's request for a substitute agenda.

There were only three ways to place items on the agenda. One was to go through the eighteen Tribal Council members from various districts who composed the advisory committee. In an emergency, the chairman or vice-chairman could introduce a by-pass provision, by-passing all the normal steps for the agenda items. And, finally, the council members could add an item with a two-thirds vote.

We knew that the opposition could not muster two-thirds support, but we didn't know if we had a majority. We tried to judge how the council delegates were changing their positions. The weaker delegates seemed to be swayed either by who among the Navajo observers was most vocal, or by which of the delegates spoke most eloquently. Nothing was clear-cut because so many were acting according to their emotions, rather than out of loyalty or a predetermined opinion.

By the end of the first day, we had provided nothing but a media show. The Tribal Council members had been yelling and screaming, including shouting obscenities. There were also vocal demonstrations outside. And all of this was being tape recorded, filmed, and noted by the media. It seemed that we might appear to be out of control to the world, since most of the people who would see this had no other contact with the Navajo or the Navajo government.

The next day we decided that it was best to give in and call for a vote on the agenda issue. However, because my supporters had dominated the previous day's speeches, the opposition was frustrated. Some of them began standing on their chairs and their desks, shouting to be heard. They understood my game plan and knew that if they made enough noise while the media were present, I would be embarrassed into doing something that might give them a chance to speak sooner. And they were right.

I explained that I would have to skip the names of my supporters and let some of them speak. I also said that we would have to vote on their motion since a substitute motion is always voted on before the original motion.

My supporters thought we still had the votes to get the original agenda, approved by the advisory committee, presented. But it turned out that everything got voted down.

I had a choice. I could reconvene the advisory council and have them prepare a new agenda, or I could do something else. By the sixteenth, we decided to have a private meeting between the two factions to discuss the issues.

The opposition faction made it clear that they were going to do whatever was necessary to get me out of office. They threatened to go to the Navajo people, to the media, and to Washington, D.C. Then one man said, "We can go to the extreme if necessary."

My position was that they shouldn't take such drastic action based on allegations against me. Nothing charged had been proven. I had faced harsh questioning. I had experienced many charges. But I had not been tried. I had not been convicted. To be so extreme over what might prove to be nothing was wrong.

That was when the opposition became brave. They didn't like me. They had failed to keep me out of office through the popular elections. They had failed to achieve two-thirds support among the Tribal Council members for my removal. But they were like a pack of wolves coming on a wounded animal. They didn't care that I was popularly elected. They intended to go back to the people and anywhere else, including "to the extreme." No one hearing what was said knows what "to the extreme" really meant, though their intensity was obvious.

I said that I was not present to fight them. It was not my nature as a leader to fight my own people. I was there to fight for the Navajo people, and the private session was meant to try to work something out, since the entire world was listening. We could not make a mockery of the Navajo Nation's government in front of the world.

The opposition said that they wanted me to leave because the reputation of the Navajo was at stake. Then they said that they would help me to clear my name. I had no money for defense, and the federal government was spending millions of dollars to put me in jail. I needed an office, a place for my papers, and the ability to do the work necessary to clear my name. I was willing to consider the issue, and I was willing to allow open discussions the next day, not just work to ensure the domination of my supporters.

We worked out an arrangement involving alternate presentations. A politician supporting me would speak, followed by a politician hostile to me. They were polite, respectful, and generally playing to the cameras and the radio stations that were broadcasting live. Everyone was courteous, though nothing was resolved.

Finally I agreed to break the deadlock by recognizing a motion that would allow me to voluntarily step down, providing we did not violate tribal laws. It would be a leave of absence, administrative leave with full pay, and I was to have Tribal Council support. I would be given an office, access to records, and the financial support I needed to work to clear my name. The vice-chairman would be the acting chairman, with full authority to run the government as I would.

Since my agenda had been voted down, I did not bring their original substitute agenda onto the floor. Instead, on February 16, I got my substitute motion onto the floor. I would accommodate their desire for me to leave, since close to 50 percent of the council delegates wanted me to leave. It was a terrible media show to present to the rest of the country, and more and more people were coming to the area from the rest of the Navajo Nation. By stepping aside, we would become the good guys, and the vice-chairman would follow the law by running the government.

Around nine o'clock that night I gave a speech. I talked of how we were Navajo, we were all one people. I said that one of the things our enemies sought was to have us be split as a people. It was the old game of divide and conquer, and we were not going to allow that.

I talked about how the opposition had brought people to rally against me. I said that I could bring my supporters for a counter rally. But all that would accomplish would be escalating tempers and probable violence, all of which would work against the Diné.

I didn't want to further the divisiveness. If I had to step down and go on administrative leave to unite the people, then I would do it. However, I wanted the vice-chairman to take over, as was the law, and I wanted them to pass my motion. No matter what, I had no intention of exacerbating the crisis, so I turned the gavel to the vice-chairman, gathered my notes, and walked off. As I did, all eighty-eight council delegates stood and applauded.

The security people helped Wanda and me into our car. Then we were driven to our home in nearby St. Michaels.

It was not more than thirty minutes later that friends came hurrying over to tell us what happened. As soon as I gave the gavel to the vice-chairman, votes were held. My plan was defeated by something like five or six votes. Then the only motion on the floor was the illegal substitute agenda that I had tried to stop.

No one was certain about the validity of the agenda, so the Justice Department and the BIA were consulted concerning the legal consequences of removing the chairman and vice-chairman. No one was certain if pro tempore leadership was possible, but the substitute agenda was passed, forcing the vice-chairman to step down.

A lawyer for the Justice Department was consulted by the vice-chairman and my supporters. Since the Justice Department lawyer was anti-MacDonald, and since the new agenda had the names of a replacement chairman and vice-chairman added, Marshall Plumber and Irving Billy, the opposing faction took control.

I was angry when I learned what had happened. Instead of staying home, I returned to may office as usual the next morning. My feeling was that everything that had happened after my request for administrative leave was voted down was illegal, contrary to what I thought was our mutual understanding. I was still the tribal chairman, and I wrote a letter to every member of the council explaining that. I said that I was still in charge as chairman.

Apparently my action on the morning of February 17 upset the vice-chairman. His few minutes of power had gone to his head. He announced that he was now the chairman and he was going to make some changes. He had plans for new staffing, new programs, new everything. When he discovered that I was staying in power, he did not know what to do.

My supporters considered the new agenda illegal. It didn't go through the advisory committee, it didn't go through the by-pass rules, and it did not get a two-thirds vote. That made it illegal, and it made the pro tempore chairman and vice-chairman illegal.

Suddenly there was a split. I had a meeting with the approximately forty council delegates who agreed with me. The pro tempore leadership had a gathering with the remaining delegates, who were against me.

Finally all the delegates reached a compromise. I would be placed on paid administrative leave with pay but no power. The BIA was consulted and refused to take a stand, telling the people to do what they wished. Then the Justice Department told the Tribal Council they could do what they wanted. The federal government was happy to support any turmoil or divisiveness among my people. As a result, there was a vote, with forty-nine in favor of getting rid of me, but the action putting me on administrative leave was not legal under tribal law.

By the time the sessions were over, rules had been suspended, the two-thirds vote regulation had been abandoned, and the law had been ignored. My attitude was that they could do what they wanted because, as their decisions were illegal, I was just going to work as usual. The attorney general for the Navajo Nation, a Navajo whom I had appointed, left the area, placing the deputy attorney general, an Anglo named Eric Dahlstrom, in charge of anything that came up. He was advising the Tribal Council, saying that anything being done to me was legal.

Finally I said that if the Tribal Council thought I was on administrative leave, then the vice-chairman was in charge. That was the way our laws worked, and no one had said anything about the vice-chairman. However, since the attorney general and the deputy attorney general serve only at the pleasure of the chairman, and since the vice-chairman was acting chairman, he had the right to fire them. This he did, not wanting to continue with either man.

Eric Dahlstrom ignored his termination, continuing to advise the Tribal Council. Then the vice-chairman went to the council chambers to assert his leadership. However, not enough delegates came over to allow for a quorum. The vice-chairman spent the eighteenth and nineteenth of February overseeing nothing while the opposing faction rented a space in the education building down the way for their meeting. The opposition also convinced enough of the delegates who had been sitting with the vice-chairman to come down so that there was a quorum at the education building. And there, once again, the vice-chairman was removed.

Suddenly we had two governments. I ran the legal government, according to Navajo law, but had few delegates offering active support. The "forty-niners," actually the forty-nine dissident council delegates who had manipulated the power shift, had their own council.

My signature was still valid. My staff was still getting paid. And the Council Delegates who were involved with legal meetings were getting their usual per diem. Any of the forty-niners who were acting separately did not get paid. As a result, they requested that the signature plate be changed from me to Leonard Haskie, who was named the interim chairman. Once that was done, they went to Citibank, the tribal banker, and arranged to have only their authorized signature recognized. All paychecks for my staff department heads and legally constituted committee members were stopped.

The Tribal Council then took the police department under their control. Then they took control of both the Finance and Justice departments. Legally constituted government was left without funds and legal help.

The battle stayed with the legal system. We went after a restraining order against the opposition, seeking a judge who was not a backer of Zah. The judge we located was Circuit Court Judge Harry Brown, and he signed the temporary restraining order. He declared that I was still the chairman, and the vice-chairman was still in power. Nothing would be changed until all legal issues could be formally resolved.

The trouble was that Circuit Judge Harry Brown was Wanda's brother-in-law. He was not otherwise related to me, and in the ways of the Navajo, the connection with Wanda was not important. However, the newspaper reporters misunderstood the relationship, assuming that he was *my* brother-in-law and would be beholden to me in some way.

Eventually the issue went to Judge Yazzie in Window Rock, a man who was a Zah supporter. Judge Yazzie stopped the temporary restraining order issued by Judge Brown and issued one against me to keep me from interfering with the forty-niners.

In 1992, when I was in court in Prescott, Eric Dahlstrom, under oath, repeated the story I told. He explained that I refused to honor the actions of the Tribal Council. The lawyers for the defendants questioned him about whether he thought I had acted illegally, which he did. Then he admitted that on February 17, when Vice-Chairman J. R. Thompson fired him in his capacity as acting chairman, he ignored the legal order. He was forced to admit that he did what I had done, defying the supposed legal authority.

The lawyer finally forced him to admit that I had been indicted for the same thing he had done, with less justification under Navajo law. However, Dahlstrom never had to face a day in court.

During this time, I was working constantly to retain as much support as possible. We were gathering backers to help regain the control we had never legally lost. The dissident Tribal Council members were doing the same, though I was accused of conspiring to overthrow the "lawful" tribal government.

We recognized that if we staged a rally of supporters, it could lead to violence and a civil crisis we wanted to avoid. Later I was accused of conspiracy for a statement to that effect, taken out of context, but fortunately recorded in context in the minutes of the Tribal Council. However, my lawyer had to point out that fact. The government wanted to ignore it.

Instead of working for the Navajo Nation, we were suddenly in the midst of political maneuverings, to the delight of the BIA and the government. This went on through the winter session, which ended in March, and that was followed by marches and demonstrations by both factions.

Shortly before May 20, 1989, the court issued an order saying me and my supporters or assigns had no right to be in any tribal building. At the same time, the Navajo were outraged, because the offices had been built with tribal money. The court could make some restrictions, but to deny the Navajo the right to their own buildings was seen as an outrage. Some Navajo decided to move into the chairman's office in a peaceful demonstration much like a sit-in. At the same time, I was working from home, trying to resolve what was taking place with a minimum of confrontations.

On May 24, 1989, when there were only a few Navajo in the building, the police sneaked in at dawn and threw them out. The next day the Navajo got a locksmith, broke in, and began working along with those council delegates and the majority of the advisory committee, all of whom were MacDonald supporters. Since the Tribal Council was not in session, under Navajo law the advisory committee becomes the executive committee, able to act in the place of the Tribal Council. Thus the real legal power was held by my supporters, but the forty-niners controlled the physical power of the police. And the advisory committee members felt that they were legally working from the chairman's office.

The forty-niners were outraged. They organized a police raid at high noon when everyone was relaxed and having lunch. Approximately fifty tribal police armed with Mace and clubs raided the office and threw everyone out. One officer videotaped the action, apparently expecting resistance and wanting evidence for court. But several of the people, including my sister, were elderly, and all the violence was one-sided, which led to the tape never being used in court.

Ultimately tempers were such that a gathering on July 20, 1989, led to two deaths and extensive violence. The situation broke my heart because it was the kind of destructiveness that played into the hands of the BIA and the politicians seeking our resources.

My supporters decided to meet on the fairgrounds, and from there went to a residence to meet. They had been hurt and did not want to risk such disruption.

The location, known as the Keeto Camp, became my headquarters when I ran for president of the Navajo Nation in 1990. The BIA was trying to force more changes on the Navajo and had effectively eliminated the position of chairman. Now we had a president to better assimilate us into the white man's culture. And the position of chairman was modified so the chairman (speaker) would be chosen by a vote of the council delegates, not directly by the people. But in 1990, the people still had a few rights.

The downfall of Peter MacDonald came in 1990. Beginning in 1988, three separate grand juries had looked into his affairs and refused to indict him. But finally, at the end of 1989, a number of different charges, primarily related to his alleged acceptance of bribes, were brought against him.

The cost of the investigation was approximately $2 million, which was paid to lawyers hired in Santa Fe, New Mexico. However, apparently there never was an original investigation independent of what had come before. Instead, there was simply a detailed analysis of the materials from the Senate subcommittee hearings, converting what had been said there into charges to be brought in tribal court. A true investigation would have started fresh, cross-checking all statements made both for and against MacDonald.

The "crimes" they claimed were such that, had MacDonald been guilty, such extra pursuit would have been foolish. Navajo tribal law considered the case a misdemeanor. The maximum penalty he *faced was six months in jail on each count, and fines which would not total more than $5,000. Guilty or innocent, the ultimate cost of prosecution greatly outweighed any potential benefit for the Navajo Nation.*

Perhaps the most serious charges brought by the Navajo tribal courts were for election-law violations. Only Navajo men and women can legally contribute to a Navajo chairman's campaign. MacDonald allegedly received more than ninety contributions from non-Navajo supporters. He could have been charged with a single count of accepting illegal campaign contributions, but the court decided instead to charge him with one count for each contribution. This decision ensured conviction and allowed the court to impose a longer sentence than would have been given to a man convicted of armed robbery, rape, or murder.

There were other charges as well. The most serious stemmed from the Big Boquillas Ranch purchase, which had been the focus of a portion of the Senate investigation. Yet despite what law enforcement claimed was overwhelming evidence against MacDonald, trials were repeatedly delayed throughout 1990.

In theory, trial delays are normal. The prosecution might build a case based on photocopies of documents that overwhelmingly prove an individual's guilt. However, only original documents can be used in court, and if they have not all been gathered by the trial date, the prosecutor may ask for an extension. Likewise, witnesses scheduled to appear may be unreachable, ill, or otherwise incapacitated, again requiring a delay.

There are other, less legitimate reasons for delaying the start of a trial. Sometimes a prosecuting attorney is able to rush indictments before the case has been properly structured. The attorney then must gather adequate evidence for conviction after the charges have been brought. This can mean that an innocent man may be put through a legal or financial nightmare because the prosecutor did not do his or her work, or that a guilty individual will walk free because the prosecutor was in too much of a rush to indict. It has been estimated that more than $5 million was spent investigating MacDonald. Not indicting him would be an embarrassment.

The delays in the MacDonald trial could have been attributed to any number of reasons. However, their timing left the impression that the prosecution was, in large part, politically motivated and determined to financially destroy the suspended chairman of the Navajo Nation. Ultimately, the proceedings that had begun in 1990 were delayed until MacDonald had survived a primary battle and was facing re-election to the position of chairman in 1990 for a fifth term. This created enormous personal and financial problems for MacDon-

ald as well as difficulties in the voting procedures, since the trial would affect the November elections.

When the first of the cases was finally heard in October 1990, the nature of the "crimes" was shocking. In addition to the charges of accepting improper campaign contributions, and regardless of the outcome, MacDonald still faced charges of bribery, conspiracy, ethics violations, and extortion. There were at least forty-two counts in all. Yet all of them revealed two distinct similarities.

First, the charges alleged that MacDonald repeatedly accepted money from individuals seeking to do business on Navajo Nation land or who were already doing business there. In some instances, subpoenaed and voluntarily supplied records from these individuals showed that they wrote off their gifts as business expenses.

The second similarity was that the people who gave the money admitted that they might have received nothing in return. Their unspoken "understanding" was that they were paying finder's fees, kickbacks, or bribes in order to ensure influence with the contracts. Yet none of them claimed that their efforts worked. Some business people felt that they did not get anything in return. One company official even testified before the Senate hearings that his business had operated without competition for the previous ten years; he had nothing to gain and nothing to lose by giving the money.

The prosecutors contended that accepting money amounted to bribery and extortion. They claimed that a threat did not have to be made verbally, that, in fact, the proof of extortion was the acceptance of the money, not the requesting of it, an interpretation some legal experts find unsatisfactory.

MacDonald's supporters laugh at the idea that the chairman took money while promising nothing. Some say that accepting gifts in such a manner fits with Navajo customs dating back many years. Others feel that MacDonald was simply "pulling the chain of some Anglos" without going against the best interests of the Navajo people. They point out that he promised nothing, gave nothing, and only created potential tax problems for the people who foolishly paid the money and then declared it as a business expense on their tax forms.

The detractors feel that the idea that MacDonald was merely acting according to Navajo custom is nonsense. They also feel that regardless of the legalities, any extra money that went into the chairman's pocket should have been used for the Navajo people. The Navajo, they felt, were too poor for any money to be wasted in such a manner.

The trial itself raised serious questions about who ultimately did what for whom. Some of the people who testified against MacDonald in the Senate hearings changed their testimony during the trial in the Navajo courts. There were strong indications that pressure had been brought to bear in Washington so that the hearings would condemn MacDonald despite what could have been evidence in his favor. Some witnesses allegedly falsified testimony to please the legislators, and others omitted details that might have changed some of the conclusions reached by the government.

In the end, the truth or misrepresentation during the Senate hearings went uninvestigated. The jury in the Navajo court case ultimately stood against the chairman. In 1990 he was found guilty as charged and sentenced to six years in Navajo jails. And while, as of this writing, appeals are in progress, the efforts to ruin Peter MacDonald, which began when he first stood against Barry Goldwater, have succeeded. MacDonald was driven from office and is unable to run for re-election.

A second trial, in January 1990, resulted in a conviction for taking money during the Big Boquillas land purchase. This time a two-year sentence was handed down.

I had been thrown out, arrested, and attacked in tribal courts, yet I managed to win the primary, facing Peterson Zah in the election. Then, three weeks before the general election, I was thrown into jail by Judge Robert Yazzie, at which time Zah wanted to win by default. Leonard Haskie, who came in third, was moved up to face Zah. However, the people wanted a write-in, adding Dr. George Lee, who I had planned to have as my vice-chairman. The result was that I could not participate but no one had a majority.

The situation was the same as that in 1963 when Raymond Nakai become chairman without the majority voting for him. It was controversial then, and it was controversial in 1990 when Peterson Zah took office with approximately 40 percent of the vote. But there was nothing to be done, my having been convicted in Navajo court for the "crimes" relative to the July violence.

The actions on the reservation became the delight of some of the media, as Peter MacDonald spent an increasing amount of time in court on one charge or another related to his years as chairman. The men he called the forty-niners sought to solidify their power any way they could, and many stories resulted. For example, the Navajo were given permission by the BIA to run their own police force with government money provided through the BIA. A man named George Johns was brought in as chief, and it was he who led many of the actions against MacDonald. Eventually other officers and MacDonald supporters turned against Johns, stripping him of his badge and weapon, then jailing him on the charge of impersonating a police officer. He was freed and reinstated, but the incident sounded humorous and could be used by the government to add further credibility to the allegation that the Navajo could not handle their own affairs.

Ironically, this was during a period when the United States vice-president Dan Quayle was being mocked for his inarticulateness, including confusing the motto of the United Negro College Fund—"A mind is a terrible thing to waste." In a speech for the fund, he commented that "It is a terrible thing to lose one's mind."

Likewise, George Bush was fending off great anger about the troubled U.S. economy, the rising cost of health care, and the fact that the "victory" in Iraq had left Saddam Hussein firmly in power. But where the stories out of Washington were treated with respect, the Navajo turmoil was seen as something to be either laughed at or greeted with pity.

Yet the truth was that Peter MacDonald was experiencing the backlash for being too good. His success with the creation of CERT, his insistence upon fair mineral leases, his demands concerning the water so precious in the desert, all made him a danger to the states where the Navajo had their reservation land.

The younger leaders, lacking a sense of history, having been born into a world where power had become an end in itself, not a means to help one's people, were readily seduced into giving up their traditions, their laws, and their minerals. The sadness of the elders was ignored. The questioning of many of their own children who were becoming curious about their past, about what it meant to be a Navajo, was likewise seen as unimportant.

While Peter MacDonald was repeatedly brought before state and federal courts, no one looked at the efforts to take full control of the Navajo water rights during a period of prolonged drought in the West. No one discussed the extensive mismanagement, waste, and occasional corruption in the BIA. No one noticed the land ownership that profited convicted bank executive Charles Keating, a friend of Barry Goldwater, and a financial supporter of Arizona's senators. No one looked at the efforts to gain cheap coal for energy plants. And no one looked at the effort to take Navajo land and use it for a possible hazardous waste dumping site.

Peter MacDonald continued his fight from home, from the courthouses during the breaks in his trials, and from jail, but his voice had sadly been muted. He looked at the new grazing rules the Navajo adopted in the early 1990s and saw the future. The permits were given for a set number of sheep, and they could be revoked if unused for a year. But the land allotted to a family could only be used if they had a grazing permit. Revocation meant that the land went back under the control of federal agencies, even though the family that lost the permit might have lived on that same acreage for generations.

MacDonald saw that the pattern of permit revocations would allow the creation of wilderness areas controlled by the government that the Navajo could not use for living or grazing. They would be forced into small communities, keeping them from traditional living arrangements. And the land they once owned, isolated from the eyes of the press and tourists, could be quietly converted to other uses. Not that such destructive measures have been taken. However, the reality is that the use of an isolated section of the Navajo Nation as a hazardous waste dumping site has been debated for several years. Even a portion of the Grand Canyon was considered, then rejected when the environmentalists were supported by the tourism industry. But the continued lack of will to fight for sovereignty and the continued changes, such as the grazing permits that strip the Navajo of control over their land, create an environment for abuse.

Yet, at the moment, only the elders and the young see the problem. The young have not yet come to power, and the elders relied upon Peter MacDonald. Even if he had been guilty under Navajo law, as he was declared to be under white man's regulations, pressure to prosecute would not have existed so strongly had he not had the vision to see the future and to seek the path that would prove most beneficial for the Diné. Jailing the Last Warrior did not still his voice. But it has ensured that he will never again rise to political prominence, and that is enough to make those who covet Navajo resources relax for the first time in almost three decades.

CHAPTER TWENTY-ONE

Despite the personal hell Peter MacDonald was experiencing, his leadership in CERT, his nationally known concern about the BIA, and his fight for assurances of sovereignty for his people impressed the leaders of other Indian tribes. Although they had little in common, their languages, religions, and histories often being quite different, their one consistent experience was destruction and exploitation by soldiers and settlers.

I don't recall the exact date, but sometime just before or just after I was removed from office, the Crow Agency's chairman, Richard Realbird, had his assistant call me. The federal government was investigating the Crow Agency because they wanted to sue the BIA for a number of problems, including negligence in handling their affairs.

The Crow Agency is located about sixty miles south of Billings, Montana, and they are important to the state because of their vast holdings of coal. The people are among the most democratic I've ever seen. The Tribal Council of the Crow Nation is actually every Crow Indian eighteen years of age and older. There are 60,000 in all, and they make their decisions based on a majority vote of however many show at the council meeting once they have the minimum number in attendance to make what they have designated a quorum.

Sometimes a special-interest faction has enough men and women to make a quorum and pass their own agenda. They call a council meeting, pass their resolution, and then another faction gets mad. Those rivals put together a quorum, call a council meeting, and counter the earlier resolution. But always the people rule their own lives without anyone being specially designated to speak for them in the manner of the Navajo council delegates.

The Crow were concerned with coal leases and the efforts of the BIA to try to run their council. The BIA apparently went so far as to try to appoint a chairman other than Richard Realbird, who had taken office by popular election. Once Realbird began challenging the BIA in the Billings federal court, the BIA started claiming that Realbird and his staff were mismanaging funds.

Somewhere in the midst of legal fights, the BIA convinced his rivals to put together a quorum and appoint a woman chairman. Realbird responded by going on the campaign trail, gaining enough support to replace the woman who had been briefly in charge.

Eventually the BIA investigation resulted in indictments against Realbird. The effort was political, and the "proof" had nothing to do with any crimes connected with Realbird's administration of the Crow Agency. As a result, I gave him my support, and together we worked to develop a plan to fight the BIA action. The chairman and his staff had hired Melvin Belli's law firm to represent the Crow, and Realbird's people and I decided to see about forming an alliance of tribal governments to stop the BIA from creating legal obstacles against tribes that didn't toe the BIA line.

I was hoping that the information from the Crow Agency and others would be used by the Senate committee in their investigation of improper actions by the BIA. Then, as a result of the meeting with the Crow, I was asked to come to New York, where the Mohawks were having difficulties with the BIA. They wanted to have gambling on the reservation to raise money, and the BIA was arguing with them about their right to do so.

The Yakima tribes were having the same problems with the BIA, so the idea of a coalition of tribes seeking to act in their own interests, not those of the BIA, made sense to all of us. We scheduled a meeting in Denver, Colorado, to which we invited as many tribal chairmen as we could bring together. Altogether we were able to get a half-dozen tribal chairmen and tribal representatives, including Russell Means, one of the founders of AIM, who was married to a Navajo woman.

The meeting occurred in 1989 around the time of the Crow fair, which was after both the July shooting in Window Rock and my being placed on administrative leave. We met in the conference room of the local Indian center in Denver, discussing our problems.

Each tribal chairman or representative made a presentation concerning the problems they were having. Then we looked at what might be done as a group to stop the problems. This meant organizing the tribes with good outside legal assistance. We would need to pool tribal resources and to create a media campaign to make the public aware of what was happening. We would also need to rally support from organizations and individuals of influence in business, Congress, and the entertainment industry.

We decided to form the First American Sovereignty Alliance. We chose our leaders from among the tribal chairmen who had not been indicted by the federal government so that there would be no suspicion of conflict of interest. A second meeting, with additional tribal chairmen, would be held before the officers were selected in order to involve as many individuals as possible.

Most of the tribes involved were energy-producing tribes from

Montana, Oklahoma, North and South Dakota, Nevada, and Arizona. The energy-producing tribes had common goals and common problems, which was why we started with this group instead of reaching out with a general call to warriors of all nations.

I was in a weak position as leader of what I called the legitimate Navajo government, the minority Tribal Council members who opposed the illegal takeover. We were outnumbered by the forty-niners, the majority of the council delegates who had seized power. Yet we wanted someone who could represent the Navajo, not just one faction, so we nominated Willy Keeto, Jr. He was on the legitimate government side, but he represented the Pro-Diné Voters, an organization that was formed to fight the split.

I was forced to spend much of my time working on my legal defense and the challenge to my position as chairman. In addition, a friend of mine made contact with Wendell Chino, the president of the Mescalero Apache tribe, to seek his help. He was sympathetic to my fight against the BIA and made two or three speeches on my behalf.

Chino shared my feelings about tribal sovereignty, but with only about 6,000 members in the state of New Mexico, his tribe had less power than the Navajo. I wanted him on my side, but other than the speeches, he did not wish to get involved, since that would mean taking sides in the Navajo tribal leadership split.

As time passed, I realized that what was happening to me and to Richard Realbird was nothing more than a tactic by the BIA. Each tribe had its own historic mechanism for leadership, and while the idea of a tribal chairman often went back no further than the 1920s, even that concept had been developed in such a manner that the tribes could live with the results. The Crow let all adult members vote. The Navajo had direct election of both the Tribal Council and the tribal chairman. And other tribes had different, equally fair procedures. However, the BIA found that when a dissident faction arose that might be friendly to the U.S. government's wishes, they could weaken the tribe by supporting one faction or another. They helped bend some rules, encouraged the creation of others, and further eroded procedures the people had declared to be fair and just. They were working to conquer us by division since, united, the people sought harmony, and that did not fit well with BIA plans.

Tragically, the BIA has been increasingly successful since the 1970s. At the time I was first involved with Navajo politics and leadership, the American press was filled with stories concerning the issues of tribal sovereignty and self-determination for all Indians. Some tribes were extremely vocal, the Crow among them, and often they had extensive energy resources that gave them power in the states where their land was located. It was against those tribes that the BIA moved first, trying to separate them.

The press was responsive to this idea. They began covering tribes as individuals, looking at local fights as if through a microscope. The Northern Cheyenne were next to the Crow Nation, and their issues were similar. Yet the press focused on the two tribes as if each were somehow unrelated to the other. They refused to see mistreatment of Indians as a problem. Rather they looked at single issues, such as education or health or unemployment or some other concern, as if it were unique to one area and one people. If an extremely vocal tribal leader was demeaned in the press because BIA public relations people made certain that a perceived weakness was publicized, no one thought anyone presenting the one-sided story was racist. Instead, it would often be balanced by a "good Indian" story discussing some tribal leader who was doing something the BIA felt should be encouraged. That this was usually either a tribe with no energy resources and thus undesirable land (by white standards) or someone who had gone along with the erosion of sovereignty was not understood by the press.

A good comparison would be to the days before the American Civil War. If the press wanted to hurt the antislavery movement among black slaves, they could do a story about a black man who was fighting for freedom and dignity, showing that he was privately a gambler or a womanizer or a thief. Whatever real or imagined sin he had would be explored in the press, implying that a bad person could not have a good cause. Then, to show there was no racial bias, there might also be a story about a slave who had helped organize other slaves to fight for the continuation of the system in which he lived. The slave might be quoted as saying that while there was some abuse, he and others on the plantation loved their master, the fact that they had food, shelter, and clothing. It was a good life, and the highest level of existence to which a black had any right to aspire.

Americans had come to see that the treatment of slaves was racist and inhumane. There was continued outrage over the lack of opportunity for blacks more than a century after the Emancipation Proclamation. And other ethnic groups were treated increasingly favorably. But Indians were treated with the same misleading reports as the blacks experienced during the period of slavery.

To make matter worse, the CERT program I created made those of us with the greatest resources the greatest targets. These included the Navajo, Crow, and Northern Cheyenne tribes.

Perhaps the greatest threat to any change is not the threat of legal action. What has been happening to me in the court system has also been the exception, not the rule. Instead, there has been a subtle subversion of the idea of consistent Indian problems through a more "efficient" bureaucracy created for dealing with Indians. This has effectively separated the tribal issues in the minds of the members of the federal government.

The BIA has a series of area offices and area directors. This is meant to allow each tribe or group of tribes to have someone who oversees their activities, is their advocate, and is the conduit for information to and from the secretary of the interior's staff. For very small tribes, with no money or resources, having a BIA area office means having a few extra jobs for tribal members. The small tribes with few resources like the idea of the BIA managing those limited funds for them. It saves them the expense of trying to educate their own people or obtaining outside expertise.

By contrast, the larger tribes and those with extensive holdings want the freedom to manage their own resources. They may have trained personnel among their people, or they may hire outsiders until their people are trained.

This is no different from the Anglo world. If people have a few thousand dollars to set aside for the future, they are quite comfortable with a neighborhood banker who knows about passbook savings accounts, certificates of deposit, and one or two other options that will bring them slow, safe growth through regular interest payments. The amount may be small, perhaps 3 percent to 5 percent, but it will be steady.

By contrast, people who have a million dollars to invest for the future want more service than the local banker can offer. What about real estate investment trusts? Stocks? Bonds? Limited partnerships in a variety of specialized investments? Rare collectibles? A combination high- and low-risk portfolio of blue chips and rapid-growth stocks? Such complex choices require greater skills than the local banker has. Such people might be content with simply placing the million dollars in the highest-interest investment normally offered to the smaller investors. The money is safe. It may even grow faster than the rate of inflation. But the potential is limited compared with that of the greater opportunities an expert can provide.

The only way for the Indian tribes to truly succeed is to eliminate bureaucratic waste by letting us work as sovereign nations, perhaps with efforts funneled, when necessary, through the assistant secretary of the interior for Indian affairs. He or she could be involved in the financial pipelines to the tribes, but instead of the money being channeled through area offices, it would go directly to the Indians for whom it was intended.

I recently read a study of what happens to every dollar Congress appropriates for the nation's Indian tribes. The cost of the BIA takes

the first 60 cents. This means that more than half the money is wiped⁻
out by those who are supposed to be advancing the Indians.

But the remaining 40 cents does not go to the tribes. Although the
exact amount will vary with the specific tribe and region of the country,
another 20 cents to 25 cents is used to pay for BIA equipment. Building
maintenance, car and truck maintenance, computers, and other equipment used by the BIA, not the tribes, requires that expenditure.

Finally there is the money that goes to the Indians. This ranges from
a high of 20 cents of that original dollar to a low of 15 cents from that
dollar.

How badly could the Indians do if given the money directly? If a
tribe is truly incompetent about money management, how much
waste will there be? Twenty percent? Thirty percent? Certainly the
least competent and skilled among the Indian tribes will never waste
80 percent of the money Congress is appropriating. Yet right now,
each time Congress authorizes a dollar for Indians, it costs 80 cents to
deliver the remaining 20 cents.

There are other problems as well. The fairest way to divide the
money appropriated by Congress is to give it on a per capita basis by
tribe. Currently the Navajo Nation comprises between a third and a
half of all the Native Americans on reservations in the United States.
Naturally a per capita arrangement will be good for the numerous
Navajo, and troublesome for the 135-member Yavapai Apache.
However, every tribe has acreage of value. In the case of the Yavapai
Apache, they have 4,000 to 5,000 acres near the city of Prescott,
Arizona, the former state capital. Without BIA intervention, the Yavapai Apache could lease the use of the land for nondestructive purposes
such as a Wal-Mart, a Sheraton Hotel, restaurants, gas stations, and
bingo or some other form of gambling. Native Americans are not the
ones who want toxic waste dumps or strip-mining operations, so there
is almost no chance that their exploitation of their land will cause
problems for anyone. They will just be business competitors like
anyone else.

There are many projects that will come to any reservation not
encumbered by BIA red tape. All the tribes are regularly approached
for business ventures, and most of the business proposals come from
men and women who are not trying to act unfairly or dishonestly.

This change would also force the states to stop trying to enforce
their morality on the tribes. The United States attorney in Phoenix has
long attacked Indians offering bingo in what is supposedly violation of
state law. However, Anglos are allowed to have highly profitable
dog-racing tracks. They are allowed to have a state lottery system.
They are allowed to have "nice" gambling such as bingo held in church
halls.

It is all hypocrisy. Small tribes can't afford to fight the states. Small tribes need to have their sovereignty protected, then be allowed to pursue what is best for them as the states are also allowed to do.

I went even further before being forced out of office. I said that the Navajo must develop the same licensing arrangements that the states have. I had our people design an auto license plate, for example. I planned to arrange to issue our own driver's licenses and to have driving tests in Navajo. The testing would be done in the same manner as the states' tests, in that a Navajo driver's license would require the same knowledge and skills as a driver's license issued in Arizona, New York, or anywhere else. The license plate would be valid anywhere in the country—just as valid California plates are also valid in Oregon.

I had hoped that my idea would be implemented after I left office, since it had been approved by the Tribal Council. Currently the Navajo have to go off the reservation to take their tests and get their licenses. The traditional people who do not speak English have to go with an interpreter. And the oldest of American natives are made to feel like the newest of immigrants.

With the change, there would be pride in the language and re- newed awareness of the young that being a member of the Navajo Nation is a source of pride, as is being a resident of Arizona, New Mexico, or Utah. Anglos living on the Navajo Nation would be forced to bring a Navajo interpreter when getting a driver's license. And the revenue from the licenses would go directly to the Navajo instead of to the state in which the Navajo are currently licensed.

Unfortunately, none of my successors have wanted to push the issue. Although there would be substantial revenue loss to the states, the issue could be positively promoted. A sovereign Indian nation would be a strong tourist attraction for any of the tribes that wished to encourage recreational development for tourists as part of the eco- nomic development program.

Many Indians also live in fear. Unnatural death has been too much a part of their history. The advances of whites, blacks, and Hispanics have often been made at the expense of the Navajo. During Black History Month each year, African-American children in the Southwest beam with pride at the stories of the heroics of the Buffalo Soldiers. These were black soldiers who proved their bravery in armed conflict throughout the West. Yet for the black soldiers to become heroes, they had to kill Indians and take their land. Likewise, the heroic Spanish missionaries and adventurers are lauded because they "tamed" the Indians.

Indian people often feel that it is easier to be quiet after making what is perceived to be a gain. They fear something they have earned being taken from them. Instead of recognizing that having more than an occasional scrap of meat is their due, they are like whipped animals who have stopped resisting the violence and started being grateful for the most minimal kindness.

The new generation of leaders, like the Navajo their age, are often complacent. They were never involved in the early fight for their treaty rights. They were born after the forced livestock reduction. They were born after the conflict between the white and *binah á dltsoziis* (Japanese) worlds when World War II challenged their traditions, religion, myths, and history. They were taught by a BIA that wanted to erase all the "savage" from their thinking. They were left without shame for accepting anything short of self-sufficiency in their own lives.

To make matters worse, current unemployment is rising too fast for the young people to stay on the reservation. The slowing of all forms of economic growth has meant that there is a 1 percent increase in jobs each year. However, there is a 3 percent growth in the number of Navajo entering the job market. This means that an ever-increasing number of young people must either leave the reservation for survival or live a life of chronic unemployment and forced welfare.

The BIA teachers are still not letting our young people get educated properly. Our people need to be trained to enter the private business sector at the management level. They must understand Mahogany Row, to see how projects work. They need to understand every phase of business, from design and manufacture to marketing and distribution. They need to understand the political decisions of the business world. And this is true for the people of all tribes, not just the Navajo.

Of course the Navajo Nation is special, one reason it is the primary target for destruction by state and federal government officials who covet our holdings. The Navajo tribal chairman is the chief executive officer and president of the largest corporation in America. When you look at the assets of that corporation, you see land, coal, water, and other resources worth hundreds of billions of dollars. The assets are worth more than the corporate assets of any business in the world, and the chairman must administer them wisely, effectively, and profitably for the people.

The tribal chairman is also the equivalent of the governor of a state or the president of a country. He is concerned with internal politics, as well as the politics of dealing with other tribes, the fifty states, and other nations.

We need to groom our people to handle such responsibilities. We need to get them the best possible educations. We need to help them gain corporate leadership experience. And we need them to return to the reservation in leadership roles that will serve all the people most effectively.

The BIA is incapable of providing the Indians with expertise or appropriate training. Many BIA workers' education was minimal, and their employment resulted from family tradition. Parents and grandparents worked for the BIA, and this is all they ever knew, much in the manner of auto, steel, and rubber workers in the so-called Rust Belt region that includes Detroit, Cleveland, Akron, and Pittsburgh. Men went into those factories when they first began opening at the beginning of the twentieth century. Their sons followed them, and then their sons' sons and, occasionally, daughters. Only a few families considered other lines of work, and often that was only when the plants began closing. Just as those workers' families must now enter new industries, it is time for the BIA employees to seek meaningful work.

At the same time, Navajo youths must learn their language, their culture, and their history. The ideal would be to keep the language alive by adding scientific and technological terms to Navajo. Scientific papers are published in English, in German, in Japanese, and in other languages, then translated into the languages of the people reading them. Why shouldn't it be normal for scientific papers relating to computer technology, medical research, the aerospace industry, or anything else that becomes part of the Navajo Nation to be published in Navajo?

Tragically, it is probably impossible to challenge the BIA without being at great personal risk. There has long been corruption among Anglo politicians. There have long been state leaders who will spend the price necessary to steal Indian water and minerals at below-market prices to benefit those whom they consider their constituents. Yet politicians go into and out of office. They change their priorities according to the mood of their constituents. The BIA, by contrast, is entrenched.

If the BIA mismanages a tribe's funds, it is the tribal chairman who is declared incompetent. When the Navajo were given the BIA law-enforcement money for funding their own tribal police, the BIA administrative staff for law enforcement remained the same as always, and additional bureaucracies were added as overseers. Then the cost of the personnel was ordered paid out of the Navajo funds before the police force was paid. This meant having to reduce service when it could have been increased and improved through better training and better equipment had the Navajo Nation been allowed to use the original funds. Then, when the police were less efficient than before, instead of anyone admitting that it was the result of the fees paid to the BIA, the Navajo were considered incompetent managers of money.

And what if the Native Americans fail in their efforts for self-determination? The white man's world is trillions of dollars in debt. American presidents, representatives, and senators cannot balance the budget. Anglo children have such poor health care that their mortality rate is one of the worst of all the developed nations. Crime, malnutrition, and poverty of the soul are rampant in urban America. Could a sovereign people allowed to follow a culture whose history was in harmony with the Great Spirit and all creation do any worse?

As this book is being completed, Peter MacDonald is fighting to appeal his convictions and to vindicate his actions as chairman of the Navajo Nation. The Navajo men and women currently in power are hostile to him. Some are convinced he is guilty of misuse of his office for personal gain. Some believe he is an anachronism, a man whose time has come and gone. Some hold him in personal disdain, the result of political fights whose hostile words prohibit the restoration of old relationships. And a tiny few, perhaps, desire his destruction.

Yet even MacDonald's enemies recognize that he is driven by a vision for the Navajo Nation, a vision with which the elders identify, making them eager to support him instead of the younger generation of leaders who were raised with ideas more in harmony with the white man's world.

Peter MacDonald is serving sentences imposed by both Navajo and federal courts. He could go to the federal penitentiary, but as you will read below, he feels that to serve his time in the relative comfort of a federal penitentiary would be to deny the sovereignty of the people for whom he has worked all of his life. He will spend what may be the rest of his life in the Navajo system, even though most of the jails on the Navajo Nation are condemned as unfit for human habitation, and the ones that are in use are little more than aged drunk tanks.

The jails were designed for the worst crimes routinely committed on the reservation—misdemeanors with penalties no greater than six months behind bars. A justice system that demands extended family involvement, that seeks harmony for all involved, does not need an elaborate prison system to ensure law and order.

MacDonald feels that he must be judged in the context of how the Navajo have lived and worked for centuries. What has he done for the people? How has he united them? How has he advanced them? And if there was impropriety involving tribal funds, a charge he rejects, how can restitution be made so that the people are in harmony again?

To MacDonald, the idea that the Navajo could be divided over their reactions to him is emotionally devastating. He firmly believes that after more than a century of being attacked by outsiders, of having their land taken from them and their homes destroyed, the Diné must stand together. (When this writer was first checking the facts to substantiate MacDonald's story, one high official of the BIA, speaking off the record, commented, "You realize that until very recent years, the official policy of the Bureau of Indian Affairs was to destroy the Navajo Nation.") The time to be concerned with legal actions by Navajo leaders against Navajo leaders is only after the Navajo Nation becomes self-sufficient, in control of their land, their destiny, and their place within the world at large.

On February 19, 1991, resting at home between trials, a convicted felon facing jail, Peter MacDonald discussed his attitude toward what he has endured. He put his suffering in the context of a Navajo whose roots transcend the centuries.

I am a man of two cultures, two worlds. I was raised a Navajo and learned to perceive the world through the history, legends, and religion of the Navajo people. I also learned the life of the white man, from the halls of the U.S. Congress and the private offices of the White House to Mahogany Row in a major American business. Because I know both worlds, I can draw strength from what I feel is the best of both cultures.

Ironically, my greatest difficulties have emerged from my fourth term in office, a length of service as Navajo chairman unequaled by any other leader in our history. Yet this should have been expected, in a way, because the number four is the most significant of all the numbers used by the Navajo.

In all the stories of conflicts between spirits or animals, there were always four questions. For example, when Coyote asks the doe how she got such beautiful children, he has to ask her four times. The first three times, she responds, "I don't know," but the fourth time, she supplies the answer.

The story of the Warrior Twins, the sons of the Sun and the Water, has the same theme. The Twins did not know that their father was the Sun, but they wanted to learn his identity so that they could go to see him. They asked the White Beaded Lady three times to tell them who their father was. Each time she said, "He lives in a place no one can get to." It was only when they asked for the fourth time that she told them that their father was the Sun.

The Warrior Twins learned from the spider spirits what blessings would be needed to overcome the obstacles at the gates that blocked the entrance way to the Sun. Among the items they needed was an eagle feather taken from a live eagle—the feather of life.

When the Twins came upon the first obstacle, a group of monster snakes the size of dragons, they escaped by holding on to the feather of life and gliding over the snakes.

The next obstacle was a man-killing hailstorm. The third was vicious lightning that shot everywhere, killing everything in its path. And the fourth was a big wind, the equivalent of the most violent tornado.

After overcoming the fourth obstacle, they met their father, the Sun. He also tested them four times to be certain that they were worthy of talking to him. He then asked them what they wanted.

The Twins told the Sun that the Navajo were under attack by many enemies. There were monsters and dragons and all manner of vicious creatures, none of which could be stopped by the weapons available on earth. Giant rocks traveled the earth, rolling over people, and huge birds constantly swooped down from the sky, snatching up men, women, and children, and smashing them against the ground. The Twins needed a weapon that would help them save the Diné.

The Sun gave the Twins lightning-bolt arrows to use as weapons. When they returned to Earth they had to use four arrows on a man-eating giant. The fourth arrow killed him.

I no longer take such stories as literal truth. But I do consider them lessons. As I look at both the emotional trials and the current court cases, I realize that all life has tests.

To the Navajo people, the Long Walk was their first test in recent times. They weathered the forced livestock reduction, followed by the post–World War II era when so many of our young men were disillusioned by their travels and the lack of opportunity on the Navajo Nation. And finally, in the present era, we face the trials of poverty, the further loss of land, the theft of our water and mineral rights, and the attack on my administration, which attempts to discredit the good while highlighting what some feel is the bad.

It is my feeling that I am experiencing my fourth test of leadership. There have been three court trials, and maybe there is one more waiting in the wings somewhere that I will have to go through. I don't know where it will end—whether I will spend more time in jail, or will go as far as the Supreme Court, or some combination thereof. Yet our history teaches that four trials must be endured, and that the man who does not tire of the fight will ultimately triumph.

The situation had been overwhelming to me. I was attacked, taken to court, and heard the traditional Navajo ways declared of no value because they were part of my beliefs. There were times I have felt that I was standing alone and that, as the only one of the older people who remains politically active, my future is the future of the Navajo Nation. But Medicine Man Dan Chee used the wisdom of his years to suggest a solution by offering a simple analogy to the Navajo Nation during these troubled times.

Dan Chee was among the elderly who were saddened by the 1989 change in the Navajo government. He experienced the installation of a Tribal Council by Standard Oil Company in the late 1920s, witnessed the creation of the position of chairman in the 1930s, and, in 1989, opposed the elimination of the position of chairman. He felt that this latest and potentially devastating change, which enabled the controlled Tribal Council to select their own leader, thereby removing him from direct responsibility to the people, was designed to stop me from spreading the concept of the sovereignty of the Navajo Nation.

Dan Chee said that in 1989, Chairman Peter MacDonald brought a large, delicious watermelon to the Navajo people. (In his analogy, the watermelon represents a program for long-term prosperity.) But the disgruntled Tribal Council, with the assistance of the BIA, took the watermelon away from Chairman MacDonald and started running with it. As they ran with it, trying to cut into it and eat it at the same time, they dropped it, and it burst open on the ground. Now they are trying to put it back together, but they don't know how.

Dan Chee said that they can't make it whole again because the pieces are scattered and some have been dirtied. It is impossible to put it together, but the question still is, How can we make the watermelon whole again?

Dan Chee suggested that the Navajo people take Chairman MacDonald's philosophy and root it in the tradition of the Diné. Then the Navajo people would not try to pick up pieces at random and put them back together. Instead, they would take the seed of the broken watermelon, find fertile land, work the ground, plant the seeds, and water the melons as they start growing. The melons would be cultivated, the weeds removed, and after a while, the plants would grow. At the end of the season, there would be huge melons that were whole and delicious, and that could be cultivated forever.

Dan Chee felt that unless you knew the culture (the seed) from which the government derived, trying to piece it together was no good. It simply would not last.

What will last are the culture and tradition of the Navajo people. These seeds will have to be nurtured, and there will always be elements, people who are like bad weeds, that will try to choke it. But if we keep hoeing these weeds so that the plants will have air and light, when the plants grow, they will bear the fruit (the watermelon, or long-term prosperity) that Chairman MacDonald had carried.

I don't know what the future will bring, but I am hoping that we can preserve that watermelon seed, the culture and tradition of the Navajo. Certainly I want to help my people gain the success that should be theirs. I feel that my bicultural experience enables me to bring effective ideas to the Diné, ideas that will benefit the people.

The use of culture and tradition, combined with the contemporary education necessary to effectively exploit the best of our land and our people, will save the Navajo from those who would let them be absorbed into a world that has spent generations trying to destroy them. My body can be imprisoned and my mouth silenced, but if the ideas I have expressed, and the programs for which I have worked, are truly the seeds of the watermelon, then perhaps my triumph will come through others, young men and women who choose to reclaim what rightfully belongs to our sovereign nation.

On December 23, 1992, Peter MacDonald was in the Window Rock jail, a little more than a drunk tank built forty years earlier by the Bureau of Indian Affairs. He described his life in confinement and the reason he feels more comfortable in the hell of the aging, foul-smelling jail than in the federal facility where he could otherwise serve his time.

The routine is: Drunks are brought in by twos, sixes, and so forth, or, if not drunk, through a bench warrant. They are logged in, issued bright orange coveralls. If they are sober, they are brought into an awful-looking jungle called the general area. The huge concrete floor and walls are a maze of steel—steel bunks side by side, double bunks to accommodate at least sixty inmates. It stinks to high heaven (recently Legal Aid lawyers sued the tribe over the jail conditions). The plumbing is half-shot. If there aren't enough two-inch-thick pads (called mattresses), then you sleep on the cold steel bunk.

Every evening, a jailer comes around with a roll of toilet paper and issues each inmate not more than six squares (too bad if you have the runs). Each evening they (jailers) come around with a tube of toothpaste—if you have a toothbrush then you get one little squirt of toothpaste. You can't have anything of your own—not even a comb. Actually this place was designed for not more than thirty to forty inmates, but I understand over the years they had as many as one hundred in here. If you are drunk, then you get thrown into a separate area where there are no beds or bunks or two-inch pads—just cold walls and steel (bars). Only after you sober up do you get transferred to the general population area.

There is no program for the inmates. Some are here for rape, drugs, assault with a deadly weapon, drunkenness, possession of liquor, DWI, fights. Many have yet to be *arraigned*. Many are awaiting trial, and then, of course, there is me (white-collar crime). But we are all here together. *No distinction!* The rules that the BIA imposed in the 1940s are still being used, such as one visitor per day for fifteen minutes through the glass window [as if the inmates are on Death Row].

No visitors allowed on Monday and Tuesday. No calls outside except on Wednesday, when you are allowed to make one call (collect) for five minutes. The only person who can call in is your lawyer. The only person who can visit you privately is your *lawyer*. You *can't* have writing tablet, pencils or pen, any paper, magazines, books, anything. As a matter of fact—no TV or even radio is allowed.

[Eventually an old television and radio were brought in, MacDonald explained.] That is it for stimulation of the mind. No outside light 'cause there isn't any window. No exercise, no candy, no soda pop— no nothing. With all of this, you probably wonder why I asked that I be allowed to return here instead of going to a federal "country club" minumum-security correction camp for white-collar criminals.

I was at Phoenix Federal Correction Facility for one week during my recent sentencing by Judge Carroll. Even though the Phoenix facility was "medium" security, it was like a Holiday Inn compared to this place. No steel or bars. You have *rooms*, two to each room, beds with springs, real mattress, desks with lamps and drawers, sheets, pillows, towels, small bureau to hang your clothes and belongings, footlocker with your own padlock to keep your valuables. No bright orange coveralls. You get khaki pants, shirts, shoes as government issue. However, during the week they have commissary merchants bring in *merchandise* where you can buy your own clothes—Nikes, sweatshirts, anything, so long as you have the money to buy it.

In the huge lobby there are games, like pool tables (good professional types), Ping Pong tables, TV rooms (literally a private twenty-by-twenty-foot room with chairs) with cable TV. Another TV outside. Inmates walk around with Walkmans plugged into their ears, and there is a walk area outside with exercise equipment. You can go in and out and walk the running path, or lift barbells any time you choose. Any time! Private baths. There are porcelain wash basins, regular toilet bowls with covers, cold and hot running water, ice machine in the lobby, microwave in the lobby for heating anything (there are snack vending machines, pop, and so forth along the walls). There's a library. They issue you writing tablets, pencils, envelopes, even postage stamps. At least five pay phones operate from 6:00 A.M. till 11:00 P.M. (it is monitored). You can call any time, anywhere from these phones. Visiting hours every day from 3:30 P.M. till 8:30 P.M., and any number can visit. There are enough kinds of snacks in the visiting area that you can skip dinner. The visiting area is decorated like the lobby of a huge Hilton with soft cushion chairs, coffee tables, and so forth. Even young children can visit. On weekends visiting starts at 10:00 A.M. and continues till 8:30 P.M. If you want to visit all that time, no problem. And this is the "medium" security facility.

Wonder what minimum security looks like or operates. I walked away from this—why?

Because I am a Navajo and I am committed to the Navajo. I have always believed in the sovereignty of the Navajo Nation and have always been very jealous of *jurisdiction*. In addition to this, all charges against me were *Navajo:* happened on Navajo land, Navajo funds, me as Navajo leader, Navajo everything. I belong here for many reasons, including that my umbilical cord is buried on the *reservation*. My people are here. My wife, my children and grandchildren are here. My relatives are here. My supporters are here. My government is here. This is a *Navajo problem* requiring a *Navajo solution*.

So how is it that I am writing to you? Well, as the great spirit never deserts you, it turns out that in this BIA "dungeon" they constructed solitary cells six feet by nine—all concrete and steel. Steel doors with a little hole for them to feed your food tray to you. Steel wash basin and commode with only cold water from the faucet. One narrow steel bunk. A small light recessed into the steel ceiling. I asked that I be placed in one of the solitary cells—they obliged. I now sort of treat it as my private room.

What MacDonald did not say was that the six-by-nine room is to be his world for the next six years, based on his sentencing at the time he wrote. Because of the length of time (no one else has ever stayed in a Navajo jail longer than six months), the guards have been kind enough to give him access to books, writing tablets, and even a small radio. He has to keep exchanging the books, but they provide enough stimulus to prevent his mind and spirit from deteriorating in the manner of his physical health. There is no way for him to retain his health, so the nurturing of his mind and spirit are essential for life. He faces fourteen and a half years in jail, his supporters working to raise money to appeal his convictions for "crimes" he did not commit.

Since the time of the pharaohs in Egypt over 5,000 years ago, white men had jails (dungeons). They had written laws, courts, and so forth. Every bit of their laws was written in terms of protecting *PROPERTY* [emphasis by MacDonald] from the peasants. Laws have been made ever since, even unto this day, by people in power not respecting human beings, but protecting property (money).

We the Navajo have lived by laws, too, for thousands of years. Our law was not written. It was given to us by the Great Spirit. It was fair, just, and equal. Our law applied to everyone evenly. The basis of our law was human beings (ones with five fingers). Compassion is the soul of justice.

Sah ah nah ghah, be keh hozohn—from the beginning to the end, the human being is more precious and sacred than material things.

On July 2, 1987, Robert Pencall made the following statement:

I Robert Pencall do recall the following as being a true statement concerning a conversation I had with Edison Wood, Navajo Tribal Appraiser. On June 30, 1987 while waiting in the Council Chambers, I was sitting at a table with John Goodfellow, Dean Moss and Edison Wood. I was talking about the Big Boquillas Ranch purchase and was saying that the appraisal and review were insufficient. That I had written some of my doubts down on paper and wanted to know if the appraiser and reviewer had considered the points covered on that paper. I showed the paper to Edison. He studied the paper and said that he felt the price had been too high. He stated that he had felt the price should be about (I for get [sic] the figure it probably was $60.00 per acre). That he had come in with a lower figure and Ninibah Cahn had instructed him to increase the figure. I think he said he had a memo instructing him to do so.

[AUTHOR'S NOTE: The statement by Pencall needs some clarification. Before it was written, he and Edison Wood had met back in April, declaring that the cost would be $68 an acre. This was done back in April, and as a result of his statement at the time, which was confirmed as accurate by the BIA, the Council voted in favor of the purchase. Apparently, if he had doubts, they were never voiced publicly when the opportunity presented itself prior to the voting. It was only mentioned to Edison Wood, who also did nothing. This memo was written approximately a week after it would have stopped the deal, had that been appropriate.]

On July 1 I called Edison to my office and told him that I had told Floyd Espinoza my supervisor about his statement and that what he had said could come out. I told him we were writing a retraction of our concurrence with his figure and that would be out as soon as possible. Edison said he felt better and that he just could not stand to live with what had been done in regard to changing the appraisal. He said he would be glad if something came out on the appraisal.

[AUTHOR'S NOTE: The tribe had approved the purchase on April 30, 1987. This effort to retract appears to be a memo meant to protect himself after the fact.]

That same day, July 2, Peter MacDonald was sent a letter by Floyd Espinoza, Pencall's superior, in the Navajo Area Office of the ARPM/ Appraisal Section. That letter read:

According to brochures and information provided to licensed real estate agents in Arizona by the Tenneco Company of Bakersfield, California, the Big Boquillas Ranch has been offered for sale for the sum of $25 million over the past two–three years.

Apparently the Big Boquillas Ranch property has been optioned by Mr. Bud Brown, et al., who have offered to sell the property to the Navajo Tribe for $33.4 million.

The significance of the above information is that the confirmed sale-option agreement of the subject Big Boquillas Ranch located near Seligman, Arizona, is the most recent and best comparable sale and measure of fair market value, that can be utilized for appraisal purposes of the subject property.

In view of this recent information the previously estimated market value of $46 per acre must be withdrawn and the $25 million listing price used as the best obtainable estimate of value, which is approximately $50.87 per surface acre.

On July 6, 1987, Michael P. Upshaw, attorney general for the Navajo Nation Department of Justice, sent a confidential memo to Peter MacDonald, chairman, Navajo Tribal Council, and to Carl Rowan, Jr., an attorney for the law firm of Milgram Thomajan & Lee, concerning the Big Boquillas Ranch purchase. He wrote:

The July 2, 1987, draft of purchase agreement for the Ranch property appears to adequately handle most of the problems attendant to a land purchase of this nature but it does not handle the issues raised by the belated letter of advise from the BIA.

The BIA letter raises issues as to the identity of the seller, the fairness of the purchase price, and the adequacy of the prior advice provided to the Navajo Tribal Council at the time the transaction was approved (approximately April 30, 1987).

From reviewing various portions of prior and current drafts of pertinent papers, it appears that:

1. A preliminary title report was obtained on December 2, 1986 by someone, but no part of that title report seems to be available showing ownership as of that time.

2. Tenneco, either directly or through controlled entities, has had title to the property since 1926.

3. Within the last six months or so, Tenneco "optioned" or conditionally sold the property to Tracy Oil & Gas Company, a company that, according to public records available in Arizona in 1987, does not seem to have sufficient financial strength to be considered a "serious" buyer. Further, that a person named Byron ("Bud") Brown, and perhaps others, are part of a syndicate or group of partners that may be a part of the Tracy selling entity.

4. According to the BIA letter, the purchase price may have been escalated from $25 million to $33.5 million in a period of less than a year, which, if true, is a "flip." Such a quick change of ownership and price may not necessarily be illegal, but can mean a very bad bargain for the buyer.

5. There will be two deeds of trust (liens) on the property after the Tribe receives title—one lien will be to protect the first seller (a Tenneco entity), and the other lien will be to protect Tracy, et all. Unfortunately, it is unlikely that the face amount of the liens will be discovered correct, the first lien would reflect a first purchase price some $8 million less than the Tracy selling price.

6. Because $500,000 was already paid outside escrow as a non-refundable deposit, this money may be completely beyond recovery.

Given these circumstances, it would be appropriate to undertake one or more of the following:

1. Since a major part of the BIA is geographically beyond reach until after the scheduled closing date, attempt to extend the closing date seven to ten days. This is not a [sic] unreasonable request in the circumstances.

2. Simply put the issues raised by the BIA directly to Tracy-Duckworth for response.

3. Add one or more provisions to the purchase agreement such as:

A. Seller warrants and represents to Buyer that no broker or finder had been engaged by it in connection with the transaction contemplated by this Agreement, or to its knowledge is it in any way connected with any of such transactions. No persons or entities, other than the current shareholders of Tracy, are entitled, either directly or indirectly, to receive or benefit from the proceeds of this sale. The current shareholders of Tracy are _____, _____, _____.

B. Prior to the closing date, Buyer shall have received a detailed appraisal of the Boquillas property at no cost or expense to the Buyer, dated as of a date between the date hereof and the closing date, prepared by an MAI appraiser, in a form reasonably satisfactory to the Buyer, showing the property to have a value of not less than

$33,417,500. Seller shall pay the fees and expenses of such appraiser, or

C. It is understood that Seller is not the owner of the Boquillas property, but that it and _____ has an interest therein as a purchaser under a contract dated February ____, 1987, with Tenneco (or the appropriate subsidiary), which contract Seller believes to be valid and binding and has been exhibited to and read in its entirety by Buyer. In the event that such contract between the Seller and Tenneco is not closed within ____ days from the date of this agreement, or if Seller does not obtain title to the property within such period, Seller shall return to Buyer all monies paid to it (or for its account in escrow), and the parties shall thereupon be mutually released from all other liability and responsibility under the contract.

The important focus here is to provide the client (Navajo Tribal Council) with adequate protection without unduly interfering with client's desire to acquire the property. It is unfortunate that the BIA was so late in making its comments known—but now that it has gone on record, it is important to either disprove the BIA allegations [sic].

Copies of the letter were sent to Nick Alrilch, Milgram, Thomajon & Lee; Mike McKenzie, Milgram, Thomajon & Lee; and Don Wharton, Department of Justice. [These were the lawyers who, along with the tribe's attorney general, reviewed and prepared the Big Boquillas land sale documents.]

Equally damning was an unsigned internal Bureau of Indian Affairs memo stamped June 26, 1987. It was used as evidence during the February 1989 Hearings Before the Special Committee on Investigations of the Select Committee on Indian Affairs, United States Senate, 101st Congress, First Session. It was reproduced in Volume 2 of the government's records and proves the BIA abdicated responsibility in this matter. None of the reporters covering the trial spotted it, but its existence shows that no matter what Chairman MacDonald's actions—honest error, desire for the restoration of land that once belonged to the Navajo, or corruption for friends—the BIA had a chance to intervene. This also reinforced testimony given before the hearing.

Review of the Boquillas Ranch Materials

I think we could have some problems on this one in the future because the price seems to me to be too high. I would hope you thought of all the stuff listed below. Think about the material and then let's talk about it.

1. Why were positive adjustments were used [sic] on comparable data in the appraisal when the appraisal contains statements that ranch prices have fallen 20 to 30% since 1980. On the sales that were adjusted by Edison the difference in between 27% and 36%.

2. If the sales were adjusted down in accordance with Edison's paragraph in his appraisal the difference in the indicated value would on average be less. That is between $9,000,000.00 and $12,000,000.00 less. That kind of money needs lots of justification and explaining.

3. The average returns on ranches vary from 2.5% to 3% the return here is 1.8% did anyone explain why the return was low. This indicates values differences of between $9,000,000.00 and $13,000,000.00.

4. The average price per A.U. was $2,791 in 1985 why are we paying $3,288.00. The figure is based on 13,000 A.U. The difference is 15% or about $5,000,000.00.

5. Why does the State require 80.2 acres for an A.U. and the owner claim or somebody claims the carrying capacity would be 6127 and the cost per A.U. would be $5,386.00. Were carrying capacities studied and the correct figures obtained? The difference here between the owners or others statement and the figure based on State carrying capacities would be 48% or $16,000,000.00.

6. If there are special commercial lands why weren't they valued.

7. Regarding the leased lands. They lease for $600,000.00 × 35% = $19,795.00 (income to the leased lands) − 23072.60 (cost of leasing the lands) + $172,722.96. Why does land that produces $172,722.96 per year have no value?

8. See comparable 3,240 × 75.68 = $775,000.00. That should have been picked up in the review.

9. Using one comparable for a review is very dangerous and when it involves another use such as coal mining it is poor judgment to use it with nothing else.

10. If leased lands do have value as demonstrated above, how can the appraiser justify using comparable with as little as 20% fee with a purchase price of only $750,000.00 when our subject has a supposed value of $34,000,000.00 that is only 2% of the value and its got 80% leased land. That just can not be done.

11. Sale 4 is adjusted for a sale date of 1981 and the comparable is dated 12984 in Goodfellow's notes. That is the date shown on the spread sheet. Woods did adjust for 1984.

12. If the Zah people [Note: Peterson Zah was tribal chairman between MacDonald's third and fourth elections] or MacDonald people want B.I.A. BLOOD [Note: emphasis in the original] and we want to defend ourselves we have to be able to explain this stuff. Do you feel comfortable or should we change our analysis?

The arrangement between Tracy and Brown was also important in understanding whether there was corruption on MacDonald's part. The implication was that he stood to gain large sums of money, and he received several thousand dollars relating to the ranch purchase. However, the sum was so small that it is difficult to consider MacDonald a "conspirator" in all this. What matters are two documents, one being the agreement between Byron T. "Bud" Brown and Tom Tracy, the other being the fees they received from their twenty-four hours of work during the transition sales. The agreement reads:

Any income derived from the sale of the Boquillas Cattle Company Ranch will be split ⅔ to Bryron [sic] T. "Bud" Brown and ⅓ to Tom Tracy.

For this purpose "income" is defined as the net profits before Income Taxes.

The income will be distributed as received.

The agreement for division of income applies whether the purchase and sale is handled by us as a corporation, partnership, or joint venture.

Dated this 20th day of February, 1987, in Phoenix, Arizona.

Finally, there was the following document:

Profits Derived fron the Sale of the Big Boquillas Ranch

PRICE OF RANCH SOLD TO NAVAJOS:	$33,417,386.00
PRICE OF RANCH SOLD TO TRACY:	$26,250,000.00
PROFITS SUBTOTAL:	$ 7,167,000.00
BROWN COMMISSION:	$ 750,000.00
TOTAL PROFITS (NOT INCLUDING EXPENSES):	$ 7,917,386.00

Division of Profits on the Sale of the Big Boquillas Ranch

BROWN—59% (NOT INCLUDING EXPENSES OR INTEREST INCOME)	$ 4,228,757.74
COMMISSION	$ 750,000.00
TOTAL:	$ 4,978,757.74
TRACY—41% (NOT INCLUDING EXPENSES OR INTEREST INCOME)	$ 2,938,628.26

February 27, 1989

Statement of William P. Ragsdale, Acting Assistant Secretary for Indian Affairs, Department of the Interior, Before the United States Senate Select Committee on Indian Affairs Special Committee on Investigations

[AUTHOR'S NOTE: Wilson Barber's letter of June, 1987, was sent several weeks after the tribe made the purchase. Thus it was of no value.]

February 17, 1989

[Ragsdale's statement covered several unrelated issues. The portion of concern for this book is that involving the Big Boquillas Ranch. This issue was addressed at the start of his comments, and reads as follows.]

During the past several weeks, this Committee has heard testimony regarding the circumstances surrounding the purchase of the Big Boquillas Ranch by the Navajo Tribe. Let me just briefly cover the Bureau's involvement in the Navajo Tribe's purchase of the Big Boquillas Ranch. I believe the Bureau acted responsibly in this matter. The then Area Director Wilson Barber is to be commended for his diligence in pursuing the matter as far as he possibly could. He made every effort to inform Navajo chairman Peter MacDonald and every council delegate that the purchase price of $33.4 million was not reasonable in view of the Bureau's own review.

In April, 1987, a Navajo Tribal Council resolution approved the purchase of the ranch. The Tribe routinely asked our Navajo Area Office to review the appraised price. The price of $33.4 million which the Tribe intended to pay, caused a concern, especially in view of the fact the same ranch had been advertised in national business publications for the last two to three years for $25 million. Our Area Office notified the Tribe that we could not agree with the appraised price which the Tribe intended to pay.

[AUTHOR'S NOTE: The BIA appraiser and the Tribe's appraiser both agreed that $68 per acre was a fair price for the land. The agreement was reported just before the Council voted to make the purchase.]

Our Area Director wrote to Chairman MacDonald advising him that the price of $33.4 million was too high and that instead of the $68 per acre the Tribe intended to pay, the property was worth only from $40 to $60 per acre, some $8 million less than the Navajo offered price of

$33.4 million. A copy of that correspondence to Chairman MacDonald was sent to every member of the Navajo Tribal Council. The Tribe apparently went ahead with the purchase and used a total of some $8 million of funds which were not held in trust.

When the Area Director was asked to approve a draw down from Navajo trust funds to complete the acquisition, he withheld approval on the basis that the full tribal council had not approved the budget amendment. He asked the Chairman for an amendment to the tribal budget stating specifically that the requested funds were to be used for the purchase of the Big Boquillas Ranch.

When presented with the authorizing resolution, the Area Director asked the Washington headquarters office for advice. He was aware that then Assistant Secretary Ross Swimmer had asked the Interior Department's Inspector General to investigate the purchase.

Additionally, the Field Solicitor stated the subsequent tribal authorization specifying the funds were to be drawn down were in order and the authorization was proper from a legal perspective. The Inspector General for the Department was also advised of the pending request to draw down funds to complete the acquisition which he had under investigation. The Inspector General advised he could not release any information which could be used for disapproving the release of these funds because of the ongoing Grand Jury proceedings.

Based upon the facts stated above, there was not sufficient reason to disapprove the amendment of the budget which was apparently used to make the second payment on the land acquisition. Committee staff of the Bureau of Indian Affairs did not disapprove the questionable acquisition. My response is that we do not exercise responsibility to approve by line items a tribal budget in this era of self-determination. The Bureau exercises its responsibility for the release of Trust funds by insuring that proper tribal authorization is given and that any items which are questionable are brought to the tribe's attention. Additionally, we ensure the funds are available and are ready to be withdrawn from government investments. We do not as a practice supervise tribal programs paid from general tribal revenues or from unrestricted trust accounts. I believe the action the Bureau took in this instance was appropriate.

Acoma, the, 264
AFL-CIO, 189, 192–94, 197
Agnew, Spiro, 216
AIM (American Indian Movement), 232, 233, 254, 313–14, 315, 321
  and Aneth oil field, 240–41, 323–27
  and Fairchild Plant, 318–20
America. *See* United States
American Indian Bank, 222
Americans for Indian Opportunity, 227
Anderson, Clinton, 256
Anderson, Larry, 319, 320
Aneth oil field (Utah), 240, 323–27
Antelope Point Marina (Ariz.), 271, 272
Apache, the, 189
Arizona, 36, 142, 182, 183, 189, 201, 202, 215, 224, 271, 274, 282, 285, 290, 308
  BVD plant in, 305–7
  expansion of, 111–13, 177, 213, 313
  land fraud in, 111, 292
  political influences in, 113–14, 199–200
  water in, 111–12, 203, 235, 288
Arizona Corporation Commission, 272
Arizona Public Service (APS) Co., 272
Arizona Republic, 144, 280
Arthur, Chester A., 183, 184
Atcitty, Wilbur, 178, 215, 239
Austin, Buck, 239

Babbitts, the, 112
Banks, Dennis, 232
Barber, Wilson, 148
Barney Old Coyote, 222
Bausch & Lomb, 107
Bear Lady, story of, 30–32
Bechtel Corp., 192, 263
Begay, Arnold, 315
Belli, Melvin, 343
Bennett, Robert L., 308–9
Bennett Freeze, 308–12
Betani clan, 1, 21
BIA (Bureau of Indian Affairs), 2, 40, 69, 73, 79, 80, 81, 82, 88, 92, 108, 121, 127, 128, 131, 149, 150, 157, 161, 166, 167, 173, 174, 177, 186, 202, 216, 251, 276, 309, 328, 332, 333, 347, 352
  area offices of, 346
  buildings of, 164, 175, 222, 232
  bureaucracy of, 129, 144, 147, 148, 152–53, 154, 179, 223
  corruption of, 277, 288, 340
  destructiveness of, 335, 336, 344–45, 354
  documents issued by, 184
  employees of, 137, 146–47, 350
  excesses of, 285–86, 291, 313
  and Fairchild Plant, 318–19
  and Hopi, 224–25, 321–23
  and Indian Self-Determination Act, 220–21
  negotiation by, 211–12, 229, 231, 233, 260, 271, 306, 327
  paternalism of, 305, 314
  power of, 136, 204, 243, 286–87, 310, 339
  and Realbird, 342–43
  regulations of, 132–33, 355
  relocation by, 116, 126
  and royalties, 210, 213
  schools and teachers of, 13, 25, 39, 41–51, 54, 58, 62, 63, 72, 75, 78, 86, 97, 106, 122–24, 156, 159, 160, 176, 279–81, 304, 349
  subjugation by, 198, 235, 257, 261, 264
Big Boquillas (Big Bo) Ranch (Ariz.), 272–79, 286–88, 291, 292–93, 295–96, 297, 328, 337, 339
Big Mountain area, 184, 196–97, 253
Billy, Irving, 332
Bingaman, Jeff, 268
Bitsie, Ashikie, 196
Black Hills of Dakota, 313
Black Mesa Power Station, 202
Blacks, 115, 142, 345, 348
Bluehouse, Milton, 242
Boileau, Oliver C., 268, 269
Bonanno, Joseph, 112
Boyden, John S., 199
Brown, Bud, 275–79, 287, 291, 293–94, 295–303
Brown, Harry, 334
Brown, Tony, 295
Bureau of Land Management (BLM), 175, 181, 283, 285

Bureau of Reclamation (U.S.), 289
Bush, George, 340
BVD Co., 305–7, 312

Cahn, Edgar, 324, 325
Cahn, Ninibah, 275, 276
California, 35, 202, 213, 235, 290, 308, 323
Canada, 308, 314
Carlucci, Frank, 183
Carroll (judge), 356
Carruthers, Garrey, 270
Carson, Kit, 8, 9, 151, 186, 199
Carter, Jimmy, 228
Cassini, Oleg, 268, 269–70
Castro, Raul, 195
Cataract, Inc., 262, 263, 264, 266
Caterpillar Equipment, 264
Central Arizona Project, 288, 289
CERT (Council of Energy Resource Tribes), 228–33, 249, 323–24, 340, 342, 345
Chee, Dan, 353–54
Cheyenne, the, 229
China, 68–70, 82
Chino, Wendell, 344
Christianity, 21, 26, 76, 78, 91, 92
Clah, David, 20, 33
Coalition for Navajo Liberation, 241
Cody, William ("Buffalo Bill"), 305
Colorado, 224
Colorado River Basin, 235
Comanche, the, 10, 117, 119, 158
Community Action Program, 156–57
Congress, 39, 123, 130, 135, 153, 155, 175, 176, 177, 178, 182, 187, 188, 192, 196, 210, 216, 220, 223, 246, 247, 253, 310
  appropriations of, 346–47
  bureaucrats in, 179
  and 1868 treaty, 36
  and Fixed Boundary, 287
  and Joint Use Area, 249
  lobbying, 170, 304
  and Navajo and Hopi Land Settlement Act (Public Law 93-531), 265, 308–9
  and Navajo Tribal Council, 40, 137
  and Paragon Resource Ranch, 282
  relocation program of, 126
  and water project, 289
COPE (Committee on Political Education), 194, 197
Coronado Francisco Vásquez de, 82
County Coalition for Abolishment of Indian Treaties, 242
Coyote stories, 4–6, 7–8, 17, 49, 52, 352
Crow, the, 229, 344, 345

Crow Agency, 342–43
Crownpoint Manpower Center, 222
Curly Haired Lefty (Clah Cheschillige), 19
Custer, Gen. George Armstrong, 147, 313

Dahlstrom, Eric, 333, 334, 335
Dailleboust, Bernard Peter, 267
Daschle, Thomas, 303
DeConcini, Dennis, 248, 265, 268, 285, 293, 303–4
DeConcinis, the, 112
Dee, John Nelson, 178
Defense Department, 103, 318
Del Webb Development Corp., 271
Denay, Inc., 256–57, 260–61, 262, 263, 264
Department of Commerce, 173
Department of Energy (D.O.E.), 228
Department of the Interior, 173, 174, 183, 189, 216, 229, 232–33, 295, 305, 309, 310
Diné. *See* Navajo/Navajo Nation
Dodge, Tom, 137
Domenici, Pete, 248, 265, 268, 269, 285
Douglas Aircraft, 99

Eastern Navajo region (Diné Anaih), 181, 272
E.G.B. Investments, 275
Egypt (ancient), 357
Ehrlichman, John, 173, 186, 187
Eisenhower, Dwight, 176, 323
Eisenhower administration, 134
El Paso Natural Gas, 97–98
Englehorn, Con, 275
Exxon Corp., 211–13, 245

Fairchild Camera & Instrument Corp., 139, 234, 318–20
Fannin, Paul, 190
FBI, 175, 205–7, 208, 301, 327
Fields, Ken, 208
52/20 (GI benefit), 71
First American Sovereignty Alliance, 343–44
Flagstaff Daily Sun, 144
Flagstaff Times, 144
Florida, 288
Forty-niners, 290, 334, 336, 339, 344
Four Corners area, 10, 19, 235, 282, 323
Four Corners Power Plant, 193, 229
Franklin, Ben, 142
Freedom of Religion Act, 20
Funks, the, 112

Gambinos, the, 112
Garment, Leonard, 173, 186, 187

General Accounting Office, 204
General Dynamics Corp., 139, 148, 269, 272
General Electric (GE), 104, 107, 229, 263
Genoveses, the, 112
Germany, 106, 142
Goldwater, Barry, 173, 174, 183, 186, 187, 194, 195, 216, 217, 224, 248, 268, 339, 340
  and AFL-CIO, 192
  allegations of, 197, 198
  and Arizona State University, 209
  and Hopi, 176–77, 188–89
  influence of, 199–200
  presidential candidacy of, 113–14, 154
  and Rainbow Lodge, 190–91
  reputation of, 196
Goldwaters, the, 112
Gorman, Howard, 116
Gorman, R. C., 160, 227
Gray Mountain Area, 217–18
Grazing District Six, 184–85, 186
Great Spirit, 16, 18, 37, 76, 124, 125, 127, 131, 132, 140, 141, 232, 351, 357
Gulf Oil, 231

Harris, LaDonna, 227
Harvey, Paul, 175
Haskie, Leonard, 328, 334, 339
Haskonhazohi clan, 1, 21
Hawkins, Michael, 295
Hawkins (police officer), 315, 316
Head Start program, 156
Hickel, Walter, 173, 174–75, 176, 183
Hollywood Canteen, 64
Home Improvement and Training Program, 165
Hopi, the, 3, 7, 116, 174, 177, 189, 253
  and Bennett Freeze, 308–12
  and Big Bo, 277, 293
  and BVD plant, 307–8, 312
  compromises of, 200–201
  and Indian Reorganization Act, 200
  and Joint Use Area, 183–85, 188, 191, 192, 197, 198, 201, 246, 266
  Kachina dolls, 191, 209
  and land dispute with Navajo, 178, 183–86, 224–26, 247–48, 254, 282, 285, 321–23
  vs. Navajo, 185–86, 230
  population of, 184
  relocation of, 199
  See also Navajo and Hopi Land Settlement Act
House of Representatives, 183, 188, 189, 199
Hughes, Howard, 101

Hughes Aircraft, 81, 99–107, 110, 122, 134, 143, 212, 236
  Mahogany Row, 107, 109, 135
  R&D division of, 99–101
  technical staff, 106–7
Hussein, Saddam, 340

Indian Health Service, 108, 164–65, 167
Indian Major Crimes Acts (IMCA), 317
Indian Reorganization Act (IRA), 40, 41, 200
Indians
  and AIM, 313–14
  and alcoholics, 72
  contributions of, 92
  as ecological threat, 305
  and mineral wealth, 228–29, 231
  and paternalism, 146–47
  prejudice toward, 115
  self-determination of, 186, 187, 216
  superstitions of, 95
  victimization by whites, 93–94
  See also Native Americans
Indian Self-Determination Act, 220–21
Inouye, Daniel, 268, 280
Iraq, 228
Irwin, Jim, 217

Jackson, Bob, 256–57, 260, 262
Jackson, Rev. Jesse, 228
Jans, Melvin, 274–75
Japanese, 54, 60, 61, 67, 68, 142, 273, 287, 293, 349
Japanese-Americans, 142
Jefferson, Thomas, 142
Johns, George, 339
Johnson, Lyndon, 113, 154, 170, 187
Johnson administration, 305
Joint Use Area, 183–85, 188, 190–92, 194, 196–201, 224, 225, 246, 249, 265, 266, 308, 310, 312
Jones, Paul, 134
Justice Department, 197, 332, 333

Karl Solomon Investments, 275
Keating, Charles, 285, 293, 340
Keating Five, 293
Keeto, Willy, Jr., 344
Kennedy, John F., 113, 134, 154
Kennedy, Ted, 189, 190
Kennedy administration, 305
Kentucky, 229
Kooros, Ahmand, 230
Kuwait, 228

Labor Department, 193
Lake Powell (Ariz.), 269, 271, 289
Landbloom, Glen, 136

LeClere, Wanda, 159–61, 162, 175, 226–27, 239, 254, 255, 262–63, 297, 332, 334
Lee, Dr. George, 339
Licavoli, Peter, Sr., 112
Lincoln, Tony, 168, 169–70
Lincoln Savings, 304
Livestock Reduction Act, 86, 156
Lockheed (aircraft), 99
Long Walk, 8–9, 11, 35, 124, 127, 149, 198, 199, 200, 304, 353
Lujan, Manuel, 256

McCain, John, 268, 269, 280, 303
MacDonald, Charity, 161–62
MacDonald, Faith, 161–62
MacDonald, Hope, 161–62, 276
MacDonald, Linda, 97, 119, 158, 161
MacDonald, Peter
    and bingo business, 263–64
    birth of, 1–2
    "crimes" of, 336–37, 338, 339
    dangers facing, 202–3
    decision to fight for Navajo, 114, 149–50
    downfall of, 277, 336
    elected tribal chairman, 179
    goals of, for Navajo, 179, 267–68
    and Goldwater's charges, 198–200
    honorable discharge for, 70
    in jail, 351, 355–57
    judgment of, historically, 351–52
    as Last Warrior, 114, 198, 340–41
    in Marines, 58–60
    as mediator opposing violence, 314–15
    mother (Glen-Habah) of, 1, 14, 33, 42–43, 54–55, 60, 108–9, 120, 128–29, 182, 237–39
    names (early) of, 29–30, 43–44, 55
    and Navajo sovereignty, 287–88, 313, 314, 327, 357
    power of, as Chairman, 239
    and Project Hope, 310–11
    and sister Betty, death of, 6–7
    tape recording clears, 292
    trials of, 337–39, 352–53
    vision for Navajo Nation, 351
MacDonald, Peter, Jr. (Rocky), 97, 98, 117, 118, 119, 158, 161, 190, 276, 294–95, 297–303
McDonnell Aircraft, 98
McGee, Kerr, 245, 246
McGovern, George, 189–90, 192, 199
McKenzie, Dr. Taylor, 241–42
Mafia, 112–13
Mao Tse-tung, 68
Marmon Group, 268
Martin Marietta, 109
Means, Russell, 232, 233, 328, 343

Mecham, Evan, 268
Meek, Phillip, 327
Mescalero Apache, 344
Mexico, 20, 308
Minneapolis Honeywell, 107
Mitchell, Ted, 167
Mohawks, the, 343
Mondale, Walter, 189, 190
Mormons, 18
Morton, Rogers C. B., 175, 183, 186, 187
Mott, Harold, 206
Mutual Help program, 166

Nakai, Raymond, 109, 110, 135, 143, 145, 157, 167, 171, 174, 177, 181, 194, 221, 224, 242, 243, 250, 261, 304, 306, 307, 339
    cooperation with MacDonald, 251–52
    and FBI, 205–6
    supporters of, 319–20
NASA (National Aeronautics and Space Administration), 217–19, 269
National Congress of American Indians, 243
National Parks Service, 271
National Tribal Chairmen Association, 243
Native American Church, 20
Native Americans
    culture of, 119–20
    and law school, 170, 171
    OPEC, 228
    programs for, 232
    tradition, 119–20
    See also Indians
NATRO (Native American Treaty Rights Organization), 242–43
NavaHopi Journal, 144
Navajo/Navajo Nation
    and alcoholism, 72–74
    arts and artists, 160, 191, 226–27
    assets, 349
    bank, 222–23
    and Big Boquillas Ranch, 274–77, 278–79
    boundaries, 35–37, 287
    businesses, 145–46, 258–61, 269–70
    ceremonies, 23–25, 43, 52–53, 77, 78, 141
    childbirth to, 1
    children, 12–13, 32–33, 118, 142–43, 164
    coal, 154, 185, 202, 211, 213, 214, 229, 247, 267, 273, 281, 283–85
    corruption, 129
    culture, 16–18, 27, 38–39, 50–53, 71–73, 77–78, 81–82, 86, 116–20, 132, 140, 141, 156, 196–97, 354–55

Navajo/Navajo Nation (*continued*)
  dances, 77–78, 116–17
  and death, 24
  deities, 21–22, 25–26, 30–32, 180
  and destruction (inner), 121–28
  driver's license, 348
  and education, 12–13, 16–17, 39, 41,
    126, 140, 161, 164, 210, 222, 227,
    243–45
  employees of, 143–44, 153, 257–58
  energy resources, 114, 179, 210–14,
    224, 227–28, 267–68, 281–82
  ethics, 257–58, 260–61
  extended families, 2–3, 8, 17–18, 23,
    26–27, 127, 309
  and farming, 3
  Fixed Boundary, 287
  four trials of, 352–53
  and hiring, 192–94
  history, 122, 142–43, 149, 156
  home improvement program, 155,
    165
  housing, 166–67, 309
  income (per capita), 215, 231
  jails, 351, 355–57
  and land dispute with Hopi, 178,
    183–86, 224–26, 247–48, 254, 282,
    285, 321–23
  language, 60–63, 126, 140, 141, 167,
    218, 350
  and laws, 131–32, 163, 284, 329, 357
  legends, 149, 218
  life span of individual, 215
  livestock, 3, 35, 36–44, 71, 82, 139,
    151–52, 199, 224–26, 321
  marriage practices, 18
  medicine men, 17, 23, 43, 51–52, 75,
    127, 218–19
  mineral rights, 139, 179, 185, 186,
    201–3, 284, 313
  and money, handling of, 146, 350
  names, 29
  and oilfields, 153, 185, 210, 323–27
  physical fitness program, 156
  political structure, 269
  population, 184, 201, 215, 273, 347
  programs, 155–57
  religion, 20–26, 39, 75–76, 81, 92,
    126, 196–97
  rituals, 6, 76, 77
  sacred lands, 324
  and self-sufficiency, 121–22, 127–29,
    153, 165
  shopping centers, 256
  skills, 17–18, 163
  social structure, 2–3
  and sovereignty, 39, 40–41, 130, 140,
    287–88, 313, 314, 327, 357
  Squaw Dances, 25, 39, 51, 141

  storytelling, 4–6, 7–8, 17, 49, 52–53,
    352–53
  taboos, 25, 50–51
  taxation, 245–46
  teenagers, 25, 72–73, 123–24, 140
  ten-year plan, 214–15, 216, 217
  and trading post, 26–27
  traditions, 12, 17, 27, 81–82, 98, 116–
    20, 131–32, 163, 196–97, 236, 354–
    55
  and treaties, 35–36, 40, 41, 130, 152,
    289
  Tribal Chairman, importance of, 3,
    132–33, 177–79, 303, 349
  Tribal Council, 40, 121, 123, 132–38,
    144, 148, 153–55, 169, 170, 177,
    181, 188, 202, 211, 212, 214, 216,
    225, 226, 233, 248, 249, 254, 257,
    259, 260, 270, 271, 278, 279, 288,
    290, 295–97, 305–8, 319, 320, 328–
    35, 344, 348, 354
  tribal courts, 82–86, 217, 336–37,
    339
  Tribal Police, 328
  and unemployment, 151, 215, 268,
    273, 349
  unique situation of, 214
  and uranium, 89, 203, 212, 233, 267
  and voting, 194–95, 199
  and water, 14, 114, 203, 235, 288–90,
    313, 340
  and welfare mentality, 122–23
  and Window Rock confrontation, 315–
    17
  See also Joint Use Area; Navajo and
    Hopi Land Settlement Act
Navajo Academy, 244–45
Navajo Assistance (office), 81
Navajo Club of Los Angeles, 116–17,
  158
Navajo Community College, 210
Navajo Cultural Center, 156
Navajo Economic Summit, 268
Navajo Fair, 204
Navajo and Hopi Land Settlement Act
  (Public Law 93-531), 196, 197, 199,
  200, 226, 247, 265, 285, 309
Navajo Justice Department, 131
Navajoland Festival of the Arts, 160,
  227
Navajo Office of Land Administration,
  275
Navajo Times, 144–45
Navajo Tribal Code, Title 2 Amendment
  to, 40
Nevada, 202, 235, 290
New Mexico, 36, 144, 181, 201, 202,
  215, 224, 235–36, 313
  See also Paragon Resource Ranch

New Mexico Public Service Co., 281, 283
New Mexico Public Services, 247
New York Times, 208
Night of the First Americans, 249
Nixon, Richard, 173, 175–76, 182, 186, 187, 188, 191, 192, 216
Nixon administration, 183, 187, 217
North American Aviation, 99
Northern Cheyenne, 345
Northern Navajo Nation Fair, 58

OEO (Office of Economic Opportunity), 157, 170, 171, 183
ONEO (Office of Navajo Economic Opportunity), 154–57, 160, 165–70, 172, 177, 178, 181, 206, 251, 256, 304
OPEC, 202, 230
Otis Elevator, 107–8
Owens, Wayne, 199

Paragon Resource Ranch (N.M.), 246–47, 281–84, 285
Patterson, Brad, 173
Paul, Frank, 242, 250
Peabody Coal Co., 202, 253, 273
Pencall, Robert, 276
Pervais, Mel, 262, 263, 264
Phillips Petroleum, 245
Phoenix (Ariz.), 112, 113, 292
Picasso, Pablo, 160
Pima, the, 3, 189
Pittsburgh Midway Mine, 231
Plumber, Marshall, 332
Polaris missile program, 104–6, 109, 143, 157
Pritzker, Robert, 268–69
Pro-Diné Voters, 344
Project Hope, 310–11
Public Law 93-531. *See* Navajo and Hopi Land Settlement Act
Pueblo, the, 7, 8

Quayle, Dan, 340

Ragsdale (BIA official), 321, 322
Reagan, Ronald, 268
Realbird, Richard, 342–43, 344
Reppel Steel, 276
Roosevelt, Franklin, 237
Rosenzweigs, the, 112

Salt River Project, 192–93, 288
San Juan River, 38, 163, 235, 289
Scott, David, 217
Scott, Hugh, 200
Sekaquaptewa, Abbott, 226

Senate, 114, 175, 183, 198, 279
Special Committee on Indian Affairs hearings, 290–93, 299–304, 313, 328, 329, 338–39, 343
Subcommittee on Indian Affairs hearings, 189–90, 199, 277, 280, 285, 286, 336, 337
Seva Development Co., 269, 271, 272
Shirley, Jim, 84
Shriver, Sargent, 145–46, 154, 157, 163, 166, 170, 183
Sidney, Ivan, 253, 265
Sioux, the, 313
Skeet, Wilson C., 180, 181
Smith, Charlie, 315
Sneed, Woody, 167
Southern Baptist Convention, 92, 93, 94
Soviets, 104
Spaniards, 81–82, 141, 151, 181, 348
Standard Oil Co., 153, 233, 257, 354
Stanford Research Institute, 138
Steiger, Sam, 173, 176–77, 183, 186, 187, 189, 190, 191, 194, 198, 199
Steigers, the, 112
Stevens, Jim, 328
Supreme Court, 246, 312, 353
Swimmer, Ross, 268

Tenneco West Corp., 274, 276, 278, 279, 293
Texaco, 245
Texas, 202, 308, 323
Thompson, Frank, 92, 93, 94
Thompson, J. R., 335
Topango Properties Co., 275
Tracy, Tom, 275, 276, 278, 279, 287, 293, 294, 296–97, 298, 299, 300, 302
Tracy Oil and Gas Co., 275
Truman, Harry, 68
Tucson (Ariz.), 112, 113, 292
Tucson Gas & Electric Co. (TG&E), 204, 208

Udall, Morris, 201
Udall, Stewart, 304–8, 309, 312
Union Pacific Railroad, 55
United Bank of New Mexico, 276
United Negro College Fund, 340
United States
adversary system of justice in, 294
and Canada, 314
checks and balances in, 259
and energy resources, 211, 227–28
ethnic groups in, 115, 142
financing in, 287
leases in, 247, 281
life expectancy in, 215
in Middle East, 202

United States (*continued*)
  and Pearl Harbor, 54
  problems mounting in, 351
  property in, 131
  reservation policy of, 313
  scandals in, 304
  schools in, 279
  and Shah of Iran, 230
  taxation in, 245
  thirteen colonies of, 41
  treaty violations of, 152, 295
  unemployment in, 273
  in World War II, 142
United States Geological Survey
    (USGS), 210
Utah, 18, 36, 144, 202, 246
Utah International, 229
Utah Sewing Operations, 269
Ute, the, 3, 7, 8, 10, 224

Vanadium Corp. of America, 90
Veterans Administration, 81
Vietnam War, 74, 113
Vlassis, George, 319, 320, 324, 325,
    326

Wallace, Ruby, 92, 161
Wall Street Journal, 204, 208
War on Poverty programs, 154
Warren, Ned, 113

Warrior Twins (story), 352–53
Washington, George, 142
Washington Post, 192
Watergate scandal, 217
Watkins, Ralph, 268
Wauneka, Annie, 134, 135, 136, 200,
    242, 261, 303
Wayne, John, 229
Westinghouse, 263
West Virginia, 201
Who Owns America (Hickel), 175
Wiley, J. Bruce, 96, 97, 99
Williams Brothers, 235, 289
Window Rock (Ariz.), 116
  confrontation at, 315–17
Window Rock Motor Inn, 144
Woods, Edison, 275–76
World War II, 60, 74–75, 142, 349

Yakima, the, 343
Yavapai Apache, 347
Yazzie, Robert, 334, 339
Yee, Dr. Sam, 68–69

Zah, Peterson, 135, 252, 253, 254, 255,
    265, 267, 269, 271, 283, 284, 285,
    315, 328, 334, 339
  administration of, 261–62
  and politics of militancy, 250–51
Zuni, the, 3, 7, 8